One Hundred Years of Argonauts

Max Planck Studies in Anthropology and Economy
Series editors:
Stephen Gudeman, University of Minnesota
Chris Hann, Max Planck Institute for Social Anthropology

Definitions of economy and society, and their proper relationship to each other, have been the perennial concerns of social philosophers. In the early decades of the twenty-first century, these definitions remain matters of urgent political debate. At the forefront of this series are the approaches to these connections by anthropologists, whose explorations of the local ideas and institutions underpinning social and economic relations illuminate large fields ignored in other disciplines.

Recent volumes:

Volume 13
One Hundred Years of Argonauts Malinowski, Ethnography, and Economic Anthropology
Edited by Chris Hann and Deborah James

Volume 12
Broken Glass, Broken Class Transformations of Work in Bulgaria
Dimitra Kofti

Volume 11
Theorizing Entrepreneurship for the Future Stories from Global Frontiers
Joost Beuving

Volume 10
Thrift and Its Paradoxes From Domestic to Political Economy
Edited by Catherine Alexander and Daniel Sosna

Volume 9
Wine Is Our Bread Labour and Value in Moldovan Winemaking
Daniela Ana

Volume 8
Moral Economy at Work Ethnographic Investigations in Eurasia
Edited by Lale Yalçın-Heckmann

Volume 7
Work, Society, and the Ethical Self Chimeras of Freedom in the Neoliberal Era
Edited by Chris Hann

Volume 6
Financialization Relational Approaches
Edited by Chris Hann and Don Kalb

Volume 5
Market Frictions Trade and Urbanization at the Vietnam–China Border
Kirsten W. Endres

Volume 4
Industrial Labor on the Margins of Capitalism Precarity, Class, and the Neoliberal Subject
Edited by Chris Hann and Jonathan Parry

For a full volume listing, please see the series page on our website:
https://www.berghahnbooks.com/series/max-planck

One Hundred Years of Argonauts

Malinowski, Ethnography, and Economic Anthropology

Edited by

CHRIS HANN AND DEBORAH JAMES

berghahn
NEW YORK · OXFORD
www.berghahnbooks.com

First published in 2024 by
Berghahn Books
www.berghahnbooks.com

© 2024, 2025 Chris Hann and Deborah James
First paperback edition published in 2025

All rights reserved. Except for the quotation of short passages
for the purposes of criticism and review, no part of this book
may be reproduced in any form or by any means, electronic or
mechanical, including photocopying, recording, or any information
storage and retrieval system now known or to be invented,
without written permission of the publisher.

Library of Congress Cataloging-in-Publication Data

A C.I.P. cataloging record is available from the Library of Congress
Library of Congress Cataloging in Publication Control Number: 2024933967

British Library Cataloguing in Publication Data

A catalogue record for this book is available from the British Library

ISBN 978-1-80539-521-8 hardback
ISBN 978-1-83695-078-3 paperback
ISBN 978-1-80539-522-5 epub
ISBN 978-1-80539-523-2 web pdf

https://doi.org/10.3167/9781805395218

Contents

List of Illustrations   vii

Introduction. Argonauts Revisited   1
    Chris Hann and Deborah James

Part I. Bronisław Malinowski and his *Argonauts* in Context

Chapter 1. Cultural Capital and Economic Stringency: Reality and Myth in Bronisław Malinowski's Socioeconomic Background   25
    Grażyna Kubica

Chapter 2. Tenerife 1921: The Writing of *Argonauts*   43
    Michael W. Young

Chapter 3. Malinowski's New Paradigm   63
    Adam Kuper

Chapter 4. Malinowski and the Politics of Economic Anthropology: Between Imperial Trusteeship and Colonial Trade   77
    Freddy Foks

Part II. Economy, Economics, and Epistemics

Chapter 5. Compulsion to Work? Malinowski and the Labor Question   97
    Rachel E. Smith

Chapter 6. On Tribal and Other Economies   117
    Richard Staley

Chapter 7. Malinowski's Place in the History of Economic Thought   137
    Chris Gregory

Chapter 8. Can Economic Anthropology Escape from Primitive Economics? Thinking Ethnographically from the Brazilian *Oikos*   161
    Benoît de L'Estoile

Part III. Cosmology, History, and Social Organization

Chapter 9. Baloma: The Spirits of the Kula in the Trobriand Islands   187
  Mark S. Mosko

Chapter 10. The Archaeology of the Kula and Malinowski's
Notion of Economy   208
  Hans Steinmüller

Chapter 11. Using Laozi to Interpret the Kula Ring: Rethinking
the Dual Chieftainship in Kiriwina   226
  Yongjia Liang

Part IV. Adaptations in Space and Time

Chapter 12. Passing On, Passing Around, and Passing Through:
Urban Inheritance in South Africa as Circulation   249
  Maxim Bolt

Chapter 13. The Anthropological Turn in the Sociology of Money   270
  Ariel Wilkis

Chapter 14. Digital Argonauts: From Kula Ring to Bush Internet
in the Western Pacific   289
  Geoffrey Hobbis and Stephanie Ketterer Hobbis

Afterword   312
  Rebecca Empson

Index   316

 Illustrations

Figures

11.1. Tabalu–OB alliance. 236

11.2. Nam–Mit dispute. 239

Map

14.1. Solomon Islands, Malaita, and Lau Lagoon. 292

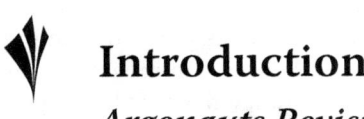

Introduction
Argonauts Revisited

CHRIS HANN AND DEBORAH JAMES

The publication in 1922 of Bronisław Malinowski's *Argonauts of the Western Pacific* inaugurated a golden age in social anthropology. Revisionist views notwithstanding, it is still widely regarded as laying the ground for modern ethnographic methods, as well as being a landmark for the subfield later known as economic anthropology. Malinowski's analysis of Kula and the canoe-paddling seafarers who exchange shell artifacts whose high value depends on their unique histories has been appropriated and reinterpreted by many later authors. Almost immediately after their first publication, Marcel Mauss drew on these materials to illustrate his theory of the gift (Mauss 2015). He also suggested that the necklaces and armbands exchanged by the Trobrianders constituted a form of money, disagreeing with Malinowski on this point. Karl Polanyi read Malinowski in the 1930s. He was inspired by the Trobriand data to propose the concepts of reciprocity and redistribution as "forms of integration" in economies that were embedded in social organization as a whole, with market exchange playing at most a subordinate role (Polanyi 1944, 1957). *Argonauts* was thus prominent in the canon of Polanyi's "substantivist" school; but Malinowski's data were also subjected to "formalist" analysis, and later to feminist reinterpretations. His ethnography continues to feature in the very latest journal articles and textbooks in the twenty-first century.

The significance of *Argonauts* in the history of anthropology is uncontested: for functionalism as a general paradigm, and for the gestation of economic anthropology in particular. This book pays particular attention to what "economy" meant for Malinowski in successive phases of his career—between his intellectual formation in the Austro-Hungarian Empire and his later fieldwork-inspired analyses. Contributors consider various works, including his 1906 Kraków dissertation on the "economy of thought" and the article on "primitive economics" he published in *The Economic Journal* in 1921. His concern with economy and economics does not end with the publication of *Argonauts* a year later. A similarly dense monograph was devoted to Trobriand gardening and property arrangements (Malinowski 1935). Finally, in the summers of 1940 and 1941, Malinowski investigated very different forms of economy in Oaxaca, Mexico (Malinowski and de la Fuente 1982), while simultaneously drafting a last review article that remained unpublished at the time of his death (Malinowski 1940–41).

We ask: what is the legacy of Bronisław Malinowski for later generations of anthropologists investigating economy? Can production, exchange, and consumption in "tribal" and "peasant" societies be investigated in the terms of modern economics? Or is it a mistake to start from these categories, because social orders such as that of the Trobriand Islanders should be approached in their own terms, through relationships grounded in kinship and politics, and practices of magic and ritual? Can these stark alternatives somehow be combined? The chapters in this volume explore these and other questions raised by *Argonauts* in the light of its rich contents and myriad contexts. They investigate the European intellectual currents on which it draws as well as the Melanesian setting, the conditions in which it was written, the importance of this monograph for the career of the author, and its lasting influence, especially for economic anthropology. Our themes are far from antiquarian, for we are also interested in the ways in which *Argonauts* continues to provide a stimulus for contemporary anthropological analysis. Beyond the theoretical and methodological issues of a (sub)discipline, contributors engage with the direction of the anthropological field as a whole. How can the kind of fieldwork pioneered by Malinowski a century ago be adapted and "stretched" to serve the agendas of contemporary, postcolonial anthropology? Does the ethnographic method remain foundational?

Malinowski's Reception and the Organization of this Volume

Bronisław Malinowski has long been celebrated as the founder of a distinctive British school in social anthropology (Kuper 1973). In two decades of often frantic activity before his premature death in 1942, he aspired to exactly this. His publications, notably a series of monographs about the Trobriand Islanders of Melanesia, were immediately influential. Many are still read today, and not just by specialists on the region and historians of anthropology. From 1924 onward, his seminar at the London School of Economics was a training ground for an extraordinary mix of scholars, many of them from outside Britain, who came to dominate anthropological research in the twilight of the British Empire. The standards he set through his long-term field research ("participant observation" as it came to be known later) have remained the gold standard of the discipline into the new century.

And yet, the reception has been uneven. Some of Malinowski's own students expressed ambivalence, for example about the ultimate grounding of functionalist theory in human biological needs. One early participant in the seminar later expressed contempt for "a futile thinker" (Evans-Pritchard 1981: 199). Arguably, the "structural functionalism" of Malinowski's contemporary A. R. Radcliffe-Brown, with its emphasis on controlled comparisons, had more influence on the discipline's later theoretical development. So did the structuralism of Claude Lévi-Strauss, which aimed to grasp universal characteristics of the human mind rather than describe how particular societies functioned to satisfy needs. Political and ethical problems came to the forefront following the publication of Malinowski's (1967) diary. Alongside the charge of personal racism, it was now alleged that Malinowski and the British school he shaped were complicit in colonial rule (Asad 1973; Geertz 1988). An influential historian of the discipline portrayed this school as exporting British folk models all around the world, especially in Africa (Kuklick 1993). Even the originality of Malinowski's field research is questioned: it has recently been argued that many others were practicing ethnographic methods in more or less scientific ways, well before Malinowski's work in the Trobriands (Rosa and Vermeulen 2022).

Even those who reached more positive verdicts on the life and work of Bronisław Malinowski sometimes did so on the basis of speculation and error. Edmund Leach attributed Malinowski's radical empiricism to a reading of contemporary American pragmatists, unaware that the innovator at the London School of Economics (LSE) had been deeply immersed in empiricist Viennese philosophy before his arrival in Britain (Leach 1957).[1] The source of his notion of needs (*Bedürfnisse*) was in Central Europe. Clouds of confusion concerning formative influences in Kraków and Leipzig before World War I were not dissipated until decades after his passing (Ellen et al. 1988; Young 2004). Anglophone scholars who had come to perceive Malinowski as an apologist for the British Empire struggled to appreciate the ways in which his worldview was decisively shaped by the continental empire of Austria-Hungary and his own identity as a Polish cultural nationalist (Gellner 1988). Those who had bemoaned Anglo-Saxon theoretical naivety in the work of Malinowski now had to recognize that in his youth he had been an outstanding philosopher; and that both his dissertation in the philosophy of science and his subsequent exposure to the economic teachings of the German Historical School contributed to the anthropology that he promoted so vigorously at the LSE from 1920 onward (Thornton with Skalník 1993). The first volume of Michael Young's definitive biography examined Malinowski's life and work up to 1918 (Young 2004). When the eagerly awaited second volume is published, there will no longer be any excuses for obfuscation and speculation in connecting the scholarly corpus to the life of the author.

This book focuses on the major work Malinowski published in 1922, *Argonauts of the Western Pacific*. This was the first of his Trobriand monographs and it has always been the best known. In addition to laying out the methods necessary for "scientific ethnology," *Argonauts* (as we shall refer to this work throughout) exemplifies Malinowski's approach to theory and is a key text in the emergence of economic anthropology. It also contains diffuse moral and political messages that can only be appreciated when placed in context: the British Empire was still a force to be reckoned with, but World War I had put an end to the empire of the Habsburgs and raised profound questions about Western civilization and the progress of humanity. These contexts are explored further in Part I of this book, in which we are pleased to be able to include a chapter by Michael Young documenting the circumstances in which Malinowski actually wrote *Argonauts* (in collaboration with his wife Elsie Masson).

We have a particular interest in how *Argonauts* gave birth to economic anthropology, which dominates Part II. Malinowski was keen to engage with the economists at the LSE, and thus with a discipline that was a great deal more powerful than his own.[2] How was he to make sense of production, distribution, and consumption in a society lacking money and markets, where these very concepts seemed to have no traction? His answers were shaped by his philosophical training as well as by his exposure to the evolutionism of historian Karl Bücher at the University of Leipzig. Although it was not the main theme of *Argonauts*, Malinowski's theorizing of *work* as it was performed within the complex whole of Trobriand society contrasted it with plantation labor and helped him to develop a concept of "tribal economy," in opposition to the market-dominated "national economies" studied by economists. This was not intended as a sharp relativizing move, since Malinowski explicitly hoped that further localized ethnographic studies like his own would open up comparative vistas and potentially lead to a rethinking of economic theory as well as concrete economic institutions. However, his inductive empiricism was at odds with the deductive models that were beginning to become dominant in mainstream (neoclassical) economics.

The Malinowskian contributions to the study of economy can be assessed from many angles. From one perspective, they are constructive provocations within the history of Western economic thought; from another, they are inadequate compromises that, due to their economic framing, end up imposing a Western view of the world where this is illegitimate. Malinowski himself must have had doubts about the work he published in the early 1920s: the concept of tribal economy was quietly dropped thereafter (Spittler 2008: 225–26). But the seeds sown here came to full fruition with the emergence of economic anthropology as a named subfield in the aftermath of World War II. We discuss these matters further below.

The very name "economic anthropology" continues to make some anthropologists uncomfortable. In Part III, contributors probe further into the contradictions of a stance that insists on the functional interconnections of all social domains but at the same time pulls them apart in analysis that is driven by the categories of the modern Western observer. For the Trobrianders, garden magicians and ancestral spirits are among the most powerful economic agents. Malinowski is also open to criticism for his neglect of recent colonial economic and political history, not to mention long-term history that was not available to him because important archaeological research had not yet been undertaken. The contributors to this section elaborate on points that Malinowski himself began to concede late in life: Kula expeditions and the exchanges that structure *Argonauts* cannot be taken out of time; they never formed a hermetically sealed, stable system. Rather, the salience of ceremonial exchange and limitations placed on accumulation in the Trobriands must be investigated comparatively with respect to belief systems, kinship organization, and a range of historical factors.

Finally, expanding on fragments of materials presented in several earlier chapters, the contributors to Part IV illustrate how the methods emphasized in *Argonauts*—including reworkings of the model developed by Malinowski to grasp Kula exchange in the Trobriand Islands—can be deployed in the contemporary world. The volume closes with an account of the continued relevance of the original Malinowskian methods for extending the boundaries of "digital ethnography" in an adjacent region of Oceania.

Argonauts, Functionalism, and the Ethnographic Method

Astute authorial self-insinuation and the sheer remoteness of the Trobriand Islands at the eastern end of Papua New Guinea have helped Malinowski's first monograph retain its place in the canon. The construction of an unsullied tribe, savage yet entirely rational in ways that neither other travelers nor armchair scholars in the metropolis could readily appreciate, was crucial to Malinowski's reconstruction of the disciplinary field on scientific foundations. But what exactly was *Argonauts* all about, and how did it establish a new theoretical paradigm as well as new methods?

Malinowski's account of the Kula has been summarized in countless anthropology textbooks. We repeat this here in schematic form, using the "ethnographic present." It involves systematic exchange between trading partners. Annual visits are undertaken by these partners, traveling in canoes, who exchange highly valued shell ornaments: necklaces (*soulava*) and armbands (*mwali*). The voyages require considerable time and effort, not to mention the dangers involved in deep-sea navigation. The main motivation was seen by Malinowski in terms of social function. Each participant is linked to two partners: one partner trading a necklace for an armband of equivalent value, and the other making a reverse exchange of an armband for a necklace. Each of those partners has an additional connection linking him to a further trader, and the system of partnerships eventually forms a circle, with necklaces circulating in one direction while armbands travel in the other. The circle links more than a dozen islands over hundreds of miles of ocean. Malinowski's analysis of its function was threefold. First, it establishes relations among the inhabitants of different islands, maintaining peaceful contact and communication over great distances with trading partners, some of whom have no language in common. Second, it enables the *gimwali* barter of more useful items, piggybacking on that of the shell valuables. Third, since hereditary chiefs own the most important shell valuables and are responsible for initiating voyages, it enhances the status of these chiefs (White 2003).

This, in briefest outline, gives a sense of Malinowski's findings. The high quality of his data was recognized from the start. Economic anthropologists have continued to mine the Trobriand corpus in putting forward their own ideas, for instance concerning money (Hart 1986) and value (Graeber 2001). *Argonauts* has been revisited by countless regional specialists in the century since its first publication. Kula expeditions continued to the end of the colonial era in 1975 and after independence. They were the subject of a large international conference in Cambridge in 1978 (Leach and Leach 1983). New generations of researchers discovered gaps, for example concerning the agency of women (Weiner 1976; Strathern 1988), and also that of the spirits (Mosko 2017, this volume). From the radical perspective of Marilyn Strathern, Malinowski's alleged demolition of "economic man" is based on erroneous premises, because he fails to realize that personhood in Melanesia is constructed on different foundations from the Euro-American individual.

But each successive critique has only cemented the iconic status of Malinowski's book in terms of the fieldwork methods it exemplified. Coming "off the veranda" and living in a tent among the natives "on the ground" enabled a detailed observation of everyday practices. Searching for the deeper significance of these made it possible to see a socioeconomic phenomenon in a far-off setting as contributing to the formation of long-lasting relationships and interdependencies. That is, it made a "functionalist" analysis possible. This approach took anthropology into the realm of methodical social science rather than leaving it as a collection of facts about obscure rituals and inexplicable practices. Crucially, as Malinowski developed it, attention needed to be paid to individual behaviors, psyches, and motivations. The ethnographic method made it possible for an anthropologist to observe discrepancies between reported custom and actual behavior, thus recognizing that individuals are not routinely governed by—or slaves to—such custom.

When Malinowski established his "Thursday seminar" at the LSE, he found a means of inculcating the importance of a fieldwork-based approach to a generation of scholars, including an inner circle of "Mandarins" (Morrow 2016: 90) but also many—like Monica Hunter and Godfrey Wilson, enrolled at Oxbridge—who attended as "guests" rather than registered students (ibid: 89). Not all accepted his style of analysis. Many had fierce debates over "whether or not to be functionalists" (ibid.: 90): some ended up opting, instead, for the "structural functionalism" of Radcliffe-Brown or Fortes's "descent theory." But while the theoretical approach was increasingly contested, the ethnographic method was abiding. These scholars went on, in turn, to hold professorial and other positions at a range of universities, both in Britain and abroad (Foks 2023).

A Century of Ethnographic Economic Anthropology

An early assessment of "The Place of Malinowski in Economic Anthropology" was provided under that title by Raymond Firth in the 1957 volume that he edited. While lauding the ethnographic accomplishments, Firth was critical of his teacher's failure to quantify any of the exchanges he documented and his general lack of sophistication in economics. He complained, for example, about Malinowski's muddled language in describing the "utility" of Trobriand labor: "This is not the terminology of economics, it is almost the language of the housewife" (Firth 1957: 220).

Malinowski has been defended against Firth's "formalist" criticism from quite different angles. On the one hand, the self-proclaimed "substantivist" Marshall Sahlins found the very lack of professional expertise attractive, since the anthropologist should be more interested in the (emic) perspective of the housewife than in the (etic) imposition of the analytic categories of a modern economist (Sahlins 1974: 186). On the other hand, Scott Cook (trained in economics and highly critical of substantivism) found Malinowski to have a shrewd grasp of the economic principles of the market system that he investigated in Oaxaca at the very end of his life (Cook 2017; Cook and Young 2016). Sahlins and Cook belonged to opposing camps in the polemical debates between substantivists and their formalist critics in the 1960s that constituted a coming of age for the field by now known as economic anthropology. Neither school took account of Malinowski's early training in continental Europe (nor indeed did his student Firth). His contribution to the emergence of economic anthropology as a (sub)discipline is generally perceived as weak, primarily ethnographic in character. The later, more intellectually focused, debates are associated primarily with another Central European, Karl Polanyi, who drew heavily on Malinowski's Trobriand data in his seminal work (Polanyi 1944). But a closer look at the background and career of the author of *Argonauts* is instructive for a more adequate grasp of theorizing in this field.

Malinowski was born in Kraków in 1884, two years before Polanyi was born in Vienna.[3] As intellectuals in the last decades of the Austro-Hungarian Empire, both were immersed in the slow consolidation of a new social order in a region that was as peripheral to the advanced centers of European capitalism then as it is today. They imbibed similar intellectual currents in their respective universities. Positivists were in the ascendant as political economy morphed into neoclassical economics in the closing decades of the nineteenth century (Gregory, this volume). Malinowski received no training in any version of economics in Kraków; but the title of his doctoral dissertation, defended at the Jagiellonian University in 1906, was "On the Principle of the Economy of Thought" (*O zasadzie ekonomii myślenia*) (Malinowski 1993: 89–115). This was a study of the limitations of positivist philosophy, particularly the ideas of Ernst Mach, who was extremely influential at the time. The same works of Mach were imbibed by Karl Polanyi almost simultaneously in Budapest. Malinowski was attracted by Mach's efforts to theorize science on the basis of concepts of minima and maxima and "least effort," though he also expressed criticisms. The excellence of this dissertation secured its author the *Habilitacja* scholarship that enabled him to move to London and begin his celebrated association with the LSE.

"Economy of thinking," according to the young Malinowski, is an invention of late nineteenth-century thinkers. But he proceeds at once to probe the Greek etymology of *oikonomia*, meaning management, be it of "livestock, a social group, or a physical system" (Malinowski 1993: 91). More specifically:

> we understand by economy not management in general but good management. Since the worth of management is measured by the magnitude of the objectives achieved in relation to the means used, we may call economy, in the specific sense of this word, namely thrift, a minimum outlay with the same gain, or a maximum gain achieved with the same means; both formulations come to the same thing. (ibid.)

Although this work focuses on the positivists, it also reveals the influence of Malinowski's early reading of Nietzsche (Thornton with Skalník 1993: 16–26). He concludes that it is impossible to do away with metaphysics altogether. Economy is the basis of Mach's philosophy of science, which posits a physiological basis in the mind of the scientist, whose task is to explain physical phenomena as efficiently as possible. Mach privileges biology and the senses, but he is simultaneously an idealist and a relativist who denies the reality of an empirical world "out there." For Malinowski, however, the "economy of thought" has to be made concrete and contextualized: in other words, connected to particular human beings and their communities. In this way, the Kraków dissertation and Malinowski's later accomplishments as an ethnographer and theoretician of functionalism in terms of biological needs were connected.

These notions of economy, thrift, and efficiency must be placed in a range of contexts. Intellectually, Ernst Mach engaged with the political economist Emanuel Herrmann (Staley, this volume). They were contemporaries of Carl Menger, one of the founders of neoclassical "marginalist" economics from the 1870s. Mach's deployment of *Ökonomie* in his philosophy of science has an affinity with the marginalism of the neoclassicals (and with a more specific Austrian tradition that later included Ludwig von Mises and Friedrich August von Hayek), notwithstanding the fact that the emerging economic science emphasized deductive methods. This tradition emphasizes the choices made by firms and individuals in ways presumed to be rational, that is, to maximize profits and satisfaction respectively.

From Mach, Malinowski also learned that "facts" depend logically on the theory that has been empirically deployed to collect and select them. But the initial theory is subject to testing (later philosophers of science would develop the concept of falsification) and Mach's perspective therefore opened up avenues to develop new ideas and theories promiscuously on the basis of empirical data. As Thornton with Skalník (1993: 35) argues: "In accepting Mach's belief that 'theory creates facts,' [Malinowski's] openness to many theoretical perspectives led him to collect and to observe a great many facts."

After the ceremonial award of his doctorate in 1908, Malinowski moved initially to Leipzig, where he was exposed to the teachings of an influential representative of very different ways of thinking about economy. The economic historian Karl Bücher taught universal laws of development, with the principles of economic organization changing in each successive stage. Bücher hypothesized an initial "pre-economic" condition. The main feature of this *Urgesellschaft* (primitive society) was the "individual search for food." This stage was followed by the "closed household economy," traces of which could still be observed in the European peasantry. But self-sufficient households had generally been overtaken by more complex forms of production and exchange, culminating in the *Nationalökonomie* of the modern state. Karl Bücher represented an empirical *Volkswirtschaftslehre* ("Teaching the People's Economy") rather than an abstract *Ökonomie*. His interest in concrete institutions placed him closer theoretically to Gustav von Schmoller and the Berlin-based Historical School, though he was respectful toward the general theories put forward by scholars based in the Habsburg empire such as Mach and Menger (Hann and Hart 2011: 39–41).

Malinowski's first explicit engagement with economic anthropology (neither the name nor the subfield yet existed) was a 1912 chapter in English in a Festschrift for Edward Westermarck. This paper, based on secondary literature, contains numerous echoes of Bücher (Firth 1957: 211). Malinowski draws an evolutionist distinction between economic and pre-economic labor to argue that only through magic and ritual can primitive man be mobilized to carry out productive activity efficiently in the modern sense (see Smith, this volume). However, following his Trobriand fieldwork, Malinowski became critical of Bücher, while simultaneously polemicizing against mainstream economics and rejecting the concept of "economic man." The complex organization of ceremonial exchange in the Trobriand "tribal economy" contradicted the assumptions of Bücher's first two stages. It was clear that the principle of least effort did not have universal validity, since the natives of Kiriwina on the Trobriand Islands toiled in their gardens to produce many more yams than they could consume (but see Gregory, this volume). This "surplus" was transferred to matrilineal kin in the form of *urigubu* payments, and to chiefs.

Before writing up his Trobriand analyses, Malinowski read two major works of mainstream economics in the English language: Alfred Marshall's *Principles of Economics* and Irving Fisher's *Purchasing Power of Money* (Young 2004: 603). His seminal publications in the early 1920s reveal a struggle to reconcile the contrasting senses of "economy" to which he had been exposed in his training in continental Europe: on the one hand, rational choice-making to maximize satisfactions; and on the other, a substantive embedding of production, exchange, and consumption in institutions that were locally rooted and regulated by custom, practices, and above all values. The bias of the Trobriand publications is to the latter. Thus, the principle of least effort is rejected again in *Coral Gardens and Their Magic* (1935). Here we learn more about the aesthetic values of maintaining a beautiful yam garden, which have implications for social emulation and "morals." It is bad manners to call a gardener lazy; yet some clearly are, and their reputation suffers in consequence. On the other hand, it is also unwise to be too proficient and diligent. This can lead to accusations of vanity, greed, and even sorcery.[4] Malinowski's lively accounts of individual agency are consistent with his own values and what might be termed his political agenda, which is to refute the notions of collective ownership and primitive communism that were current in early twentieth-century Europe, inside anthropology as well as outside it. Malinowski showed that the "tribal economy" was made up of individual actors who interacted in complex ways. The key to social organization was to be found in the property system, above all in how land was held and used by persons and kin groups. Much of this fitted very well with what was later consolidated in the substantivist school of Karl Polanyi.

However, at his academic base in the 1930s the discipline of economics was developing quite differently. Whether or not Malinowski interacted with John Maynard Keynes through his Bloomsbury connections, or with Lord Lionel Robbins and Friedrich Hayek in the senior common room at the LSE, he must have had some awareness of developments in the larger discipline. The LSE was a stronghold of the emerging neoclassical orthodoxy, in which it was taken for granted that this version of economics had universal validity. Raymond Firth applied this paradigm to the Polynesian island of Tikopia (Firth 1939). Junior members of the LSE seminar working in less remote locations such as the African colonies were even more attracted to the neoclassical approach to economy, in terms of individuals making choices in conditions of scarcity. After the outbreak of World War II, extending his stay in the United States, Malinowski himself undertook field research with the help of a local partner in peasant marketplaces in Mexico (Malinowski and de la Fuente 1982). He found an equivalent of Trobriand Kula in the regional marketing system of the Oaxaca Valley, an institution that integrated far-flung communities, many of them economically more specialized than those of the Trobriands (Cook 2017). Oaxaca commodity markets were highly monetized, yet dominated by peasant-artisans whose sociocultural relations were as complex as those of Melanesia. Malinowski died in 1942 and never wrote up this work in a theoretical framework comparable to that of the "tribal economy" he had proposed two decades earlier for the case of the Trobriand Islands.

While engaging with this new material, Malinowski wrote a lengthy review of a landmark volume by Melville Herskovits (Herskovits 1940; Malinowski 1940–41). His major critique of Herskovits was an echo of the Machian arguments he analyzed in his Kraków dissertation: Malinowski insisted on the primacy of the empirical complexity uncovered by the fieldworker; theorization should only follow later. Yet in the same document he went out of his way to praise the new work of Firth, together with that of David Goodfellow in South Africa (Goodfellow 1939). This represented a more "aggressively neoclassicist" approach than anything advocated by Herskovits (Cook and Young 2016: 668, 671). To judge from this evidence, influenced both by what he had observed on the ground in the monetized economy of Oaxaca as well as the neoclassical approaches that dominated in London, by the 1940s Malinowski was probably ready to grant the rational choice principles of microeconomics more general, perhaps even universal validity. Yet he simultaneously upheld an institutionalist, substantivist approach to understanding particular economies and the relationships between them. He maintained the position that fieldwork should be a basis for fresh theorizing. Yet, for all the rich detail in his notebooks from Oaxaca in 1940 and 1941, there is no sign that the unfinished research in Mexico would yield a new theoretical paradigm.[5]

The arguments of both Herskovits and Malinowski are replete with inconsistencies, even contradictions (Cook and Young 2016). Malinowski tended to see strategizing, maximizing individuals everywhere (Parry 1986: 454), a penchant that may have owed at least as much to his intellectual trajectory in Central Europe as to later influences at the LSE. Toward the end of his life, having embarked on research into peasant markets in Mexico, he seems to have been more willing to endorse theories extrapolated from mainstream economics. He stops short of postulating a new subdiscipline called "economic anthropology." In place of "primitive economics" and "tribal economy," his framework when writing *Argonauts*, by the time of his death, with the Oaxaca project still unfinished, in his unpublished review of Herskovits he offers "ethnographic economics" (Malinowski 1940–41; Cook and Young 2016: 659–60).

Malinowski never used the concept of "embeddedness," which later became the mantra of the substantivist school.[6] He never recommends a strong relativism, in which the world consists of incommensurable local models. He does not reduce economics to culture (Gudeman 1986). Like Polanyi, he was interested in generalizations and the comparison of types of economy. Both were uncomfortable about defining these types simplistically in terms of evolution. Malinowski would surely have objected to the attempt by Janet Tai Landa (representative of the so-called "new institutionalism" that built on earlier "formalist" approaches and enjoyed considerable popularity in the last decades of the twentieth century) to rationalize Kula exchanges from the point of view of an evolutionary economics driven by rational choices to minimize transaction costs (Landa 1994).[7] What Malinowski accomplished in *Argonauts* and repeated in *Coral Gardens* was to demonstrate that the study of economy must be adapted to prevailing institutions. It must include the study of beliefs and values as well as material flows. This is why Malinowski's "ethnographic economics" was congenial to the Polanyians; and why it was defended by Sahlins against the reservations expressed by Firth; and why it continues to inspire anthropological approaches to economy in the twenty-first century.

The Chapters

We have found it convenient to organize the volume in four parts, even though some chapters touch on multiple themes and might have been classified differently. The first four chapters situate *Argonauts* in a series of contexts. Grażyna Kubica provides insight into Malinowski's family background, supplementing the information presented by Michael Young (2004) in his biography with archival material from the Archive of the Jagiellonian University and other sources. She demolishes the common assumption (even "myth," possibly promoted by Malinowski himself) that he was a Polish aristocrat. In fact, he belonged to the emerging, "post-noble," intelligentsia—a social *stratum* rather than a *class*—whose cultural capital far outstripped their wealth but who remained aloof from the masses. The son of a poorly paid professor of Slavic linguistics at the Jagiellonian University who died when his only child was still a schoolboy, Malinowski grew up practicing "snobbery on a shoestring." This background, argues Kubica, affected the way he interacted with white settlers and colonial officers in Melanesia—and perhaps also his understanding of the sociopolitical hierarchies of Trobriand society.

Moving on to the moment of post-fieldwork, Michael Young's chapter discusses the writing of *Argonauts* in 1921, when Malinowski and his wife Elsie, together with their new baby, took up residence on Tenerife. Malinowski had initially planned a comprehensive volume on the life of the islanders entitled "Kiriwina," but soon realized that this would be impossible. What was originally intended as a mere chapter of that volume turned into a volume of its own; its contents and approach are carefully summarized in the chapter. Elsie assisted with the writing in crucial ways, as he acknowledged by writing on the flyleaf of the copy he eventually gave her—she "had half the share at least and more than half the merit"—but her name was missing, along with those of many others who assisted, from the publication. With what appears, in retrospect, to be an extraordinary lack of foresight, Macmillan declined to take it on, on the grounds that "it is very difficult to get a sale" for "these anthropological books." *Argonauts* has been in print in the Routledge catalogue ever since.

Delineating the functionalist approach that, first outlined in *Argonauts*, would go on to become a hallmark of the Malinowskian school (albeit one that attracted criticism from the beginning), Adam Kuper's chapter shows how the other features of Malinowski's "new paradigm" informed and underpinned that approach. In setting out the "function" of rituals and institutions, Malinowski saw the individual as logically prior to the community. Averse to Durkheimian-style holism, he saw the "give and take" of exchange, although it contributed to solidarity and was "organized and regulated by custom," as being initiated by individuals who manipulate rules to suit themselves. Here, the "imponderabilia of actual life" (especially those aspects that appeared not to fit with homogenizing views of custom) were important. The chapter also points to a key "flaw" of such work, namely Malinowski's ignoring of "external influences."

While this may have been true of *Argonauts* itself, as Freddy Foks shows in his chapter, Malinowski was well aware of the "extractive economic regime" that was unfolding in the Western Pacific during this period. Foks characterizes Malinowski's attitude toward plantation labor as "ambivalent." He postulates the Kula as the "mirror image" of that system of production, and thus a critique of the utilitarian or profit-driven economics that undermined evolved native economies. To draw labor away from this system via recruitment would necessarily degrade the economy. Malinowski, shows Foks, supported a protectionist approach called "trusteeship." He supported chiefly rule (up to a point) in the "interests of the natives," and was, in effect, an "anti-colonial imperialist."

Several chapters explore the nature of economy and economic explanation. The fact that production, exchange, and consumption were regulated by custom and kinship rather than money and markets did not mean that natives were not "economically minded." This fundamental point is explored further by Rachel Smith in the first chapter in Part II. Her particular focus is on "incentives to work," and on Malinowski's distinction between the drudgery of labor for white plantation owners and the fulfilling character of work done in the local setting where work "makes life worth living." Drawing (as do Foks and Staley) on evidence given by Malinowski in 1916 to a parliamentary commission investigating the Labor Question, Smith highlights the problematic boundary between the "economic" and the "non-economic" or what Malinowski called "not purely economical." If the "incentive" to cooperate with others in productive activities lay in magic, religion, or kinship organization, the implication was that these activities would have to be recognized as "economic." Malinowski evidently felt that the motives of Indigenous peoples were structured according to an entirely different and incompatible social system.

Richard Staley traces continuities in Malinowski's concept of the economic from his dissertation work in Kraków through to the fieldwork-based publications that culminated in *Argonauts*. Respecting the native point of view in its own terms will, Malinowski argues at the end of the book, provide the basis for a true "Science of Man" and for a better understanding by Europeans of their own culture. According to Staley, while the Trobriands are presented as an allegory of the world economy with its industrial, agricultural, and fishing centers and international trade, Malinowski nonetheless relativizes Euro-American assumptions (both expert and lay) about economy and economics. But although his concept of tribal economy enabled him to represent the integrity of native life and customs, it limited his ability to recognize and represent critical elements of its engagement with other economies.

The dichotomy of knowability versus uncertainty is central to Chris Gregory's chapter. He takes us back to debates about economy in the early years of the twentieth century concerning the predictability of economic outcomes and demonstrates that Malinowski played a key role in these. John Maynard Keynes and Malinowski were both concerned to demonstrate how people deal with the unknowable. Keynes, like others in the Bloomsbury group, was opposed to cold Benthamite calculation. His "theory of the knowability of the unknowable reveals a paradox that lies at the heart of mainstream theory of entrepreneurial decision-making, namely, that the necessity for action in the face of incalculable economic uncertainty leads to the paradox of having to measure the unmeasurable" (see p. 154). Economists such as Frank Knight could not grasp uncertainty (though their successors have presumed to do so down to the present day). The solution in the Trobriand Islands lies in "meaningless words:" magical chants help the islanders to cope with uncertainty in verbal rather than numerical terms.

Benoît de L'Estoile challenges the framework in which, he claims, economic anthropology has been trapped since the pioneering work of Malinowski. Despite the best efforts of Malinowski to open up new horizons for anthropology by studying primitive economic life alongside later forms, anthropology has thrived as the study of 'other economies,' largely on the periphery of capitalist markets. Both in *Argonauts* and in his programmatic article in *The Economic Journal* published in the previous year, Malinowski argued that the Trobriand Islanders had a form of organized economy both equivalent to and different from the one in the modern West. To analyze this economy, he used familiar terms such as production, work, consumption, and division of labor. For de L'Estoile, this betrays an inability to shed "our own Western native ontological beliefs and categories" (p. 153) accentuated by anthropologists' keenness to be taken seriously by "real" economists. In place of this distorted "economic framing," he proposes fieldwork-based emic visions of economic life that he interprets in terms of the ancient Greek word *oikonomia*, emphasizing not rational management but the dimensions of "government" and "autonomy." In contemporary Latin America, it is precisely people's vulnerability to the imposition of random government forces that makes "control" within the house so important.

In addition to considering political issues such as control, might Malinowski have paid more attention to other, seemingly "non-economic," aspects of the systems he plotted, such as the magic spells and incantations he detailed? And can modern-day anthropologists think more seriously about the broader topic of time and how changes have been—and perhaps still are—incorporated in system-oriented (once called "synchronic") analyses like that of the smoothly operating Kula? The exploration of how colonial arrangements enabled and influenced Malinowski's views on exchange, labor, and the like opens up questions such as: what happened earlier—and why have we not consulted the archaeological record to find out? Broadening the discussion beyond Papua New Guinea, might Kula-type arrangements be found in other settings? The three chapters of Part III revisit Malinowski's Trobriand ethnography from these perspectives.

Mark Mosko looks again at the relation between economic and non-economic with reference to cosmology. Based on long-term fieldwork on Kiriwina, his chapter suggests that Malinowski's determination to find something "economic" in all Trobriand activity led him to underestimate otherworldly economic agency and thus portray "tribal economy" in narrowly materialist terms. Mosko sees Malinowski's understandings of the meaning of "labor" as pragmatic and as underpinning a rigid divide between the economic and the non-economic (more or less equivalent to the divide between living beings in the here-and-now and those that exist beyond). The dense verbiage used by magicians that Gregory notes in his chapter did not, claims Mosko, work in the quasi-mechanical manner Malinowski presumed. Rather, it functioned to communicate with ancestral spirits (*baloma*). Acknowledging this allows one to recognize that spirits have their own Kula and thereby to shed new light on the celebrated "virgin birth" debate. Mosko concludes by noting that Malinowski's neglect of this dimension was only obliquely critiqued in Marcel Mauss's *The Gift*.

Many critics of Malinowskian functionalism, and of *Argonauts* in particular, have complained about the neglect of history. Hans Steinmüller draws on both archaeological and ethnographic data to argue that "the ethnographic Kula was a relatively recent invention, and that the history of the Kula was intimately tied in with changes in ecology, warfare, and memory." He shows that for Malinowski "to emphasize rational rule-following, it was necessary to downplay violence and creativity": specifically, the warring between islanders that was brought to an end by colonial "pacification." This suppression of warfare likely released valuables into the exchange system, thus inflating the worth of Kula valuables and setting the stage for the emergence of "big men." The rules of the Kula reflect long-term creative adaptations. Neglecting such changes, according to Steinmüller, serves to simplify and abstract the nature of this exchange system. It led to a model called "reciprocity" that mistakenly presupposed the equality of the various parties involved in exchanges.

Yongjia Liang also pursues a historical approach to the Kula, in this case through the lens of the *Laozi*, a Chinese literary work of the sixth century BCE. Here, too, the attribution of high value to goods that cannot be accumulated but must be circulated functions to integrate societies while keeping them small and peaceful. The chapter explores parallels between Laozi's idealized political system and "dual chiefship" in the Trobriands, where there is a paradoxical opposition between kinship-based exchange and land-based administration. Matrilineal kinship dilutes the potential for monopoly by allowing for alternative social orders. At least temporarily, it held these internal tensions in balance, where resolving them would have moved the system irrevocably toward patriliny (and hierarchy). At a metatheoretical level, Liang argues that introducing a Sinic civilizational perspective alongside the dominant Greco-Roman episteme (cf. de L'Estoile, whose radical critique of "economic framing" remains within the Western universalist tradition) can make anthropology more truly global. He rejects a relativist collapsing of analysis into a plethora of non-Western exceptionalisms.

We close with three more chapters illustrating how the influence of *Argonauts* has traveled and continues to make itself felt in space and time. Maxim Bolt seizes on the idea of "circulation," a notion with a long history in political economy and central in very literal ways to Malinowski's analysis of the Kula. In Bolt's study of newly instantiated private property in urban South Africa, in a postapartheid setting formerly characterized by communal or family ownership, houses are transferred from the hands of a group in one generation into the hands of a specific individual in the next. In a context of fracture and dispute, pathways of value can create circuits (or fail to do so); conceptions of movement and circulation can coexist within a single field; and forward movement and change can coexist with reversal and repetition. While "folk models" of circulation imply quasi-automatic processes of flow and onward movement in a single direction, the ethnographer is able to show how much more complicated possession and ownership are in reality—not unlike Kula circulation itself.

Sociologists, too, have drawn on *Argonauts* for inspiration, particularly in South America. A Malinowskian-style ethnographic approach informs Ariel Wilkis's analysis of money in Argentina, although he departs from Malinowski in identifying a range of diverse types (or "pieces") of money in the two contrasting settings he has investigated. Among the poor of Buenos Aires, a householder parcels her finances up into separate conceptual bundles ("pieces") occasionally converting one into the other strategically, in a manner informed by moral calculation, political necessity, or the need for social continuity. In the countryside, at a time when the peso was subject to wild fluctuations and the US dollar was seen as "healthy" by contrast, farmers used the soybean for speculation, alternately converting or cannily withholding it to maximize returns. Overall, the chapter explores how "social ties, economic transactions, and political actions are configured by monetary hierarchies that organize and classify the uses, meanings, and functions of money."

Finally, we return to the Pacific, in this case to Solomon Islands, where Geoffrey Hobbis and Stephanie Ketterer Hobbis report on latecomers to digitalization, delayed by a range of environmental, infrastructural, and geographic barriers. The digital practices they investigate turn out to be both "in but also beyond" capitalism. To understand them, "digital ethnography" is not sufficient. Like the Argonauts of Malinowski's account, their interlocutors "surf the world wide web to build, maintain, and strengthen relationships of perpetual mutual indebtedness." Wealth earned through enterprise is valued, but must be redistributed rather than hoarded; doing so enables them to acquire relational fortune and fame. The economic lives of city-dwellers and the inhabitants of remote Malaita are very different: in the latter, the "bush internet" consists of a unique human infrastructure in which people download files and move them along Kula-like pathways. In a human–object communications network that brings the country into a new sort of "ring," these files are carried in pockets, bags, and wallets and transported on trucks and in ships, dugout canoes, and banana boats, creating and affirming relationships of perpetual mutual indebtedness.

Acknowledgments

We are indebted to our respective institutions for their support in the organization of a centennial workshop "Malinowski and the Argonauts" at the LSE in early July 2022. Most chapters of this book are revised versions of papers presented in person at this meeting. Rebecca Empson participated as a discussant and we are grateful to her for contributing the Afterword. We are also indebted to Isaac Stanley for his assistance at the workshop, to three anonymous reviewers, to Anke Meyer in Halle for her assistance in preparing the manuscript, and to Tony Mason at Berghahn Books.

Chris Hann is Emeritus Director at the Max Planck Institute for Social Anthropology (Halle/Saale). He has worked as an economic anthropologist in provincial Hungary since the 1970s and has also carried out fieldwork in Poland, Turkey, and China (Xinjiang). His publications include *Repatriating Polanyi: Market Society in the Visegrád States* (Budapest, 2019) and

Economic Anthropology: History, Ethnography, Critique (with Keith Hart, Cambridge, 2011).

Deborah James is Professor of Anthropology at LSE. Her book *Money from Nothing: Indebtedness and Aspiration in South Africa* (Stanford, 2015) explores the lived experience of debt for those many millions who attempt to improve their positions (or merely sustain existing livelihoods) in emerging economies. She has also done research on advice (especially debt advice) encounters in the context of the UK government's austerity program and is coauthor (with Insa Koch) of "The State of the Welfare State: Advice, Governance and Care in Settings of Austerity" (in *Ethnos*, 2022).

Notes

1. Adam Kuper (this volume) continues to find merit in Leach's account on the grounds that American pragmatism was "fashionable" in England before World War I.
2. In the early 1920s, the subject was still popularly known as ethnology and Malinowski followed this usage. However, the designation "social anthropology" was gaining ground thanks to James Frazer, who chose this name for his chair at Liverpool in 1907, and also to R. R. Marett in Oxford. Given his formation in Central Europe, Malinowski might have been inclined to opt for cultural anthropology when specifying the title of his LSE readership in 1923; but the concept of culture was claimed (in quite specific ways) by local rivals at University College; see Firth (1988: 38–39).
3. Polanyi, though born in Vienna, grew up in Budapest. Like Malinowski, he was a cultural nationalist: a patriotic Hungarian throughout his life, most of which was spent in exile. Polanyi's bourgeois family was prosperous in comparison with the academic household in which Malinowski was raised in Kraków, but much of the family's wealth disappeared with a bankruptcy in 1906. Malinowski's family experienced financial pressures following the death of his father, a university professor (see Kubica, this volume).
4. Malinowski (1935, vol. 1: 175–176). Nowhere does Malinowski use the concept of a moral economy. But in the second volume of *Coral Gardens* he does write of "the moral tradition of a tribe"; he puts "economic values and morality" on a par with hunger and sex as determinants of "vital interests" (ibid., vol. 2: 47; cited in Spittler 2008: 239).
5. Malinowski's concerns in the unfinished Oaxaca project can be glossed as Weberian (Cook and Young 2016: 673). It is perhaps more accurate to state that the lasting legacy of his studies of Mach was a functionalism that was compatible with quite different traditions in social and political theory. Scott Cook finds the contributions of Herskovits to be confused and contradictory; it is hard to avoid reaching the same conclusion about the work of Malinowski himself.

6. The first anthropologist to use this metaphor was Malinowski's contemporary Richard Thurnwald (Firth 1972; Thurnwald 1932). Polanyi drew heavily on both Malinowski and Thurnwald in proposing his own concepts for the comparative analysis of economies not dominated by market exchange, namely reciprocity and redistribution; see Polanyi (1957).
7. Stephen Gudeman has repeatedly critiqued the work of Landa; see, e.g., Gudeman (2005: 138–40).

References

Asad, Talal, ed. 1973. *Anthropology and the Colonial Encounter*. London: Ithaca Press.
Cook, Scott. 2004. *Understanding Commodity Cultures: Explorations in Economic Anthropology with Case Studies from Mexico*. Lanham, MD: Rowman and Littlefield.
———. 2017. "Malinowski in Oaxaca: Implications of an Unfinished Project in Economic Anthropology." *Critique of Anthropology* 37(2): 132–59 (Part One) and 37(3): 228–43 (Part Two).
Cook, Scott, and Michael W. Young. 2016. "Malinowski, Herskovits, and the Controversy over Economics in Anthropology." *History of Political Economy* 48(4): 657–79.
Ellen, Roy, Ernest Gellner, Grażyna Kubica, and Janusz Mucha, eds. *Malinowski between Two Worlds: The Polish Roots of an Anthropological Tradition*. Cambridge: Cambridge University Press.
Evans-Pritchard, Edward. 1981. *A History of Anthropological Thought*. London: Faber and Faber.
Firth, Raymond. 1939. *Primitive Polynesian Economy*. London: Routledge.
———. 1957. "The Place of Malinowski in Economic Anthropology." In *Man and Culture: An Evaluation of the Work of Bronislaw Malinowski*, ed. Raymond Firth, 209–28. London: Routledge & Kegan Paul.
———. 1972. "Methodological Issues in Economic Anthropology." *Man* 7(3): 467–75.
———. 1988. "Malinowski in the History of Social Anthropology." In *Malinowski between Two Worlds: The Polish Roots of an Anthropological Tradition*, ed. Roy Ellen, Ernest Gellner, Grażyna Kubica, and Janusz Mucha, 12–42. Cambridge: Cambridge University Press.
Foks, Freddy. 2023. *Participant Observers: Anthropology, Colonial Development, and the Reinvention of Society in Britain*. Oakland: University of California Press.
Geertz, Clifford. 1988. *Works and Lives: The Anthropologist as Author*. Stanford, CA: Stanford University Press.
Gellner, Ernest. 1988. "'Zeno of Cracow' or 'Revolution at Nemi' or 'The Polish Revenge: A Drama in Three Acts.'" In *Malinowski between Two Worlds: The Polish Roots of an Anthropological Tradition*, ed. Roy Ellen, Ernest Gellner, Grażyna Kubica, and Janusz Mucha, 164–94. Cambridge: Cambridge University Press.
Goodfellow, D. M. 1939. *Principles of Economic Sociology*. London: George Routledge & Sons.
Graeber, David. 2001. *Toward an Anthropological Theory of Value: The False Coin of Our Own Dreams*. Basingstoke: Palgrave.

Gudeman, Stephen. 1986. *Economics as Culture*. Oxford: Blackwell.
———. 2005. "Realism, Relativism, and Reason: What's Economic Anthropology All About?" In *Peopled Economies: Conversations with Stephen Gudeman*, ed. Staffan Löfving, 111–55. Uppsala: Interface.
Hann, Chris, and Keith Hart. 2011. *Economic Anthropology: History, Ethnography, Critique*. Cambridge: Polity.
Hart, Keith. 1986. "Heads or Tails? Two Sides of the Coin." *Man* 21(4): 637–56.
Herskovits, Melville J. 1940. *The Economic Life of Primitive Peoples*. New York: Knopf.
———. 1952. *Economic Anthropology*. New York: Knopf.
Kuklick, Henrika. 1991. *The Savage Within: The Social History of British Anthropology, 1885–1945*. Cambridge: Cambridge University Press.
Kuper, Adam. 1973. *Anthropology and Anthropologists: The British School, 1922–1972*. London: Allen Lane.
Landa, Janet Tai. 1994. *Trust, Ethnicity, and Identity*. Ann Arbor: University of Michigan Press.
Leach, E. R. 1957. "The Epistemological Background to Malinowski's Empiricism." In *Man and Culture: An Evaluation of the Work of Bronislaw Malinowski*, ed. Raymond Firth, 119–37. London: Routledge & Kegan Paul.
Leach, Jerry W., and Edmund Leach, eds. 1983. *The Kula: New Perspectives on Massim Exchange*. Cambridge: Cambridge University Press.
Malinowski, Bronisław. 1921. "The Primitive Economics of the Trobriand Islanders." *The Economic Journal* 3(121): 1–16.
———. 1922. *Argonauts of the Western Pacific: An Account of Native Enterprise and Adventure in the Archipelagos of Melanesian New Guinea*. London: Routledge & Kegan Paul.
———. 1935. *Coral Gardens and Their Magic: A Study of the Methods of Tilling the Soil and of Agricultural Rites in the Trobriand Islands*. 2 vols. London: Allen & Unwin.
———. 1940–41. "Review of *The Economic Life of Primitive Peoples*, by Melville J. Herskovits." Typescript (Malinowski Archive at the London School of Economics, MPLSE 13/21).
———. 1967. *A Diary in the Strict Sense of the Term*. New York: Harcourt, Brace, and World.
———. 1993. *The Early Writings of Bronislaw Malinowski*, ed. Robert J. Thornton and Peter Skalník. Cambridge: Cambridge University Press.
Malinowski, Bronisław, and Julio de la Fuente. 1982. *Malinowski in Mexico: The Economics of a Mexican Market System*, ed. Susan Drucker-Brown. London: Routledge.
Mauss, Marcel. 2015 [1925]. *The Gift: Expanded Edition*, trans. Jane Guyer. Chicago: Hau Books.
Morrow, Sean. 2016. *The Fires Beneath: The Life of Monica Wilson, South African Anthropologist*. London: Penguin.
Mosko, Mark S. 2017. *Ways of Baloma*. Chicago: Hau Books.
Parry, Jonathan. 1986. "The Gift, the Indian Gift and the 'Indian Gift.'" *Man* 21(3): 453–73.
Polanyi, Karl. 1944. *The Great Transformation: The Political and Economic Origins of Our Time*. New York: Rinehart.

———. 1957. "The Economy as Instituted Process." In *Trade and Market in the Early Empires*, ed. Karl Polanyi, Conrad M. Arensberg, and Harry W. Pearson, 243–70. Glencoe: Free Press.

Rosa, Frederico Delgado, and Han F. Vermeulen, eds. 2022. *Ethnographers before Malinowski: Pioneers of Anthropological Fieldwork, 1870–1922*. New York: Berghahn.

Sahlins, Marshall. 1974. *Stone Age Economics*. London: Tavistock.

Spittler, Gerd. 2008. *Founders of the Anthropology of Work: German Social Scientists of the 19th and Early 20th Centuries and the First Ethnographers*. Berlin: Lit.

Strathern, Marilyn. 1988. *The Gender of the Gift: Problems with Women and Problems with Society in Melanesia*. Berkeley: University of California Press.

Thornton, Robert J., with Peter Skalník. 1993. "Introduction: Malinowski's Reading, Writing, 1904–1914." In *The Early Writings of Bronislaw Malinowski*, ed. Robert J. Thornton and Peter Skalník, 1–66. Cambridge: Cambridge University Press.

Thurnwald, Richard. 1932. *Economics in Primitive Communities*. Oxford: Oxford University Press.

Weiner, Annette B. 1976. *Women of Value, Men of Renown: New Perspectives in Trobriand Exchange*. Austin: University of Texas Press.

White, Eric. 2003. "Bronislaw Malinowski, Identifying the Kula Ring of the Trobriand Islanders: The Role of Ethnographic Field Observation in Pattern Recognition." *CSISS Classics*. Retrieved 24 October 2023 from https://escholarship.org/content/qt4rg9t7wv/qt4rg9t7wv.pdf.

Young, Michael W. 2004. *Malinowski: Odyssey of an Anthropologist, 1884–1920*. New Haven, CT: Yale University Press.

Part I

Bronisław Malinowski and His *Argonauts* in Context

1

 ## Cultural Capital and Economic Stringency
Reality and Myth in Bronisław Malinowski's Socioeconomic Background

Grażyna Kubica

Bronisław Malinowski has often been presented in British and American publications as a Polish aristocrat. It is not clear whether this was a result of deliberate attempts on his part to raise his social status in the eyes of anglophone readers, or simply a consequence of the impenetrability to outsiders of Polish social structure and its cultural dimensions. This chapter analyzes the socioeconomic standing of the Malinowski family in the context of the formation of the intelligentsia, a distinctive social stratum in Central and Eastern Europe. I build on information about Malinowski's background presented by Michael Young in his brilliant biography (Young 2004), and on my own earlier papers (Kubica 1988, 2002, 2015), by analyzing documents from the Archive of the Jagiellonian University and other sources, as well as presenting a historical-sociological, processual account of the intelligentsia phenomenon.

The sociocultural background of Bronisław Malinowski exemplified that of the Polish gentry (*szlachta*). All his ancestors were respectable nobility who owned estates. Some of them still did so during his lifetime, but his paternal grandfather lost his lands when his sons were still young. They were well educated and moved to the cities, where such men formed a new social class, the post-noble intelligentsia. This phenomenon has been widely discussed in history and the social sciences. Józef Chałasiński (an outstanding Polish sociologist who co-translated Malinowski's works into Polish in the 1930s) pointed out the importance, from a sociological point of view, of the form of collective life shared by members of the intelligentsia and their moral model. The intelligentsia created "a common social milieu with a clear tendency to separate from the rabble" (commoners)

(Chałasiński 1946: 35).[1] Its members played the role of "social lawmakers." They formed specific "social ghettos": just as commoner migrants formed new ghettos abroad, so the ghettos of the intelligentsia resulted from internal emigration and the transfer of "the noble element from the countryside to the cities" (ibid.: 46). Chałasiński characterized the situation whereby the intelligentsia continued the noble tradition without a foundation in landed property as "empty grandness." At the same time, fear of social degradation led to an intensified gulf vis-à-vis the common people, buttressed by their education. This gave members of the post-noble intelligentsia a sense of superiority over the emerging bourgeoisie, while reducing their distance from the aristocracy. The intelligentsia's ghetto could admit new members from a non-noble (peasant) background, but only if they broke their ties to their social class; and even if they did, access to social salons was sometimes withheld.

Chałasiński's stance was more critical than that of the Polish-American sociologist Aleksander Gella, who gave the following definition: "The old intelligentsia was a culturally united, though not homogeneous stratum of educated people, characterized by a charismatic sense of vocation and a certain syndrome of values and manners" (Gella 1989: 132–33; see also Gella 1976). The sense of vocation was inter alia a civilizing mission toward the people (*lud*). Recent analysis of the intelligentsia in Eastern and Central Europe, much of it inspired by Pierre Bourdieu, has highlighted the late impact of the industrial revolution on this region (see Zarycki 2008: 29). Social stratification therefore exhibits a distinctive duality, with a modern (capitalist) class hierarchy coexisting alongside traditional (feudal) stratification. If modernization consists in displacing the logic of social capital (group membership) by the logic of economic capital (contracted, institutionalized, and rationalized), in Central and Eastern Europe cultural capital plays an important but ambiguous role: it is a factor in the development of modern class structures, but it simultaneously strengthens traditional stratified structures (Eyal, Szelenyi, and Townsley 1998: 24–36).

In a premodern society, social capital dominates. It is capital that cannot be exchanged for any other type. It is supported by cultural capital as shared social knowledge that marks group membership (Zarycki 2008: 32). The autonomy of cultural from economic and political capital has lingered in Central and Eastern Europe due to the incomplete nature of modernization in this region (Martin and Szelenyi 1987; Zarycki 2008). Hybrid social systems privilege both informal types of social capital and embodied ("post-noble") forms of cultural capital. According to Zarycki: "On the one hand, the intelligentsia, being in a certain sense the heir of noble traditions, undoubtedly aspires to the role of connoisseur in the field of high culture, mainly its Western canons, and also to set the standards for a refined lifestyle and sophisticated cultural tastes. On the other hand, its ethos also has clear anti-establishment, anti-elite aspects, and sometimes strong egalitarian and democratic elements" (2008: 79; see also Zarycki 2003). Thus the intelligentsia and its various incarnations can at the same time be both conservative and progressive.[2]

An Impecunious Professor

Malinowski's paternal grandfather owned an estate in the Russian part of partitioned Poland.[3] When he filed for bankruptcy, his son Lucjan (1839–98) had to interrupt his gymnasium education. A few years later he managed to return to school, supporting himself by tutoring younger schoolmates. Later he studied linguistics at Szkoła Główna, a short-lived Polish university in Warsaw that was closed down by the Russian authorities. Thanks to the Szkoła Główna scholarships, he was able to visit institutions for Slavic philology in Prague, Jena, Berlin, Saint Petersburg, and Leipzig. In 1869, Lucjan conducted dialectological research in Silesia (then divided between Prussia and Austria-Hungary). He worked for much of this period as a gymnasium teacher in Kraków and Warsaw while longing to obtain a position at the oldest Polish university, the Jagiellonian University (UJ) in Kraków.

In the late nineteenth century, the UJ was governed in much the same way as other Austro-Hungarian universities. Running costs were covered by the central government in Vienna. It was, however, a very Polish institution as a result of the Polonization that accompanied the political autonomy of the Austrian province of Galicia, formally legislated in 1867. The UJ was comparable in size to the universities of Graz or Innsbruck. It was provincial, but its professors were well acquainted with leading centers of scholarship (Stinia 2014). Lucjan Malinowski's efforts to obtain a position at the UJ did not bear fruit for a long time (Taszycki 1974). He was finally appointed to a chair in Slavic philology in 1877. He also became a member of the Academy of Arts and Sciences and the secretary of its Language Commission. In 1883 he became a full professor, which meant a significant increase in salary. Only when he was sure of this promotion did he marry and start a family (at the age of 44). Having previously lived as a bachelor in a flat in a tenement house close to the railway station (24 Lubicz Street), after their marriage he and his new wife Józefa moved to 12 Podwale Street. Their son was born here. Later they moved to 36 Krowoderska Street, which was also within the Kleparz district, outside the historic center.

Józefa Łącka (1848–1918) came from a noble family that still possessed some land and estates. It was a fairly large family whose members maintained close relations with each other. Józefa was an educated person who probably attended a school for girls in Warsaw. In Malinowski's papers, I found a notebook containing essays written by her in beautiful handwriting, which revealed broad, humanistic views. "She was a woman of outstanding intellect, great determination and utter devotion to her gifted son" (Wayne 1984: 190), as her granddaughter noted.

It was not easy to uncover how much Lucjan Malinowski actually earned as a young professor, but documents in the Jagiellonian University Archives provided some answers and illuminated problems of bureaucratization and the relative pauperization of academia in this era. The financial situation of university professors seems to have deteriorated in the 1890s, leading to a kind of soft rebellion among academics (not only in Kraków, but also in other Austrian Universities). Academic discontent led to an anonymous report "On the Social Position and Improvement of the Material Conditions of University Professors" that opened with the statement that "Unfavorable conditions are preventing Austrian universities from gaining a leading position in science." The authors added that "The position of university professors is not properly defined by law, and the material remuneration is too modest."[4] The main problem lay in the fact that, according to Austrian protocols, professors were classified as civil service staff (they were even required to wear uniforms on official occasions). A full professor qualified for the sixth grade, an extraordinary professor for the seventh; further promotion in this hierarchy was not foreseen. The authors argued that professors should not be treated as civil servants, because academia was a separate domain (an autonomous field as Bourdieu would say). They gave the example of a professor transferred to a ministerial post who, if he returned to the academy, would suffer a massive decline in salary. The problem, it was argued, could only be addressed by a doubling of the basic remuneration and automatic increases with every five years of service.[5] A list of all UJ professors and their annual income was drawn up to illustrate the situation. Lucjan Malinowski earned 2,855 Austrian florins: an income that was comparable to that of other professors of the Faculty of Philosophy of the UJ.[6]

How did Lucjan himself assess his financial situation? He must have been accustomed to difficult economic conditions, having had to support himself from an early age. He could not count on any family inheritance. Only his full professorial position made his marriage possible. In letters to a friend, there are hints of dissatisfaction with his situation. In 1889, referring to his holiday plans, he wrote: "And I would so like to be by the sea! Unfortunately: kein Geld—kein Kompliment" (L. Malinowski in Sochacka 1975: 111). Later, he wrote with respect to his young son: "We shall not leave him a fortune; we want at least to ensure his health" (ibid.: 112). It seems that he was glad to finance frequent stays in the mountains for his wife and son, but even in this context, he calculated material gain. In 1890 he bought a piece of land in Zakopane for 1,700 florins (half of his yearly income) to build a house, the total cost of which was 9,000 florins. This villa was fitted out with eleven rooms with a view to generating rental income. Later they started building a second house. I do not know how they financed these investments.

Lucjan Malinowski's salary could have been increased by the award of a "personal allowance" but he declared in another letter dated 1894 that "I will not ask for it, because the Faculty might not support me and I would look like a fool, which is the last thing I want. They will give it to someone who lives in a lordly way, and needs a lot; and as for me—'skinny lackey'—I live frugally, what do I need?—so they can reason. Sokołowski wears monocles, holds a liveried butler, he is in need . . ." (L. Malinowski in Sochacka 1975: 158). The irony here reveals that Lucjan was critical of professors who aspired to an aristocratic lifestyle without having the means to support it. Two years later, Lucjan complained that "social relations among the professors have ceased entirely. Some aspire to aristocracy, while others are shrinking, burdened with families, with no time for anything" (ibid.: 156). Eventually, in 1896, Lucjan (along with twenty other professors of the Faculty of Philosophy) was awarded a substantial personal allowance.

The aspiration to aristocracy displayed by some members of the intelligentsia, criticized by Chałasiński and scorned by Lucjan Malinowski, at the UJ could in practice mean associating with Count Stanisław Tarnowski, professor of Polish literature, whose main home was a palace on Szlak Street.[7] He was also the owner of a large estate. For Tarnowski, working at the Jagiellonian University was more a hobby than a way to earn his living. The university was one of the few places where a person of his rank could devote himself to professional activity. Most professors were post-noble intelligentsia, like Malinowski. A minority stemmed from the bourgeoisie, including several of German or Jewish background. For these professors, working at the university was the main, and often the only, source of income. Only a generation later does one come across professors of peasant background in the Faculty of Philosophy (Banach 2009).

To sum up at this point, Lucjan Malinowski was a member of the post-noble intelligentsia for whom social stratification was obvious and natural. But he rose to his position on the basis of his own hard work and evidently did not appreciate the aristocratic aspirations of some of his colleagues. He was hardly a snob and seems to have taken good care of students from the countryside, often asking for their help in documenting regional dialects. Much of this interaction took place when Lucjan was a "senior" at the Bursa Akademicka (Academic Dormitory; the modern equivalent in Britain would be a hall of residence), where he and his wife had an apartment for many years. Bronisław looked back on this apartment as his Kraków home in the diaries that he started to keep much later.[8]

The Bursa was located on Mały Rynek (Little Marketplace), in the immediate vicinity of the city's central square (Rynek Główny), in a building that had formerly belonged to the Jesuit Order. It provided accommodation for about one hundred students of Kraków secondary schools and a dozen or so students of the university who lacked the means to rent rooms elsewhere. The university calendar specified how this institution operated: "Only poor students who are diligent and well behaved shall be admitted for an entrance fee of 6 crowns 50 h per year; they shall receive lodging, fuel, light, and service; food and other needs are to be covered from their own funds. For those wishing to eat at home, there is a shared kitchen, in which a cook, appointed and paid for by the institution, provides food."[9]

The regulations of the Bursa stated inter alia that:

[Students in the Bursa] should get up to the sound of the bell in summer at 5 o'clock, in winter at 6 o'clock, and after washing themselves and getting dressed, they should go to morning prayer, which is to be held kneeling in the presence of the senior and vice-senior. . . . Each student of the Bursa should be in the hall before 9 o'clock in the evening, and after praying, go to bed directly, except for students of higher grades who, with the permission of the senior or vice-senior, might remain until 10 o'clock in the reading room for study. . . . When in need, they should seek advice from the vice-senior, who, either directly or by consulting with the senior, will devise appropriate measures. In the event that the issue exceeds the authority of the senior, he will notify the Inspector, and finally the Academic Senate. . . . Everyone should avoid even the slightest relationship of familiarity with the staff of the Bursa and refrain from visits to the kitchen except when necessary, in order to avoid developing inappropriate habits.[10]

This reveals the importance of the position of the senior, his power over pupils, but also his responsibilities, which included waking up early to participate in morning prayers (it is possible that Lucjan's wife and son were exempted from this obligation).

Lucjan Malinowski served as the senior of the Bursa from 1892, having been proposed by the Dormitory Inspector Józef Rostafiński, Professor of Botany and a personal friend. Nowadays the building is again in Jesuit hands. It extends over four stories (a result of connecting together six gothic townhouses in the seventeenth century), and has a cozy internal doorway and a courtyard that is adjacent to the church of St. Barbara. Compared with the busy square outside (formerly the location of a food market), it is peaceful and secluded. A wide staircase leads up to the first floor, which features a corridor overlooking the courtyard. The senior's tied apartment was probably here, while pupils lived on the second and third floors.

Documents in the Jagiellonian University Archives reveal how seriously Lucjan Malinowski took his responsibilities, for example, by ensuring free health care from a doctor who would come to the dormitory to examine and treat residents as required. Kraków experienced epidemics of cholera every few years, and tuberculosis was also a constant threat. The dormitory, where poor students lived in high density, was a potentially dangerous place where diseases could spread easily. Lucjan tried to convince the Senate of the necessity to pay this doctor a salary, but in this he was unsuccessful.[11] This initiative might well have been prompted by Bronisław's contracting an eye disease from coresidents at the Bursa (Matlakowski 1962).

On the other hand Lucjan was a very strict senior, who at least on one occasion expelled a resident for sneaking out to the theater, because attending theater was strictly forbidden. Expulsion from the dormitory resulted in this young man's not being able to afford continuing his education.[12]

How, then, is one to characterize the financial and social situation of Professor Lucjan Malinowski and his family? Their main source of income was his professorial salary at the Jagiellonian University. His freelance work at the Academy of Arts and Sciences was prestigious but unpaid (at the most, he might have earned modest royalties from his not very numerous publications). Józefa Łącka probably brought some dowry, but we know nothing about its size or form. Michael Young mentions some "family money" but without offering detail (Young 2004: 45–46).

As for expenses, before moving to the Bursa the family had to pay for a flat. They probably employed some servants there: a cook or a maid (or both), and perhaps, after the birth of their son, a nurse.[13] Every week on Thursdays, a "servants market" was held in the Rynek Główny at the foot of the monument to Adam Mickiewicz (celebrated poet of the Romantic era), where poor girls from nearby villages came to be assessed and selected by city ladies. Every intelligentsia and bourgeois family could afford such domestic help (and some could even afford a butler in livery, as Lucjan mocked). The appointment at the Bursa meant that the Malinowskis no longer had to pay rent or the wages of their servants, since they could use the services of the dormitory staff.[14]

Due to the poor health of their son,[15] and their belief in climatic treatment, the Malinowski family often led a divided life: mother and son would stay in peasant cottages in a village to the south of the city and in Zakopane in the Tatra Mountains, to be joined there during vacations by Lucjan. The Malinowskis also paid frequent visits to Józefa's family in Warsaw and to the estates of her relatives in regions governed by Russia.[16] Contrary to the impression of isolated frugality sometimes conveyed by Lucjan, they also led lively social lives in the circles of professorial families and as participants in the rich cultural life of Kraków: concerts, theater, and exhibitions.

In short, the Malinowskis led the typical life of an intelligentsia family. While they could not afford luxury, they were able, especially after 1892 when Lucjan took up his appointment at the Bursa, to enjoy a rich cultural and social life, keep domestic servants, and spend vacations out of town and, increasingly, even abroad. It goes without saying that good manners and decorous behavior were expected from all family members. The daughter of a colleague and friend of Lucjan's recalled the high standards professorial families had to meet, ranging from intellectual acuity to etiquette and social skills, morality, proper behavior of children, and not least patriotism. "These requirements were imposed because it was about creating an elite that could really appeal to the young" (Zofia Krzyżanowska, quoted in Truszkowski 1984: 3–4). This summed up the ethos of the intelligentsia, which saw itself not as a mere "cultural stratum," but as "a leading intellectual elite" (Chałasiński 1946: 57).

Educating Bronio

Providing one's children with a good education was essential for intelligentsia families. Bronio (the name by which Bronisław was known from an early age to intimates inside and outside his family) attended the King Jan Sobieski classical gymnasium, the best in the city, where he studied both Latin and ancient Greek (in addition to the usual subjects). Due to his frequent illnesses, he also received much home tutoring from his mother. In 1899, when Bronio was 14, Józefa reported:

> so far, he is going through gymnasium as an excellent student. He is gifted, clever, and quick-witted, but lazy and negligent. It seems to me that I am to blame for his faults, but having an only child, I took excessive care and made his studies too easy for him.... But if he does not like work, he is passionate about reading and serious conversations. For a book, even a demanding one for him, he is ready to give up eating and sleeping. He also learns to play the violin and has some talent to do so, but because of his indolence, the results of his lessons are mediocre. On the other hand, he listens to music with the greatest pleasure and does not miss a single concert. His character is righteous, very honest and simple, but without too much tenderness. (Malinowska in Sochacka 1975: 195)

Young Bronio's reading habits were indeed remarkable, as testified by countless fragments in his own later writings. When he was 10 or 11 he read *Ogniem i mieczem* (With Fire and Sword) by Henryk Sienkiewicz in secret. The author was widely revered, but Józefa held that Bronio was too young to tackle such literature (Wayne 1995, vol. 1: 108). While still a gymnasium pupil, he read Fredric Amiel and Michel de Montaigne. He read *Hamlet* in the original.[17] He read the *Odyssey* in Greek while holidaying on the Adriatic (Malinowski 2002: 138; Young 2004: 50).

A girlfriend, the painter Zofia Dembowska, who later married into the aristocracy, wrote in a memoir when informed of his death:

> Bronio Malinowski! It was 36 years ago.... magnolias were blooming in Grandpa's garden on Krupnicza 18 [a street in Kraków], sprinkling large white petals on the grass ... Aunt Ela (Grosse) was playing Beethoven's sonnets, and we were siting on a bench, having long, essential conversations. We were reading Wilde's *Dorian Gray* at the time. And *Einleitung in die Philosophie* by Cornelius for a sort of mental gymnastics; and we marveled at the poetry of Zarathustra by Nietzsche. I had the impression that Bronio was taking me by the hand and leading me into the realm of the spirit—higher and higher. (Romer in Rosner and Rosner 1992: 268–69)

Michael Young is right to point out that, for Bronio, the links between intellectual activity and eroticism were always very close (Young 2004: 201).

Lucjan Malinowski's death in 1898 when Bronio was 14 changed the situation of the family, though not dramatically. Józefa and her son were allowed to stay in their apartment at the Bursa. A few months after her husband's death, his widow wrote to a friend:

> I am still staying in the dormitory to care for the poor students who live here. My family, especially my eldest brother, wanted me to move back to Warsaw. My son would have been able to study privately and pass his examinations in Kraków. This scheme was attractive for many reasons, but I felt sorry to leave the dormitory. So I decided not to leave. (Malinowska in Sochacka 1975: 194)

Insight into their new situation is provided in a "Report on Filling the Position of a Senior of the Academic Dormitory at the Senate Session on 17.1.1906" prepared by the Reverend Stanisław Spis, Professor of Theology. It states that the Senate (at the request of Professor Rostafiński) had allowed Józefa Malinowska to continue to occupy part of the senior's apartment in return for her continuing to oversee the pupils of the dormitory. The position of senior had thereafter rotated frequently, which was presumably related to the continued residence of the widow. At the beginning of 1905,

> Mrs. Malinowska resigned from her occupation and residence in the Bursa. In her letter [which has not survived], she lists her substantial deeds and dedication to the Bursa—including the very large expenses (on one occasion 1,000 florins) she had incurred for the benefit of the pupils; she says that residence in the Bursa was not a sinecure for her, and that only her sense of service to underprivileged children had held her back from departing earlier.[18]

The Senate of the UJ accepted the resignation of Mrs. Malinowska and thanked her for her maternal dedication, before immediately proceeding to advertise for a new permanent senior.

In October 1905, after thirteen years of living in the Bursa, including seven years as a widow, Józefa Malinowska and her son moved to a third-floor apartment at 19 Radziwiłłowska Street. She did not give up her matron's role entirely and rented a large apartment near the railway that functioned as a kind of unofficial boarding house for pupils. One of her tenants here was Stanisław (Staś) Ignacy Witkiewicz, a student at the Academy of Fine Arts and Bronio's best friend. Witkiewicz later achieved fame as an avant-garde painter and playwright.

After the death of her husband, Józefa Malinowska was entitled to a widow's pension of 500 florins a year (one quarter of the basic professorial salary) from the UJ (Kasparek 1885). It is possible that Bronisław received additional support as an orphan. During his studies at the UJ, where he matriculated in 1902, as the son of a professor he was exempted from tuition fees. He was also the recipient of scholarships. In 1905, when he was a third-year student, the Potocki Foundation for students of noble birth awarded him 315 crowns. In the following year, this was converted into a scholarship from the Barczewski Foundation (similarly restricted to students of noble descent) worth 600 crowns, which he also received in 1908 (Kubica 1985: 264).

At the UJ one could study at the Faculty of Law, Medicine, Theology, or Philosophy. The last offered access to a wide range of courses in science and humanities. One graduated from the faculty and not in a specific discipline. After four years one had to sit final examinations (*rigorosa*) and write a dissertation to obtain the title of doctor (PhD). Bronisław focused initially on mathematics and sciences, but in his final years he also took courses in philosophy and humanities.[19]

Józefa Malinowska probably continued for some time to receive rent from her houses in Zakopane, but one was destroyed in a fire and the other seems to have been sold.[20] Malinowski mentioned in his diary that his mother invested in a business of her brother Bronisław Łącki, who later went bankrupt (Malinowski 2002: 244, 249). She must have had some reserves, on which she drew to pay for numerous trips southward to improve Bronio's health. In 1902 they traveled to Trenczen in Slovakia, before proceeding to Lido and Lake Garda, and the Dalmatian Coast. In 1904, they spent several months in North Africa. In 1906, they returned to Italy. They also traveled to Finland, where Bronio was enchanted by the landscape.[21] After Bronisław had finished his studies at the UJ, they spent almost two years in the Canary Islands to improve his health in the unique climate and spa atmosphere there.

Snobbery on a Shoestring

One may ask: how could the widow of a university professor afford such extensive travels to distant places? Young writes that Józefa's family and friends of her husband contributed to the funding of these trips. However, irrespective of such support, we should note that Józefa and Bronisław did not travel in the luxurious style of the young Polish aristocrat Tadzio and his mother who figure in Thomas Mann's *Death in Venice*. The Malinowskis were quite used to living in peasant cottages in Galicia, and the costs of modest hotels around the Mediterranean were affordable. Their main expenses were travel costs, but within the Habsburg Monarchy, that is, from Kraków to the Adriatic Sea, they were entitled to half-price rail tickets as members of the family of a civil servant. They always traveled third-class.

Their lifestyle, then, might have appeared grand, but it was carefully budgeted in the cheapest way possible. Money must have been a constant element in the life of young Bronio, even if he pays almost no attention to it in his diary. He knew full well that his parents (later his widowed mother) could not afford to indulge all his whims. Kiejstut Matlakowski, another lodger at Mrs. Malinowska's boarding house, remembered how Staś Witkiewicz would mimic a dialogue of Bronio, who "hissed through clenched teeth," with his mother, who "spoke very slowly, in a nice voice, with impeccable diction": "Mum, why is there no toilet paper? Bronio, my deeer chiild! Wee caaan't buuy toooilet paaper" (the implication being that they could not afford it) (Matlakowski 1962: 7). This mockery on the part of Staś Witkiewicz must have been funny not only because of his acting skills, but also because the performer put his finger on a real problem: a fastidious Bronio valued basic comforts, while his mother had to make ends meet (toilet paper could be substituted by pieces of newspaper).

How did Bronisław Malinowski see his family's position in the social hierarchy? Michael Young writes at the beginning of his biography that

> Malinowski was proud of his noble ancestry. To the supremely class-conscious British he often claimed to be an aristocrat ("with his Polish aristocratic background, he prided himself on his good horsemanship," wrote his pupil Hilda Beemer Kuper, recalling his visits to Swaziland). (Young 2004: 6)

It is not obvious from this quotation whether Malinowski introduced himself as a Polish aristocrat, or whether Hilda Kuper merely surmised this to be the case when observing that he was proud of his horsemanship. In the early 1930s, Malinowski himself summed up his sociocultural background as follows: "We belonged to the dispossessed, impoverished small Polish nobility, shading into the inteligencja" (also cited by Young 2004: 15). This was supplemented by the characterization: "Shabby genteel withal really cultured world not without dignity and heroism (see Joseph Conrad's recollections)."[22] His Polish students never described him as an aristocrat or even as having aristocratic background. Józef Obrębski and Andrzej Waligórski knew full well that his sociocultural background was the same as their own: the post-noble intelligentsia. Feliks Gross, who had Jewish bourgeois ancestry, described him as "a real Krakauer, no professorial moods, but Cracovian sentiments, a sense of humor; he was nasty in the most intelligent way" (Bator and Łukasiewicz 2000). Malinowski taught a blue-blooded representative of European royalty at the LSE, Prince Peter of Greece and Denmark, who later wrote that "his manners resembled '*grand seigneur*'" (Piotr, książę Grecji i Danii 1953: 1). But this "resemblance" does not imply that Malinowski presented himself as an aristocrat, which is the myth to which some anglophone readers have tenaciously clung.

It seems to me likely that this myth was created not by Malinowski himself but by Western European and American acquaintances unable to grasp that being of "noble ancestry" was not the same as being an aristocrat. Western publics did not perceive the autonomy of cultural capital, because this no longer existed in their modern societies. Malinowski invoked Joseph Conrad's *A Personal Record* as probably the only work available in English at the time that adequately conveyed the characteristics of the Polish *szlachta* (Conrad 1912; see Young 2004: 15).

However, while the charge of posing as an aristocrat does not bear close scrutiny, unlike his father Bronisław as a young man had a pronounced snobbish streak, on which he reflected critically in later life. Young writes: "His pride in origins sometimes manifested itself as snobbery, sometimes as arrogance and condescension, and sometimes as disdain if not contempt for servants, peasants and other members of the 'lower orders'" (2004: 6). There was a rhyme circulating in Kraków about young Bronisław: "On his table, Romi's card lies on top," the point being that Bronio kept the visiting card of a young aristocrat prominently on his table, so everybody could see that he had had a visitor of distinction (Romer in Rosner and Rosner 1992: 105).[23] Karol Estreicher, a prominent art historian, pointed out that being the descendants of noble families and having relatives who possessed estates, both Malinowski and Staś Witkiewicz tended to see others as socially inferior; but Malinowski was the first to free himself from such snobbery (Estreicher 1971: 11–17).[24] In 1918, he wrote critically to his fiancée Elsie Masson about his friendship with Henryk Józef Sienkiewicz, the son of the celebrated writer Henryk Sienkiewicz: "He is a very nice, perfectly gentlemanly character with a distinct pose to be English, but perfectly anaemic mentally and absolutely uninteresting. My friendship with him is one of the saddest pages in my mental history, because I stuck on to him out of pure snobbishness" (Wayne 1995, vol.1: 108–9).

Despite this self-criticism in a letter to Elsie, at roughly the same time he noted in his diary a dream in which he and Elsie made a *grande entrée* at the ball at the "Pod baranami" palace (Malinowski 2002: 612).[25] This Renaissance palace on the Rynek Główny was owned by the aristocratic Potocki family; it was the epicenter of cultural, social, and also political life in Kraków at the time. The youthful snobbery of Malinowski and his friends reflects their aspirations and hierarchical values in the process of cultural capital formation. Later, having achieved some recognition themselves, they could afford to distance themselves from their earlier deference to the aristocracy.

Conclusion

Bronisław Malinowski was and remained throughout his life an authentic representative of the post-noble Polish intelligentsia, persons who stressed their noble ancestry and, in their lifestyles, displayed embodied forms of cultural capital that distanced them from other citizens. Malinowski's family lacked significant economic capital, but their social and cultural capital was high. Even without a manor house and land, one retained one's *szlachta* (gentry) standing. The "dispossessed" nobility retained its overall position in the social hierarchy by forming a new stratum, the intelligentsia. His own family after marriage to Elsie functioned in the British social structure of the time, which did not recognize such a phenomenon. He was simply an academic who lived from a modest (only gradually increasing) income as a member of the upper middle class. As a breadwinner, he was responsible for the family budget. In a 1926 letter to Elsie he wrote: "our finances are sound, even if you spend over the margin which you had fixed. Do not stint yourself dearest. I am as you know temperamentally economical, but I do never worry now abt. a pound note or so . . ." (Wayne 1995, vol. 2: 87).

It has been suggested that Malinowski "internalized class-based distinctions of hierarchy" (Weston and Djohari 2020: 51). In this he resembled virtually all contemporaries: the European culture of his era was certainly classist. What makes Malinowski's internalized hierarchy distinctive is that the *stratum* formed by the carriers of cultural capital was at least as important as economically defined *class*. This Polish background was arguably of great relevance to his later understanding of the hierarchy he found in Trobriand society. The chief Touluva resembled a Polish aristocrat, surrounded by his retinue. The fact that Malinowski pitched his tent close to the chief's hut indicated that he understood the meaning of the hierarchy and knew how to manipulate it for the purposes of his research. His enduring critical sensitivity to hierarchy in white colonial society comes through in a diary entry written in Port Moresby in September 1914, when a woman he met at the Governor's residence is described as "a kindhearted, horsy Australian woman who treated me with the deference of a socially inferior person" (Malinowski 1967: 8–9). On the other hand, his noble ancestry enabled him to empathize with those who valued honor and prestige above material gain. He could appreciate "Native Enterprise and Adventure" (as the subtitle of his first monograph reads) among the Kula players, whose ultimate concerns were renown and perhaps even immortality. His classical education in Kraków inspired him to name them *Argonauts*.

But it is important to recall that the worldview of the Eastern European intelligentsia also had antiestablishment, democratic elements. This is reflected in Malinowski's anthropological goal to recognize the humanity of "natives" and the importance of grasping the "point of view" of those classified at the time as "savages." In the last paragraph of his introduction to the *Argonauts* Malinowski justified his project in universalist terms: "Perhaps as we read the account of these remote customs there may emerge a feeling of solidarity with the endeavours and ambitions of these natives. Perhaps man's mentality will be revealed to us, and brought near, along some lines which we never have followed before" (Malinowski 1922: 25).

Acknowledgments

This chapter derives from a project sponsored by Poland's National Science Center (2019/33/B/HS3/00272). I would like to thank Maria Stinia, a historian of the Jagiellonian University, for her help in my research.

Grażyna Kubica is a Professor in the Social Anthropology Section of the Institute of Sociology, Jagiellonian University, Kraków. One of her specializations is the history of anthropology. She coedited the volume *Malinowski between Two Worlds* (Cambridge University Press, 1988) and authored the introduction and annotations of Malinowski's diaries in their original language, *Dziennik w ścisłym znaczeniu tego wyrazu* (2002). Kubica has recently published an anthropological biography of another Polish-British anthropologist: *Maria Czaplicka: Gender, Shamanism, Race* (2020). She is co-editor of *Bronislaw Malinowski and His Legacy in Contemporary Social Sciences and Humanities* (2024).

Notes

1. All translations from Polish sources are mine.
2. See Jakubowska (2017) for analysis of the resilience of the Polish gentry in socialist and postsocialist times.
3. From the late eighteenth century until 1918, Poland was deprived of its statehood; its territory was divided by three neighbors: Russia, Prussia, and Austria.
4. See Uposażenie profesorów 1849–1917, sygn. S II 930 and S II 931, and S II 1080, Archive of the Jagiellonian University.
5. The income of the average professor approximated that of a doctor or a municipal counselor in Kraków at this time (see Małecki 1994: 321). The city president earned three times as much.
6. His income was made up of a basic salary of 1,800 florins, supplemented by 480 for assuming responsibility for a hall of residence, and other smaller allowances that increased with length of service.
7. After World War II, Radio Kraków was housed in this building, which is nowadays falling into disrepair.
8. Bronisław Malinowski began to keep a personal diary on 6 January 1908 while sojourning on the Canary Islands. Entries during the next ten years were irregular. His diaries have been published in their entirety in Polish (their original language) with my extensive annotations and an introduction (Malinowski 2002, see also Kubica 2024). The dormitory was a regular port of call when he gave his Warsaw mistresses sightseeing tours of his home city. In New Guinea, when he drafted a plan to write the "sketch of my life," the Bursa was the starting point (ibid.: 214, 285, 422, 656; Kubica 2015).
9. "Skład Uniwersytetu w roku szkolnym 1898/99." [The University Calendar 1898/99] The Archive of the Jagiellonian University.
10. Regulamin Bursy, Bursa św. Barbary, potem Akademicka, sygn. S II 930, Archive of the Jagiellonian University. I have also found a yearly "payroll" (in Austrian crowns): senior—350; vice-senior—270; dormitory caretaker—1,241; assistant caretaker for winter—127; cook—225; cook's helper—120; laundress—100.
11. Bursa św. Barbary, potem Akademicka, sygn. S II 931, Archive of the Jagiellonian University.
12. Fortunately, this did not prevent Władysław Orkan from becoming a distinguished writer (Pigoń 1958).
13. According to Young (2004: 18) they could not afford a nurse. However, this judgment does not take into account the cheapness of domestic service in this era.
14. Bronisław Malinowski maintained contacts with a maid called Władysławowa Świderska, whom he helped financially from London many years later (Kubica 1985: 283).
15. Young Bronisław was a very sickly child. In his childhood he had an intestinal abscess operated on, and later he was threatened with blindness; see Young (2004: 37–38).
16. See Kubica (in progress): "The Two Worlds of Bronisław Malinowski's Polish Youth in His Own Writings. The Anthropologist's Historical Autoethnography."

17. Letters of Bronisław Malinowski to Józef Liwiniszyn and memoirs of the latter, copies in the author's archive.
18. Bursa św. Barbary, potem Akademicka, sygn. S II 931, Archive of the Jagiellonian University.
19. His doctoral thesis (completed in 1906, handwritten, comprising about eleven thousand words, hardly comparable to a modern PhD) was titled "On the Principle of the Economy of Thought." For an English translation, see Malinowski (1993).
20. This villa still exists (it was identified only recently by Magdalena Kwiecińska, an ethnologist working in the Tatra Museum in Zakopane).
21. This information comes from Malinowski's correspondence with his friend, Józef Litwiniszyn, and his mentor, Rev. Prof. Stefan Pawlicki, and from Malinowski's diary. These trips are also listed by Young (2004: 45–47).
22. Bronisław Malinowski, An Outline of a Book ABC of Culture, Malinowski Papers, LSE Archives.
23. The young aristocrat in question was Hieronim Mikołaj Radziwiłł (1885–1945) of Balice near Kraków, who studied at the Jagiellonian University from 1904.
24. A caricature of that early snobbishness can be found in the autobiographical novel of Staś Witkiewicz *622 Downfalls of Bungo*, where all the main protagonists are aristocrats, including Malinowski as Duke Edgar of Nevermore, who lived with his mother, the Duchess, in Birnam Palace, the description of which fits the tenement house on Radziwiłłowska Street. The novel was first published in 1972, but it was written in 1910–11 (Witkiewicz 1972).
25. This fragment appears in the translated *Diary*, but it is not properly annotated (Malinowski 1967: 254).

References

Banach, Andrzej K. 2009. *Kariery zawodowe studentów UJ pochodzenia chłopskiego 1860/1861–1917/1918* [Professional careers of students of the Jagiellonian University of peasant origin 1860/1861–1917/1918]. Kraków: Księgarnia Akademicka.

Bator, Joanna, and Sławomir Łukasiewicz. 2000. "Najgorsze jest okrucieństwo" [Cruelty is the worst], an interview with Feliks Gross. *Gazeta Wyborcza* 2–3.18.

Bourdieu, Pierre. 1986. "The Forms of Capital." In *Handbook of Theory and Research for Sociology of Education*, ed. John G. Richardson, 241–60. New York: Greenwood Press.

Chałasiński, Józef. 1946. *Społeczna genealogia inteligencji polskiej* [The social genealogy of the Polish intelligentsia]. Warsaw: Czytelnik.

Conrad, Joseph. 1912. *A Personal Record: Some Reminiscences*. London: Doubleday.

Estreicher, Karol. 1971. *Leon Chwistek: Biografia artysty* [Leon Chwistek: Biography of an artist]. Kraków: Państwowe Wydawnictwo Naukowe.

Eyal, Gil, Ivan Szelenyi, and Eleanor Townsley. 1998. *Making Capitalism without Capitalists: Class Formation and Elite Struggles in Post-Communist Europe*. London: Verso.

Gella, Aleksander, ed. 1976. *The Intelligentsia and the Intellectuals*. London: Sage.

———. 1989. *Development of Class Structure of Eastern Europe*. Albany: State University of New York Press.

Jakubowska, Longina. 2017. *Patrons of History: Nobility, Capital and Political Transitions in Poland*. London: Routledge.

Kasparek, Jan Rudolf, ed. 1885. *Zbiór ustaw i rozporządzeń administracyjnych w Królestwie Galicyi i Londomeryi z Wielkiem Księstwem Krakowskiem obowiązujących* [Collection of laws and administrative regulations in force in the Kingdom of Galicia and Londomeria with the Grand Duchy of Krakow]. Vol. 5. Lwów.

Kubica, Grażyna. 1985. "Listy Bronisława Malinowskiego" [Letters of Bronisław Malinowski]. In *Antropologia społeczna Bronisława Malinowskiego* [Social anthropology of Bronisław Malinowski], ed. Andrzej Paluch and Mariola Flis, 153–300. Warsaw: Państwowe Wydawnictwo Naukowe.

———. 1988. "Malinowski's Years in Poland." In *Malinowski between Two Worlds: The Polish Roots of an Anthropological Tradition*, ed. Roy Ellen, Ernest Gellner, Grażyna Kubica, and Janusz Mucha, 88–104. Cambridge: Cambridge University Press.

———. 2002. "Wstęp" [Introduction]. In Bronisław Malinowski, *Dziennik w ścisłym znaczeniu tego wyrazu* [A diary in the strict sense of the term], 1–90. Kraków: Wydawnictwo Literackie.

———. 2015. "A Flâneur and Ethnographer in Their Home City: The Krakow of Bronisław Malinowski and Feliks Gross; Remarks of a Historian of Anthropology." In *Rytíř z Komárova: K 70. narozeninám Petra Skalníka* [Knight from Komárov: To Petr Skalník for his 70th birthday], ed. Adam Bedřich and Tomáš Retka, 71–82. Prague: AntropoWeb.

———. 2024. "A Notorious Diarist - Bronisław Malinowski, and His Sinful Publics. Polish Editor's Remarks," in Aleksandar Bošković and David Shankland (eds.), *Argonauts of the Western Pacific and The Andaman Islanders: A Centenary Study in Social Anthropology*. Canon Pyon: Sean Kingston Publishing.

Malinowski, Bronisław. 1922. *Argonauts of the Western Pacific: An Account of Native Enterprise and Adventure in the Archipelagoes of Melanesian New Guinea*. London: Routledge & Kegan Paul.

———. 1967. *A Diary in the Strict Sense of the Term*. Translated by Norbert Guterman. London: Harcourt, Brace & World.

———. 1993. "On the Principle of the Economy of Thought." Translated by Ludwik Krzyżanowski. In *The Early Writings of Bronisław Malinowski*, ed. Robert Thornton and Peter Skalník, 89–116. Cambridge: Cambridge University Press.

———. 2002. *Dziennik w ścisłym znaczeniu tego wyrazu* [A diary in the strict sense of the term]. Annotated and prefaced by Grażyna Kubica. Kraków: Wydawnictwo Literackie.

Małecki, Jan M. 1994. "W dobie autonomii galicyjskiej (1866–1918)" [In the era of Galician autonomy (1866–1918)]. In *Dzieje Krakowa: Kraków w latach 1796–1918* [The history of Krakow: Krakow in the years 1796–1918], ed. Janina Bieniarzówna and Jan M. Małecki, 225–394. Kraków: Wydawnictwo Literackie.

Martin, Bill, and Ivan Szelenyi. 1987. "Beyond Cultural Capital: Towards a Theory of Symbolic Domination." In *Intellectuals, Universities, and the State in Western Modern Societies*, ed. Ron Eyerman, Lennart G. Svensson, and Thomas Soderquist, 16–49. Berkeley: University of California Press.

Matlakowski, Władysław Kiejstut. 1962. *Wspomnienia: Kraków matematyka* [Memories: Krakow mathematics]. A typescript, sygn. 9835 III, Manuscript Department, Jagiellonian Library.

Pigoń, Stanisław. 1958. *Władysław Orkan: Twórca i dzieło* [Władysław Orkan: Author and his work]. Kraków: Wydawnictwo Literackie.

Piotr, książę Grecji i Danii [Prince Peter of Greece and Denmark]. 1953. "Wspomnienie o Bronisławie Malinowskim" [Memories of Bronisław Malinowski]. *Wiadomości* 8(25): 1.

Rosner, Anna, and Andrzej Rosner. 1992. *"Pasmo czynności ciągiem lat idące . . ." Z dziejów Romerów na Litwie* ["A series of activities over the years . . ." From the history of the Romers in Lithuania]. Warsaw: Wydawnictwo Krąg.

Sochacka, Stanisława, ed. 1975. *Listy Lucjana Malinowskiego do Jarosława Golla* [Lucjan Malinowski's letters to Jarosław Goll]. Opole: Wydawnictwo Instytutu Śląskiego.

Stinia, Maria. 2014. *Uniwersytet Jagielloński w latach 1871-1914. Modernizacja procesu nauczania* [Jagiellonian University in 1871-1914. Modernization of the teaching process]. Kraków: Towarzystwo Wydawnicze "Historia Iagellonica."

Taszycki, Witold. 1974. "Malinowski Lucjan." In *Polski Słownik Biograficzny* [Polish biographical dictionary], vol. 19, 348–50.Kraków: Polska Akademia Nauk.

Truszkowski, Witold. 1984. "Jak Bronisław Malinowski został ocalony dla nauki" [How Bronisław Malinowski was saved for science]. Typescript in my archive.

Wayne, Helena. 1984. "Bronisław Malinowski: An Influence of Various Women on His Life and Works." *Journal of the Anthropological Society of Oxford* 15(3): 189–203.

———. 1995. *The Story of a Marriage: The Letters of Bronislaw Malinowski and Elsie Masson*. Vols. 1–2. London: Routledge.

Weston, Gavin, and Natalie Djohari. 2020. *Anthropological Controversies: The "Crimes" and Misdemeanors that Shaped a Discipline*. London: Routledge.

Witkiewicz, Stanisław Ignacy. 1972. *622 upadki Bunga, czyli demoniczna kobieta* [622 downfalls of Bungo, or a demonic woman]. Warsaw: Państwowy Instytut Wydawniczy.

Young, Michael W. 2004. *Malinowski: Odyssey of an Anthropologist, 1884–1920*. New Haven, CT: Yale University Press.

Zarycki, Tomasz. 2003. "Cultural Capital and the Political Role of the Intelligentsia in Poland." *Journal of Communist Studies and Transition Politics* 19(4): 91–108.

———. 2008. *Kapitał kulturowy: Inteligencja w Polsce i w Rosji* [Cultural capital: Intelligentsia in Poland and Russia]. Warsaw: Wydawnictwa Uniwersytetu Warszawskiego.

2

Tenerife 1921

The Writing of Argonauts

Michael W. Young

Malinowski, Elsie, and baby Józefa sailed for the Canary Islands in early January, having spent the previous months in London and Edinburgh. Their vessel called at Lisbon, Madeira, and Las Palmas, and they finally disembarked at Puerto de la Cruz on the north coast of Tenerife. In contrast to the desiccated southern portion of the island the north is green and fertile, moistened by the trade winds and notable for its vineyards, orange groves, and banana plantations. From everywhere along this coast with its black-sand beaches can be seen the snow-capped, gently smoking volcanic peak of El Teide, at over 12,000 feet the highest mountain on Spanish territory.

Avoiding the English colony in Puerto de la Cruz, the Malinowskis went inland to Icod de los Vinos, which had been recommended to them in Edinburgh. With its shady squares graced by laurels, palms, and jacarandas, it was locally renowned for its white wine and a thousand-year-old dragon tree. "We have hired a villa standing at about 400 meters overlooking the valley of Icod," Malinowski wrote to Sir James Frazer. "We have also two Spanish servants and we live quite comfortably on very little indeed."[1]

Perched above the terraced slopes, "El Boquín" was a rambling, terra-cotta-roofed villa, at least two centuries old, which commanded an estate of 17 hectares. There were banana groves on the terraces and goats roamed the lava-strewn hillside. The villa had a kitchen on the ground floor and several awkwardly shaped rooms on the main story above, two of them bedrooms. Throughout the villa uneven wooden floors sloped erratically. Water had to be drawn from a nearby well, cooking and heating was provided by wood-burning stoves, lighting by paraffin lamps, and the maids washed clothes in a nearby stream. Malinowski created a compact study for himself in one of the two narrow, enclosed balconies that jutted from one side of the villa.[2]

Despite the strain of his self-imposed work Malinowski would be happy here, Elsie even happier. By mid-February she had learned enough Spanish to conduct her housekeeping in the vernacular. Although Malinowski spoke Spanish quite fluently, he tried not to use it too much, as he quaintly explained to Frazer: "English is not my mother tongue and yet I have to work in it, so I do not want to mix it up with another language."[3]

Fifty years later there were people in Icod who still remembered the foreign scholar and his beautiful long-haired wife. A local lawyer recounted seeing, as a youth, Malinowski "taking the sun" on the black-sand beach of San Marcos, and sometimes he was to be seen astride a horse, riding up to "El Boquín" from Icod, where he had visited the bank. But mostly he secluded himself in the villa, where the young sons of *criada* Antonia Gonzales remembered glimpsing him reading or writing in the *escritorio*. They remembered particularly the green visor he wore to shade his eyes. The noise of their games often disturbed him, and he would bid them to be quiet: "even so, he was amiable with those children who approached him."[4]

The Ever-Expanding Kula

"I am working fairly well," Malinowski reported to Frazer on 10 February, "but my health still gives way from time to time, especially when I work too long hours." He assured Frazer he would take his advice and remain in Tenerife until he had finished "writing out" all the Trobriand material. It is not clear what he had in mind by "all." To complete the volume on the Kula was an ambitious enough project in itself, though he was still insisting it was "a sort of *preliminary* account on intertribal trading and sailing" (emphasis added)—the subject matter of his LSE lectures the previous year. He summarized his progress:

> I am through about half of the work—that is I have written out the first eight Chapters. As I am able to skim my information, to omit heavy matter and to foreshorten duller subjects—for it all will be republished in extenso later on—the book, though strictly scientific and containing a mass of information, promises to make quite attractive reading. It will be some 200,000 words, that is, some 400 pages.[5]

This statement raises some interesting questions. What sort of "heavy matter" was Malinowski omitting from his text? How could he expect a publisher to republish "in extenso later on" the material that he had left out of this one? More pertinently, could he really have been only halfway through, when he had completed his manuscript just ten weeks later? There would appear to be no reason for him to tell Frazer anything but the truth, as he was not writing to a given deadline, nor was he beholden to Frazer for an account of his progress.

As published by Routledge, *Argonauts of the Western Pacific* consists of twenty-two chapters and a chapter-length introduction. Excluding preliminaries, there are 518 pages comprising about 220,000 words of text. If we accept his claim to have completed eight chapters, he would have been about to begin Chapter 9 ("Sailing on the Sea-Arm of Pilolu"). Allowing that he had also completed the introduction (a rough draft survives from Edinburgh days), he would have written almost one hundred thousand words—still ten thousand short of the halfway mark. On his account he still had another fourteen chapters (some three hundred pages) to write. Yet just ten weeks after he had written to Frazer, he took his completed manuscript to the typist he had engaged in La Orotava. "How very nice to think that the book is actually at that stage now," Elsie wrote to him from Icod that day, "a new created being which didn't exist four months ago! It takes you less time to make a child than it does me."[6] Four months earlier would have been 21 December 1920; about the time they took up residence at "El Boquín." To take Elsie literally would mean that Malinowski had written more than five hundred pages in sixteen weeks, an almost unbelievable output.

But the book had expanded considerably in scope since he began it, whether this was July 1920 (as some correspondence suggests) or indeed earlier. He had been working on it intermittently since his return to Edinburgh in September. He also had his LSE lectures and the earlier *Man* article to draw upon, the latter completed during the voyage from Australia. In addition there were the drafts of material on the Kula he had written in Melbourne in 1916–17, beginning with the "chapters" of "Kiriwina" that he had taken with him on his return to the Trobriands and supplemented during his last ten months of fieldwork. Granted, too, some of the later chapters in *Argonauts* are devoted to the presentation of Kiriwina texts, many of which he had translated and analyzed in 1919 in Wangaratta and Whitfield. But whatever he wrote during these earlier stages would surely have needed extensive rewriting for the book as he conceived it in 1920 and reconceived it in early 1921. So it becomes slightly more credible that Malinowski could write three hundred pages in ten weeks—even taking into account, as he told Frazer, that his health gave way if he worked for too many hours. While it is not impossible to maintain an average output of two thousand words a day for a six-day week over a ten-week period, it is still a staggering achievement worthy of Frazer himself.

We must bear in mind Malinowski's method of working, based on what is known of his daily habits. Never an early riser by choice, he would begin work after breakfast between 9–10 a.m., then break for lunch at about

2 p.m., before continuing until about 7 in the evening. Sometimes, surely, he would have succumbed to the temptation to take a *siesta* in the afternoon. If the Malinowskis followed the Spanish hours of *comida*, they would eat dinner or supper quite late, between 9–10 p.m., so it is possible that he worked even later than 7 p.m. This routine would have allowed for up to eight or nine hours of writing a day. We need also to consider Elsie's role as amanuensis whenever her mothering tasks permitted. With two *criadas* in the household (Antonia to cook and Dolores to mind Józefa) Elsie was released from the drudgery of housework and constant baby-care. Her main assistance, when she gave it, would have consisted in taking down his dictation in longhand, correcting his English as she went. As an accomplished "visual" thinker, Malinowski didn't need to see his words on the page to maintain a narrative or pursue an argument, though as his draft notes for books, articles, and lectures testify, it helped him to set out his thoughts under numbered headings, subheadings, and sub-subheadings, using colored pencils for further visual guidance. Having thought about and jotted down in this manner what he wanted to say, he could dictate without putting pen to paper. This would explain the fact that many chapters of the *Argonauts* manuscript are in Elsie's hand. After all, Elsie had helped him to "write up" his Trobriand ethnography as early as 1917, when he was assembling a rough draft of the monumental monograph on "Kiriwina" that he eventually abandoned. With three or more years' practice of serving Bronio in this way, Elsie must have become quite accomplished at polishing his prose as she took down his dictation.

Six weeks before its completion, Elsie told Hede Khuner that Bronio "has now nearly finished the Kula book." Later in the letter she added: "Bronio— very unshaven, even by the Dago standard—tells me to send you his love, & says he would write to you if it were not that he has to put in 4000 words a day on the Kula, & all other writing is therefore hateful to him."[7] Even with a clear structure in mind, copious notes for guidance, and many drafted passages to hand, this seems an impossible daily target, and it would have required more robust health than Malinowski enjoyed to maintain such an output. Yet, somehow, he evidently did "dash off" the final version of this lengthy monograph with astonishing speed.[8]

A Reluctant Publisher

In a gently manipulative move, Malinowski advised Frazer in his February letter that he had already contacted Macmillan (Frazer's publisher), "telling them that you have done me the honor of listening to my lectures and that therefore you know my material" and he hoped that Frazer would "put in a word or two" in his favor. He had informed Macmillan that by late April his manuscript would be ready, with maps, tables, and some fifty illustrations. "I think its publication ought to be really a paying proposition," he told Frazer.

> That is, if a firm like Macmillan takes it and if some publicity is given to it in the press ... I believe in the value of my stuff, and naturally I would like that it should be read ... Moreover, I am now very much in need of becoming known and even, if possible, of earning a few pounds. I believe that if Macmillan published it for me even on the worst financial terms, i.e. half-profits, I might get something out of it. Forgive me putting it so directly and crudely, but since I am making bold enough to ask your help in the matter, this is best.[9]

Frazer duly wrote to George Macmillan on 2 March, testifying to the "novelty and interest" of the book and saying of Malinowski: "I consider him decidedly the ablest, the most philosophical, and the most penetrating of the younger anthropologists with whom I am acquainted. I expect great things of him ... He is perhaps the first observer to recognize the extreme importance of an accurate study of primitive economics" (cited by Ackerman 1987: 287). Macmillan agreed to look at it, but while it helped "to know what a high opinion you have of him ... the trouble is that however good these anthropological books may be, it is very difficult to get a sale for them under present conditions."[10]

Frazer forwarded this discouraging letter to Malinowski. Meanwhile, Seligman wrote to Malinowski to tell him that he had asked Frazer for assistance in placing the book.

> I suggested he might write an introduction, pointing out that it was not your idea, but purely a scheme of my own to help your book along. I send you his letter. He will not write the introduction and regards the chances of Macmillan taking the book as minimal; so do I.[11]

Frazer's letter to Seligman has not survived, but on 8 May Malinowski wrote disarmingly to Frazer to apologize for any "misunderstanding" concerning Seligman's requests on his behalf:

> As to the Preface, I entirely share your views and feelings, which are averse to prefacing books of other people, as I gather. Of course, I would have valued it very highly to enter the world of literature, introduced by you so to speak—and indeed I am grateful to Seligman for his suggestion—but I am convinced that a Preface ipso facto gives the effect of artificially strengthening something that is inherently weak.

Some months later, however, both men changed their minds: Frazer's preface would endorse and ornament the book, while Malinowski's subsequent enthusiasm for writing introductions to the works of others is evident from his final record of three forewords, four prefaces, and eleven introductions.

Referring to Macmillan's equivocal letter, Malinowski told Frazer that he was disappointed:

> That a type of scientific work which has to be done now or never and which entails at present real sacrifices—for there is no career for an Ethnologist, few endowments and the work itself is hard—that it should be even difficult to find a publisher for it, is discouraging! But nowadays "culture" is altogether considered a useless luxury.[12]

He was showing characteristic impatience: whenever he completed a task at top speed, he expected the world to respond with similar alacrity. He had barely completed the manuscript and was already despondent because the first publisher he approached had said, in effect, "we must proceed with caution." He seemed to expect Macmillan to accept his baby with open arms, sight unseen. His pessimism was not misjudged, however, and Macmillan did turn the book down. It was "very well written" and had "high scientific value," the publisher conceded, but it was not popular enough to pay.

As for their living in "these happy islands," Malinowski told Frazer, he and Elsie were still enjoying "a really good climate and wonderful scenery"; they were prospering in health and his working conditions were "admirable."

> If one could have a good library here—then the only reasonable plan would be to leave the trouble and irritation of Europe and settle here forever, even if one had to live on bread, water, and sunshine.[13]

He added that with "Kula" out of the way he had now begun "on the working out of my full material. In about 18 months I hope to finish all I know about the Trobriands." This astonishing claim suggests that he had not abandoned the idea of "Kiriwina," the comprehensive ethnography that would present everything he had recorded in the Trobriands. Yet he must have realized that in writing *Argonauts* he had already bitten off and chewed a very large chunk of that data; and he must also have been aware that if he faced any difficulty in getting publishers to show interest in what he intended to be a semipopular monograph, how much more would they resist an entirely technical, multivolume work. That he saw *Argonauts* as a potential money-spinner there can be no doubt: "I still hope my M.S. may be accepted [by George Macmillan], not because of its scientific value (whatever this might be) but because it ought to be a book that *sells*."[14] This too is an extraordinary claim, though perhaps less surprising if we bear in mind that he was addressing the most prolific, successful, and widely read anthropological author of the century: Sir James Frazer. The notion that he could write up everything that he knew about the Trobriands and package it as "Kiriwina" within eighteen months was unrealistic, to say the least, and he would spend countless months over the next fourteen years "working out" his Trobriand material. He would never "finish" it, nor even attempt to, after completing *Coral Gardens and their Magic* in 1935.

"Kula" Alias "Argonauts"

"Kula" the book grew out of what Malinowski had originally planned as Chapter 13 ("Kula and External Trade") in Part IV ("Economics") of "Kiriwina."[15] A handwritten, four-page outline or synopsis of "Kula" survives. Although it is undated, it's likely that Malinowski used it in Icod: its chapter headings differ only slightly from those in the published version of *Argonauts*, and with a couple of exceptions the Roman numberings of the chapters are the same. The internal evidence of the outline (with its cramped insertions and references to page numbers of his field notebooks) also strongly suggests that he referred to it while composing the final draft of his book. On the back of the first page are hopeful doodles of how he imagined the book's spine might appear, with its title and subtitle at the top, "B. Malinowski" in the middle, and "Macmillans" at the bottom.[16]

With this preamble, let us proceed to a synopsis of *Kula: A Tale of Native Enterprise and Adventure in the South Seas* (anticipating, I shall continue to refer to the book as *Argonauts*). It traces, in an episodic fashion, the contours of an overseas Kula expedition. Following a methodological introduction—an engagingly candid fieldworker's manual—the first two chapters set the ethnographic scene, initially from a panoramic view of insular eastern New Guinea with descriptions of the changing landscape and Frazerian *mise-en-scène*, then to a close-up inspection of the Trobriand Islands. The transition is presented as a travelogue of a coast-hugging boat journey from west to east, recapitulating the author's own. Malinowski creates narrative suspense by recounting his first contact with villagers on Kiriwina Island (or Boyowa). He sketches their physical appearance and the principal features of their society. The third chapter outlines "essentials of the Kula"— describing the types of valuables transacted and the rules governing their exchange—to enable the reader to follow the unfolding complexities of the system as presented in the rest of the book.

The meandering Kula story within the broader narrative begins in the fourth chapter and continues in fits and starts until the penultimate one. There are many aspects of the Kula and its associated practices to describe. First is the building of a seagoing canoe, with its accompanying magic, its sociology of ownership, and its ceremonial launching. This is followed by a lengthy disquisition on tribal economics, including a classification of gifts, payments, and other transactions; here Malinowski takes issue with classical economic theory, and demonstrates his thesis that *"the whole tribal life is permeated by a constant give and take"* (Malinowski 1922a: 167, italics in the original). The Kula is a magnificent instance of this principle.

When the overseas expedition gets underway we accompany it south from Sinaketa to Dobu. The narrative is soon interrupted by descriptions of the magic used in sailing, of the perils of shipwreck, of the cannibal witches who lie in wait for sailors. The expedition's landfall in the Amphlett Islands entails further digressions on the sociology of the Kula and provides the opportunity for an ethnographic account of the islanders and the pottery-making for which they are renowned. Passing the islands of Tewara and Sanoroa, we embark on a chapter-length account of mythical Kula heroes and the mythology that validates the magical systems. After a "ritual halt" for magical preparations to woo the favors of their Dobuan hosts, the expedition members disperse to the hamlets of their respective exchange partners. Kula transactions begin in earnest at this point, and Malinowski describes them in all their technical complexity. Then we join the traders for their return voyage to Kiriwina, stopping along the way to fish for the shells from which Sinaketa people manufacture necklaces.

The return expedition of Dobu and Amphlett traders to Sinaketa is the subject of Chapter 16, with detailed accounts of the magic that punctuates the conduct of Kula. In the two lengthy chapters devoted to magic that follow, Malinowski is at pains to stress how the Kula is aided and validated at every stage by incessant magical spells intoned, muttered, sung, or shouted. The book draws to a close with a local diversion through the inland districts of Kiriwina, and a more speculative appraisal of distant branches of the Kula on islands that Malinowski did not manage to visit. The final chapter, "The Meaning of the Kula," concludes the allegorical journey into the mind of the native, conjectures on the value of the Kula, and assesses the significance for Ethnology of this novel institution. The work ends, as the author's foreword began, on a note of elegiac regret with an impassioned plea for the study of Ethnology—"before it is too late."

The very *strangeness* of the Kula must strike the reader, not least the sheer elegance of its basic model: a system of ceremonial exchange in which shell necklaces circulate clockwise and armshells anticlockwise around a ring of a dozen islands (with an outer perimeter of approximately 750 miles) and in which these curious ornaments exalt and confer dignity on the men who temporarily possess them. In Trobriand idiom, the movement of Kula valuables between partners is along roads or paths (*keda*), whether on land or over the sea. The metaphor that Malinowski employs, however, is a liquid one; the "flow" of Kula valuables between communities is sometimes a "trickle," sometimes a "flood," while his trope refers to "eddies," "currents," and "leaks" within the larger Kula ring (Malinowski 1922a: 480, 489, 495, 505–6). The system is not only exotic but beautiful in the way a chess game, an orchestral symphony, or a mathematical solution can be aesthetically satisfying in its complexity. Part game, part ritual, part economic exchange, part serious political pursuit in which men may triumph or die, the Kula operated in a marvelously intricate way that no individual genius could have devised. A social institution par excellence, it depended on the more or less harmonized, more or less conscious acts of those who self-interestedly kept the interminable cycle of transactions in motion. The Kula is greater than the sum of its transactions, bigger than the totality of its participants—who numbered, after all, a mere few thousand souls. Kula traders formed not a community but rather a guild, an association of men (and a few women) of a certain rank who respected the same rules, followed the same protocols, and strived for the same ends across village and tribal boundaries. As a political institution the Kula was an elegant solution to maintaining the peace of the market for the exchange and barter of essential commodities. The men of a village who crewed a canoe to visit potentially hostile foreign shores were internally *divided* in their competitive desire for Kula valuables, and for the short duration of their stay each was under the protection of his foreign host, *allied* with his exchange partner against fellow-villagers. Such countervailing relationships created—to use the coinage of one of Malinowski's later pupils, Max Gluckman—"peace in the feud" (Gluckman 1963; see also Uberoi 1962).

Theory and Method in Argonauts

Although Malinowski frequently refers to "theory" its place in *Argonauts* is ambiguous. He clearly wished to avoid overloading his book with "theory" in case it deterred the general reader. As he had told Frazer, he hoped it would be "a paying proposition." What he did not tell Frazer was that ethnography in this literary mode would also serve his ambition to become a man of letters, a Conrad of anthropology. In his 1918 diary he envisaged a "general theoretical 'sauce' in which my concrete documentations are to be dressed up"—as if he was willing to subordinate theory to description (Malinowski 1967: 158).[17] On occasion he uses the word "theory" to refer to the paradigms of evolution and diffusion (which had yet to gain their status as "isms"), though he quickly retreats from engaging them, claiming that it is not the Ethnographer's task to venture grand deductions. "I cannot enter into any theoretical speculations myself," he announced at the end of his book, a protestation of "methodological puritanism" that has been regarded by at least one critic as an abrogation of scientific responsibility

(Malinowski 1922a: 515).[18] His methodological purity forbade historical speculation in particular: "all questions of origins, of development or history of the institutions have been rigorously ruled out of this work. The mixing up of speculative or hypothetical views with an account of facts is, in my opinion, an unpardonable sin against ethnographic method" (ibid.: 100n).

When Margaret Mead first met Raymond Firth (on a Sydney dockside in 1929) she told him she had found "no *ideas*" in *Argonauts*. "Well," Firth recalled, "I couldn't explain that the ideas were buried in the text, in the way Malinowski had expressed things. He didn't label them; you found them if you were interested in his topics."[19] Malinowski's ideas are indeed implicit rather than explicit in *Argonauts*, so the ratio of descriptive ethnography to theoretical generalization is difficult to gauge. He often interleaves and integrates theory and description—in effect collapses them—just as he frequently dissolves the distinction between theory and method. Even his technical description of that vital item of Trobriand material culture—the seagoing canoe—is teasingly discursive. The example is instructive in demonstrating his method of presentation. He breaks with the "curio-hunting," "antiquarian" tradition of museum-based Ethnology by widening his descriptive angle of vision to include social context. "A pulling to pieces of a lifeless object will not satisfy us," he says, for it is necessary to provide the contextual background of the material object in order to represent what he called its "deepest ethnographic reality" (Malinowski 1922a: 106). In this particular case the "reality" encompasses the entire social and cultural ambience of the making, launching, and sailing of a canoe. His description of the canoe—informed, perhaps, by his youthful study of mechanics at the Jagiellonian University and aided by diagrams and photographs—is easily accessible to the general reader (ibid.: 108–13). He provides just enough technical detail to satisfy someone like Seligman, if not a die-hard technologist like Haddon, who had to extract more details from him when compiling his synoptic work *The Canoes of Oceania*. But Malinowski never loses sight of what the canoe means to the men who build and sail it, and he dwells on the "emotional attitude" they have toward their canoes. He wants his reader to see the canoe through Trobriand eyes, and his descriptions shift constantly between "etic" and "emic" viewpoints. Thus does "theory" cunningly infuse his descriptions.

Malinowski's attacks on current views of utilitarian Primitive Economic Man—"a fanciful, dummy creature" motivated by enlightened self-interest—are among the strongest theoretical statements in the book, and in advancing a new theory of value they introduce a moral dimension into the work (Malinowski 1922a: 60, 166ff., 516). He believed that his account of the Kula would help dismember this straw figure and "dispel such crude, rationalistic conceptions of primitive mankind" (ibid.: 516). Kula "shows us that the whole conception of primitive value; the very incorrect habit of calling all objects of value 'money' or '*currency*;' the current ideas of primitive trade and primitive ownership—all these have to be revised in the light of our institution" (ibid.). On value he writes: "The Kula is the highest and the most dramatic expression of the native's conception of value" (ibid.: 176). Again, "Value is not the result of utility and rarity, intellectually compounded, but it is the result of a sentiment grown around things, which, through satisfying human needs, are capable of evoking emotions" (ibid.: 172). Values, needs, emotions: three key terms that recur in his functional anthropology as in his own psychic economy.

In *Argonauts* "function" is not yet an explicit theoretical concept, however. There is a naïve, nascent functionalism in statements such as the following concerning obligatory gift-giving: "The function of these ceremonial re-payments is, on the surface of it, to thicken the social ties from which arise the obligations" (Malinowski 1922a: 182). Proto-functionalism lurks in his use of synoptic charts, too, for the imaginative manipulation of "aspects" of an institution as visually represented in such charts brings them into conjunction. "The method of reducing information, if possible, into charts or synoptic tables ought to be extended to the study of practically all aspects of native life," he advised (ibid.: 14). Charts do not "explain" by indicating causation (there are no directional arrows in his charts); they are a discovery procedure, rather, and what one sees in them are connections, correlations, and correspondences.

The Ethnographic Persona

If we distinguish method from theory we are on more solid ground. As befitting the work of a student of Mach and Rivers, *Argonauts* is rich in methodological insights. The introduction ("The Subject, Method and Scope of this Inquiry") defined a mode of research that would be pursued by subsequent generations of anthropologists. It has even been called "the book of Genesis in the fieldworker's bible" (Van Maanen 1988: 10). Malinowski's clear intention was to raise ethnographic fieldwork to a professional art. The essential rule, he emphasized, was to study the "tribal culture *in all its aspects*," making no distinction "between what is commonplace, drab or ordinary" and what may seem novel, astonishing, or sensational. He insisted on the collection of three kinds of documents or texts: (1) "concrete, statistical documentation" of the "organization of the tribe and the anatomy of its culture"; (2) "minute, detailed observations, in the form of some sort of ethnographic diary" in order to record "the imponderabilia of actual life";

and (3) a *corpus inscriptionum* of vernacular statements, typical utterances, myths and folklore narratives, magical spells, and so on to be used as "documents of native mentality" and to illustrate "typical ways of thinking and feeling" (Malinowski 1922a: 10–11, 24).

Other prescriptions for effective fieldwork might involve "the personal equation of the observer." Putting aside notebook and camera on occasion to participate "in what is going on" is not easy for everyone, he admitted, and "perhaps the Slavonic nature is more plastic and more naturally savage than that of Western Europeans" (Malinowski 1922a: 21). It was perhaps also his "Slavonic nature" that enabled him to break with current Anglo-American ethnographic convention in other respects. What must have seemed outlandish to Malinowski's British colleagues, for instance, was the presence of a central character called the Ethnographer who tugs persistently at readers' sleeves and never lets them forget not only that he was *there* as a participant observer, but also that he is the one, in a fully contextualized first-person sense, who is doing the writing. It is the ethnographic persona—patient, empathetic yet ironic—who was given a tentative outing in the "*Mailu*" report and reached maturity in the "*Baloma*" essay (Young 2004: 371–72, 430). While this intrusion of Malinowski's authorial self blurs the distinction between Romantic travelogue and ethnographic monograph, one that had been hardening steadily during the late nineteenth century (Thornton 1983), it was done in the service of "methodic sincerity." In Ethnography, "the writer is his own chronicler," Malinowski reminds us, and chides those whose works offer "wholesale generalizations" without informing the reader according to "what actual *experiences* the writers have reached their conclusion" (my italics). There is, after all, an "enormous" distance between "the brute material of information—as it is presented to the student in his own observations, in native statement, in the kaleidoscope of tribal life—and the final authoritative presentation of the results" (Malinowski 1922a: 3–4). George Stocking puts it concisely: Malinowski's "own experience of the native's experience must become the reader's experience as well. And that was a task that scientific analysis yielded up to literary art" (Stocking 1995: 270).

In one of his most conspicuous attempts to lay his own cards on the table, Malinowski (1922a: 16) presents a "Chronological List of Kula Events Witnessed by the Writer." This document, offered in a spirit of "methodological candor," purports to enable the reader "to estimate with precision the degree of the writer's personal acquaintance with the facts which he describes, and form an idea under what conditions information has been obtained from the natives" (ibid.: 3). Although his readers were not to know, the exercise is vitiated by a number of careless factual errors. Malinowski presumably did not bother to check his field diaries in allowing his cavalier approach to dates off the leash. He tacks a month onto each end of the three periods he spent in the field (as if travel to and from the actual field constituted fieldwork) and was in conspicuous error as to when he was in Woodlark Island (February not March 1915) and the month in which he returned to Australia in 1916 (March not May). Obviously, fieldwork *seemed* longer to him than it really was.[20]

A Deskbound Ethnographer

While Malinowski says a great deal in his introduction about "the proper conditions for ethnographic work" by adducing his own exemplary fieldwork practice, he says nothing whatsoever about the conditions under which he wrote his monograph as a deskbound Ethnographer. As we have seen, some of it was produced piecemeal over a period of years, but there is no doubt that the longest, most sustained and intensive stint of writing was during the four-month period in Icod de los Vinos. The problem of how to reconcile the emotional demands of love and the intellectual demands of work that had preoccupied him throughout his early manhood, he had apparently solved by his marriage to Elsie. The "proper conditions" for the final crafting of *Argonauts* appear to have been happily settled ones, in an environment of Spanish-Canary culture, more domestic than erotic. If Elsie, baby Józefa, and the two *criadas* created a quotidian distraction of household clamor, he was sufficiently focused on his writing to ignore it. The conditions for desk work, in short, were as close to optimum as he could hope for, and he would replicate them in the Italian Tyrol the following year. The sweeping views from his veranda study at "El Boquín" would have been conducive to contented contemplation; the elevation, too, must have helped one who believed that his lungs functioned better in slightly thinner air. Yet one searches *Argonauts* in vain for any sign or symptom of daily life at "El Boquín." The local color and background hum of Tenerife seem not to have inflected his writing nor infiltrated his remembered vistas of the Trobriands.

It is tempting to read *Argonauts* through the lens of the *Diary*, and I have described elsewhere some of the personal experiences that Malinowski exploited for ethnographic purposes, such as the "unmitigated funk" and superstitious terror that gripped him when he was almost shipwrecked by a violent squall in the Amphletts (Young 2004: 531–32). Examples could be multiplied, but this is not to say—as James Clifford has proposed—that the *Diary* and *Argonauts* constitute "a single expanded text" (Clifford 1986; Geertz 1988). I am more inclined to agree with Raymond Firth, who points out that this judgment is to overlook the years that elapsed between them and the fact that they were written for very different purposes under very different conditions. They were also written in different languages in quite different styles, and no amount of "blurring" of genres can make them coextensive. Crucially, only *Argonauts* was written for publication by—as Firth puts it—"a happily married man, in a time of relative tranquility. Of course they are poles apart" (Firth 1989: xxx). Firth's pun was perhaps inadvertent, but there is an unmistakably Polish flavor to the *Diary* that is not evident in *Argonauts* except where Malinowski deliberately draws attention to his "Slavonic nature."

The *Diary* is characterized by a dark thread: not only that of its author's melancholic moods reflecting his personal crises and that of a world savagely at war, but also in its intimations of a Papuan "heart of darkness."[21] Despite its final falling cadences, the dominant air of *Argonauts* is a fairly sunny one; the dark thread is absent—unless in those passages that castigate "the minor cast of cramped minds" (Payne 1981: 422)—misguided missionaries, rapacious traders, and ignorant colonial officials—for bringing about the demise of traditional ways. The two texts are certainly "complementary," however, as Malinowski certainly would have acknowledged.[22] On an intertextual level, indeed, one would expect some of the experiences he recorded in his private diaries to be reproduced (with suitable cosmetic modifications) in his public writings, just as one would expect the confessional tenor of the diaries to leak on occasion into the monographs. But the objective, scientific stance of *Argonauts* is not compromised unduly by the Ethnographer's subjective lapses.

Today there are many modes of ethnographic writing, and it is not too fanciful to claim that in *Argonauts* Malinowski anticipated most of them: the "realist," the "confessional," and the "impressionist" modes, for example.[23] As a perspicacious authority on Malinowski's style has remarked: "He is at once expert guide, romantic yarn-spinner, and pedantic moralist" (Payne 1981: 421). His writing is lavish with adjectives, adverbs, and figures of speech, though they are not often strikingly original: the apt cliché and the familiar simile served his general purpose better than the ostentatious turn of phrase and attention-seeking trope. His persistent use of the present tense helped to create what came to be known as "the ethnographic present."

Some of these stylistic devices were undoubtedly endorsed by Elsie, with her penchant for clear prose and abhorrence of the passive voice. In the copy of *Argonauts* he presented to his wife, Malinowski wrote: "To my collaborator, who had half the share at least and more than half the merit in writing this book—Its nominal author. Cassis, 20.7.22."[24] Yet it is a curious fact that he does not acknowledge her in print, neither in his foreword nor in the formal acknowledgments page. Her name is not the only conspicuous omission, however. Haddon, Rivers, and Westermarck are missing, and so too are Murray and other officers of the Papuan administration such as Bellamy and Champion. Of the missionaries who helped Malinowski in the Trobriands—Gilmore, Johns, and Ethel Prisk—there is no mention.

The End of Ethnology

In the very first sentence of his introduction, Malinowski purports to peer into the future: "The coastal populations of the South Sea Islands, with very few exceptions, are, *or were before their extinction*, expert navigators and traders" (Malinowski 1922a: 1, my italics). From the Riversian opening paragraph of his foreword, deploring the dying away of the inhabitants of "savage countries" ("Ethnology is in the sadly ludicrous, not to say tragic position . . ."), to the closing Frazerian paragraph of the book with its elegiac lament ("Alas! the time is short for Ethnology . . .") there is a strain of Romantic regret and pastoral nostalgia haunting the work (ibid.: xv, 518). Throughout, Malinowski quaintly refers to "olden days," as if to some innocent Arcadian past. By these devices, in a subtly subversive way, the book transcends its subject matter. Just as the circuit of the Kula is closed in the penultimate chapter with the description of the "remaining branches of the Kula," so does the author close the circle of his book's journey by evoking an identical mood, repeating the same sentiments of Romantic pessimism. Although empirically Machian in intent and method, *Argonauts* hints at greater mysteries: not only ancient ones evoked by the title—Jason's quest has archetypal resonances—but also entropic ones of death and decay. The thoughtful positioning of photographs cleverly conveys the book's message. The frontispiece establishes the subject matter (Chief Tolouwa ceremonially receiving Kula valuables); the first photograph in the text establishes the authoritative presence of the author (the Ethnographer's tent on a beach in the Amphletts); but the very last photograph depicts a *pieta*: an emaciated corpse adorned with "life-giving" Kula valuables, surrounded by mourners. This stark image subtly conveys the covert theme of dissolution, the demise of the Savage, and the end of Ethnology.

Let us join the introduction to the finale (as the last chapter was originally entitled) and make "its two ends meet" (Malinowski 1922a: 509). Malinowski restates his claim that the Kula is "something unusual, something not met with before in ethnological studies" (ibid.). Among its many uniquely interesting features, he draws particular attention to the theoretical importance of an aspect of Kula that he had brought to the fore in *The Economic Journal* the previous year (1921). This was the demonstrable fact that "economic enterprise and magical ritual form one inseparable whole, the forces of the magical belief and the efforts of man molding and influencing one another" (ibid.: 515). The irrational and the practical were two sides of the Trobriand coin. The way "in which these two aspects of culture functionally depend on one another might afford some interesting theoretical reflection," he writes. "Indeed, it seems to me that there is room for a new type of theory." This modest announcement bows toward functionalism waiting in the wings. But still center-stage—as he quickly acknowledges—are the "evolutional" theories of the "classical school of British Anthropology" as practiced by Tylor, Frazer, Westermarck, Hartland, and Crawley, and the "ethnological" school of "Ratzel, Foy, Gräbner, W. Schmidt, Rivers, and Eliott-Smith [sic]." He then ventures to prophesy the revolution to come, led by himself:

> The influence on one another of the various aspects of an institution, the study of the social and psychological mechanism on which the institution is based, are a type of theoretical studies which has been practiced up till now in a tentative way only, but I venture to foretell will come into their own sooner or later. This kind of research will pave the way and provide the material for the others. (Ibid.: 516)

The last two pages of the book contain a rhetorical appeal for a disinterested Ethnology. (That it is not entirely disinterested in placing the science at the service of Western civilization's quest for universal knowledge would, in the 1920s, have given Malinowski no cause for apology.) It is the psychology of primitive man that he wants to understand, not just his sociology. "Thus the details and technicalities of the Kula acquire their meaning only in so far as they express some central attitude of mind of the natives, and thus broaden our knowledge, widen our outlook and deepen our grasp of human nature" (Malinowski 1922a: 517). In the passage that follows, he offers an anthropologist's personal credo:

> What interests me really in the study of the native is his outlook on things, his *Weltanschauung*, the breath of life and reality which he breathes and by which he lives. Every human culture gives its members a definite vision of the world, a definite zest of life ... [I]t is the possibility of seeing life and the world from the various angles, peculiar to each culture, that has always charmed me most, and inspired me with real desire to penetrate other cultures, to understand other types of life. (Ibid.)

The rhetoric hints clearly at his *humanistic* concern. Recall his vision of a "New Humanism" that would replace the moribund humanism of "dust and death" based on the civilizations of antiquity (which he was happy nevertheless to exploit for the title of his book) (see Young 2004: 547). The philosophy of the New Humanism would be vitalized by the Ethnology of living, breathing savages displaying the broadest spectrum of human nature. The beginning and the end of *Argonauts* are affirmations of Malinowski's belief in the noble aims of Ethnology, with its potential to be a "deeply philosophic, enlightening and elevating" scientific discipline.

In his cabin trunk at "El Boquín" was the essay, drafted in Edinburgh the previous autumn, that Seligman had shrugged aside, and Rivers had failed to place. The argument of that essay and the final pages of *Argonauts* are convergent, almost interchangeable, with the difference that the essay gives more practical spin ("save the savage from extinction") as a cogent reason for the study of Ethnology (Malinowski 1922b).

Following another swipe at the antiquarian's attitude toward curio-collecting, Malinowski continues:

> Some people are unable to grasp the inner meaning and the psychological reality of all that is outwardly strange, at first sight incomprehensible, in a different culture. These people are not born to be ethnologists. It is in the love of the final synthesis, achieved by the assimilation and comprehension of all the items of a culture and still more in the love of the variety and independence of the various cultures that lies the test of the real worker in the true Science of Man. (1922a: 517)

After this explanation of his ideal vocation, Malinowski turns up the rhetorical volume another notch. The ultimate aim is to convert knowledge of other modes of life into wisdom.

> Though it may be given to us for a moment to enter into the soul of a savage and through his eyes look at the outer world and feel ourselves what it must feel to *him* to be himself—yet our final goal is to enrich and deepen our own world's vision, to understand our own nature and to make it finer, intellectually and artistically. In grasping the essential outlook of others, with the reverence and real understanding, due even to savages, we cannot but help widening our own. (Ibid.: 518)

Anthropology is an Enlightenment project. The Science of Man must lead to "tolerance and generosity, based on the understanding of other men's point of view." Ethnology can administer an antidote to ethnocentrism. The "final Socratic wisdom of knowing ourselves" is achieved by transcending the "narrow confinement of the customs, beliefs, and prejudices" into which we are born. More than ever is tolerance needed in the aftermath of a terrible war, "when prejudice, ill-will and vindictiveness are dividing each European nation . . . when all the ideals, cherished and proclaimed as the highest achievements of civilization, science, and religion, have been thrown to the winds." With a fine rhetorical flourish, Malinowski ends the book, as he began it, with an elegiac appeal that carries the same broad message of the still unpublished article he had written a few months earlier:

The study of Ethnology—so often mistaken by its very votaries for an idle hunting after curios, for a ramble among the savage and fantastic shapes of "barbarous customs and crude superstitions"—might become one of the most deeply philosophic, enlightening, and elevating disciplines of scientific research. Alas! the time is short for Ethnology, and will this truth of its real meaning and importance dawn before it is too late? (1922a: 518)

I return, finally, to the remarkable introduction of *Argonauts*, which famously concludes with a passionate peroration concerning the Ethnographer's "final goal" (cited *ad nauseam* in textbooks), which is "to grasp the native's point of view, his relation to life, to realize *his* vision of *his* world. We have to study man, and we must study what concerns him most intimately, that is, the hold which life has on him" (1922a: 25).

Acknowledgments

I should like to thank my wife Elizabeth C. Brouwer for her assistance in preparing this account for this publication.

Michael W. Young is a social anthropologist with fieldwork experience in Papua New Guinea and Vanuatu. He is currently Emeritus Honorary Associate Professor in the School of Culture, History & Languages at the Australian National University. His books include *Fighting with Food* (Cambridge University Press, 1973), *The Ethnography of Malinowski* (Routledge, 1979), *Magicians of Manumanua* (California University Press, 1983), *Malinowski among the Magi* (Routledge, 1988), *Malinowski's Kiriwina* (Chicago University Press, 1998), *An Anthropologist in Papua* (Hurst, 2001), and *Malinowski: Odyssey of an Anthropologist* (Yale University Press, 2004).

Notes

1. Malinowski to Frazer, 10 January 1921. Frazer Papers, Trinity College Cambridge (FPTCC). b.36/178.
2. See the photograph in Wayne (1995: 15).
3. Malinowski to Frazer, 10 February 1921. FPTCC b.36/179.
4. Cuscoy, a local historian at the Universidad de La Laguna, who collected oral accounts of the Malinowskis in Tenerife.
5. Malinowski to Frazer, 10 February 1921. FPTCC b.36/179.
6. Elsie to Malinowski, 21 April 1921 (Wayne 1995: 18).
7. Elsie to Hede Khuner, 5 March 1921. Malinowski Papers, LSE (MPLSE).

8. A conservative calculation would allow that if he maintained an average output of about 2,200 words a day he could have written, or rewritten, the whole of *Argonauts* in one hundred days.
9. Malinowski to Frazer, 10 February 1921. FPTCC b.36/179.
10. George Macmillan to Frazer, 3 March 1921. Malinowski Papers, Yale (MPY), I/203.
11. Seligman to Malinowski, 26 April 1921. Verso of notes on "Social Ideas." MPLSE, f. Mal.111.
12. Malinowski to Frazer, 8 May 1921. FPTCC b.36/180.
13. Ibid.
14. Ibid.
15. Materials in "Culture boxes" and "Coral Gardens boxes," MPLSE.
16. MPY, II/155.
17. According to this culinary image, as James Urry noted, "Ethnographies were obviously things to be consumed, with the ethnographic material providing the basic dish and the theory the piquant flavouring" (1993: 53).
18. Harry Payne asks: "Did Malinowski-Conrad really live in fear of Malinowski-Newton?" (1981: 419).
19. Raymond Firth, personal communication June 1993. See Young (2003).
20. Malinowski made two annotations in the margin of page 16 of his author's copy of *Argonauts* (MPY II/156). He wrote "1 week" opposite "March 1915," as if to correct the impression that he had spent a month in Woodlark; but the month itself he left uncorrected. Opposite "Third Expedition, October 1917–October 1918," he wrote "10 months." Too late his methodological conscience had caught up with him.
21. See Thornton (1985). Thornton makes much of Malinowski's reading of Conrad's novella, *Heart of Darkness*, assuming that he read it while in the field. While he may well have done so in Mailu (which Thornton confuses with Woodlark Island), I believe that he had read it first in London before embarking for Australia.
22. See Young (2004: 416, 484) concerning Malinowski's observation that his diary and his ethnography were "well-nigh as complementary as complementary can be."
23. These are the three principal modes identified by Van Maanen (1988).
24. The copy now resides in his Yale archive (MPY: II/157).

References

Ackerman, Robert. 1987. *J.G. Frazer: His Life and Work*. Cambridge: Cambridge University Press.

Clifford, James. 1986. "On Ethnographic Self-Fashioning: Conrad and Malinowski." In *Reconstructing Individualism: Autonomy, Individuality and the Self in Western Thought*, ed. Thomas C. Heller et al., 140–62. Palo Alto, CA: Stanford University Press.

Firth, Raymond. 1989. "Second Introduction, 1988" in Bronisław Malinowski, *A Diary in the Strict Sense of the Term*. pp. xxi–xxxi. London: Athlone Press.

Geertz, Clifford. 1988. *Works and Lives: The Anthropologist as Author*. Palo Alto, CA: Stanford University Press.

Gluckman, Max. 1963. *Custom and Conflict in Africa*. Oxford: Basil Blackwell.

Malinowski, Bronisław. 1921. "The Primitive Economics of the Trobriand Islanders." *The Economic Journal* 31(121): 1–16.

———. 1922a. *Argonauts of the Western Pacific: An Account of Native Enterprise and Adventure in the Archipelagoes of Melanesian New Guinea*. London: Routledge & Kegan Paul.

———. 1922b. "Ethnology and the Study of Society." *Economica* 6: 208–19.

———. 1967. *A Diary in the Strict Sense of the Term*. London: Routledge & Kegan Paul.

Payne, Harry. 1981. "Malinowski's Style." *Proceedings of the American Philosophical Society* 125(6): 416–40.

Stocking, George W. 1995. *After Tylor: British Social Anthropology 1888–1951*. Madison: University of Wisconsin Press.

Thornton, Robert. 1983. "Narrative Ethnography in Africa: 1850–1920; The Creation and Capture of an Appropriate Domain for Anthropology." *Man* 18(3): 502–20.

———. 1985. "'Imagine Yourself Set Down . . .': Mach, Frazer, Conrad, Malinowski and the Role of Imagination in Ethnography." *Anthropology Today* 1(5): 7–14.

Uberoi, S. J. 1962. *Politics of the Kula Ring*. Manchester: Manchester University Press.

Urry, James. 1993. *Before Social Anthropology: Essays on the History of British Social Anthropology*. Chur: Harwood Academic.

Van Maanen, John. 1988. *Tales of the Field. On Writing Ethnography*. Chicago: University of Chicago Press.

Wayne, Helena, ed. 1995. *The Story of a Marriage: The Letters of Bronislaw Malinowski and Elsie Masson*. Vol. 2. London: Routledge.

Young, Michael W. 2003. "Raymond William Firth, 1901–2002." *Journal of Pacific History* 38(2): 277–80.

———. 2004. *Malinowski: Odyssey of an Anthropologist, 1884–1920*. New Haven, CT: Yale University Press.

3

 Malinowski's New Paradigm

ADAM KUPER

Three classics of anthropology appeared in 1922: Bronisław Malinowski's *Argonauts of the Western Pacific*, A. R. Radcliffe-Brown's *The Andaman Islanders*, and the one-volume abridged edition of James George Frazer's *The Golden Bough*. Malinowski invited Frazer to write a preface to his *Argonauts*, but he and Radcliffe-Brown were turning away from speculative reconstructions of large sweeps of history in favor of what both called a "functionalist" approach. In 1929, Radcliffe-Brown wrote: "I believe that at this time the really important conflict in anthropological studies is not between the 'evolutionists' and the 'diffusionists,' nor between the various schools of the diffusionists, but between conjectural history on the one side and the functional study of society on the other" (Radcliffe-Brown 1929: 53).

What then was "functionalism," and where did it come from? The short answer is that it came from biology. Its use in the social sciences went back at least to Herbert Spencer's mid-nineteenth-century "organic analogy" between social and biological processes. By the early twentieth century, various notions of function were current in psychology and sociology. During his postgraduate studies in Leipzig, Malinowski was influenced by the pioneering social psychologist Wilhelm Wundt. Wundt's *Völkerpsychologie*, published in 1904, drew from ethnographic sources and offered a functional approach to what he termed *Kultur*:

> those mental products which are created by a community of human life and are, therefore, inexplicable in terms merely of individual consciousness, since they presuppose the reciprocal action of many ... the various mental expressions, particularly in their early stages, are so intertwined that they are scarcely separable from

one another. Language is influenced by myth, art is a factor in myth development, and customs and usages are everywhere sustained by mythological conceptions. (1917: 7)

At each stage of social evolution, Wundt wrote, "there are certain ideas, emotions, and springs of action about which the various phenomena group themselves" (ibid.). Malinowski echoed Wundt in the closing pages of *Argonauts*: "The influence on one another of the various aspects of an institution, the study of the social and psychological mechanism on which the institution is based, are a type of theoretical studies which have been practiced up till now in a tentative way only, but I venture to foretell will come into their own sooner or later" (Malinowski 1922: 516).

Durkheim drew on Wundt in developing his conception of a "collective consciousness." In his early publications in Polish, Malinowski wrestled with Durkheim's ideas about the functions of totemism (Malinowski 1993). But did institutions, taboos, and rituals serve the needs of the individual or the community? Radcliffe-Brown adopted the Durkheimian view that individuals were thoroughly indoctrinated with local ideologies, Malinowski insisted that sane persons put their individual interests first, manipulate the rules, and twist myths, rituals, and customary practices to suit themselves. Traditional ethnography represented its subjects as the slaves of custom. The Trobrianders used myths to make property claims, rituals to extend their power, marriages to gain influence. Malinowski used the term "savage" ironically. He was the first ethnographer to represent "savages" as rational actors, no more liable to be bamboozled than the average European.

Pragmatism and Linguistics

Edmund Leach suggested that Malinowski was influenced, even inspired, by the Pragmatism of William James, which was fashionable in England when he turned up as a graduate student at the LSE in 1910. Leach quoted a commentator who explained that in James's view "the sole function of thought is to satisfy certain interests of the organism, and that truth consists in such thinking as satisfied these interests." There "in a nutshell," Leach remarked, we have "the whole essence of Malinowski's functionalism" (Leach 1957: 122).

Pragmatism had a more particular interest for Malinowski, in its interrogation of language. His father was a linguist and he knew very well that among the new developments in science there was a reorientation in the study of language. He did not have in mind the linguistic revolution of Saussure, but perhaps rather the pragmatism (or pragmatics) of Charles

Sanders Peirce and William James and developments of German linguists, notably the work of Philipp Wegener, who dubbed his approach *Situationstheorie*.[1] In *Argonauts*, Malinowski insisted that translation was impossible without cultural contextualization, and that language was a mode of action. (Wittgenstein's *Tractatus Logico-Philosophicus*, also published in that magical year, 1922, launched the linguistic turn in British philosophy.)

The new theory that meaning is above all a matter of context was given a great impetus by the publication in 1923 of *The Meaning of Meaning: A Study of the Influence of Language upon Thought and of the Science of Symbolism*. The authors, a linguist, C. K. Ogden, and a literary critic, I. A. Richards, commissioned a 'Supplement' from Malinowski. Malinowski's theme, one he had already broached in *Argonauts*, in a chapter on "The Power of Words in Magic," was that "it is impossible to translate words of a primitive language or of one widely different from our own, without giving a detailed account of the culture of its users and thus providing the common measure necessary for a translation." Moreover, the "primitive function" of language is as a "*mode of action*" rather than "*a countersign of thought*" (Malinowski 1923: 296). Just as Lévi-Strauss's structuralism was inspired by the Prague school of linguistics, so Malinowski's functionalism was imbued with ideas drawn from pragmatic linguistics.

Tribal "Give and Take"

Malinowski presented *Argonauts* not only as an exemplar of a new theory but also as a contribution to a new field: the study of production, consumption, and exchange in societies without markets or money, but where, nevertheless, "*the whole tribal life is permeated by a constant give and take*" (Malinowski 1922: 167, italics original). According to Malinowski, "the Kula presents to us a new type of phenomenon, lying on the borderland between the commercial and the ceremonial and expressing a complex and interesting attitude of mind" (ibid.: 513).

In fact, the study of gift exchange was not all that new. It was central to the research project of Karl Bücher, another famous Leipzig professor whose lectures Malinowski attended as a graduate student. The luminaries of the modern German school of historical economics, Friedrich List, Max Weber, and Werner Sombart, developed models of precapitalist economies. In the 1890s, as the German overseas empire grew, Bücher came up with the conception of a "primitive" stage, in which an economic sphere could not easily be isolated for purposes of analysis (see Liebersohn 2011: 40–61). In 1914 a doctoral thesis at Leipzig University by Wilhelm Gault identified a type of exchange mechanism that, though widely reported by travelers among *Naturvölker*, "has not yet been the object of a cohesive description: *the gift in its form and contents* . . . in its various manifestations and motives" (quoted in Liebersohn 2011: 55; Gault's italics). Gault insisted that, in its traditional form, the gift always required a return gift. At the end of World War I Bücher published a major essay that drew on Gault, and which emphasized the return of the gift and extended the range of gifts to the offering of hospitality, the reimbursement of magicians and performers, and marriage, itself a form of gift. He insisted that gift-giving is a moral act, contributing to social solidarity.

In a paper on the Trobriand economy, published in *The Economic Journal* in 1921, Malinowski dismissed Bücher's conclusions as "a failure, not owing to imperfect reasoning or method, but rather to the defective material on which they are formed." Drawing on his Trobriand material, he argued that "production, exchange and consumption are socially organized and regulated by custom, and . . . a special system of traditional economic values governs their activities and spurs them on . . . This state of affairs might be called—as a new conception requires a new term—Tribal Economy" (Malinowski 1921: 1, 15).

Malinowski did not concede that Bücher was the first to formulate a theory of the gift. Nor did he point to the fine descriptions of gift exchanges published by a new generation of fieldworkers who had been stimulated by Bücher's challenge. Among them was Franz Boas, who encountered the potlatch in British Columbia in the winter of 1895–96 and published detailed accounts of potlatch ceremonies. More immediately relevant was the work of a disciple of Bücher, Richard Thurnwald, on the exchange of marital and extramarital sexual favors among the Banaro, who lived along the Sepik river in what was then German New Guinea (see Liebersohn 2011: 104–22). Thurnwald's initial report appeared in the *American Anthropologist* in 1916. Following Bücher, and like Malinowski, Thurnwald argued that gift-giving pervaded social relations in Papuan societies. (By a bizarre coincidence, Thurnwald, like Malinowski, was stranded in the Pacific by the outbreak of World War I, and like Malinowski he took advantage of an enforced stay to engage in more intensive field research.) Surprisingly, Malinowski did not cite Boas or Thurnwald in the *Argonauts*.

The "Imponderabilia of Actual Life"

Argonauts is celebrated above all as an exemplar of a new method of ethnographic research. Ernest Gellner remarked that Malinowski and his disciples "insist that anthropology differs from 'mere' ethnography by also having theory; on investigation of this theory, called Functionalism, it turns out to be in large part the doctrine that anthropology should be nothing but ethnography. Or rather—good ethnography" (Gellner 1973: 98).

The Royal Anthropological Institute's *Notes and Queries on Anthropology*, an extended questionnaire, went through four editions between 1870 and 1920. It was written for "men in the field": colonial administrators, missionaries, and scientific travelers, who would summon native experts to their verandas and take them through the checklist of queries about food taboos, totems, ghosts and witches, funeral customs, or ideas about conception, as required. Even in the first decades of the twentieth century, when the first professionally trained ethnographers went into the field, they seldom spent more than a few weeks in any one field site, and they still relied on native experts, whom they questioned with the help of translators.

Malinowski had no faith in this way of doing fieldwork. Before going to the Trobriand Islands he undertook an apprentice field study in Mailu on mainland New Guinea. Writing it up, he organized his material to fit the standard format of *Notes and Queries*. He wrote to Haddon that his Mailu fieldwork was "a time of trial and learning of method and I made of course lots of blunders and wasted half my time" (Young 2004: 373). The mechanical listing of customs and beliefs may have facilitated cross-cultural comparisons, but it obscured the connections between different activities and institutions. As a student of Wundt and Bücher, Malinowski was not comfortable with the treatment of institutions as independent silos. In a small-scale society without a developed division of labor it was necessary to tease out the various strands—magic, economics, kinship, politics—that were woven together in even the most ordinary activities, such as house building, sailing, or gardening.

Above all, Malinowski wanted the ethnographer to record instances where people bent or broke the rules, or manipulated customs. Getting the rules from some expert did not tell you how the game was played. Witch doctors disagreed among themselves, like medical doctors. And people tend to say one thing but do another: "Whenever the native can evade his obligations without the loss of prestige, or without the prospective loss of gain, he does so, exactly as a civilized businessman would do" (Malinowski 1926: 30). To understand what was really going on, the ethnographer must relinquish his comfortable position on the verandah, pitch a tent in the village, cultivate a garden, exchange gifts, listen in to conversations, flirt, argue, and generally hang about. Intimate personal histories, neighborhood feuds, the tug of personal loyalty against formal duties: all this was accessible only to an observer who was immersed in the everyday life of the village (Malinowski 1922: 6–7).

In a letter to his fiancée, Elsie Masson, Malinowski described his delight at going fishing with "real *Naturmenschen*" and remarked:

> It was another cardinal error in my previous work that I talked too much in proportion to what I saw. This one expedition ... has given me a better idea of Kiriwinian fishing than all the talk I heard about it before. It was also a more fascinating though not necessarily an easier method of working. But, it is *the* method. (Wayne 1995: 6–7)

In the opening pages of *Argonauts*, Malinowski made a claim for "this ethnographer's magic, by which he is able to evoke the real spirit of the natives, the true picture of tribal life" (1922: 6). Yet fieldwork was not simply a matter of immersion or participation. In the introductory chapter of *Argonauts*, Malinowski distinguished three distinct classes of ethnographic documentation. "*The organisation of the tribe, and the anatomy of its culture* must be recorded in firm, clear outline" (ibid: 24). Then, since people say one thing and do another, "the *imponderabilia of actual life, and the type of behaviour*" have to be filled in. They have to be collected through "minute, detailed observations, in the form of some sort of ethnographic diary, made possible by close contact with native life." Third, "A collection of ethnographic statements, characteristic narratives, typical utterances, items of folk-lore and magical formulae has to be given as ... documents of native mentality"(ibid.). But not all kinds of data are equally valuable. "The most conclusive and deepest insight," Malinowski wrote, "must always be obtained by a study of behaviour, by analysis of ethnographic custom and concrete cases of traditional rules" (ibid.: 177). All this was in the service of "the final goal, of which an Ethnographer should never lose sight. This goal is, briefly, to grasp the native's point of view, his relation to life, to realize *his* vision of *his* world" (ibid.: 25).

"Of the Very Exceptions"

How innovative was this kind of ethnographic research? Frederico Delgado Rosa and Han F. Vermeulen (2022) document several hundred ethnographic studies carried out by individual fieldworkers in the half century before 1922. But in the early twentieth century there was growing discontent with the *Notes and Queries* style of research, typically carried out on short expeditions, often by teams, operating with a one-size-fits-all toolkit, organizing findings into set categories. Shortly before Malinowski went to the Pacific proposals to reform field methods were published by two of the leaders of anthropology in Britain: by R. R. Marett in 1912 and W. H. Rivers in 1913.

Instead of survey studies, Rivers advocated "intensive work."

> A typical piece of intensive work is one in which the worker lives for a year or more among a community of perhaps four or five hundred people and studies every detail

of their life and culture; in which he comes to know every member of the community personally; in which he is not content with generalized information, but studies every feature of life and custom in concrete details and by means of the vernacular language ... It is only by such work that it is possible to discover the incomplete and even misleading character of much of the vast mass survey work which forms the existing material of anthropology. (Rivers 1913: 7)

Rivers and Marett agreed that this type of research would recast the way in which social life was understood. Rivers suggested that the ethnographer who undertook "intensive work" would soon come to recognize that "among peoples of rude culture, a useful art is at the same time a series of religious rites, an aesthetic occupation, and an important element in the social organization" (ibid.: 11).

Marett was more specific. He argued that intensive immersion in the life of a community would make the ethnographer conscious of individual variation and changing mores: "even where the regime of custom is most absolute, the individual constantly adapts himself to its injunctions, or rather adapts these to his own purposes, with more or less conscious and intelligent discrimination. The immobility of custom, I believe, is largely the effect of distance. Look more closely and you will see perpetual modification in process ... manifesting itself through individuals as they partly compete and partly cooperate one with the other" (quoted in Wallis 1957: 790).

This reads almost as if it were a vision of a book review of *Argonauts*, which was published ten years later. Indeed, Malinowski rephrased Marett's argument in the introduction to *Argonauts*. In "survey work," he remarked:

> we are given an excellent skeleton, so to speak, of the tribal constitution, but it lacks flash and blood. We learn much about the framework of their society, but within it, we cannot perceive or imagine the realities of human life ... In working out the rules and regularities of native custom ... from the collection of data and native statements, we find that this very precision is foreign to real life, which never adheres rigidly to any rules. It must be supplemented by the observation of the manner in which a given custom is carried out, of the behaviour of the natives in obeying the rules so exactly formulated by the ethnographer, of the very exceptions which in sociological phenomena almost always occur. (Malinowski 1922: 17)

"Swamped by Detail"

"The main principle of my work in the field: avoid artificial simplifications," Malinowski wrote in his diary toward the end of his stay in the Trobriand Islands. "To this end, collect as concrete materials as possible: note every informant; work with children, *outsiders, and specialists. Take side lights and opinions*" (Malinowski 1967: 290). But he was not a vulgar empiricist. Working in the Trobriands, he sometimes felt himself "almost swamped by detail" (Young 2004: 558). Experience had to be shaped; theory must come before description.

As an undergraduate in Kraków, studying physics and chemistry, Malinowski specialized in the philosophy of science. Revolutionary neopositivist programs for scientific research were being developed in the early twentieth century. He wrote his doctoral thesis on the ideas of Ernst Mach, an Austrian physicist and philosopher. Mach influenced Einstein. He became a central figure in the Vienna Circle of neopositivists. His reflections on individual perception made him a father figure to Gestalt theorists in psychology. Franz Boas, who also studied physics, drew on Mach for his doctoral thesis on the perceptions of individual experimenters in the physics of water.[2]

From Mach, Malinowski took a crucial lesson. Facts are constructs. Reviewing Frazer's *Totem and Taboo* in a Polish publication, he wrote: "The fewer hypothetical assumptions and postulates to be found in a given description of facts, the greater the value of this description, but because every precise description of facts requires precise concepts, and these can be provided only by theory, every description and classification must thus be based of necessity on a theoretical formulation" (Malinowski 1993: 127).

A Professional Émigré

If the postmodernist critique taught us anything about ethnographic studies, it is that the ethnographer's situation and personal background require interrogation. Lévi-Strauss described this immersion in the field as a technique for deracination. The ethnographer is a displaced person, a professional émigré—a role to which Malinowski was born. He once wrote that his family belonged "to the dispossessed, impoverished small Polish nobility, shading into the *inteligencja*" (Young 2004: 15). Kraków was the capital of a cosmopolitan province of the Austro-Hungarian Empire. Graduating from the Jagiellonian University, Malinowski was awarded the Imperial Prize for his doctoral thesis.[3] As his father had done, he proceeded to the University of Leipzig. But educated Poles were at best ambivalent in their attitudes to Vienna and to German culture. Their allegiance was to a vanishing Poland, and they imagined that its authentic spirit might still be captured in isolated villages. The intellectuals of Kraków spent long summer holidays in the mountain resort of Zakopane, where they admired and imitated local crafts; Malinowski's father collected folktales; some artists and writers married peasant women. As a sickly child, Malinowski was packed off to live with peasants in a reputedly healthy but remote Carpathian village.

> By the time I was eight I had lived in two fully distinct cultural worlds, speaking two languages, eating two different kinds of food, using two sets of table manners, observing two sets of reticencies and delicacies, enjoying two sets of amusements. I also learned two sets of religious views, beliefs and practices, and was exposed to two sets of morality and sexual mores. (Ibid: 16.)

Malinowski mixed in Young Poland circles in his student days in Kraków, but he did not become a Polish nationalist. In 1923 he turned down a chair in ethnology at the Jagiellonian University in order to take up a permanent position at the LSE, and in a letter to his future wife he confessed to a "highly developed Anglomania, an almost mystic cult of British culture and its exponents" (Wayne 1985: 532).

Malinowski was an outsider many times over in Australia and New Guinea. He went to Australia in 1914 to attend a grand imperial meeting of the British Association for the Advancement of Science. Trapped by the outbreak of war, he found himself an enemy alien. The Australian authorities allowed him to carry out his research as planned in their colonial territory of Papua, and even helped to finance his work, but although he talked of his "voluntary captivity" he was under continual surveillance. The colonial boss of Papua remarked that there was "something wrong about him." Local gossip reported that he was a spy, a seducer, and a pederast. His future father-in-law, a distinguished Australian professor, was set against what he called "mixed marriages" (see Young 2004: Chapters 15 and 16).

Malinowski never tried to go native. In London he liked to play the part of the Central European intellectual. In Melbourne, his closest friends were fellow exiles. In the Trobriand Islands, he spent more time with white traders than he acknowledged in his accounts of his fieldwork. He lodged for weeks at a time in the rowdy compound of the pearl trader Billy Hancock. Hancock's wife was the daughter of another trader, Mick George, and his Trobriand wife. Malinowski's closest friends were Raphael Brudo and his wife: French-speaking Levantine Jews, in whose house he would eat French food, listen to readings from Racine, Hugo, and Chateaubriand, and daydream over back numbers of *La vie parisienne*.

Malinowski took it for granted that the ethnographer is very like any immigrant—a young Polish intellectual, for example, making his way in London. In a letter to Frazer, written from the Trobriands in 1917, Malinowski remarked that a foreigner coming to England would need to understand the language, grasp the temperament, become familiar with current ideas, tastes, and fads, learn to enjoy native sports and amusements: in short, he had to make himself at home if he was "to penetrate into the depths of the

British mentality... The same refers, *mutatis mutandis*, to native society, as far as I can see" (Young 2004: 475).

A good case can be made that an ethnographer should maintain something of an outsider's point of view. Modern ethnography is the product of a movement backward and forward between the field and various explicit and implicit sources of comparison. Malinowski kept a diary intermittently for years, since first reading Nietzsche as a teenager. Now it became an instrument of research, as he monitored his physical and spiritual condition and urged himself to work harder. "Main thing to do," one note reads, "is to reflect on the two branches: my ethnological work & my diary.... They are well-nigh as complementary as complementary can be" (Young 2004: 416).

Detachment could shade into revulsion. Malinowski's diary and his letters to his fiancée were punctuated with outbursts of irritation, even rage, against the Trobrianders:

> I had a row with some of the niggs—they crowd round the tent: to ask them to get away is of no avail, to swear at them in fury or to hit them is dangerous, because they'll swear back or even hit back & as you have more to lose by loss of prestige than they have, you are the weaker in the contest. No, Elsie, I see no way out of this problem—it is either slavery for them or for us & out of the two, I prefer slavery for them. (Wayne 1995: 161)

Malinowski could be equally scathing about colonial officials, missionaries, colonists, and Australian professors. Nor did he spare himself. "I know my character is not very deep," he wrote to Elsie. "Small ambitions & vanities & a sense for intrigue & spite are more rampant there than the real, true feelings" (ibid.). His closest friend, the artist and writer Witkiewicz, accused him of cynicism—"a total lack of faith in any noble impulses whatsoever ... and the conviction that at bottom human motives are always petty and mean" (Young 2004: 305–6). Malinowski did not dissent. Nor did he doubt that the Trobrianders were much like everyone else. Self-reflection and observation fed off each other, yielding not only aversion and self-disgust but also new insights. "What is the deepest essence of my investigations? To discover what are [the native's] main passions, the motives of his conduct, his aims? ... His essential, deepest way of thinking. At this point we are confronted with our own problems: What is essential in ourselves?" (Malinowski 1967: 119).

"Everything is Explanatory of the Main Theme"

Finally, Malinowski came up with a new way of "writing up" ethnographic research. Marc Manganaro suggests that Malinowski was inspired by

Frazer himself to introduce pace and drama into ethnographic description. His stronger claim is that Malinowski combined two genres: ethnographic scene-setting and analysis are set off against, contextualized by, a narrative of the Kula voyages. *Argonauts* follows the route of a typical Kula expedition, beginning in the Trobriands and moving out around the ring of Kula islands. Each destination is described, its peculiar habits, customs, dangers evoked. Digressions explore the types of gift exchange, the techniques of boat building and sailing, the magical spells. As the complex panorama unfolds, the reader may come to see the Kula as it appears to a Trobriander. "Much of the power of the book," Manganaro (2002: 78) writes, "has to do with how the momentum of anthropological knowledge gathering on the one hand and of narrativized voyaging (both of the native and of the anthropologist) on the other so fittingly and complexly combine."

Malinowski's field diaries and letters reveal a fascination with the writings of Joseph Conrad and Émile Zola, two of the great realist novelists. He himself once remarked that he would be the Conrad of anthropology while Rivers would be the Rider Haggard, and his field diary sometimes invokes Conrad. (One entry quoted the words of a raging Kurtz in *Heart of Darkness*: "At moments I was furious at them, particularly because after I gave them their portions of tobacco they all went away. On the whole my feelings toward the natives are decidedly tending to *'Exterminate the brutes'*" (Malinowski 1967: 69).)[4]

It was Zola, however, who influenced the writing of *Argonauts* more directly. In 1917 Malinowski sent his future wife, Elsie Masson, a copy of Zola's *La terre*, which he had been reading in the field, suggesting that it was "somewhat akin in its tendency to my Kiriwinian efforts." In reply, Elsie reported that she had begun to read the novel, which immediately "interested me a hundred times more than the Balzac ... I see already what you mean about the Zola resembling your work. It has a tremendous central idea, and everything expresses this idea, and has a bearing on it ... nothing seems trivial ... everything is explanatory of the main theme. The reader is not just presented with a jumble of fact but a philosophy is constantly placed before him. It *is* just the same in your work" (Wayne 1995: 20). That is the best capsule account of Malinowski's expository style that I have come across.

"Transformed by These Influences"

While Malinowski promised an account of the realities of Trobriand life, the Government Officer, the Missionary, and the Trader appear as shadowy stereotypes in his academic texts. His diaries "permit a better view of the colonial context of his fieldwork than do any of his monographs," Malinowski's biographer, Michael Young (2004: 315), remarks. In a confessional appendix to his final Trobriand monograph, *Coral Gardens and Their Magic*, published in 1935, Malinowski wrote: "The empirical facts which the ethnographer has before him in the Trobriands nowadays are not natives unaffected by European influences but natives to a considerable extent transformed by these influences." His neglect of the colonial reality was, he admitted, "perhaps the most serious shortcoming of my whole anthropological research in Melanesia" (Malinowski 1935: 479–81). At the LSE in the 1930s, he promoted a new brand of anthropology, which he called "the anthropology of the changing native."

In retrospect, this neglect of the radical changes in Melanesia is the more surprising, since Rivers had highlighted the crisis in the way of life of the Pacific Islanders. In 1922, that magic year once more, T. S. Eliot, no less, noted:

> In a most interesting essay in the recent volume of *Essays on the Depopulation of Melanesia* the great psychologist W. H. R. Rivers adduces evidence which has led him to believe that the natives of that unfortunate archipelago are dying out principally for the reason that the "Civilization" forced upon them has deprived them of all interest in life. They are dying from pure boredom. (Eliot 1922: 659–63)

Colonial policy addressed social changes by trying to turn the clock back. Nineteen twenty-two was also the year in which the colonial grandee Lord Lugard set out the policy of "Indirect Rule" in *The Dual Mandate in British Tropical Africa*. This mandated government of "tribes" through the "chiefs." Malinowski scribbled a triumphant note to himself: "[Lord Lugard's] Indirect Rule is Complete Surrender to the Functional Point of View" (Cell 1989: 483). But the Trobriand monographs were written as though the society was traditional, its institutions set in aspic.

Conclusion

Argonauts launched a new way of doing anthropological research. Functionalist theories were well established in sociology and psychology at the time, but ethnological research was still dominantly historical, in search of a pristine primitive baseline. Changing the focus to the functioning of society, Malinowski shifted the emphasis of fieldwork to long-term participant observation. This was new, although his mentor Rivers had begun to preach the necessity for what he called intensive field studies. It was the combination of a functionalist theoretical perspective and a new design for field research that delivered a new paradigm for ethnographic studies.

The great flaw in this functionalist program was that it downplayed—even ignored—external influences, and was uncomfortable when dealing with social change. Malinowski's ethnographies nevertheless retain their power in large part because the cosmopolitan Malinowski regarded the Trobriander as being essentially rather like himself. The ethnographer in Papua and the immigrant in London are similarly situated, but then all societies have a great deal in common. When he started as an anthropologist, Malinowski once remarked, the emphasis had been on the differences between peoples. "I recognized their study as important, but underlying sameness I thought of greater importance & rather neglected. I still believe that the fundamental is more important than the freakish" (cited in Young 2004: 76).

Adam Kuper was most recently Centennial Professor of Anthropology at the London School of Economics and a visiting professor at Boston University. A Fellow of the British Academy and a recipient of the Huxley Medal of the Royal Anthropological Institute, Kuper has appeared many times on BBC TV and radio and has reviewed regularly for the *London Review of Books*, the *Times Literary Supplement*, and the *Wall Street Journal*. His new book, *The Museum of Other People: From Colonial Acquisition to Cosmopolitan Exhibition*, appeared in 2023.

Notes

1. Hann and James (this volume) point to the influence of empiricist Viennese philosophy.
2. For a fascinating account of what Boas and Malinowski took from their studies of physics, see Schaffer (1994).
3. For more on his early education see Hann and James (this volume); Kubica (this volume); Young (2004).
4. See also Thompson (1995: 53–75).

References

Cell, John W. 1989. "Lord Hailey and the Making of the African Survey." *African Affairs* 88: 481–505.
Eliot, T. S. 1922. "London Letter." *The Dial* (New York) 73(6): 659–63.
Gellner, Ernest. 1973. *Cause and Meaning in the Social Sciences*. London: Routledge & Kegan Paul.
Leach, Edmund. 1957. "The Epistemological Background to Malinowski's Empiricism." In *Man and Culture: An Evaluation of the Work of Bronislaw Malinowski*, ed. Raymond Firth, 119–38. London: Routledge & Kegan Paul.

Liebersohn, Harry. 2011. *The Return of the Gift: European History of a Global Idea.* Cambridge: Cambridge University Press.

Malinowski, Bronisław. 1921. "The Primitive Economics of the Trobriand Islanders." *The Economic Journal* 31(121): 1–16.

———. 1922. *Argonauts of the Western Pacific: An Account of Native Enterprise and Adventure in the Archipelagoes of Melanesian New Guinea.* London: Routledge & Kegan Paul.

———. 1923. "The Problem of Meaning in Primitive Language." In C. K. Ogden and I. A. Richards, *The Meaning of Meaning,* 451–510. London: Routledge.

———. 1926. *Crime and Custom in Savage Society.* London: Routledge & Kegan Paul.

———. 1935. *Coral Gardens and Their Magic.* Vol. 2. London: Routledge & Kegan Paul.

———. 1967. *A Diary in the Strict Sense of the Term.* London: Routledge & Kegan Paul.

———. 1993. *The Early Writings of Bronislaw Malinowski,* ed. Robert J. Thornton and Peter Skalník. Cambridge: Cambridge University Press.

Manganaro, Marc. 2002. *Culture, 1922: The Emergence of a Concept.* Princeton, NJ: Princeton University Press.

Radcliffe-Brown, A. R. 1929. "A Further Note on Ambryn." *Man* 29: 50–53.

Rivers, W. H. R. 1913. "Report on Anthropological Research Outside America." In W. H. Rivers, A. E. Jenks, and S. G. Morley, *The Present Condition and Future Needs of the Science of Anthropology.* 5–28 Washington, DC: Carnegie Institute of Washington.

Rosa, Frederico Delgado, and Han F. Vermeulen, eds. 2022. *Ethnographers before Malinowski: Pioneers of Anthropological Fieldwork, 1870–1922.* New York: Berghahn.

Schaffer, Simon. 1994. *From Physics to Anthropology and Back Again.* Cambridge: Prickly Pear Press.

Thompson, Christina A. 1995. "Anthropology's Conrad: Malinowski in the Tropics and What He Read." *Journal of Pacific History* 30: 53–75.

Wallis, Wilson D. 1957. "Anthropology in England Early in the Present Century." *American Anthropologist* 59: 781–90.

Wayne, Helena. 1985. "Bronislaw Malinowski: The Influence of Various Women on His Life and Works." *American Ethnologist* 12(3): 529–40.

———, ed. 1995. *The Story of a Marriage: The Letters of Bronislaw Malinowski and Elsie Masson.* Vol. 1. London: Routledge.

Wundt, Wilhelm. 1917 [1904]. *Elements of Folk Psychology: Outlines of a Psychological History of the Development of Mankind.* London: Allen and Unwin.

Young, Michael W. 2004. *Malinowski: Odyssey of an Anthropologist, 1884–1920.* New Haven, CT: Yale University Press.

4

Malinowski and the Politics of Economic Anthropology

Between Imperial Trusteeship and Colonial Trade

FREDDY FOKS

Most interpreters of *Argonauts* look to the very biggest structures with which Malinowski's text was engaged: colonialism, the politics of method, the history of the self, and so on. It is much less common to interpret *Argonauts* as an intervention in a political context that Malinowski thought he was engaged in. This chapter situates Malinowski's economic anthropology alongside his contemporary comments on colonialism and economic development. The chapter begins by examining the evidence given by Malinowski at an inquiry on Pacific trade held in 1916 and then argues that these remarks relate to his writings on economic anthropology. Read in this context, Kula exchange represents a mirror image of the extractive economic regime that Malinowski witnessed in the Western Pacific. After making this argument, the chapter then discusses Malinowski's later economic anthropology, his teaching methods, his criticisms of Lionel Robbins, and his fieldwork in Oaxaca, Mexico. The chapter concludes with some broader reflections on the relationship between histories of anthropology and histories of economics.

Argonauts and Colonial Trade

After his first period of intensive fieldwork in the Trobriand Islands in 1916, Malinowski traveled to Sydney and then on to Melbourne, where he gave evidence at a government inquiry on trade in the Pacific (Young 2004: 418; Stocking 1992: 253–55). This inquiry took place two years after Australian troops had pushed the German Empire out of New Guinea.

Commonwealth forces had been ruling the former German colony ever since (Storr 2018).

The Australians found themselves governing a system of plantation labor in the region, mostly supplying copra (dried coconut used for oil and animal feed) for the world market.[1] The inquiry at Melbourne was tasked with finding out about labor, transport, and commodities and with gathering and publishing statistics about German and British trade. Malinowski's evidence at this inquiry offers some sense of his views about the politics of imperialism in the Pacific.

Malinowski expressed his concern that the plantation system in the Western Pacific was significantly disrupting community life. The absence of men for long periods was leading to demographic problems. The birth rate was falling and, on workers' return from the plantations, venereal diseases and alcohol were being brought into their villages. On the subject of what he called the "development of the country," he questioned whether increasing exports was in the islanders' self-interest (Australia Interstate Commission 1918, vol. 2: 107–8).[2] These comments need to be seen in the context of local labor practices (Smith, this volume). For decades, European settlers in the Pacific clashed with islanders, colonial authorities, European humanitarians, and missionaries. Legal proceedings raged as a result and dwelt on the fraught questions of forced labor and economic development (Gregory 1979). Hubert Murray, the Lieutenant-Governor of Papua, fought a campaign against planters and settlers who wished to indenture islanders. In general, the planters wanted islanders to work on long contracts and they wished to keep the costs of labor down as far as possible. Murray sought to balance the interests of planters and Papuans and to hold employers to a minimum legal standard for contracts, payments, and standards at work (Lewis 1997: esp. Chapters 10 and 11).

These disputes continued during Malinowski's fieldwork. A few years before his arrival in the Trobriand Islands, the Assistant Resident Magistrate R. L. Bellamy made a coercive plan for peasant production within and between village communities. Bellamy explained his policy at the same Melbourne inquiry that Malinowski attended. He explained that he compelled Trobriand Islanders to plant coconuts along tracks between villages and punished islanders who did not comply (Australia Interstate Commission 1918, vol. 1: 61). The authors of the inquiry suggested that this might be a policy worth emulating elsewhere, "since," they wrote, compelled planting may prove to be "a valuable aid in correcting the prevailing indolence and deterioration of the natives" (ibid.). Malinowski seems to have agreed with Bellamy's policy, up to a point. He told the Melbourne inquiry that administrators should be able to compel islanders to plant coconuts in their villages. These crops might spur unambiguously "economic" activity: responding to market stimuli by increasing production in order to obtain cash income. Equally, they might not, since Malinowski explained that most of the islanders he had met had "plenty of work on hand" already. "I think that the native Papuan is not very keen on working for the white man," he explained, before adding, "it is quite evident he does his own work, and if he is left to his own conditions he has plenty of work on hand, work which is not exactly of a purely economical description, but which for him makes life worth living" (Australia Interstate Commission 1918, vol 2: 107–8). This was at odds with the inquiry's idea that islanders were "indolent." What looked like laziness to European planters could also be interpreted as an unwillingness to work for an employer rather than for oneself (see Smith, this volume). The implication was that a more sustained development program would have to rely on ever more coercion to plant more cash crops or the migration of men for long periods of time to plantations far from home, with deleterious consequences for them and their communities. Malinowski did not agree with either of these options, so he proposed his studied support for the status quo.

Malinowski's testimony at the Melbourne inquiry reveals skepticism about the compatibility of economic development with relative political freedom under conditions of imperial overrule. He criticized the businesses encouraging labor migration and he ended his deposition by comparing the policy of the German Empire's Pacific plantations with the Nama and Herero genocides in South West Africa. There, German colonial authorities had, Malinowski said, "transplanted numerous tribes from one place to another, and decimated them." The Germans, he stated, "did not discuss at all whether that was a fair way to treat the natives." In light of these dangers, he proposed some measure of administrative amelioration, bleakly concluding: "once the natives come into contact with white civilization it is always better to take some measures to prevent their dying out" (Australia Interstate Commission 1918, vol. 2: 107–8).

What can this testimony about coconuts, coercion, and violence tell us about the relationship between *Argonauts* and colonialism? George Stocking thought the "ambivalence" of Malinowski's testimony in 1916 rendered it mostly useless to historians (Stocking 1992: 255). I want to make the opposite case: it was precisely Malinowski's ambivalence about economic development that makes his comments in Melbourne so valuable for our understanding of *Argonauts*. Malinowski's Melbourne testimony is significant because of its timing relative to the research that led Malinowski to discover the Kula. Malinowski gave his testimony in between his two main periods of fieldwork in the Trobriand Islands. When he returned to the field after Melbourne, he must surely have had in mind the interest he explained at the inquiry in work "which is not exactly of a purely economical description." It is at least plausible that his public pronouncements in Melbourne about plantations reflected his views as he began to piece together the functioning of the Kula ring. Of course, he had developed an interest in economics before his move to London and embrace of anthropology. But this interest in economics was now brought into renewed focus when he was called on to report on plantations and economic development. Subsequently arriving back on Kiriwina, he was more competent in the local language and he had processed many of his earlier observations. He was ready to formulate his findings about the Kula: the ultimate non-"economical" economic system.

The Kula represents the mirror image of the colonial labor complex Malinowski had criticized in Melbourne in 1916. The Kula is maintained by "uneconomical" work rather than by cash wages. It is controlled and directed by islanders themselves rather than by European planters. Whereas Kula has great value for islanders, work in the plantation system (although considered "economical" by European planters) had little or no value for islanders, even if islander labor had huge value for the Europeans who employed it. The Kula represents a world of exchange and labor totally inimical to Europeans and their sense of value.

Malinowski's argument about the resilience and significance of the Kula is simultaneously an argument for its protection. Malinowski suggests as much in his long commentary on Chief Tu'uluwa's diminished prestige as a result of "the interference of Government officials and the influence of Mission work ... [which means that] There are reasons to fear, and even natives express their misgivings, that in a generation or two the Kula will become entirely disorganised" (Malinowski 1922: 464, 465). The implication is that it would be singularly unjust to disrupt the Kula and substitute waged work for the extensive "uneconomical" labor that Trobriand Islanders carried out in the course of maintaining and reproducing their culture. This is typical of functionalist arguments more generally, which most often implicitly argue for the protection of the institution being analyzed (Pettit 1996). He even made an explicit commentary on colonial policy when he wrote:

> A wise administration of natives would, on the one hand, try to govern *through* the chief, using his authority along the lines of old law, usage, and custom; on the other hand it would try to maintain all which really makes life worth living for the natives, for it is the most precious inheritance, which they have from the past ages, and it is no good to try to substitute other interests for those lost. (Malinowski 1922: 466)

Politics and Economic Anthropology

When we contextualize Malinowski's view about the Kula in light of the politics of trade and labor he discussed in Melbourne, *Argonauts* can profitably be read as an implicit argument against both extensive labor migration to plantations and authoritarian development (beyond Bellamy's existing plans of minimal cash cropping for export). *Argonauts* is not an explicitly political text, but it has a politics. Malinowski linked anthropological ideas to his politics throughout his career, from his earliest writings to the essays and lectures that appeared in print only after his death (Gellner 1987; Mucha 1988). In light of the contrast he drew between the German Empire's treatment of the Nama and Herero and his desire for protectionism, it seems clear that two political poles characterize his writings: an investment in a politics of protectionism that contemporaries called "trusteeship," and a rhetorical contrasting of this policy to what would later be termed genocide. Trusteeship and genocide were the two options facing colonized peoples, Malinowski implied, and colonial administrators had to choose between them.

This context left little room for the possibility that colonized peoples might accomplish full political, economic, and military self-determination.[3] War-making was a "custom" that should not be allowed by colonial administration (see Steinmüller, this volume). The colonial administration should retain a monopoly on legitimate force within a given territory. This, of course, is why he and his disciples have been so roundly criticized by postcolonial theorists and politicians who sought to escape colonial dependence through nationalist self-strengthening or via federations of self-governing states.[4]

Malinowski's political views mark him out as an ameliorist liberal: a kind of anti-colonial imperialist. It was commonplace for reformist liberals, Fabians, and assorted "humanitarians" in Britain during the 1920s and 1930s to be pro-empire and anti-colonial in just this way (Saville 1988). Many metropolitan liberals were united in opposition to the "elimination" (Wolfe 2006) of colonized peoples through the invasion and settlement by Europeans of Indigenous lands. But opposing "elimination" did not necessarily entail anti-imperial politics. On the contrary, the protection of colonized peoples could be imagined as a core mission of the British Empire itself: to steward colonized peoples toward self-government under imperial overrule (Hyam 1999; Mantena 2010; Roberts 1986). Susan Pedersen (2005: 120) has helpfully called this ideology "autocratic paternalism" and associated it with the interwar politics of the League of Nations (see also Foks 2018, 2023: Chapter 2).

Malinowski was an ardent supporter of the League of Nations, which sought to govern former German and Ottoman territories in a manner that would secure, as Article 22 of the League Covenant stated, the "well-being and development" of their populations under foreign rule as a "sacred trust" (Pedersen 2015).[5] When Lord Lugard, Britain's permanent representative on the League's Mandates Commission, lobbied for a policy of "indirect rule" in the European empires, Malinowski commented approvingly that "Indirect Rule is a Complete Surrender to the Functional Point of View" (Stocking 1992: 261). This does not mean that Lugard agreed with Malinowski's functionalist anthropology, of course, or that anthropologists wholeheartedly supported indirect rule or had much influence over policymaking (Foks 2018, 2023: Chapter 2).

Nevertheless, Malinowski made public interventions in support of indirect rule throughout his career. Perhaps the clearest statement of this argument can be read in an article published in 1930 in the BBC's magazine *The Listener*. Malinowski argued that rule "for the benefit of the natives" was not compatible with what he called "the 'get rich quick' principle ruthlessly followed by settlers or exploiters." Rather than going "full steam ahead . . . native interests should be regarded as supreme" (Malinowski 1930: 1). This meant that development must be "slow, gradual, and constantly subordinated to the question of whether it does not deplete and permanently cripple the native supply of labor." Too much emphasis on "development," he thought, would disturb the labor supply and lead to gluts of "over-production" (ibid.: 2). The kind of labor regime necessary to support "full steam ahead" development would, in effect, create what he called a "new kind of slavery" (ibid.: 5). There are clear echoes here of Malinowski's testimony in Melbourne fourteen years earlier.

Malinowski's argument in 1930 is also consistent with his critique of utilitarian economics in *Argonauts*. Throughout the 1920s and 1930s Malinowski argued that the happiness of colonized peoples would not necessarily be increased by driving them into waged labor. Since there was no market-based price-setting in the Trobriands, administrators could not read off the preferences of time-constrained individuals from the price of wages in the labor market. This was because there was a difference, he explained in his 1921 contribution to the *The Economic Journal*, between a "national economy" characterized by the circulation of goods through the use of money and a "Tribal Economy" functioning according to a logic of "reciprocal obligations and dues, one constant flow of gift and counter-gift" (Malinowski 1921: 8), in which "production, exchange and consumption are socially organised and regulated by custom" (ibid.: 15). Kinship ties, customary usages, and magical rites interacted to generate values in the Trobriand Islands. A lack of an extensive market system with cash exchange did not make the islanders *uneconomically* minded. What Malinowski was interested in was a kind of economic analysis of a non-money economy.

If employers drew labor away from village communities to boost profits in plantations this would degrade the functioning of the "Tribal Economy." The implication was that islanders' movement between the Tribal Economy and the plantation system would mean moving between two worlds structured by different, and opposing, values. To ignore the different system of values between the Tribal Economy, on the one hand, and national economy, on the other, would risk more than merely an academic misunderstanding. Malinowski did not discuss these issues explicitly in *The Economic Journal*, but he did make such an argument five years earlier in Melbourne and nine years later in *The Listener*. Read in the context of his contemporary political statements about forced labor and migration, Malinowski's economic arguments implicitly supported a politics of "trusteeship." His economic anthropology was thus entirely consistent with his more explicitly political writings.

Hubert Murray, Lieutenant-Governor of Papua (under whose authority Malinowski had done his fieldwork), seems to have understood the thrust of this logic, too. He wrote in 1931 that "[t]he principals of the functional school [he seems to mean Radcliffe-Brown and his students at Sydney here, but presumably also Malinowski] if pressed to their logical conclusion must end in a refusal to admit 'that the white race can under any circumstances govern the black or the brown'" (quoted in Bashkow 1995: 11–12). Malinowski did not go as far as that, but some of his students did, including Jomo Kenyatta (Matera 2015: Chapter 6).

Prices, Markets, and the Politics of Method

Teaching posed fresh problems for Malinowski's economic anthropology, especially as so many of his students worked in such different areas of the world. During the 1930s his students' research was focused mainly on Eastern, Central, and Western Africa. Their research called into question the clarity of the conceptual and empirical division Malinowski drew in the 1920s between "tribal" and "national" economies, given that his students were often studying societies undergoing rapid social change.

One such student was Lucy Mair, who wrote to Malinowski from Ngogwe, southern Uganda, in 1932 that "there is no opportunity of testing either my favorite theories or yours." She put this down to the ubiquity of cash money. "They can't remember enough about the cowry-shells for one to get anything of value," she explained. Money is taken "so much for granted now that it is far too late to analyze what specific results it produced."[6] Clearly, Malinowski's neat distinction between two separate spheres of value and exchange—one "tribal" and based on gifts and one "national" and intermediated by money—did not pertain in 1930s Uganda.

Another problem that Malinowski faced was how to turn his functionalist methodology into a teachable practice. In *Argonauts* he had written of the necessity of studying social phenomena in their "concrete manifestations" and that "the results ought to be tabulated into some sort of synoptic chart" (Malinowski 1922: 17). *Argonauts* did not contain such a chart. But his professional papers deposited at the London School of Economics reveal that he had devised one for teaching his students by the early 1930s (for a more extensive discussion of the charts see Foks 2020: 724–27). "Economics" was one of eight topics listed under a column heading that split culture into other "Functional Aspects": "education," "political constitution," "law and order," "art," "knowledge," and "recreation." Economics was split into further subheadings: "resources," "ownership," "production," "exchange," "consumption." This reveals something important about Malinowski's view of economics. The study of resources, ownership, production, exchange, and consumption could be analytically separated from other aspects of a society, but, in the last instance, they would have to be understood alongside other functional aspects of culture. Economic activities were "embedded" in the wider social structure. *Argonauts* made this clear in prose. Malinowski's pedagogical chart represented this insight in an operationalizable and heuristic methodological prompt: "economics" was literally embedded in the chart he handed his students alongside other functional aspects of culture.

To get a grip on the distinctiveness of this kind of economic analysis it is instructive to compare Malinowski's functionalist ideas with those of his contemporary at the LSE, Lionel Robbins, author of the celebrated *Essay on the Nature and Significance of Economic Science* (Robbins 1932). Because "we have been turned out of paradise," Robbins argued, and humans have "neither eternal life nor unlimited means of gratification," economists must study how people allocate their finite time and finite means. Economics is thus, he famously argued, "the science which studies human behavior as a relationship between ends and scarce means which have alternative uses" (ibid.: 15). Economics is therefore a science of value that studies the "relinquishment of other desired alternatives" (ibid.: 16). The way that economists generally worked out what people desired and what they thought worth relinquishing was to study the price that people pay to buy and sell goods and services.

Economics is thus best fitted to study societies where prices are set more or less freely. Economists might also study other forms of society, where, for example, "the organization of production must depend on the valuation of the final organizer," Robbins (1932: 18) wrote, or where "a patriarchal estate unconnected with a money economy" is structured "depend[ing] on the valuations of a patriarch." The values set in societies like these would flow from some "final organizer" (Robbins is probably thinking of planning in the USSR) or a patriarch of a household. Economics, in those cases, would involve a study of these coercive decision-makers, not the collective decision-making of market actors revealing their preferences via the price mechanism.

Malinowski and his students posed a number of problems in response to Robbins. In lecture notes dated October 1932, the year Robbins's *Essay* was published, Malinowski wrote that "problems of production, exchange value etc. are not an autonomous body of customs and institutions in every community." His next remarks are hard to understand—the notes are sketchy and paraphrased—but he mentions Robbins by name, writing, "we are not arbitrary in this division [between economic and non-economic institutions], but there is no dictatorial step afterwards. If we are arbitrary in this, we are in good company from Adam Smith to Professor Robbins." He went on:

> Gradual growth of economic interests corresponds definitely to the fact that the more we advance in so-called civilization, the more certain institutions crystallize out. In our modern world economic institutions are pretty definite, e.g. we recognize a bank as such. . . . What really matters is that we should recognize in our tribe a certain department of activities which are grouped or organized on a special principle, that this is the interest in material possessions, in value, in consumption, in display and uses of goods. . . . once we recognize that there is this field, our further steps are no longer arbitrary.[7]

In modern capitalist societies it is usually obvious where "economic" activity takes place (Malinowski gave the example of a bank). However, one could not so easily point to the place where economic activity is carried on in a "tribal economy," because economic functions have not, as he put it, "crystallized" out through the division of labor. Economic activities are thus mixed together through many other institutions with other functions. Thus, whereas Robbins could study economic institutions—banks, finance ministries, firms, and so on—this was much more difficult for an anthropologist working in a society with less division of labor and less functional "crystallization" of separate institutions. Anthropologists should not make the "arbitrary" division between economic and non-economic institutions without first doing empirical study.

Another problem Malinowski must have had with Robbins was the latter's description of alternatives to free market economies. Recall that Robbins's only counterexamples were a totally planned society or a patriarchal household economy. The Kula was neither: it was a relatively non-authoritarian, non-money economy. As Raymond Firth, Malinowski's first PhD student, explained in direct response to Robbins's own terms quoted above: "there is *no final organizer* in primitive societies in the sense of a single individual or ruling group of individuals who are in a position to dictate all choices" (Firth 1939: 23, emphasis added). Behavior in the Trobriand Islands and in many other societies studied by anthropologists "tends ... to follow the conception of reward for the social advantages conferred by participation in production, instead of a quantitative return for the material advantage obtained" (Firth 1938: 81). Value, in short, is determined by a broader scale than pecuniary advantage or by the price one would pay in a market for a good or receive as a wage.

Almost all of Malinowski's students worked in societies marked by various degrees of non-market production and exchange. Thus, prices could not provide the kind of information that anthropologists needed to infer about how people chose to use their time and allocate their scarce means. Without a price mechanism intermediated by a stable unit of exchange (money), anthropologists would have to explain economic behaviors by recourse to other functional aspects of culture. To cope with this issue, anthropologists would have to develop "among other things, a set of 'substantial' as well as 'formal' economic categories" of analysis when explaining production, exchange, ownership, and consumption (Firth 1939: 27). Because anthropologists could very rarely rely on governments, financial newspapers, and statisticians to produce price data for them, they were thrown back on empiricism: only observation of behavior directly would allow them to infer reasoning about means and ends.

Not only that, but production, exchange, and consumption were often differentiated between settler and colonized in regions where anthropologists worked. Firth gave the following example to illustrate the point: why could a "native" buy only three sticks of tobacco for a shilling whereas a European could buy five sticks? Clearly the price of tobacco depended on the status of the purchaser, and he explained that this status was evidence of "one of the inscrutable privileges which accompany white domination." "On the whole," Firth (1937: 55) concluded, "these different rates are operative and seem to require more than pure economic theory for explanation." Firth thought that economists would have to learn to collaborate with other social scientists to find out why inequalities and differential prices were generated. Like Malinowski, his interest in explaining economic behavior had a political slant, signaled by the tangible sense of injustice he felt at the immiserating effects of "white domination" and the unequal exchanges that deepened poverty and inequality.

Malinowski's final fieldwork in Mexico carried through a line of political and methodological critique that is recognizably continuous with his earlier economic anthropology. He traveled to Mexico in 1940 while based at Yale University (Cook 2017a). During this time, he carried out research on market trading in Oaxaca that was linked to a political program of reform and economic development. "[R]aising the standard of living of Indians and peasants, townsmen and artisans," he wrote, "ought to be in the mind of the anthropologist as the lodestar of his investigation" (Cook and Young 2016: 673). He gave a critical talk in Mexico City on the treatment of the Indigenous people of the country.

During this research Malinowski maintained an interest in economics via intensive fieldwork and by reconstructing the values expressed in production, exchange, and consumption (Cook 2017a, 2017b). His surviving notebooks reveal a great many observations about life in the valleys of Oaxaca. Weights and measures were a topic of particular concern, reflecting, once again, Oaxacans' refusal to take stated "prices" at face value. Market traders used shorthand terms for quantities of raw materials sold at market associated with the size of a trader's basket. But Malinowski found that there were further distinctions based on quality that could only be understood by empirical investigation (Cook 2017b: 8). This was research based on direct observation and note-taking: very much the same as his fieldwork two decades earlier in the Trobriand Islands.

Malinowski did not do any statistical sampling in Oaxaca, nor did he conduct systematic household surveys. Perhaps his research might have moved in these directions if he had not died in 1942, shortly after beginning this new project. After all, by the late 1930s he had moved beyond the sharp division he had made in 1921 between "tribal" and "national" economies and he had begun to take an interest in the transition from a non-money to a cash-based society, anticipating later research in economic anthropology (Cook and Young 2016: 666).

There is evidence that he thought neoclassical economics might be useful to study transitional cases like Oaxacan markets (Cook and Young 2016: 667–68). But he did not wish to preempt the issue. Ethnographers must observe economic life in their embedded contexts before applying economic analysis. In this sense Malinowski's work perhaps transcended later debates among economic anthropologists, between so-called "formalists" who sought to apply economic analysis to ethnographic materials and so-called "substantivists" who denied the applicability of economic models to much anthropological research (Cook and Young 2016; Plattner 1989).

Malinowski did not seem opposed to the possibility that economic methods could be used to isolate and analyze motivations, values, and behavior. He was not interested in critique of the discipline of economics for its own sake. His approach to different social science methodologies was much more pragmatic than that and he seems to have pushed some of his students to combine economics and anthropology (Cook and Young 2016: 668). But he did reserve his judgment and thought that anthropologists should seek to observe which institutions and practices created values first before presuming that prices and market exchange could be used to infer actors' choices. In his own work and in his pedagogy he urged others to avoid the "dictatorial step" of presuming that it was obvious which institutions were properly "economic" and which methods were best fitted to understand them.

Conclusion

Argonauts is a landmark in at least two ways. First, it stands as a monumental achievement of observation and description. Second, *Argonauts* made a substantial theoretical advance in anthropologists' understanding of non-money economics. Both of these aspects of *Argonauts* have contributed to its lasting impact. Malinowski's account of how exchange is given value by its embeddedness in other institutions influenced many later analyses of welfare and markets, prominently in the work of Karl Polanyi and E. P. Thompson (Foks 2023: Chapter 7).

This chapter has shown that Malinowski's attentiveness to the embeddedness of economic life spanned his career. He was invested in the empirical study of value and motivation in order to explain the lives of peoples living in very different cultures. He thought that this research was important because it might guide government administration of colonized populations. Trusteeship was liable to go awry, Malinowski thought, if presumptions formed in capitalist societies were employed in so-called "primitive" societies without first observing how people in colonial situations formed their own values.

Malinowski came to share a concern with later development economists that anthropologists should direct themselves at "raising the standard of living of Indians and peasants, townsmen and artisans" (Cook and Young 2016: 673). He died in 1942, just before economists began turning their attention to the question of how to raise standards of living in the areas where anthropologists traditionally did their fieldwork. It is intriguing to ponder what he would have made of models about economic "takeoff." As it turned out, many of those who drew on Malinowski's ideas, like Karl Polanyi and E. P. Thompson, set their faces against the idea that economic growth could be read as a proxy for raised standards of living (Foks 2023: Chapter 7). More sensitive critics, like Raymond Firth and the economist Phyllis Deane, took a more pragmatic approach and investigated development as an empirical problem in need of careful study (ibid.; Deane 1962; Messac 2018; Morgan 2011). Anthropologists are, after all, especially attuned to the way that autonomy and ethics are impinged on by larger structures of power and inequality (Bear et al. 2015). A flight from "the economy" (de L'Estoile, this volume) may well open up a space for engagement between anthropologists and other critical social scientists who dwell on the importance of governing the household (Owens 2015).

It strikes me (as a participant observer in academic events with anthropologists) that a generosity of thinking across disciplinary boundaries is one part of Malinowski's legacy that remains relevant a century after *Argonauts*. Another part is the comparative exploration of standards of living, in all their interpretive subtlety and ethnographic complexity. Economists, in this regard, may not be so alien from anthropologists. At least some economists do think about the goods necessary for living a good life (e.g., Sen 1979, 1987 on "capabilities" and "functionings").

After a century of critique, will the steam ever run out of anthropologists' attacks on economics (to riff on Latour 2004)? Has anything come of all the challenges they have leveled? What would a post-critique economic anthropology look like? Having a capacious sense of the welfare of humans living at the margins seems like a worthwhile pursuit. Insisting on the importance of empirical study rather than solely deductive model-making also seems sensible. Asking the people who are the subject of development programs what they value and what makes their lives worth living is a worthy endeavor. In these terms, Malinowski remains a pioneer.

But there are likely to be many frustrations for anthropologists moving along this line of inquiry. At the most banal level, letting go of the critique of economics may leave anthropologists bereft of one of the key organizing principles of their tribe and one of the main sources of charisma for their leading ritual practitioners. In addition, many anthropologists would feel queasy at Malinowski's desire to improve the administration of government. Another sort of nausea might strike anthropologists if they were ever to find out that academic economists do not actually wield the power that anthropologists think they do.

Of course, modern governance is built out of the "crystallization of institutions" (as Malinowski put it) that prioritize the numerate, quantitative, and abstracted kinds of knowledge that economists study and anthropologists so often find frustratingly unempirical, simplifying, and more-or-less stupid. This is more than merely about empirics, it is also about power. As Talal Asad writes: "statistics is much more than a matter of representation; it is a tool of political intervention. And as a political tool it is infinitely more powerful than ethnographic representation—for good or for ill" (Asad 2002: 82).

So much of the anthropological critique of economics seems grounded in the idea that economists are the main makers of statistics, their main interpreters, and the main deciders of what to do with them. Of course, this is wrong. Spies, accountants, armies, finance ministries, oil companies, defense contractors, bankers, advertising agencies, and telecoms firms all produce statistics in far greater volumes with far greater reach and importance. These actors have far more social power than economics professors, even economics professors seconded into government administrations.

Anthropologists today approach economists from a relatively subaltern position within the academy. But when we zoom out to scan the wider topology of social power (Mann 2012), both anthropologists and economists are huddled close together relative to the far distant peaks of the power elite who make the decisions that affect the lives of millions. Perhaps anthropologists have something valuable to offer humanity from this relatively humble and yet relatively elevated position. Perhaps they can share with other social scientists the labor of imagining a better world together with their interlocutors in a more-or-less equal exchange. That would carry forward the spirit of *Argonauts* into a new age.

Acknowledgments

My thanks to Richard Staley who provided helpful comments on a draft of this chapter.

Freddy Foks is a Simon Research Fellow at the University of Manchester. His first book *Participant Observers: Anthropology, Colonial Development and the Reinvention of Society in Britain* (2023) is about the history of social anthropology in the twentieth century.

Notes

1. I have found Kris Manjapra's (2018) work a very helpful overview of the global dynamics of this labor regime.
2. All quotations in the following paragraphs are from Australia Interstate Commission (1918). Further comments by Malinowski can be found in the Appendix, i.e., vol. 2. pp. 107–8, paginated in the online page scans as #279–80. Parts of this evidence are also used in the main body of the report, i.e., vol. 1: p. 61/#67 and p. 102/#108.
3. Although Malinowski seems to have changed his mind somewhat in the 1930s, when he appears to have supported some kind of cultural nationalism in sub-Saha-

ran Africa. He wrote in an undated (likely mid–late-1930s manuscript), about "culture contact": "The goal or end result. African nationalism, not exactly on Europe's pattern but same type." "Dynamics of Contemporary Diffusion," B. Malinowski pamphlet, n.d., corrected in pencil, Malinowski Papers, LSE Library, Box 11, Folder 5. For more on Malinowski's engagement with African nationalism see Berman and Lonsdale (2010); Mucha (1988).
4. *Pace* Raymond Firth, who "shook his head in a mixture of pretended and real confusion," according to James Clifford, in 1970, before going on: "'Not so long ago we were radicals. We thought of ourselves as gadflies and reformers, advocates for the value of indigenous cultures, defenders of our people. Now, all of a sudden, we're handmaidens of empire!'" (Firth quoted in Clifford 2012: 419). Firth and his colleagues were not exactly radicals, more center-left reformers. The "radicals" in the 1920s would surely be the Bolsheviks associated with the Third International who supported anti-imperial national liberation movements (Riddell 2019).
5. German New Guinea became a "C" Mandate. The League's Article 22 famously stated:
"To those colonies and territories which as a consequence of the late war have ceased to be under the sovereignty of the States which formerly governed them and which are inhabited by peoples not yet able to stand by themselves under the strenuous conditions of the modern world, there should be applied the principle that the well-being and development of such peoples form a sacred trust of civilisation and that securities for the performance of this trust should be embodied in this Covenant. The best method of giving practical effect to this principle is that the tutelage of such peoples should be entrusted to advanced nations who by reason of their resources, their experience or their geographical position can best undertake this responsibility, and who are willing to accept it, and that this tutelage should be exercised by them as Mandatories on behalf of the League" (Covenant of the League of Nations n.d.). The best study of the way that the League influenced British imperialism is Pedersen (2018).
6. Lucy Mair to Bronisław Malinowski, 24 February 1932, Malinowski Papers, LSE Library, Box 7, Folder 16.
7. "Seminar on Primitive Economics 6 x 1932," Malinowski Papers, LSE Library, Box 6, Folder 9.

References

Asad, Talal. 2002. "Ethnographic Representation, Statistics, and Modern Power." In *From the Margins: Historical Anthropology and Its Futures*, ed. Brian Keith Axel, 66–91. Durham, NC: Duke University Press.

Australia Interstate Commission. 1918. *British and Australian Trade in the South Pacific*. Report, Parliament of the Commonwealth of Australia. Retrieved 30 October 2023 from http://hdl.handle.net/2027/uc1.c2755247.

Bashkow, Ira. 1995. "'The Stakes for Which We Play Are Too High to Allow of Experiments': Colonial Administrators of Papua on Their Anthropological Training by Radcliffe-Brown." *History of Anthropology Newsletter* 22(2): 3–14.

Bear, Laura, Karen Ho, Anna Lowenhaupt Tsing, and Sylvia Yanagisako. 2015. "Gens: A Feminist Manifesto for the Study of Capitalism." *Society for Cultural Anthropology*, 30 March. Retrieved 31 October 2023 from https://culanth.org/fieldsights/gens-a-feminist-manifesto-for-the-study-of-capitalism.

Berman, Bruce, and John Lonsdale. 2010. "Custom, Modernity, and the Search for Kihooto: Kenyatta, Malinowski, and the Making of *Facing Mount Kenya*." In *Ordering Africa: Anthropology, European Imperialism and the Politics of Knowledge*, ed. Helen Tilley and Robert Gordon, 173–98. Manchester: Manchester University Press.

Clifford, James. 2012. "Feeling Historical." *Cultural Anthropology* 27(3): 417–26.

Cook, Scott. 2017a. "Malinowski in Oaxaca: Implications of an Unfinished Project in Economic Anthropology; Part I." *Critique of Anthropology* 37(2): 132–59.

———. 2017b. "Malinowski in Oaxaca: Implications of an Unfinished Project in Economic Anthropology; Part II." *Critique of Anthropology* 37(3): 228–43.

Cook, Scott, and Michael W. Young. 2016. "Malinowski, Herskovits, and the Controversy over Economics in Anthropology." *History of Political Economy* 48(4): 657–79.

"The Covenant of the League of Nations." n.d. Yale Law School, Lillian Goldman Law Library. Retrieved 30 October 2023 from https://avalon.law.yale.edu/20th_century/leagcov.asp.

Deane, Phyllis. 1962. "The Industrial Revolution in British Central Africa." *Civilisations* 12(3): 331–55.

Firth, Raymond. 1937. "Anthropology Looks at Economics." *Science and Society: A Journal of Human Progress* 1(2): 48–55.

———. 1938. *Human Types*. London: Thomas Nelson.

———. 1939. *Primitive Polynesian Economy*. London: Routledge.

Foks, Freddy. 2018. "Bronislaw Malinowski, 'Indirect Rule,' and the Colonial Politics of Functionalist Anthropology, ca. 1925–1940." *Comparative Studies in Society and History* 60(1): 35–57.

———. 2020. "Constructing the Field in Interwar Social Anthropology: Power, Personae, and Paper Technology." *Isis* 111(4): 717–39.

———. 2023. *Participant Observers, Anthropology, Colonial Development and the Reinvention of Society in Britain*. Oakland: University of California Press.

Gellner, Ernest. 1987. "The Political Thought of Bronislaw Malinowski." *Current Anthropology* 28(4): 557–59.

Gregory, Chris. 1979. "The Emergence of Commodity Production in Papua New Guinea." *Journal of Contemporary Asia* 9(4): 389–409.

Hyam, Ronald. 1999. "Bureaucracy and 'Trusteeship' in the Colonial Empire." In *The Oxford History of the British Empire: Vol. 4; The Twentieth Century*, ed. Judith M. Brown and Wm. Roger Louis, 255–79. Oxford: Oxford University Press.

Latour, Bruno. 2004. "Why Has Critique Run Out of Steam? From Matters of Fact to Matters of Concern." *Critical Inquiry* 30(2): 225–48.

Lewis, D. C. 1997. *The Plantation Dream: Developing British New Guinea and Papua; 1884–1942*. Canberra: Journal of Pacific History.

Malinowski, Bronisław. 1921. "The Primitive Economics of the Trobriand Islanders." *The Economic Journal* 31(121): 1–16.

———. 1922. *Argonauts of the Western Pacific: An Account of Native Enterprise and Adventure in the Archipelagoes of Melanesian New Guinea*. London: Routledge & Kegan Paul.

———. 1930. "Race and Labour." *The Listener* 4(8).

Manjapra, Kris. 2018. "Plantation Dispossessions: The Global Travel of Agricultural Racial Capitalism." In *American Capitalism: New Histories*, ed. Sven Beckert and Christine Desan, 361–88. New York: Columbia University Press.

Mann, Michael. 2012 [1986]. *The Sources of Social Power*. Vol. 1. Cambridge: Cambridge University Press.

Mantena, Karuna. 2010. *Alibis of Empire: Henry Maine and the Ends of Liberal Imperialism*. Princeton, NJ: Princeton University Press.

Matera, Marc. 2015. *Black London: The Imperial Metropolis and Decolonization in the Twentieth Century*. Oakland: University of California Press.

Messac, Luke. 2018. "Outside the Economy: Women's Work and Feminist Economics in the Construction and Critique of National Income Accounting." *Journal of Imperial and Commonwealth History* 46(3): 552–78.

Morgan, Mary S. 2011. "Seeking Parts, Looking for Wholes." In *Histories of Scientific Observation*, ed. Lorraine Daston and Elizabeth Lunbeck, 303–25. Chicago: University of Chicago Press.

Mucha, Janusz. 1988. "Malinowski and the Contemporary Problem of Civilisation." In *Malinowski between Two Worlds: The Polish Roots of an Anthropological Tradition*, ed. Roy F. Ellen, Ernest Gellner, Grażyna Kubica, and Janusz Mucha, 149–63. Cambridge: Cambridge University Press.

Owens, Patricia. 2015. *Economy of Force: Counterinsurgency and the Historical Rise of the Social*. Cambridge: Cambridge University Press.

Pedersen, Susan. 2005. "Settler Colonialism at the Bar of the League of Nations." In *Settler Colonialism in the Twentieth Century: Projects, Practices, Legacies*, ed. Caroline Elkins and Susan Pedersen, 113–34. London: Routledge.

———. 2015. *The Guardians: The League of Nations and the Crisis of Empire*. Oxford: Oxford University Press.

———. 2018. *Internationalism and Empire: British Dilemmas, 1919–1939*. Columbia Academic Commons. Retrieved 31 October 2023 from https://academiccommons.columbia.edu/doi/10.7916/d8-m672-1p02.

Pettit, Philip. 1996. "Functional Explanation and Virtual Selection." *British Journal for the Philosophy of Science* 47(2): 291–302.

Plattner, Stuart, ed. 1989. *Economic Anthropology*. Stanford, CA: Stanford University Press.

Riddell, John. 2019. "Origins of the Anti-Imperialist United Front: The Comintern and Asia, 1919–1925." In *Left Transnationalism: The Communist International and the National, Colonial, and Racial Questions*, ed. Oleksa Drachewych and Ian McKay, 99–124. Montreal: McGill-Queen's University Press.

Robbins, Lionel. 1932. *An Essay on the Nature and Significance of Economic Science*. London: Macmillan.

Roberts, A. D. 1986. "The Imperial Mind." In *The Cambridge History of Africa, Vol. 7: From 1905 to 1940*, ed. A. D. Roberts, 24–76. Cambridge: Cambridge University Press.

Saville, John. 1988. "Britain: Internationalism and the Labour Movement between the Wars." In *Internationalism in the Labour Movement: 1830–1940*, ed. L. van Holthoon and Marcel van der Linden, 565–83. Leiden: E. J. Brill.

Sen, Amartya. 1979. "Equality of What?" Tanner Lecture on Human Values, Stanford University, May 22. Retrieved 31 October 2023 from https://tannerlectures.utah.edu/_resources/documents/a-to-z/s/sen80.pdf.

———. 1987. *Tanner Lectures in Human Values: The Standard of Living*. Cambridge: Cambridge University Press.

Stocking, George, Jr. 1992. *The Ethnographer's Magic and other Essays in the History of Anthropology*. Madison: University of Wisconsin Press.

Storr, Cait. 2018. "'Imperium in Imperio': Sub-Imperialism and the Formation of Australia as a Subject of International Law." *Melbourne Journal of International Law* 19(1): 335–68.

Wolfe, Patrick. 2006. "Settler Colonialism and the Elimination of the Native." *Journal of Genocide Research* 8(40: 387–409.

Young, Michael W. 2014. *Malinowski: Odyssey of an Anthropologist, 1884–1920*. New Haven, CT: Yale University Press.

Part II

Economy, Economics, and Epistemics

5

 Compulsion to Work?
Malinowski and the Labor Question

RACHEL E. SMITH

Introduction

What "drives man to strenuous, prolonged, and often unpleasant effort?" This was one of the questions that Bronisław Malinowski would continue to return to throughout his career. His answer was that "the psychological problem of value" is key (Malinowski 1925: 927), but grounded in kinship and social organization, magic and religion.

Compared with his influence on anthropological theories and debates over exchange, the question of work in Malinowski's writings has garnered relatively little attention (apart from contributions by his own students). Malinowski, from the time of his earliest publications (Malinowski 1993) and initial fieldwork, posed the question of incentives and stimuli to work in different ways. In his Trobriands ethnography he investigated the question in a more systematic and empirical way in order to dispel the caricature of isolated, self-interested "economic man" in prevailing economic and social theory, and simultaneously the idea that labor in "savage" societies was compelled by bare necessity, with minimal social organization.

At the time Malinowski was pursuing his fieldwork in the Western Pacific, the "Labor Question"—how to ensure a sufficient supply and reproduction of labor power on plantations and in other enterprises—was a pressing concern for British colonial authorities. The Labor Question encompassed a range of concerns including questions of depopulation, disease, and biological reproduction, conditions and incentives, as well as the suitability of local people for hard labor in view of a racialized characterization of the indolent "native." In October 1916, during a hiatus from his Trobriand fieldwork, Malinowski was called upon to contribute to a deposition by the Commission on "British and Australian Trade in the South Pacific in Melbourne," where he discussed plantation labor in New Guinea.

For Malinowski, the "psychological problem of value" as applied to the Trobriand "Tribal Economy" and the colonial Labor Question (the practical problem of how to mobilize "native" labor in the colonies) were not unrelated. In the deposition he departed from the common colonial presentation of labor mobilization as being in the interests of the "natives" themselves. Instead, he argued that the islander was better left to his own conditions and to a form of "work which is not exactly of a purely economical description, but which for him makes life worth living" (Malinowski in Australia Interstate Commission 1918: 107; see also Foks, this volume). And a year after the deposition, he mused in his private diary: "What is the deepest essence of my investigations? To discover what are his [the native's] main passions, the motives for his conduct, his aims. (Why does a *boy 'sign on'*? Is every *boy*, after some time, ready to '*sign off*'?) His essential, deepest way of thinking. At this point we are confronted with our own problems: What is essential in ourselves?" (Malinowski 1989: 119; see also Stocking 1986). Clearly, for Malinowski, the questions of stimuli to work were fundamental human ones. But questions of why a "native" would work for the "white man" were more vexed. Perhaps he found them too difficult to answer through his functionalist framework and his model of the "Tribal Economy" (Malinowski 1921: 15).

In this chapter, I track how Malinowski raised the question of incentives to work in different ways over the course of his career, including his approach in *Argonauts*. I also explore aspects of the Labor Question that he overlooked in his early monographs, but that later figured prominently in his call for a new "Practical Anthropology," in which anthropologists would contribute to, and influence, colonial policy.

Early Influences

Malinowski's inquiry into incentives to work was a concern he adapted from numerous influences in German scholarship, including Eduard Hahn, Richard Thurnwald, Max Weber, and above all Karl Bücher, whose classes Malinowski attended in Leipzig in 1908–10 (Spittler 2001; 2008: 222). Before the end of the nineteenth century, Bücher had asked what incentives and stimuli enabled people in preindustrial societies to endure tedious and strenuous labor. Malinowski (1925: 928) admired Bücher's attention to how rhythm, music, and aesthetic aspects of work were crucial motivating factors, alongside social organization, camaraderie, competition and emulation, and forms of leadership. Many of these were factors that Malinowski would take up in his own work and recommend to others (Firth 1957: 209; Spittler 2008: 224).

To a greater extent than Bücher, Malinowski was interested in social incentives for communal work, and particularly the role of magic and religion as stimuli (Spittler 2008: 223). In an early publication on ritual practices in Central Aboriginal Australia, he critiqued J. G. Frazer's argument that totemism and magic represented a fallacious misapplication of the principle of division of labor, rendering it "barren." Rather, he argued, magic and religion provided a motivation and organizing principle for coordinated effort aimed at fertile increase (Malinowski 1993: 209; Thornton and Skalník 1993: 55–56; Spittler 2008: 221). Magic and religious thought acted as "coercive ideas and other powerful mental incentives, which compel man to work, and to work ... economically in savage societies when no rational motives or outward coercion are able to move him" (Malinowski 1993: 226–27; see Firth 1957: 212).

This quotation evinces prevailing racist and evolutionist assumptions, including that of a "pre-rational" stage. Like Bücher, Malinowski saw the development of communal work as a step toward the development of more systematic organized "economical labor." Malinowski (1922a: 157, 167n) rejected several aspects of Bücher's (1901) evolutionary schema, including the individual hunt for food and the isolated autarkic household, substituting for them the notion of a "Tribal Economy" (Malinowski 1921: 15; see Firth 1957: 209; Hann 2021: 5–6; Spittler 2008: 225; Thornton and Skalník 1993: 56). Nonetheless, Bücher's work helped Malinowski transcend prevailing evolutionary models and take up a more comparative and functionalist approach to labor, even in his early work (Thornton and Skalník 1993: 53, 57).

Malinowski returned to the question of motivation for work in his early ethnographic fieldwork among the Mailu of southeast Papua in 1914. In his 1915 report from this fieldwork (seen as a "trial run" for *Argonauts* (Young 2002: 2)), Malinowski regretted his failure to address questions of labor in a systematic way hitherto:

> In order to give any facts which would speak convincingly for themselves, it would be necessary to observe the natives at work for a long time; to study the conditions under which they are capable of strenuous work; to see under what circumstances they work willingly and effectively; to investigate the stimuli to their work, aims, incentives, and so on. Such a task is, of course, beyond the capacity of an ambulant ethnologist on a short visit. (Malinowski 2002: 249; see Firth 1957: 214; Spittler 2008: 228)

Here Malinowski highlighted the importance of sociological "problems of labor," and the potential contribution if they were to be approached empirically, through long-term fieldwork (Malinowski 2002: 250). Some of these observations prefigured his later analyses of work in the Trobriands, particularly the incentive of social approbation (Firth 1957: 214).

In the report, he provided observations—albeit limited ones—on labor incentives and organization, concluding that both men and women were clearly capable of sustained work (ibid.: 249; see Firth 1957: 214; Spittler 2008: 227). Comments on laziness were at least in part directed at colonial administrators, who often charged local people in racist terms with indolence and apathy (Fitzpatrick 1980: 75; Young 1983: 75, 1984: 4).[1] "Mere general statements that the natives are lazy and slack, or that they are good workers, really have very little value," argued Malinowski (2002: 249), adding, "Lazy is an adjective having a meaning or value on a moral background only, and as such ought to be strictly excluded from scientific language" (ibid.: 251). On the other hand, paraphrasing Oscar Wilde (and perhaps evoking Thorstein Veblen), Malinowski elevated the choice to enjoy leisure as reflecting a refined aesthetic appreciation (rather than evidence of "savagery"): "All this does not mean that the natives do not understand 'the perfectly aristocratic art of doing absolutely nothing.' On the contrary, I formed the impression that they have a great deal of artistic feeling for the beauty of the *dolce far niente*" (Malinowski 2002: 251). While Malinowski was deeply interested in motivations for work, he did not consider a Weberian work ethic to be universal, or intrinsically desirable.

In the same fieldwork report, Malinowski also shows an interest in how Mailu people were adjusting to plantation labor regimes, and also the potential relevance of observations by European plantation managers:

> Much valuable information on such points could be gathered by those who have to deal with natives on the plantations, especially as regards the way in which the natives are adaptable to European methods of working. More difficult, perhaps, would be the attempt to picture the native's way of working under his own natural conditions. (Malinowski 2002: 249)

Conditions on Papuan plantations in this period were exploitative, unfree, and often violent (Fitzpatrick 1980). Nonetheless some Papuans did appear to sign on of their own volition and adapt local institutions to accommodate indentured labor, raising the question of what motives might induce them to do so (e.g., Young 1983: 75–76).

"Why Does a Boy 'Sign On'?"

In the early part of the twentieth century, the "Labor Question"—the practical problem of how to mobilize people to work for colonial masters and thus solve labor shortages—reposed more philosophically as a conflict between "European" and "Native" conceptions of and attitudes to work—was a question at the forefront of colonial agendas (Spittler 2008: 215; Jacomb 1920). Colonial administrators and observers alike deliberated over acute labor shortages in the Western Pacific and the importation of "coolie" labor (Young 1984: 4). The option to import indentured labors was further diminished by a withdrawal from indentured labor schemes by the Indian and Chinese governments (the predominant labor reserves for indentured labor in British colonies from the mid-nineteenth century, following the abolition of slavery) (Stocking 1992: 253).

The commission to which Malinowski contributed in 1916 in Melbourne reported that the Labor Question in the region was a matter of "supreme importance" (Australia Interstate Commission 1918: 57). The authors of the report appeared to agree that islanders were not innately lazy, but "generally could be capable of work and sustained effort" (ibid.: 60), and that post-contact changes were partly to blame for the changes in attitude to labor. They cited a former missionary to Fiji, Rev. Burton, who described the "protracted and tedious labor" carried out with "infinite patience" by islanders before colonization and European trade, following which manufactured conveniences and tools had replaced local craftsmanship (ibid.: 58).

On the other hand, the report's authors blamed much of the reluctance to participate in indentured labor on aspects of the native's "own conditions" and local custom and mores. First, islanders already enjoyed abundant resources, and could not be moved to labor by hunger and scarcity. But secondly, "the prevailing communal custom by which all property is shared in common" together with the obligation to redistribute one's earnings (wage or truck) on return to the village acted as disincentives to sustained labor. Increasing islanders' wages was not deemed effective, "since they have little idea of the value of money, and usually squander what they receive on useless articles, the personal possession of which . . . they lose as soon as they return to their island" (Australia Interstate Commission 1918: 59). Some, however, had a love of adventure, which explained the preference to engage on plantations far from their home islands (ibid.: 58).

By the time of the deposition, Malinowski had written his essay on the Mailu, and completed his first fieldwork stint in the Trobriands. As in his Mailu report, his contribution began with hesitation about his lack of "facts," but he immediately added his opinion that, under his own conditions, the "native Papuan" had his own impetus to work:

> My researches may throw some light on the labour question, but I have not made a special study of it because I had not the facts before me. Speaking broadly, I think that the native Papuan is not very keen on working for a white man. It is quite evi-

dent he does his own work, and if he is left under his own conditions he has plenty of work on hand, work which is not exactly of a purely economical description, but which for him makes life worth living." (Malinowski in Australia Interstate Commission 1918: 107)

This paragraph was quoted in full in the report, the authors of which also quoted Malinowski's diagnosis of which aspects of plantation life made labor tolerable:

I think the Papuan is induced to work for the white man not out of any deep-seated reasons or motives, but simply because of the personality and behaviour of the recruiter, and his putting before him very interesting matter. I think that after a few weeks any native would desire to leave if it were not for the penalty, but after a year he gets to like the life on the plantation ... A helpful demeanour on the part of the manager, firmness, and making their lives pleasant, has an effect on the natives. I know that is so from the natives' point of view. (Ibid.: 61)

Malinowski was also quoted on the policy of encouraging coconut planting in the region, a regulation the report seemed to endorse as a potential strategy for boosting production across the Pacific, where it seemed doubtful that sufficient plantation labor could be recruited domestically (assuming "forced labor" was out of the question) (Australia Interstate Commission 1918: 63). In pacified areas, including the Trobriands, the regulation to plant a certain number of coconuts was already being implemented. A 1913–14 evaluation from the Lieutenant Governor stated:

The regulation is not easy to enforce: difficulties arise not only from natural indolence, but also in some cases from the established custom of generations, whereby certain villages and districts confine themselves to the production of certain commodities, so that the community that makes canoes is rather insulted by the suggestion that it should plant coco-nuts. (In ibid.: 60)

Whether or not the canoe-crafting Trobrianders were being referred to here, Malinowski argued that the policy had been relatively successfully implemented in their case:

I know that in Trobriand Island the Resident Magistrate was an exceedingly good official, and he compelled the natives to plant a number of coconut trees each year ... I do not think it would be possible to induce the natives to engage in any other form of industry. No native will plant coconuts voluntarily, but this experiment on Trobriand Island shows that they are extremely glad for having done so .... [T]hey will be very well off when they reap these crops if they have a fair return. The native Papuan cannot really see even seven or eight days ahead, though he may be very intelligent in many matters; he has no mental grasp of a further perspective ... There is no incentive to the native except some present desire. (Ibid.: 108)

This statement betrays latent racialized and evolutionist stereotypes, including the inability to plan for a future. Later, in *Argonauts*, Malinowski (1922a: 60) would refute the idea that traditional work was motivated solely by "present wants."

The Labor Question in the Pacific was closely linked to the problem of depopulation. Clearly, there was a concern that labor shortages would be exacerbated by the "dying out" of local people (Stocking 1986: 6). The report tried to dispel the narrative that the post-contact "extinction" of Polynesians and Melanesians was "inevitable" in light of the vices of white settlers, particularly nefarious "beach-combers" and "blackbirders"[2] who had taken advantage of local people, and introduced new vices (such as alcohol) as well as diseases: "The type of civilization meted out to the native in the Pacific has largely been of a character not only altogether unsuitable for, but in many respect fatal to his well-being" (Australia Interstate Commission 1918: 60).

Recurring themes included perceptions of depression, despondency, and "race despair" (or "race suicide") ensuing from the rapid transformation of society, and the loss of "anything to live for" (Young 1984: 4). This position was epitomized by another anthropologist and pioneer of fieldwork, W. H. R. Rivers, who attended the meeting in Australia in 1914 alongside Malinowski:

> the labour traffic continues to act as a cause of depopulation. It acts directly by taking men and women away from their homes when they should be marrying and producing children, while other evils are that, as at present conducted, the traffic tends to spread disease and to undermine an influence which I believe to be at the present time the most potent for good in Melanesia, the work of the missionaries. Moreover, the use of natives as labourers on plantations fails to give that interest in life which, as I have tried to show, forms the most essential factor in maintaining the health of a people. (Rivers 1922: 106)

For Rivers (ibid.: 46), this analysis did not entail that local labor should not be used. Rather, the "native" should be involved in industrial development and trade.

Similarly, the authors of the 1916 deposition felt that involving islanders in appropriate forms of productive work would imbue them with a sense of life-giving purpose, citing again Rev. Burton's view that "the Fijian must work again or perish." The report implied that the populations of the islands could be revived with a greater share in domestic production and better education, as had been demonstrated in British African colonies (Australia Interstate Commission 1918: 60, 62): "If the native can be reconverted to labor, his condition of life will vastly improve and he will survive, otherwise he must certainly perish" (ibid.: 60).[3] Stemming depopulation was also the motivation for measures to extend medical services and clamp down on "abortionists" (ibid.: 62).

A major theme omitted from the main report (but included in the appendix) was Malinowski's lengthy discussion of the significance of sex and marriage for the recruitment and retention of native labor, including the availability of sex for plantation workers, the reluctance of married men to leave their wives, and the potential conflicts arising if wives were present (Australia Interstate Commission 1918: 107–8). Whether allowing workers to take their wives would aid recruitment and retention of workers or only create more problems was a matter of debate (ibid.: 59). For Stocking, Malinowski's foregrounding of the "sexual question" was not only an instance of quandaries about the relationship between depopulation and the Labor Question, but also of what would become an enduring intellectual interest in the relationship between sex and work (Stocking 1987: 27n3). Stocking suggested that Malinowski's contention that it was "almost impossible to think that a young native would spend three years of his life without having sexual intercourse without degenerating into sexual abnormality" may be more than a reflection of the "native point of view"; it might also be an expression of Malinowski's own repressed desire during his fieldwork (ibid.: 26–27n3; Stocking 1992: 253).[4]

Overall, Malinowski concurred with the gist of the report (Australia Interstate Commission 1918: 108). The problems lay in depopulation and "contact with Western civilization," including the introduction of alcohol and disease via plantation labor, but also depression and despondency (see also Foks 2023: 22–23; Foks, this volume). However, while the deposition's authors seemed to suggest that education and labor practices could be brought into better alignment with the islander's existing interests and incentives to work (Australia Interstate Commission 1918: 60–62), Malinowski seemed to suggest that the islander's motives and stimuli were structured according to an entirely different and incompatible social system (Foks 2023: 49–50). Another aspect of Malinowski's position not reproduced in the main body of the report was his more radical contention that it might be preferable to cease recruitment and leave the islanders left uncontaminated (see Stocking 1986: 9; Foks, this volume):

> There is not much likelihood of the native Papuans and of the natives of the other Pacific Islands dying out if left alone, and if they do not come in contact with the white man's civilization. Once the natives come into contact with the white civilization it is always better to take some measures to prevent their dying out. Broadly speaking, I think it would be best to leave them to their own conditions. (In Australia Interstate Commission 1918: 108)

This was indicative of Malinowski's tendency toward a preservationist stance (Stocking 1992: 258; cf. Foks, this volume). In the same year that

Rivers published a collected volume on depopulation, Malinowski followed up on *Argonauts* with an article in *Economica* attributing the "gradual dying out" of Pacific Islanders mainly to "the destruction of all vital interest for the native, by taking away from him of all that was dear and valuable to him, of all that gave him the joy of living." It was tradition (including tribal law and morality) that represented a form of "collective adaptation" of a community to its conditions: "Destroy tradition, and you will deprive the collective organism of its protective shell, and give it over to the slow but inevitable process of dying out" (Malinowski 1922b: 214; see Staley, this volume).

But Malinowski's tendency to curb a "romantic primitivism" with a pragmaticism or "real politik" (Stocking 1992: 271–72) was also evident in his simultaneous appeal to colonial interests, and the potential for an anthropological contribution:

> The survival of natives—apart from humanitarian, aesthetic or moral considerations—is a matter of vital importance for practical purposes. Are the South Sea colonies to be repeopled by imported yellow or Hindu labour or are they going to be left to waste, since white labour seems absolutely inadequate? The first course creates a serious political danger, the second means ruin. Millions of money—if we overlook the millions of human lives—are at stake and yet no serious effort has been made by the administrators to assess the danger and try to find out a cure for it. (Malinowski 1922b: 209)

Dispelling "Economic Man"

The colonial Labor Question was neglected in Malinowski's most celebrated monograph. Nonetheless, as in his Mailu report and the 1916 deposition, in *Argonauts* Malinowski argued implicitly that motivations for work under local conditions were inseparable from the will to live. As we have seen, the backdrop to Malinowski's work was the common European characterization of the native as lazy, individualistic, and ill-disposed to sustained effort. This, Malinowski (1922a: 156) wrote, was "a constant refrain of the average white settler, but even ethnography and travel books." Malinowski (ibid.: 156–57) noted that Europeans were puzzled as to why economic gain was not a sufficient incentive to induce local people to labor (see also Malinowski 1965: 20). In *Argonauts*, he suggested that the removal of a man from his "own conditions" was the most probable explanation for planters' accusations of laziness: "If you remove a man from his social milieu, you eo ipso[5] deprive him of almost all his stimuli to moral steadfastness and economic efficiency and even of interest in life. If then you measure him by moral, legal or economic standards, also essentially foreign to him, you cannot but obtain a caricature in your estimate" (Malinowski 1922a: 156–57).

Whether or not Malinowski (1922a: 60) was indirectly addressing colonial authorities when seeking to dispel the myth of the "lazy" native (as Foks suggests in his contribution to this volume), in *Argonauts* he was famously determined to address the caricature among scholars of "Primitive Economic Man." Students are commonly taught that this monograph is concerned with trade and exchange, the takeaway theoretical message being that the Trobriand Kula player was not motivated (as economic utilitarians would supposedly have it) by the maximization of material gain according to his economic self-interest. But in fact, in the passage in which Malinowski evokes that "fanciful dummy creature" of scholarly textbooks, his main goal is to refute the parallel assumption that work was conducted according to the "principle of the least effort" (Hann 2021: 6): "On the contrary, much time and energy is spent on wholly unnecessary effort, that is, from a utilitarian point of view. Again, work and effort, instead of being merely a means to an end, are, in a way an end in themselves" (Malinowski 1922a: 60).[6] The Trobriander "works prompted by motives of a highly complex, social and traditional nature, and towards aims which are certainly not directed towards the satisfaction of present wants, or to the direct achievement of utilitarian purposes" (ibid.).

As he had for the Mailu, Malinowski stressed that the Trobriander was perfectly capable of sustained and energetic work, albeit not motivated by utilitarian gain, but by values and aspirations shaped by custom (Malinowski 1922a: 58, 156–57). While the title of the monograph focuses on the islander as an intrepid voyager, Malinowski was keen to highlight that he spent half his working life in the garden, and that the title *tokwaybagula*, or "good gardener," brought renown and was borne with pride. Garden work was non-utilitarian in the sense that much of it was motivated by aesthetic considerations, emulation and competition, and complex social obligations (Malinowski 1922a: 58–61). Likewise, objects were valued not simply for their "utility" but for their rarity and their craftsmanship, which elicited an emotional attachment. Artists would work excessively to accomplish excellence in their craft. They drew deep satisfaction from their workmanship, though they would often attribute their design to magical inspiration. Value and wealth did not conform to "laws of supply and demand," nor to notions of scarcity or utility (ibid.: 172).

Alongside this critique of crude utilitarianism, Malinowski argued against a second fallacy in the textbook portrayal of Primitive Economic Man: that work was unsystematic and disorderly. Contrary to this depiction, Malinowski stressed that Melanesian societies maintained complex labor systems (Firth 1957: 210; Malinowski 1922a: 166). The cooperation necessary for canoe-building belied the myth that, in small-scale societies, work was carried out individually or in autarkic household groups. Rather, work was systematic and often communal in organization, overseen by a chief as well as technical specialists. But the overriding influence was adherence to custom, which not only regulated the division of labor, but acted on people's psychology and moral sense. As with gardening, magic and ritual imbued craft activities with extra force (Malinowski 1922a: 158–59). Malinowski distinguished between work and magic but saw them as deeply intertwined. In canoe-building, both work and magic were designed to ensure a speedy and safe passage and a successful Kula (ibid.: 414). Magic augmented workmanship, lending a "superadded quality" of swiftness to even the most finely built vessel (ibid.: 420). Thus, as he had found in his earlier investigation of the Intichiuma rituals, for the Trobriander, magic was a crucial factor in the motivation and regulation of work. It shaped the timing and division of tasks and in itself motivated further effort, providing both a principle of leadership as well as a psychological influence and assurance of success (ibid.: 114–16).

Despite these insights, stereotypes of "primitive labor" persisted after 1922. The release of a book of that title in 1924 by physical anthropologist L. H. Dudley Buxton (1924) demonstrates how relatively progressive Malinowski's idea were at the time. Buxton's book was based on the idea of "races" of man advancing along evolutionary stages. Reviewing it gave Malinowski (1925: 926) a chance to reiterate his critique of many evolutionist assumptions, and to make a case for the "new anthropology" based on a sociological approach to culture and empirical fieldwork, while at the same time acknowledging the work of German predecessors such as Hahn and Bücher (see Firth 1957: 209). In this review Malinowski distilled many of the ideas and analyses he had been developing of labor, which he now defined "as purposeful systematic activity standardized by tradition and devoted to the satisfaction of wants, the making of means of production, and the creation of objects of luxury, value, and renown" (Malinowski 1925: 927). Labor was the link between the "psychological problem of value" (motivations) and economic value, thus bringing economic questions into relationship with those of religion:

> It is obviously futile to discuss labour except as a part problem of economics. The early forms of labour are intimately correlated with the manner in which economic value came into existence. In fact, the inquiry has to burst the bounds even of the widest economic analysis and to consider how other motives, above all those of magical and religious character, have pushed man towards certain pursuits, established new values for him, and thus given him new forms of labour. (Ibid.: 927)

From Coral Gardens to Plantation Labor

Later in life, Malinowski (1965: 457) reflected on how his deep interest in the relationship between magico-religious belief and work was present even in his early essay on the Intichiuma ceremonies (Malinowski 1993: 226–27). This interest was to become the "dominant motive" for *Coral Gardens and Their Magic*, which was based on a draft manuscript from 1916–17. *Coral Gardens* can be seen as the culmination of Malinowski's effort to connect psychological and economic value through careful ethnography of the deep intertwining of magic and garden work (Thornton and Skalník 1993: 57).[7]

In a way, *Coral Gardens* can also be seen as a more general affirmation that daily work belongs at the center of ethnographic research. Malinowski acknowledged that mundane gardening might not capture the reader's imagination in the same way as trading expeditions or sexual lives. But gardening was at the forefront of the working life of the Trobriand Islander: "Whatever he might appear to others, to himself he is first and foremost a gardener. His passion for his soil is that of a real peasant" (Malinowski 1965: xix). In his appendix to this monograph, Malinowski (ibid.: 481) expressed regret at having largely ignored the colonial context, an oversight that "is perhaps the most serious shortcoming of my whole anthropological research in Melanesia."[8] In a 1926 entry for the *Encyclopaedia Britannica*, Malinowski wrote: "By inquiring into savage economic organization, the functional method can teach how to manage indigenous labor and how to trade with the natives" (cited in Spittler 2008: 241).

Later, especially after he became a British citizen, Malinowski wrote of the potential for functional anthropology to contribute to colonial issues (Spittler 2008: 241). He admitted that he had not done enough to address such matters in his previous ethnographic work, but "Practical Anthropology" (1929) and "Rationalisation of Anthropology and Administration" (1930) were intended in this way (Malinowski 1965: 481). In the 1929 article, having again defined labor as purposeful and systematic activity, Malinowski approached the colonial Labor Question in terms of his long-standing interest in incentives for work and the "psychological problem of value." Returning to the question of motivations for strenuous and prolonged toil in tribal society, he wrote:

> The problem of labour can be treated only against the background of the psychological problem of value. What are the effective incentives to effort? In what way are they related to the individual, and how far are they transformed by culture? We see thus, that exactly as it would be useless to investigate land tenure without asking to

what uses land is being put, so it is impossible to understand native labour except as part of the problem of their system of values, incentives, and utility. Early forms of labour are obviously correlated with the manner in which economic value comes into existence. *The wise entrepreneur and administrator will be interested to know what were the old tribal values and what forms economic ambition took in their area.* (Malinowski 1929: 34, italics added)[9]

As Foks (2018: 40; 2023: 33; this volume) has argued, in the latter stage of his career Malinowski came to advocate a "hands-off" form of indirect rule and trusteeship, more radically and explicitly opposed to "ruthless" settler colonial policies of land dispossession and forced labor. In his 1930 reply to a critique by a Mr. Mitchell, an administrator in East Africa, of the use of functionalist anthropology for a civilizing and pacifying colonial administration, Malinowski referred him to the violent history of forced labor and punitive expeditions in the area that he knew best:

> unfortunately I could quote numerous cases from the South Seas in which the practical man, having "regretfully" and unintelligently violated native customs by the mere right of his ignorance and moral zeal, has brought whole native tribes to grief. Let Mr. Mitchell read the report of the Goaribari massacres in New Guinea; the history of "black-birding" in the South Seas; or even the data referring to the repatriation of the black-birded Kanakas to their Melanesian homes; for that matter the antecedents of any of the numerous punitive expeditions in the South Seas. Africa is not my special field, but I have a vague idea that "punitive expeditions," wholesale massacres of natives by whites, strange retaliations in the name of "justice," "prestige", and "the white man's honour" did also occur in the Dark Continent, and that it is not only the coloured African there who deserves the title of "murderer" nor is it the white European who should use such terms of abuse as marks of his own racial superiority. (Malinowski 1930a: 411; see James 1973: 57)

By this time, Malinowski's return to the question of what compels someone to work provided important grounds for critique of compelling labor under direct rule (see also Foks 2018: 40; 2023: 22–23, 49–50). In a magazine article of 1930 addressing questions of forced labor in Africa, he echoed his earlier work in arguing that far from being "lazy," the "native" has a passion for work in his own conditions, but is equally averse to difficult, degrading, and unrewarded toil and drudgery as the white European:

> Why is it, then, that the labour supply is not sufficient? . . . It is because the white colonist, while he needs labour and demands labour, compels the African to work under handicaps, to work with insufficient inducements, and to work without any economic outlook and aims, without any hope of raising his standard. Under such conditions, only force can supply labour. (Malinowski 1930b: iv)

Conclusion

In this chapter, I have discussed a question that preoccupied Malinowski from his earliest writings on Intichiuma, through his fieldwork among the Mailu, and then in the Trobriand ethnography for which he is most remembered: the question of motives and incentives to work. As articulated in *Argonauts*, the work question was simultaneously a question of value—"the problem of labor can be treated only against the background of the psychological problem of value" (Malinowski 1925: 927). In so doing he sought to connect psychological motivation, social and religious values, and economic value. It seems that for Malinowski, the question of work was at the heart of his search for the "native's" "*Weltanschauung*, the breath of life and reality which he breathes and by which he lives" (Malinowski 1922a: 517).

Answers were to be empirical, and not based on a priori assumptions about the nature of Primitive Economic Man. Concrete ethnography was to be combined with a functional approach that connected economy to aesthetic, religious, and social considerations. Raymond Firth (1957: 216) later reflected that one of Malinowski's great contributions to economic anthropology was to have given "easily the most penetrating analysis of incentives of production yet made for a non-European society." According to Firth (ibid.: 215), Malinowski had "demonstrated how the Trobriander was spurred on to the expenditure of a great amount of time and energy in work, the product of which went to other people, because of his status interests and ambitions, his response to legal and moral rules and to the expected norms of a structural framework." His exploration of the relationship between magic and the economy was another important contribution.

Malinowski's Trobriand ethnography, alongside the writings of his student Firth and their Austrian colleague Richard Thurnwald, formed key sources for Karl Polanyi's critique of economic Formalism, and for "Substantivist" arguments about the economic embeddedness of non-market societies (Polanyi 2001: 50n; Cook and Young 2016: 658). Firth (1957: 212) later criticized his mentor Malinowski for insufficient grasp of formal economics. The "Formalist–Substantivist" debate was a relatively brief period in the history of economic anthropology, but the same problems have continued to haunt the discipline. As Graeber (2001: 12) put it:

> It seems to me that these basic issues have never been resolved. Those who start by looking at society as a whole are left, like the Substantivists, trying to explain how people are motivated to reproduce society; those who start by looking at individual desires end up, like the Formalists, unable to explain why people chose to maximize some things and not others (or otherwise to account for questions of meaning).

For Malinowski, economic questions were to be explored through a deeply ethnographic investigation of value and motivations, connecting economy to aesthetic, religious, and social considerations. In this respect, foregrounding embeddedness in social institutions, and customs and values, Malinowski was a proto-Substantivist, suggests Hann (2021: 4–6), though he struggled to reconcile this more Substantivist view of the economy with the universalist idea of "economizing" he had originally imbibed as a student of philosophy in Kraków.[10] Whether or not he ever fully succeeded, this tension allowed Malinowski to circumvent extremes, maintaining a strong interest in questions of individual psychological motivations and incentives (ibid.: 3) while continuing to emphasize the institutional specificities of a non-market economic system. Had Malinowski's inquiry into motives for work inspired as much enthusiasm among subsequent anthropologists as his descriptions of Kula inspired theories of exchange, perhaps more of this balance (i.e., sufficient attention to personal motivations while avoiding utilitarian pitfalls of the "maximizing individual") would have remained more clearly foregrounded.

Malinowski found it difficult to resolve the question of incentives and motivation for labor on colonial plantations. In 1917, it seems he was already privately connecting "the deepest essence" of his ethnographic work, that is to uncover the Trobriander's "main passions ... his essential deepest way of thinking," with a seemingly jarring digression: "Why does a *boy* '*sign on*'?" (Malinowski 1989: 119; Stocking 1986: 6; 1987: 26–27n3). If, as he wrote in his 1916 deposition statement, work under the islander's "own conditions" "makes life worth living" (Malinowski in Australia Interstate Commission 1918: 107), what did that say about the conditions of labor under the colonial regime, under which he was removed from the social milieu that was the source of meaning and value? As Malinowski would later regret, the colonial Labor Question was largely omitted from his ethnographic fieldwork. But one can see in his 1916 deposition, and in his 1917 diary entry, precursors to his later call for a "Practical Anthropology" that would influence and intervene in colonial policy (Stocking 1987: 26–27n3).

Questions of incentives and motivations to work, including the question of free versus unfree labor, remain relevant today, for example in debates surrounding the conditions faced by Melanesian seasonal workers on modern day farms and orchards in Australia and New Zealand (Bailey 2009; Connell 2010; Petrou and Connell 2023; Smith 2019; Stead 2019). More generally, there seems to be a renewed interest in questions of labor, not only in forms of exploitation, precarity, and labor politics (Kasmir and Carbonella 2008, 2014; Lazar and Sanchez 2019; Parry 2018; Prentice 2020), but also in the "meaning" and motivations of work for those performing it (Dobler 2016; Graeber 2019; Sanchez 2020). In uncovering and reflecting on how Malinowski dealt with these questions throughout his career, we can see that questions of compulsion to work, both in terms of political economic conditions structuring labor under global capitalism and psychological motivations and meanings for work, have been there from the beginning of anthropological interest in the "economic."

Rachel E. Smith is a Lecturer in Anthropology and Museum Studies at the University of Aberdeen. Her core research has focused on local perspectives on development and social change in Vanuatu, an island nation in the Western Pacific. Her doctoral project (2011–16) focused on the "domestic moral economy" in a rural community undergoing rapid social and economic transformation due to an overseas labor mobility programme.

Notes

1. The Austrian-born anthropologist Richard Thurnwald had already written several papers advising colonial authorities on the recruitment of native labor, in both the Western Pacific and later East Africa (Spittler 2008: 207). In 1910, Thurnwald refuted any straightforward characterization of the islander as "lazy": "When he is at home, the native is always active, and he occasionally interrupts this activity with entertainment when he is tired. He is subject to no force and scarcely any constraint, he works 'at his own whim' . . . . And from his point of view the European is right when he calls the native 'lazy'. But the native considers that what the white man demands of him is a heavy, tedious, dull and dreary burden" (in ibid.: 215). For Thurnwald, work at "one's own whim" was not conducive to colonial efforts to mobilize labor, and his essay attempted to suggest some practical solutions. But while this quotation shows some sympathy for the "native point of view," ultimately Thurnwald clung to the model of successive stages of work, and the need to inculcate natives into sustained working in order to justify colonialism (ibid.: 215–16, 244).
2. "Blackbirding" refers to the late-nineteenth-century "labor trade" in which Pacific Islanders, especially Melanesians, were treated as a labor reserve for indentured labor on the colonial plantations of Queensland, Fiji, and other locations. While the extent to which the labor trade was "free" or coerced has been hotly contested, we have numerous well documented accounts of kidnappings, deception, and violence in recruitment, as well as exploitation, disease, brutality, and poor working and living conditions on the plantations (see Smith 2021: 33).
3. Although he would later admit similarities of the indentured system to slavery (Young 1983: 74), Hubert Murray, Lieutenant Governor of Papua, 1908–40, argued that it was in the Papuan's own interests to "learn to work" through plantation labor (Stocking 1992: 243). See also Young (1984: 4) on the "industrial ideal" proposed by Murray: that laboring for whites would give Papuans "something to live for."

4. According to Stocking, commenting on Malinowski's later monograph *Sex and Repression*, the passage from "savagery" to "civilization" was understood by the ethnographer as part of a move from a free sexuality to a more repressed state: "For mankind as a whole, the long-run evolutionary consequences of 'signing on' might be interpreted as involving loss as well as gain—and the loss might be even more sharply felt by a European living on a tropical island but denying himself the sensual pleasures that cultural exoticism usually associated with such primitive realms. Denied the compensating gains of civilization, why, indeed, would the native 'boy'—or anyone else—'sign on'?" (Stocking 1987: 26–27n3; see also 1986: 9).
5. Latin: "by that itself: by that fact alone" (*Merriam-Webster* 2023).
6. According to Hann (2021: 3–4), Malinowski would have been taught to accept the "universal" principle of "least effort" by his teachers in Leipzig, but came to refute the assumption following his ethnographic fieldwork.
7. Malinowski wrote, "One aspect of Trobriand gardening is very prominent and may raise problems of wider implication: I mean the relation between purely economic, rationally founded and technically effective work on the one hand, and magic on the other . . . It comes out more clearly there than in the relation of magic to work found in the kula or in the conduct of native courtship, although these cast valuable light on the role of magic in human affairs" (Malinowski 1965: xx). Magic and work had distinct aims; magic accounted for the good or bad luck in outcome despite the work put in. Unlike Frazer and Weber, Malinowski did not see magic as an illusionary impediment to prosperity, but rather a structuring principle for the organization of work, and inspiring confidence in its ultimate success. Magic was effective in gaining mastery over good and bad fortune (Spittler 2008: 230–32).
8. Although the Trobriands were not much impacted by the labor trade, pearling, copra (dried coconut flesh) production, and the use of local labor in colonial production regimes were well underway at the time of Malinowski's fieldwork (Firth 1957: 226; Stocking 1992: 249–51). Malinowski (1965: 20) discussed Trobrianders' reluctance to engage in pearling, despite the inducements of white traders offering far higher recompense than they could make through fishing: "Obedience to tradition and the sense of tribal honour make him invariably put his gardens first, his fishing for exchange second, and pearling last of all." Elsewhere he discussed relative incomes from plantation labor versus local production, the use of "surplus" crops to feed laborers, and broader impacts of European colonialism (Firth 1957: 226).
9. It is, however, instructive to note that, at least in Australia, Malinowskian functionalism was perceived less as a "handmaiden of colonialism" than as an obstacle (Bashkow 1995: 13). Soon after his arrival at Sydney in 1926, Radcliffe-Brown began correspondence with the Australian government to suggest that they employ anthropologists to assist with "native administration" in Papua New Guinea, as other colonial powers had in Africa. He met with some success, with colonial officials being sent to attend anthropology courses in his department (Murray in Bashkow 1995: 12; Gray 2003: 320; Kaberry in Malinowski 1945: x). But some administrators took a dim view of Malinowski's influence and the potential of functional anthropology to aid their activities—particularly the functionalist assumption that custom is worth preserving and the "refusal to admit 'that the white race can under any circumstances govern the black or the brown'" (Murray in Bashkow 1995: 12).

10. Prior to his "enslavement" to anthropology, Malinowski completed a thesis on "economy of thought," based on the ideas of philosopher-physicist Ernst Mach (Malinowski 1993: 89–116; see Staley, this volume; Stocking 1992: 240–41).

References

Australia Interstate Commission. 1918. *British and Australian Trade in the South Pacific*. Report, Parliament of the Commonwealth of Australia (Melbourne: Government printer for the state of Victoria, A. J. Mullett).
Bailey, Rochelle. 2009. "Unfree Labour? Ni-Vanuatu Workers in New Zealand's Recognised Seasonal Employer Scheme." MA thesis. Christchurch: University of Canterbury, School of Social and Political Sciences. Retrieved 31 October 2023 from http://ir.canterbury.ac.nz/handle/10092/2957.
Bashkow, Ira. 1995. "'The Stakes for Which We Play Are Too High to Allow of Experiments': Colonial Administrators of Papua on Their Anthropological Training by Radcliffe-Brown." *History of Anthropology Newsletter* 22(2): 3–14.
Bücher, Karl. 1901. *Industrial Evolution*. New York: Henry Holt.
Buxton, L. H. Dudley. 1924. *Primitive Labour*. London: Methuen.
Connell, John. 2010. "From Blackbirds to Guestworkers in the South Pacific: Plus Ça Change . . . ?" *Economic and Labour Relations Review* 20(2): 111–21.
Cook, Scott, and Michael W. Young. 2016. "Malinowski, Herskovits, and the Controversy over Economics in Anthropology." *History of Political Economy* 48(4): 657–79.
Dobler, Gregor. 2016. "'Work and Rhythm' Revisited: Rhythm and Experience in Northern Namibian Peasant Work." *Journal of the Royal Anthropological Institute* 22(4): 864–83.
Firth, Raymond. 1957. *Man and Culture: An Evaluation of the Work of Bronislaw Malinowski*. London: Routledge & Kegan Paul.
Fitzpatrick, Peter. 1980. "Really Rather Like Slavery: Law and Labor in the Colonial Economy in Papua New Guinea." *Contemporary Crises* 4: 77–95.
Foks, Freddy. 2018. "Bronislaw Malinowski, 'Indirect Rule,' and the Colonial Politics of Functionalist Anthropology, ca. 1925–1940." *Comparative Studies in Society and History* 60(1): 35–57.
———. 2023. *Participant Observers: Anthropology, Colonial Development, and the Reinvention of Society in Britain*. Oakland: University of California Press.
Graeber, David. 2001. *Toward an Anthropological Theory of Value: The False Coin of Our Own Dreams*. New York: Palgrave.
———. 2019. *Bullshit Jobs: A Theory*. New York: Simon and Schuster.
Gray, Geoffrey. 2003. "There Are Many Difficult Problems." *Journal of Pacific History* 38(3): 313–30.
Hann, Chris. 2021. "One Hundred Years of Substantivist Economic Anthropology." *Max Planck Institute for Social Anthropology Working Papers*, No. 205. Halle: Max Planck Institute. Retrieved 31 October 2023 from https://www.eth.mpg.de/pubs/wps/pdf/mpi-eth-working-paper-0205.

Jacomb, Edward. 1920. "The Future of the Kanaka." *Anti-Slavery Reporter and Aborigines' Friend* (London) 9(4): 115–17.
James, Wendy. 1973. "The Anthropologist as Reluctant Imperialist." In *Anthropology & the Colonial Encounter*, ed. Talal Asad, 41–70. London: Ithaca Press.
Kasmir, Sharryn, and August Carbonella. 2008. "Dispossession and the Anthropology of Labor." *Critique of Anthropology* 28(1): 5–25.
———. 2014. *Blood and Fire: Toward a Global Anthropology of Labor*. New York: Berghahn.
Lazar, Sian, and Andrew Sanchez. 2019. "Understanding Labour Politics in an Age of Precarity." *Dialectical Anthropology* 43(1): 3–14.
Malinowski, Bronisław. 1921. "The Primitive Economics of the Trobriand Islanders." *The Economic Journal* 31(121): 1–16.
———. 1922a. *Argonauts of the Western Pacific: An Account of Native Enterprise and Adventure in the Archipelagoes of Melanesian New Guinea*. London: Routledge & Kegan Paul.
———. 1922b. "Ethnology and the Study of Society." *Economica* 6: 208–19.
———. 1925. "Primitive Labour." *Nature* 116(2930): 926–30.
———. 1929. "Practical Anthropology." *Africa: Journal of the International African Institute* 2(1): 22–38.
———. 1930a. "The Rationalization of Anthropology and Administration." *Africa: Journal of the International African Institute* 3(4): 405–30.
——— 1930b. "Race and Labour." *The Listener* 4: i–vi (16 July, Supplement 8).
———. 1945. *The Dynamics of Culture Change: An Inquiry into Race Relations in Africa*. New Haven, CT: Yale University Press.
———. 1965. *Coral Gardens and Their Magic, vol. 1. Soil-Tilling and Agricultural Rites in the Trobriand Islands*. Bloomington: Indiana University Press.
———. 1989. *A Diary in the Strict Sense of the Term*. Stanford, CA: Stanford University Press.
———. 1993. "The Economic Aspects of Intichiuma Ceremonies." In *The Early Writings of Bronislaw Malinowski*, ed. Robert J. Thornton and Peter Skalník, 209–42. Cambridge: Cambridge University Press.
———. 2002. *Malinowski among the Magi: The Natives of Mailu*. Abingdon: Routledge.
Merriam-Webster. 2023. "Eo Ipso." Retrieved 31 October 2023 from https://www.merriam-webster.com/dictionary/eo+ipso.
Parry, Jonathan. 2018. "Introduction: Precarity, Class, and the Neoliberal Subject." In *Industrial Labor on the Margins of Capitalism: Precarity, Class, and the Neoliberal Subject*, ed. Chris Hann and Jonathan Parry, 1–38. New York: Berghahn.
Petrou, Kirstie, and John Connell. 2023. *Pacific Islands Guestworkers in Australia: The New Blackbirds?* Singapore: Palgrave.
Polanyi, Karl. 2001 [1944]. *The Great Transformation: The Political and Economic Origins of Our Time*. Boston: Beacon Press.
Prentice, Rebecca. 2020. "Work after Precarity: Anthropologies of Labor and Wageless Life." *Focaal* 88: 117–24.
Rivers, W. H. R. 1922. *Essays on the Depopulation of Melanesia*. Cambridge: Cambridge University Press.

Sanchez, Andrew. 2020. "Transformation and the Satisfaction of Work." *Social Analysis* 64(3): 68–94.

Smith, Rachel E. 2019. "Be Our Guest/Worker: Reciprocal Dependency and Expressions of Hospitality in Ni-Vanuatu Overseas Labour Migration." *Journal of the Royal Anthropological Institute* 25(2): 349–67.

———. 2021. "The Meaning of 'Free' Work: Service as a Gift, and Labor as a Commodity for Ni-Vanuatu Labor Migrants." In *Work, Society, and Self: Chimeras of Freedom in the Era of Neoliberalism*, ed. C. Hann, 27–48. New York: Berghahn.

Spittler, Gerd. 2001. "Work: Anthropological Aspects." In *International Encyclopedia of the Social & Behavioral Sciences*, ed. Neil J. Smelser and Paul B. Baltes, 16565–69. Oxford: Pergamon. Retrieved 31 October 2023 from http://www.sciencedirect.com/science/article/pii/B0080430767009864.

———. 2008. *Founders of the Anthropology of Work: German Social Scientists of the 19th and Early 20th Centuries and the First Ethnographers*. Berlin: Lit Verlag.

Stead, Victoria. 2019. "Money Trees, Development Dreams and Colonial Legacies in Contemporary Pasifika Horticultural Labour." In *Labour Lines and Colonial Power: Indigenous and Pacific Islander Labour Mobility in Australia*, ed. Victoria Stead and Jon Altman, 133–57. Canberra: ANU Press.

Stocking, George W. 1986. "Why Does a Boy 'Sign On'? Malinowski's First Statement on Practical Anthropology." *History of Anthropology Newsletter* 13(2): 6–9.

———. 1987. *Malinowski, Rivers, Benedict and Others: Essays on Culture and Personality*. Madison: University of Wisconsin Press.

———. 1992. *The Ethnographer's Magic and Other Essays in the History of Anthropology*. Madison: University of Wisconsin Press.

Thornton, Robert J., with Peter Skalník. 1993. "Introduction: Malinowski's Reading, Writing, 1904–1914." In *The Early Writings of Bronislaw Malinowski*, ed. Robert J. Thornton and Peter Skalník, 1–66. Cambridge: Cambridge University Press.

Young, Michael W. 1983. "'The Best Workmen in Papua': Goodenough Islanders and the Labour Trade, 1900–1960." *Journal of Pacific History* 18(2): 74–95.

———. 1984. "The Intensive Study of a Restricted Area, or, Why Did Malinowski Go to the Trobriand Islands?" *Oceania* 55(1): 1–26.

———. 2002. "Editor's Introduction." In *Malinowski among the Magi: The Natives of Mailu*, 1–76. Abingdon: Routledge.

6

 On Tribal and Other Economies

RICHARD STALEY

Introduction: "Returned in Really Good Value"

When he returned from Kiriwina and the Trobriands to Australia in late 1918, Bronisław Malinowski was looking forward to marriage with Elsie Masson but also to the eighteen months or so he thought he would need (with Elsie's help) to write out his material and think it through in the big book that would present his methodological mission. A further six months would be required to see it through the press, and he was very worried about the time this would all take and "the sordid questions of lucre," as his letters to his academic mentor Charles Seligman show (Young 2004: 580, citing Malinowski to Seligman, 21 January 1919). Malinowski told Seligman that learning that the next instalment of Robert Mond's grant might, like the previous one, require him to engage once more in Trobriand fieldwork (and thereby delay publication) sent a chill through his bones. All the alternatives—bar a return to Europe—seemed too difficult. In response Malinowski wrote to Mond to explain that, convinced of the value of his work, he knew he should "be able to make a fundamental contribution to the problems of method and scope of ethnology," rendering it a "definite branch and adjunct discipline of theoretical social science" rather than idle speculation. But that would require Mond's further investment, so, he wrote,

> To put it crudely: I feel confident that the money spent on me so far and the future assistance I am asking for will be returned in really good value of scientific fact and method. But if I am compelled now to earn my living by other means, the result of

my four years work assisted by your generosity may be seriously jeopardized. (Malinowski to Mond, 21 January 1919, in Young 2004: 582)

Such are the gifts, grants, and exchanges that sustained Malinowski's academic life, with its long cycles of field and other work. He was thoroughly relieved that Mond signaled his assent to the further two years' funding that would allow him time to digest his material. Yet as Malinowski prepared *Argonauts of the Western Pacific* for publication, returning to Britain in 1920 after an intensive period writing on the Canary Islands with Elsie, and then taking up a lectureship at the London School of Economics in 1921, he put more than that single book and more than ethnology in play, publishing a significant series of papers that signaled his growing concern with a particular field of activity and a second major discipline. This chapter will explore how Malinowski's concerns with the economic activities and institutions he found in the Trobriand Islands became a significant foil in his work to render ethnology a form of theoretical social science, and in particular led him to flank *Argonauts* with two papers that he published in economics journals.

The seeds for Malinowski's approach had been sown much earlier, in at least two different respects. For a start, if Seligman or Mond had wanted some idea of Malinowski's methodological aims, they would have thought first of the groundbreaking discussion of the spirits of the dead he had published in 1916, where he concluded his complex, multifaceted account of Trobriand beliefs and customs with methodological reflections articulating the sociological rules necessary to deal with the complex ways in which beliefs were reflected in native groups. He had begun to work on these ideas as early as in his 1906 dissertation "On the Principle of the Economy of Thought." They were to be elaborated further in his engagement with the discipline of economics. Malinowski thought it was critical to understand the variation in respondents' expression of beliefs, embodied in each mind but also reflected in many social customs, but argued that one shouldn't seek "an average opinion" (Malinowski 1916: 421). Instead, understanding the distinctions between private opinions, information gathered through consulting many informants, and public ceremonial practices, one had to look for the answers in corresponding customs, in which beliefs like those surrounding the dead would be unmistakably documented. Malinowski insisted on a difference between his own approach and what he described as Durkheim's metaphysical use of a "collective soul." He nevertheless argued that native beliefs could be treated as invariably fixed. They were the dogma or "social ideas of a community" rather than individual ideas. "Believed and acted upon by all," he thought that because customary actions did not permit individual varieties, "this class of belief is standardized by its social embodiments." The one qualification necessary was to note that, among the many social institutions, only those ideas that natives explicated and recognized themselves could be regarded as social ideas (ibid.: 423). In further reflections Malinowski engaged the interrelations between belief, behavior, and opinions, and the different contexts in which they occurred. While natives recognized classes of specialists who represented orthodox and authoritative understanding of particular topics, Malinowski argued for the need to distinguish specialist views from those of the profane public, and also between "the general opinion of a given community" and "the private speculations of individuals" (ibid.: 428). As we shall see, the distinctions Malinowski began developing in understanding belief in its diverse social manifestations will also help us understand key elements of the relations between ethnology and economics, and yet also point to important limits in the extent to which Malinowski thought his ethnological investigations could bear upon the economics of his own society.

Secondly, although Malinowski's work on Baloma referred only glancingly to economic concerns in a passage on Trobriand treatment of the yam harvest, he signaled his interest in these issues with the promise that in another place he would describe the complex and fascinating feature of "Kiriwinian social economics" that was represented in their system of mutual garden duties (Malinowski 1916: 372). Similarly, the subject matter of each of Malinowski's next two articles led him to comment briefly but insistently on the salience of economic features. Writing for *Man* in 1918 he offered an account of Trobriand fishing as a significant economic pursuit that was entwined with magical customs, drawing attention to the prescriptive rights that were expressed in the diverse ways that different catches were distributed among participants and villagers with different ownership rights over coral patches, the canoe and equipment used, or rights stemming from participation in expeditions on the fringing reef or open sea shark fishing (Malinowski 1918: 89–90). With fish plentiful, it was the privilege of giving that animated customary ceremonial distributions of the catch. Once these were completed, everyone in the village could get as much as they wanted—even "dogs, cats, pigs, white men, and their native cooks" (ibid.: 90). Two years later, Malinowski followed this with his first detailed description of the elaborate expeditions and exchange of valuables in the Kula, "a special system of trade with a remarkable bearing on questions of primitive economics" (Malinowski 1920: 97). Malinowski emphasized the highly unusual form of ownership this involved, with each article, whether an armshell or string of shells, being held for a year or two at most before it was passed on. The renown it conferred was far more important than any use value. Delicate questions of trust and honor were engaged in the way each gift gave rise to the obligation to return a counter-gift in due course (ibid.: 100). On this occasion Malinowski emphasized the preliminary character of his account and underlined that, while economic in the sense that they concerned the desire for wealth and ownership, the conception of value and kind of ownership displayed were so different from those current "amongst us" that a more detailed analysis of Trobriand economic ideas would be required (ibid.: 105).

This, then, confers significant interest in the fact that Malinowski preceded and followed *Argonauts* with papers published in *The Economic Journal* (1921) and *Economica* (1922b). Devoted respectively to the primitive economics, or what he called the "Tribal Economy," of Trobriand Islanders, and to the application of ethnology to the study of society, in the first Malinowski made an argument for an anthropological contribution to economics in the journal of the Royal Economic Society, while in the second he drew on his own expertise and experience to raise major questions about colonial administration and the public role of anthropology in the newly founded house journal of the London School of Economics. To give a sense of the company Malinowski courted and kept, other articles in these issues concerned the history of corn prices and the corn law (Fay 1921), international labor legislation (Bauer 1921), postwar wholesale and retail prices (Bowley 1922), and the theory of progress (Ginsberg 1922). Morris Ginsberg had recently joined LSE as a sociologist, having collaborated with L. T. Hobhouse and G. C. Wheeler in a comparative study of the material culture and social institutions of "the simpler peoples" (Hobhouse, Wheeler, and Ginsberg 1930). In 1923 Malinowski and Seligman supported his gaining a readership at the same time as Malinowski. Malinowski's two articles promoted incipient cross-disciplinary conversations between economics and anthropology, and about the public significance of anthropology; and they did so in new terms. Over time and in concert with *Argonauts*, they helped found economic anthropology as a field of study. More immediately, they were central in helping Malinowski articulate the academic value of anthropology outside its customary bounds, to a different implied reader than his work in anthropological journals or even the broad audience he envisaged for *Argonauts*.

Having briefly set the scene for Malinowski's work linking ethnography and economics by charting its gradual unfolding in his early papers, the rest of this chapter will develop in four stages. I will first consider the principal precedents, both positive and negative, that Malinowski identified for his pioneering approach, and then turn to a significant stimulus about which he said very little, his earliest work in the philosophy of science. This will help clarify central features of the epistemology underlining Malinowski's methodological mission. Turning to an account of the papers themselves, my final two sections will reflect on what these papers show about

Malinowski's understanding of disciplinary knowledge and its relation to lay thought; and on what Malinowski described as the "New Humanism" imbuing his scholarly ideals. Once more a key point will be to observe revealing silences in Malinowski's work; complementing the intellectual histories and rich biographical studies of Robert J. Thornton, Peter Skalník, and Michael Young with recent historical accounts of shells in circulation and the concept of "the economy" will allow me to develop an account of the significance and limits of Malinowski's engagement with Trobriand and (critically) other economies.

Precedents: Exemplars and Foils

Malinowski's article "The Primitive Economics of Trobriand Islanders" offered a "resumé" of a series of lectures given at the LSE in the summer term of 1920. Its opening observation was that very little had been written about the economics of primitive races and that this was devoted principally to the origins of economic institutions (especially property), stages of development, questions of exchange and "primitive money," and the division of labor. Malinowski refers directly to only one other writer, strongly critiquing Karl Bücher's conclusion in *Industrial Evolution* that savages are in pre-economic stages, committed at the lowest level to an individual search for food and at a higher level to self-sufficient household economies, but in any case lacking economic organization (Malinowski 1921: 1).[1] Malinowski had been a student of Bücher's in the three semesters he spent in Leipzig in 1909–10. He argued that it was insufficient evidence rather than faulty logic or method that had misled Bücher. The burden of his article was to provide "some data" bearing on economic life in the Trobriands. Like Bücher, Malinowski accepted hierarchies of culture and savagery, but he would show that, although they might be less developed culturally than some others, Trobriand Islanders displayed distinct forms of economic organization. Given these findings, he thought one could infer that facts of economic interest would be found among all levels of culture (ibid.: 2). In fact Malinowski had developed a similar perspective in earlier work on Australian Aboriginal customs, drawing on the work of Baldwin Spencer, Francis Gillen, and Carl Strehlow to argue that Aboriginal ceremonies had economic implications even though there was no money involved (Malinowski 1993b). Perhaps because he wished to rest his work on his own empirical foundations, these arguments went unmentioned as Malinowski developed instead a portrait of the resources involved in Trobriand life, with its extensive produce gardens and fishing enabling perennial abundance in foods. He noted their industrious manufactures, but also the need to import stone and pottery given the absence of these on the coral archipelago (Malinowski 1921: 2–3).

After a brief general economic outline covering resources, pursuits and crafts, and material technologies, Malinowski developed his own approach, which highlighted the complexities of Trobriand social organization mediated by magic and mythical ideas. He unfolded his perspective by discussing in sequence materials bearing on several concepts integral to economic thought, in each case showing how differently they must be understood in the Trobriands: first ownership or land tenure, then production and labor (its rhythms dictated by the garden magician), and then the apportioning of food, which involved the authority of the chief and different kinds of wealth, which could be treated as forms of finance and banking.

In this 1921 article, as in *Argonauts* and "Ethnology and the Study of Society," Malinowski conveyed a clear sense of traditional approaches and his intention to disrupt them. However, the introductory chapter of *Argonauts* began by pointing to two positive ethnological exemplars in earlier studies of several New Guinea trade networks, notably the *hiri*, in which the Motu of Port Moresby sailed hundreds of miles along the Papuan coast, and trade routes pursued by the Southern Massim. Both had been described in Seligman's major book *The Melanesians of British New Guinea* (Seligmann 1910; note that Seligman shortened his name after 1914). Following Seligman, Malinowski praised the wealth of detail and clarity of Captain Francis Barton's chapter on the *hiri* (Barton 1910; Malinowski 1922a: 1). He went further in describing the methodological importance of Seligman's own careful tracing of the circulation of valuable axes (Malinowski 1922a: 1–2, 14). Yet although both men and their writings were extremely important—and more than foundational—for Malinowski, as we shall see, their work also illustrated the limitations of earlier research on primitive economy.

In his chapter on the trade carried out by the Southern Massim in the southeast of British New Guinea, Seligman (1910: 527) described Tubetube as "an island of merchant venturers." He used a British Museum catalogue to abstract a list of sixteen or more items and materials that were or had formerly been imported to Tubetube quite regularly, including obsidian slivers used for shaving, stone blocks used for hearthstones (and previously whetstones), and the *igo* reed from which flutes were manufactured (ibid.: 536). As well as providing a methodological example, the subject matter of Seligman's chapter was extremely important to Malinowski. Seligman noted the Rev. M. K. Gilmour's brief discussion of voyages and expeditions in the 1904–5 *Annual Report of British New Guinea*, some of which were purely for trade, while others involved circulating articles of native wealth (ibid.: 529). This led Seligman to suggest the research that would lead to

Malinowski's identification of the Kula (and in the closing pages of *Argonauts*, Malinowski (1922a: 500–2) pointed to the accuracy of Gilmour's understanding of Kula). Seligman also carefully stipulated what had been traded for named ceremonial axes in different places. The stone axe named Budia "was sold to a Yanaba man for one canoe, one *sapisapi* belt and certain other articles, and then to an Egum man for one pair of *masiwaru*, two pigs and certain other unspecified articles" (Seligmann 1910: 532; see also 517–20). Malinowski was to attempt still more rigorous accounting in nailing down significant details of the Kula.

Yet Seligman was not as sure of the quality of his work on the Massim as he was of that on the Koita. He described his sixteen chapters on the latter as "probably the most trustworthy" because the information had been provided by the hereditary chief Ahuia Ova, who had learned English and could write Motu (Seligmann 1910: ix). Their discussions had mostly taken place on the veranda of the house in which Ova lived, surrounded by contemporaries with a lively interest who could explain any difficulties; and the chapter had also been checked by Barton. In sum, these were unusually favorable conditions for writing on people in the region. Seligman's chapters followed methods that W. H. R. Rivers had helped pioneer and considered many features of Koita life, such as midwifery, property and inheritance, morals, and ceremonial feasts. In four pages on "Trade," he described one or two earlier markets that had often led to intergroup conflict; but these were insignificant and had been discontinued before the advent of the white man. He noted that the opening of a store in Port Moresby had increased trade, and led some communities to abandon their gardens and rely on imported food. It paid white traders to spend four or five weeks sailing up the Papuan coast and then beating down against the monsoon, selling sago for cash. But most of Seligman's discussion detailed the trades carried out by particular groups, such as the rich variety of goods from coconuts and petticoats to shell ornaments and smoked fish that the Hula would bring (many obtained from tribes still further away) in order to receive pots and sago from the Koita and Motu (ibid.: 92–95: see 92 for recent trade, 93 for the Hula, 94–95 for markets).

Having provided this account of ordinary trade, Seligman deferred to Barton's account of the *hiri* expeditions of the Motu for a reliable guide to Koita customs (Seligman 1910: 92). In fact Barton's chapter was very different in character. It described the elaborate myth that pointed to the origins of the *hiri*, the taboos that kept the husband and crew member as far apart from his wife as possible in preparation for the journey (as well as other food taboos), the songs and ceremonial practices that accompanied different steps of the journey, and a vocabulary of the trading language used. But

Barton's chapter was also marked by the author's linguistic uncertainty, especially pertaining to the songs (the meaning of which was often unknown to the participants), and by the fact that he had not himself witnessed the arrival of trading canoes in the Gulf, but instead relied on the testimony of many men who had (Barton 1910). In short, the writings of those who had worked in New Guinea before him offered helpful guides but also served Malinowski as an inducement for more rigorous and comprehensive research; and we should also note that they often illustrated a concern with colonial as well as native trade.

In addition to these ethnographic exemplars, in each of these different settings Malinowski established significant negative examples. In "Primitive Economics" and more explicitly *Argonauts* he identified foils that he claimed were haunting both the specialist literature and popular thought. In "Ethnology and the Study of Society," Malinowski railed against the superficial understanding and harmful prejudices of some colonial administrators and missionaries (while carefully pointing to several exceptions). Expanding on his 1921 critique of Bücher, the most significant foil in *Argonauts* was the idea of Primitive Economic Man that Malinowski argued could be found throughout the economic literature—popular and semipopular, as well as in some economic textbooks—but also inhabited the minds of anthropologists. Malinowski aimed to "explode" the image of an imaginary savage motivated by rationalistic conceptions of self-interest, achieving his aims directly, with minimum effort. In his discussions of garden work, he also repeatedly challenged preconceptions about native laziness. Instead of such misconceptions, he argued that the activities of Trobriand Islanders were guided by "highly complex motives of a social and traditional nature and ... aims which are certainly not directed towards present wants" (Malinowski 1922a: 60). Their garden endeavors, fueled by extensive display and produced to a large extent for the chief and their sister's (or mother's) husband and family, showed that time and effort were spent on work that was superfluous from a short-term utilitarian point of view. This work was both an end in itself and a means to elicit the praise and renown of being known as a good gardener. Malinowski elaborated on such preconceptions in considering primitive trade (developing his arguments against Bücher in greater detail in this context), and in discussing ideas about wealth and value (or possessions and gift and counter-gift giving). He showed how deeply the social and moral obligations of Trobriand Islanders contradicted Western assumptions about crude barter. Stereotypes of possessive greed untrammeled by social convention were as wide of the mark as idealizations of "primitive communism" (ibid.: 84–85, 95–98, 167–76). He returned to the limitations of Primitive Economic Man in summarizing his conclusions at the end of *Argonauts* (ibid.: 516).

Origins and Guiding Orientations

Before engaging more fully with the outcomes of Malinowski's work as reflected in his publications for economists, I want to note two important respects in which we might recognize significant origins and guiding orientations for his approach in his earliest work. It has frequently been observed that the fieldwork era of anthropology in the late nineteenth and early twentieth century was often driven by scientists who developed ethnographic interests in the course of expeditions initially pursued with other aims (e.g., Kuklick 2011). One of the best known examples is the zoologist-turned-ethnographer Alfred Cort Haddon, who led the 1898 Torres Strait expedition that introduced the physician and pathologist Seligman to ethnographic work. In some ways Malinowski's path to ethnography was more direct, but his university work in Kraków and 1906 doctoral thesis "On the Principle of the Economy of Thought" did begin with significant work in the laboratory sciences as well as with philosophy of science. Robert Thornton and Peter Skalník have argued that his examination of the work of the Austrian physicist Ernst Mach in his dissertation was particularly important in orienting Malinowski's concerns, alongside his reading of Friedrich Nietzsche (Thornton and Skalník 1993, esp. 26–38; see also Young 2004: 82–90). In a recent chapter on "The Economic Explanation" (Staley 2023), I have considered how Malinowski absorbed and then transformed Mach's epistemological stances in the context of a new discipline. Mach argued that science was principally concerned with the convenience and saving of thought, a view he had found expressed particularly clearly by the political economist Emanuel Herrmann (Mach 1911: 55, 88). Mach first expounded it at length in an account that warned against fetishizing science as magic, or mythologizing mechanics; and he developed his argument that the aim of science was (merely) to provide the most economical description of phenomena in discussing the relations between physics, physiology, and psychology (Mach 2014, where reference is made to Herrmann 1873 on p. 192; Mach 1883: 452–66; 1919: 481–94). This helped Malinowski write with such clarity about the methodological strictures of the physical sciences when introducing his approach to ethnography in *Argonauts* (1922a: 2–3). Mach is also known for his rigorous empiricism, a stance that Malinowski replicated in developing robust sociological perspectives in the face of the bewildering variety of testimony he met in the field. It is revealing, then, that Malinowski's primary critique of Mach (following Richard Avenarius) was that, in focusing on the demand for economy of thought in mathematical and physical principles and the psychological treatment of scientific law, he had neglected the sociological dimensions of scientific work. Malinowski (1993a: 104, 112–13) argued that science is a collective social process that does not depend on the psychological insight of a typical, normal man, or a plebiscite of humanity. This was an early example of the strategy he pursued in critiquing the concept of Primitive Economic Man and other idealized images of putatively typical perspectives; science is socially collective, not psychologically individual, and so is primitive economics.

Analysts have commonly focused on Mach's strictures against metaphysics without recognizing that his epistemology was specifically designed to yield an understanding of science that did not have to be abandoned when moving from one discipline to another—such as from the physical to the social sciences. For Mach, the processes of thought were similar in all fields. Achieving economy in the household was no different from doing so in scientific work. In Malinowski's argument against assumptions and his insistence on developing ethnographic facts—guided by theory (or leading questions) but always tested by the widest field of phenomena possible—we can see a creative development of Mach's approach in quite new contexts, with a stronger emphasis on the role of theory and metaphysical commitments (as Michael Young argues in his discussion in this volume of the relations between them). Mach had also insisted that physical knowledge should be approached within the frame of biological evolution, and argued for the need to approach relations functionally, rather than through monocausal arguments. Malinowski's readiness to see scientific knowledge in the pragmatic activities of Trobriand Islanders mirrored Mach's discussions of the power of instinctive knowledge, and his efforts to relate social phenomena to their functional roles echoed Mach's concerns in new ways.[2]

In short, although Mach's economies of thought and things were concerned with efficiency rather than exchange, recognizing long-term continuities in Malinowski's concerns helps us to grasp his ability to see economic relations in tribal contexts where other observers would see no place for modern economic thought. It is time, now, to examine more closely the arguments Malinowski developed for the economists of his time.

Disciplinary and Lay Thought—and Gaps and Side-Steps

Malinowski framed his 1921 discussion of primitive economics principally in terms of conventional economic concepts. At the most general level these were production, apportionment, and exchange. In each case Malinowski showed that customs in the Trobriand Islands involved complex social rights and obligations that introduced new layers of meaning for standard economic theory. These would be misunderstood if native testimony was approached superficially through the lens of concepts such as ownership or money. Malinowski had become aware of complexities of this kind in receiving diverse answers to questions about the ownership of garden plots, when informants might point to the village chief, the garden magician, or different individuals as the owner of the very same plot. In early passages on land tenure, intended to convey to his economist readers the subtlety and rigor of ethnological methodology, Malinowski (1921: 3) stressed the need to avoid giving "our own meaning of 'ownership' to the corresponding native word." The native concept involved several different legal and economic senses that needed to be distinguished from one another. The solution was a layered concept recognizing over-rights and particular rights to garden plots, with the authority of the chief, the prestige of the magician, and magical rites all important in the rhythms of production. Magic helped to establish the organization of work (its ordering, systematization, and regulation), in ways that Malinowski thought force and reason could not have done in a culture at this stage of development (ibid.: 6). This allowed him to assimilate his empirical findings into an implicit framework of cultural evolution. The investigations of yam production, taken up again in loving detail in his last Trobriand monograph, *Coral Gardens and Their Magic* (Malinowski 1966), are the outstanding example of the complex interweaving of factors that Malinowski regarded as central to tribal life. He argued that the same was true of fishing, house and canoe-building, and big trading expeditions. They were all socially organized by legal norms and custom along with magical and mythical ideas—and just as understanding economic activity required recognizing this complexity, one could not approach any single element of tribal life without also considering the economic perspective (Malinowski 1921: 7).

I wish to highlight two features of the way Malinowski addressed economists in this 1921 article. The first is the extent to which his discussion was framed in terms of the mutual benefits that ethnologists and economists would gain *as specialists* from these new empirical materials. On the one hand, the ethnologist considering any aspect of tribal life would fail if they did not take account of economic features. On the other, with more accounts of native economics of similar detail to Malinowski's pioneering effort, comparative analysis might enable the economist "to grasp the nature of the economic mechanism of savage life, and incidentally we might be able to answer many questions referring to the origins and development of economic institutions." Given the stimulation and broadening of "wide comparison and sharp contrast," Malinowski thought economic theory, the explicit subject of his concerns, would be refreshed and fertilized by the study of primitive economic institutions (Malinowski 1921: 12).

The second feature I wish to note is that these specialist dividends depended upon the integrity of the dense interrelations between economic and other facets of tribal life that Malinowski had articulated. These led Malinowski (1921: 15) to give a name to what he regarded as a novel empirical reality: Tribal Economy.[3] However, this conceptual innovation reflects both a strength of and subtle limitations to Malinowski's approach. His considerations tended to isolate tribal from other economies, treating them apart without asking how they were enmeshed in other economic and commercial relations empirically. Nor did he pursue how understanding tribal economies might relativize Western economics itself, generating critical new perspectives on its concepts. Unlike Seligman's descriptions of trade, Malinowski barely considered the implications of colonial relations and trade. In describing the chief's wealth in specific ornamental and other objects he states that about 80 percent of *Vaygu'a* in the village remained in the chief's hands—or at least that was the proportion before the white man's influence had undermined their power and all tribal law; similarly he writes that the chief "is (or more correctly, in olden days was) the owner of three-quarters of all the pigs, coconuts and betel nuts in the district" (ibid.: 10). He devoted considerable care to showing why the trade and gift exchanges he observed among Trobriand Islanders should not be assimilated to the concept of money, and then simply commented briefly that "Of course, when a savage community comes into commercial relations with a higher culture—as in Africa, where trading between Arabs and Europeans has long taken place—then money can and even must exist," without considering how money and other exchanges were interrelated among the groups concerned (ibid.: 14–15).

These points will remind many readers that in the well-known "Confessions of Ignorance and Failure" in Appendix II to *Coral Gardens and Their Magic*, in which Malinowski set out "Gaps and Side-Steps" and "Errors of Omission and Commission" from which his work had suffered, he also expressed regret at the fact that he had done so little to analyze the significance of the colonial setting on the changing character of Trobriand life, having early in the book considered the varied ways that the pearl trade had shaped Trobriand economics (Malinowski 1966: 18–20 (on pearl-fishing), App. II, esp. 479–81). But leaving the matter with this later explicit recognition would not do justice either to the analytic complexity of Malinowski's work, or the extent to which *Argonauts* and his paper on colonial administration show that in 1922 Malinowski did, in fact, consider the difficulties of recognizing native integrity and colonial power. Critically, he treated both groups in similar terms, but tracing several revealing silences in his work will help me point to important limitations in the extent to which Malinowski was able to acknowledge significant relationships that bore on economic relations in the region, and on his vision of tribal economy. In the terms of Foks (this volume), this work will offer a means of knitting together the politics of method and imperialism in Malinowski's work, by exploring fissures and absences.

I have shown here that, from as early as his *Baloma* paper, methodologically Malinowski approached the varied statements obtained from informants when asking about native belief with a careful recognition of distinctions between lay opinions and specialist perspectives (such as those of the magician or industrial manufacturer), together with an insistence on the need to understand all the circumstances and behavior in which particular ideas were implicated. The opening sections of his account of methodology in *Argonauts* work through a similar set of distinctions—but this time in the position of the Ethnographer introduced to a particular region, initially in the company of "some white trader or missionary," encountering also their beliefs about the natives (Malinowski 1922a: 4–11; Malinowski routinely capitalized Ethnography and Ethnographer). Michael Young has shown that the Trobriand Islands were undoubtedly the most organized and efficiently administered part of the region, under the control of R. A. Bellamy (whose handling of food also meshed with Trobriand conceptions of wealth) (Young 2004: 382–90). Malinowski's (1922a: 4–8) famous sketch of the Ethnographer's arrival does not mention any colonial official, but argues that the limitations of this mode of engagement through white company must be surmounted by living alone in the native village and becoming fluent in the native's language, and notes the necessity of being prepared with foreshadowed problems to bring scientific aims into gathering material and surpass any preconceptions.

There are both conceptual and practical correlates of this methodological argument in Malinowski's treatment of the relations among which the Ethnographer is embedded. On the one hand he argues that the trustworthiness of ethnographic description depends on giving a much more careful account of sources than is customary, one that makes the distinctions between native informant perspectives and the Ethnographer's authorial interpretations clear (Malinowski 1922a: 3, 15). We can regard this care for the relations between native and ethnographic vision as a necessary precondition and complement to Malinowski's somewhat abstract but rhetorically brilliant concluding argument that understanding the native point of view in its own terms has its ultimate dividend in the wisdom that a true "Science of Man" may confer on European understanding of its own culture, for "our final goal is to enrich and deepen our own world's vision, to understand our own nature and make it finer, intellectually and artistically." The rest of this penultimate paragraph makes clear that in the aftermath of World War I this was also a moral argument (ibid.: 517–18).

On the other hand, in *Argonauts* Malinowski does describe some of the specific economic and scholarly relations that enabled him to carry out his work in ways invisible in "The Primitive Economics of the Trobriand Islands." These are first outlined in his foreword and elaborated in the acknowledgments, but they also enter his discussions of methodology and the body of the text. They centered on his debts to Mond and also Seligman, to whom the volume is dedicated as both friend and teacher, yet went much further—while also being marked by revealing omissions (even in the act of disclosure), side steps that point to the interrelated complexities of imperial trade, colonial administration, and personal relationships in a period of war. In particular, Malinowski notes the financial assistance and "on the spot" help of Atlee Hunt, C. M. G., secretary of the Home and Territories Department of the Commonwealth of Australia (who he actually met in Melbourne). He does not note any local colonial officials, not even Bellamy (Malinowski 1922a: xvii). Similarly, the aid received from Paul Khuner of Vienna is acknowledged warmly. Malinowski describes him as "an expert in the practical affairs of modern industry and a highly competent thinker on economic matters," without noting the character of his business interests. They became friends in Melbourne in 1917, after Khuner and his wife (like Malinowski, Austrian subjects) were rounded up when war broke out while they were visiting a German New Guinea copra plantation (now under Australian control). Khuner's family manufactured chocolate, soaps, and margarine from coconuts (Young 2004: 457). As for Bellamy, he had induced coconut planting by natives on a large scale on Kiriwina with rewards for meeting quotas and jail for failing to do so, thereby abrogating the chiefly monopoly (ibid.: 386).[4] Addressing the British and Australian commission on Pacific trade in 1916, Malinowski was critical of the system of plantation labor and migration that was being introduced in northern and eastern regions of New Guinea, but spoke favorably of Bellamy's work (Australia Interstate Commission 1918: App. G, 107–8; Foks, this volume; Smith, this volume). It is fruitful to follow Foks in reading Malinowski's arguments about the Kula (depending principally on later fieldwork) as a mirror-image of his 1916 critique of the colonial treatment of plantation labor, yet it is also revealing that in 1921 and 1922 Malinowski wrote about tribal economy without referring to coconut growing. This is despite the fact that Malinowski expressed regret at the diminution of chiefly power, describing this as due to the colonial prohibition of polygamy, which cut the chief off from the wealth required to hold the expected feasts, core to native life, and to the increased relative wealth of coastal villages through their participation in the pearl trade (Malinowski 1922a: 464–68).

Another key relationship was Malinowski's long-term friendship with the pearl trader Billy Hancock, who made it possible for him to present a collection of ethnographic materials to the Melbourne Museum and who was the source for the photos Malinowski published of the working of the

Kaloma or spondylus shell into the necklaces that circulated in the Kula (Malinowski 1922a: xvii, xix, and plates L–LII).⁵ Dániel Margócsy has recently offered a brilliant account of the tension between understanding shell specimens as unique or duplicate in regulating their exchange both commercially and among museums, arguing that a common concern and sometimes similar dynamic must be recognized among Melanesian participants in the Kula and European natural historians and collectors. Margócsy shows how Malinowski's interpretation of Trobriand economics depended on his argument that the division of labor was also critical in what he regarded as premodern Trobriand life; and that in 1914 the regional administrator C. B. Higginson had been called in to adjudicate questions arising from the breakdown of specific exchanges that mixed Kula and barter, something Malinowski denied was possible (although we should note that he also recognized that trade and barter accompanied Kula expeditions and similar items) (Margócsy 2022: 397–98 on division of labor and 405–0820 on Kula and other exchanges).

Like the coconuts that Bellamy counted but Malinowski left unmarked, Margócsy's discussion of a mixed but global trade in spondylus shells is a valuable illustration of the extent to which we may follow Malinowski's methodological and analytic lead, and yet set tribal and other economies in still fuller conceptual and practical relations by understanding them more deeply historically, extending further the rich anthropological and colonial contexts in which Young has embedded his biography of Malinowski.

Malinowski's work can also be invoked to relativize mainstream Euro-American economics. For example, Chris Gregory has suggested that unsatisfactory ideas about the market mechanism today can be critiqued via the thought of Malinowski and John Maynard Keynes on uncertainty and risk (Gregory 2017: 1; Gregory, this volume). My study of "The Economic Explanation" sought to further this goal by showing that Malinowski's 1921 conception of national economy is as revealing historically as his innovative use of the concept of Tribal Economy (Staley 2023). Malinowski (1921: 15) drew on Bücher's accounts of national economy in arguing that Trobriand Islanders certainly did not possess one, if this meant "a system of free competitive exchange of goods and services, with the interplay of supply and demand determining value and regulating all economic life." Leading economists of the era such as Frank Knight (and, somewhat later, Friedrich von Hayek) were well aware that this conception of the market was best understood as an ideal, a prevalent Western model, and in their eyes a desirable one (Knight 1933: 9; Hayek 1937, 1945). Historians Timothy Mitchell and Daniel Hirschman have argued persuasively that, in the English language, a singular concept of "the economy" as a bounded mechanistic whole was consolidated only in the 1920s and 1930s with the management of colonial economies like that of India and the development of concepts of Gross Domestic Product (Mitchell 2002: 81–82; 2005; Hirschman 2016). Following Mitchell, I argued that historical work on general, framing concepts like the economy and less explicitly marked but nevertheless formative concepts like mechanism and system—shared by both economists and anthropologists, Malinowski, Knight, Keynes, and Hayek, and running through popular and lay thought—might set our understanding of economic and anthropological thought in mutual interplay (Staley 2023). Addressing similar aims, in this section I have underlined the analytic and methodological significance of Malinowski's work with concepts and behavior across lay and specialist realms in both fields, but also argued for the possibility of achieving this still more comprehensively than Malinowski could in the early 1920s.

Conclusion: Malinowski's "New Humanism" and the Future of Scholarship

In 1935 Malinowski used an appendix to incorporate an explicit discussion of limitations to his work on *Coral Gardens and Their Magic*. It is telling that it was in a note referring to his section on the magic of coconuts that Malinowski (1966: 479–81) made his general argument that the attitude with which he had previously observed the facts of contact and change "was false," both in theory and practice. Given this turn of mind, it is revealing to see that very soon after the publication of *Argonauts* he addressed the same question of the decay of custom under European influence, in ways that show the strength of his moral response, but also some of its intellectual limitations. While the closing pages of *Argonauts* set an ideal goal for ethnology in enriching and deepening "our own world's vision," "Ethnology and the Study of Society" (Malinowski 1922b) engages a dichotomy similar to the contrast I have developed in considering the conceptual and practical features of Malinowski's analytic and methodological stance. Although seldom considered, the article articulated more fully and directly than *Argonauts* both how ethnology might be practically useful to colonial administration by providing greater insight into specific customs in different settings and "savage morality" more generally (the bulk of its argument), and how it might simultaneously widen perspectives on human nature by providing a new theory of society (the concern Malinowski took up in its final four pages). It offered a significant expansion of the context-contingent judgment of colonial administration that Malinowski had expressed in his 1916 testimony, but was oriented in particular toward the problem of the gradual dying out of native races, rather than problems of labor and immigration (ibid.: 209). He raised these questions from the perspective of colonial politics, but moved straight on to consider the destruction of all that was precious in native life through the introduction of superficial legislation. The argument was that ethnological insight would have prevented many of the worst crimes of colonial administration, so often occasioned by overly hasty responses to sexual customs, dancing, even warfare and cannibalism; and it is striking that his rhetoric on crime so effectively reversed the customary perspective (ibid.: 211). The answer to these problems was gradual change based on scientific ethnology, "preserving the integrity of native life so far as possible so as to prevent complete extinction" (ibid.: 214–15).

In the final pages Malinowski turned to his more general aim, outlining key elements of the empirically based Science of Man that he thought should pursue real utility in the conduct of affairs. He cautioned against relying on modern historical methods for this empirical material, for the contemporary sociologist needed insight into more obscure realms: "the fundamental forces of human society, the forms of social constitution, the types of economic organization, the great moral, religious and philosophic tendencies of an age." History was too oriented toward great men and courtiers, whereas for Malinowski "To speak of leaders and forget the led is an error of method" (Malinowski 1922b: 216). He argued that what was hidden in time was made visible in space in the extraordinary variety of phases of civilizations now accessible, as far distant as the Middle Ages, Homeric Greece, or the Neolithic. Ethnology now enabled a broadening as significant as the Renaissance and justified the call for a "New Humanism" (ibid.). While his right method might have led Malinowski to a new form of history, this also expresses very clearly the approach to history writ large that he was later to describe as the source of his false attitude: the attempt to read the history of mankind in the variety of customs still existing (Malinowski 1966: 480). In 1922, Malinowski used his argument for a New Humanism to point to specific material concerns for anthropology: the breadth in kinds of civilization had to be matched by a new breadth in the kind of data considered, and Malinowski concluded with a plea for the orientation his own work had represented. While a whole school of philosophers regarded the primary cause of social change as lying in economic organization, the best work on native races had almost without exception neglected the economic aspect. This showed the need to reform the methods of fieldwork "still more thoroughly in the direction of a *comprehensive treatment of all aspects of tribal life and their correlation*" (Malinowski 1922b: 218).

Despite the rhetorical vigor of Malinowski's innumerable public writings, here I have traced a critical irony in his work—and explored its implications for his vision of economics. He interpreted the Trobriands as an allegory of the world economy with its industrial, agricultural, and fishing centers and international trade (Hann and Hart 2011: 51), but although his formulation of the concept of Tribal Economy enabled Malinowski to represent the integrity of native life and customs, it also limited his ability to recognize and represent critical elements of its engagement with other economies. We can do more.

Acknowledgments

I am grateful to Freddy Foks, Dániel Margócsy, and Simon Schaffer for their careful reading and wise advice, and to Chris Gregory for the inspiration of his work.

Richard Staley is Professor in the Department of History and Philosophy of Science at the University of Cambridge and the Department of Science Education and Niels Bohr Archive at the University of Copenhagen. Since *Einstein's Generation and the Origins of the Relativity Revolution* (2008), he has developed a long-term project on physicist anthropologies and the cultural history of mechanics, while also leading collaborative projects on climate history and the histories of AI.

Notes

1. Bücher's *Industrial Evolution* was a translation of the third edition of a book that in its original German title examined "The Rise of National Economy." According to its translator's preface its first two chapters "emphasised the kinship between economics and ethnology" in a realistic portrait of prominent features of pre-economic life in the tropical zone, before outlining developmental stages of household, town, and national economy (Bücher 1901: iv).
2. In 1906 Malinowski argued that the concept of function expressed the interrelations and mutual dependence of phenomena (Malinowski 1993a). Young (2004: 87) has pointed to a similar tension between this understanding and the second sense in which both Mach and Malinowski referred to biologically or socially functional knowledge.
3. The term was certainly not new. Spittler (2008: 225–26) has linked it to Gustav Schmoller's work on mercantilism, but it was also used in English in the late nineteenth century (Gomme 1890: 24, 127; Bates 1878: 417).
4. Their first coconut crop was expected in 1922, but as Andrew Connelly (2018) has shown, the bottom fell out of the copra market. While one of Bellamy's successors continued a similar program, later Assistant Resident Magistrates had been trained in anthropology at the University of Sydney and did not pursue it.

5. It is also important to note one key economic resource: much of Malinowski's ability to gain information depended upon payments to interpreters, in particular donations of tobacco (Malinowski 1922a: xix, 4, 8).

References

Australia Interstate Commission. 1918. *British and Australian Trade in the South Pacific*. Report. Parliament of the Commonwealth of Australia (Melbourne: Government printer for the state of Victoria, A. J. Mullett).

Barton, F. R. 1910. "The Annual Trading Expedition to the Papuan Gulf." In *The Melanesians of British New Guinea*, ed. C. G. Seligman, 96–120. Cambridge: Cambridge University Press.

Bates, Henry Walter, ed. 1878. *Central America, the West Indies and South America*. London: Edward Stanford.

Bauer, Stephan. 1921. "Past Achievements and Future Prospects of International Labour Legislation." *The Economic Journal* 31(121): 28–37.

Bowley, Arthur L. 1922. "The Relation between Wholesale and Retail Prices since the War." *Economica* 6: 195–207.

Bücher, Karl. 1901. *Industrial Evolution*. New York: Henry Holt.

Connelly, Andrew. 2018. "To'uluwa and the Magistrates: Coconuts and Yams, Governance and Indigenous Agency in the Trobriand Islands, Papua New Guinea, 1912–41." *Journal of Pacific History* 53(4): 1–24.

Fay, C. R. 1921. "Corn Prices and the Corn Laws, 1815–1846." *The Economic Journal* 31(121): 17–27.

Ginsberg, Morris. 1922. "The Theory of Progress." *Economica* 6: 228–37.

Gomme, George Laurence. 1890. *The Village Community: With Special Reference to the Origin and Form of Its Survivals in Britain*. London: Walter Scott.

Gregory, C. A. 2017 [1982]. *Gifts and Commodities*. Chicago: HAU Books.

Hann, Chris, and Keith Hart. 2011. *Economic Anthropology: History, Ethnography, Critique*. Cambridge: Polity.

Hayek, F. A. von. 1937. "Economics and Knowledge." *Economica* 4(13): 33–54.

———. 1945. "The Use of Knowledge in Society." *American Economic Review* 35: 519–30.

Herrmann, Emanuel. 1873. *Prinzipien der Wirthschaft*. Vienna: Lehmann und Wentzel.

Hirschman, Daniel Abramson. 2016. "Inventing the Economy. Or: How We Learned to Stop Worrying and Love the GDP." PhD thesis. Ann Arbor: University of Michigan.

Hobhouse, L. T., G. C. Wheeler, and Morris Ginsberg. 1930 [1915]. *The Material Culture and Social Institutions of the Simpler Peoples: An Essay in Correlation*. London: Chapman & Hall.

Knight, Frank H. 1933 [1921]. *Risk, Uncertainty and Profit*. London: London School of Economics and Political Science.

Kuklick, Henrika. 2011. "Personal Equations: Reflections on the History of Fieldwork, with Special Reference to Sociocultural Anthropology." *Isis* 102: 1–33.

Mach, Ernst. 1883. *Die Mechanik in ihrer Entwickelung historisch-kritisch dargestellt*. Leipzig: F.A. Brockhaus.

———. 1911 [1872]. *History and Root of the Principle of the Conservation of Energy.* Chicago/London: Open Court/Kegan Paul, Trench, Trübner & Co.
———. 1919 [1902]. *The Science of Mechanics: A Critical and Historical Account of its Development.* Chicago: Open Court.
———. 2014 [1882]. "On the Economical Nature of Physical Inquiry." In *Popular Scientific Lectures*, ed. Ernst Mach and Thomas J. McCormack, 186–213. Cambridge: Cambridge University Press.
Malinowski, Bronisław. 1916. "Baloma: The Spirits of the Dead in the Trobriand Islands." *Journal of the Royal Anthropological Institute of Great Britain and Ireland* 46: 353–430.
———. 1918. "Fishing in the Trobriand Islands." *Man* 18: 87–92.
———. 1920. "Kula: The Circulating Exchange of Valuables in the Archipelagoes of Eastern New Guinea." *Man* 20: 97–105.
———. 1921. "The Primitive Economics of the Trobriand Islanders." *The Economic Journal* 31(121): 1–16.
———. 1922a. *Argonauts of the Western Pacific: An Account of Native Enterprise and Adventure in the Archipelagoes of Melanesian New Guinea.* London: Routledge & Kegan Paul.
———. 1922b. "Ethnology and the Study of Society." *Economica* 6: 208–19.
———. 1966 [1935]. *Coral Gardens and their Magic, Vol. 1: Soil-Tilling and Agricultural Rites in the Trobriand Islands.* London: Allen & Unwin.
———. 1993a [1906]. "On the Principle of the Economy of Thought." In *The Early Writings of Bronislaw Malinowski*, ed. Robert J. Thornton and Peter Skalník, 89–115. Cambridge: Cambridge University Press.
———. 1993b [1912]. "On the Economic Aspects of the *Intichiuma* Ceremonies." In *The Early Writings of Bronislaw Malinowski*, ed. Robert J. Thornton and Peter Skalník, 209–27. Cambridge: Cambridge University Press.
Margócsy, Dániel. 2022. "Malinowski and Malacology: Global Value Systems and the Issue of Duplicates." *British Journal for the History of Science* 55(3): 389–409.
Mitchell, Timothy. 2002. *Rule of Experts: Egypt, Techno-Politics, Modernity.* Berkeley: University of California Press.
———. 2005. "Economics: Economists and the Economy in the Twentieth Century." In *The Politics of Method in the Human Sciences: Positivism and Its Others in the Social Sciences*, ed. George Steinmetz, 126–41. Durham, NC: Duke University Press.
Seligmann, C. G. 1910. *The Melanesians of British New Guinea*, ed. E. L. Giblin. Cambridge: Cambridge University Press.
Spittler, Gerd. 2008. *Founders of the Anthropology of Work: German Social Scientists of the 19th and Early 20th Centuries and the First Ethnographers.* Berlin: Lit.
Staley, Richard. 2023. "The Economic Explanation." In *Beyond Description: Anthropologies of Explanation*, ed. Paolo Heywood and Matei Candea, 125–41. Ithaca, NY: Cornell University Press.
Thornton, Robert J., and Peter Skalník. 1993. "Introduction: Malinowski's Reading, Writing, 1904–1914." In *The Early Writings of Bronislaw Malinowski*, ed. Robert J. Thornton and Peter Skalník, 1–64. Cambridge: Cambridge University Press.
Young, Michael W. 2004. *Malinowski: Odyssey of an Anthropologist, 1884–1920.* New Haven, CT: Yale University Press.

7

Malinowski's Place in the History of Economic Thought

Chris Gregory

> We find a state of affairs where production, exchange and consumption are socially organised and regulated by custom, and where *a special system of traditional economic values* governs their activities and spurs them on to efforts. This state of affairs might be called—as a new conception requires a new term—Tribal Economy.
> —Bronisław Malinowski, "The Primitive Economics of the Trobriand Islanders" (emphasis added)

> Too large a proportion of recent "mathematical" economics are merely concoctions, as imprecise as the initial assumptions they rest on, which allow the author to lose sight of the complexities and interdependencies of the real world in a maze of pretentious and unhelpful symbols.
> —John Maynard Keynes, *The General Theory of Employment, Interest and Money*

Bronisław Malinowski's documentation and analysis of the early twentieth century Trobriand Islands economy as presented in *Argonauts* (1922), *Coral Gardens* (1935), and other monographs and articles are rightly seen as pathbreaking contributions to the history of anthropological thought. For Malinowski, the economy was inseparable from society and culture. Few ethnographers of the past century have been able to produce concrete analyses of non-European economies of comparable quality. The hallmark of his functionalist method of economic analysis was a concern to grasp the "native point of view" via a close linguistic analysis of the magical chants that punctuated all key phases of the economic process, be it in the annual cycle of yam production, overseas Kula expeditions, or fishing in the safety of the lagoon and in the dangerous open seas.

As indicated by the quotation above from his 1921 article in *The Economic Journal* summarizing his findings for the benefit of economists, Malinowski clearly considered his work to be a novel contribution to the history of economic thought generally. What distinguished his approach to comparative economic analysis, he argued, was his firsthand observations on the functioning of a "tribal economy" and his ability to question his informants about the motives for their actions in their own language. Not for him the construction of speculative economic histories based on secondary source material collected by missionaries and other visitors to non-European economies; not for him either the unrealistic assumptions that informed the economic theories of his day.

While Malinowski's place in the history of anthropological thought is secure, his concept of "tribal economy" has had no impact on the history of economic thought.[1] It is tempting to put the blame for this state of affairs on the arrogance and insularity of mainstream economists and their preference for mathematics over history, anthropology, or sociology. Raymond Firth, however, sees it otherwise. While acknowledging the "novelty of [Malinowski's] first-hand observations," the "verve and sincerity of his concrete exposition," and his concern with the "relationship between the economic and other aspects of the social system," Firth's overall judgment is harsh. In his opinion Malinowski's "knowledge of formal economics was always very limited; his approach to economic analysis began largely on a descriptive, common-sense level and for the most part continued to be unsophisticated" (Firth 1957: 209). This judgment must be taken seriously because few scholars are better qualified to make this assessment. Firth was initially trained in economics in New Zealand in the early 1920s. He then traveled to London to do a PhD in economics, met Malinowski, became his student, and wrote a library-based thesis on the economic life of the New Zealand Maori. Subsequently, Firth went to the Polynesian island of Tikopia to carry out pathbreaking anthropological fieldwork of his own. His theoretical approach was informed by an uncritical acceptance of the assumptions of the mainstream Marshallian tradition of economic thought in which he had been trained. This was the basis of his claim that Malinowski's understanding of economic thought was "unsophisticated."

With the benefit of hindsight more than half a century later, Firth's judgment can be questioned. As his early writings in Polish reveal (Malinowski 1993; Thornton and Skalník 1993), Malinowski understood key developments in nineteenth-century European intellectual thought very well. The 1870s was a turning point in the history of economic thought, often known as the "neoclassical revolution." As this term suggests, this tradition of thought stands opposed to the "classical" period, one defined by the works of theorists such as Adam Smith (1723–90), David Ricardo (1772–1823), and Karl Marx (1818–83). While the differences between the approaches of these three theorists are many, all drew on the labor theory of value in their analyses of price determination and the distribution of income. In Marx's hands, the labor theory of value became a theory of capitalist exploitation. While this theory appealed to revolutionaries such as Lenin (1870–1924), alternative theories of value based on the utilitarian theories of Bentham (1748–1832) and others attracted policymakers concerned with the efficient functioning of capitalism rather than its overthrow. Soon after Marx's *Capital* was published in German in 1867, W. Stanley Jevons (1835–82) and Carl Menger (1840–1921) published their alternative theories of value (in English and German respectively) in 1871. Léon Walras (1834–1910), a mathematician, published his version of essentially the same theory in French in 1872 (Gregory 2021).

The near simultaneous emergence of the marginal utility theory of value, the basis for the "neoclassical revolution," saw the birth of *Homo economicus*, a creature whose ways have been the subject of much fierce debate ever since. The proponents of this approach assert its superiority on the grounds of its universality. For Marxists, by contrast, this universality is precisely the problem because, for them, the task is to understand the workings of geographically and historically specific economies and to develop general theories grounded in cultural geography and political history. But neither Marxists nor mainstream economists speak with one voice. Many schools contend as different variations of the utility theory paradigm have risen and fallen in the changing political and economic environment of the world of which they are part.

Malinowski, like all of us, was a product of his time. If we are to grasp his place in the history of economic thought, we must contextualize him. We can get our bearings if we take John Maynard Keynes as our lodestar. Keynes's place in the history of European economic thought is beyond question. His *The General Theory of Employment, Interest and Money* (1936) defined the "Keynesian revolution" in mainstream economics. His aim was to develop a new theory of capitalism that would "knock away" the Ricardian foundations of Marxism with a new theory of time and economic uncertainty (Keynes 1937). It also eroded the foundations of neoclassical thought. Keynes was implacably opposed to Benthamite value theory and the unrealistic assumptions that informed neoclassical marginal utility theory. In this respect, Keynes and Malinowski were in full agreement. Both were pioneers when it came to the problem of economic uncertainty. The other key protagonist in this context was Frank Knight, whose *Risk, Uncertainty, and Profit* was published in 1921, the same year as Keynes's *Treatise on Probability*.

In September 2021, the *Cambridge Journal of Economics* published a special issue to mark the centenary of the first publication of these works by

Knight and Keynes. One of the questions the editors (Faulkner et al. 2021) rightly address in their introduction is that of the "parallels" in the distinction they draw between risk and uncertainty. Who was the first to make this distinction? They conclude that "Keynes and Knight are sufficiently close to be considered joint fathers of the risk/uncertainty distinction" (ibid.: 864). What the editors—and indeed all contributors to this issue—failed to notice is that Malinowski published an article for *The Economic Journal* in 1921 that was concerned with the very same distinction. Indeed, he was the first to discuss the relationship.

Frank Knight, unlike Keynes and Malinowski, vigorously defended the assumptions and methods of the neoclassical revolutionaries. Whereas Keynes argued that government regulation was necessary for the efficient functioning of capitalist market economies, Knight argued the contrary. Knight was the founder of the Chicago School of Economics, and his student, Milton Friedman, played a key role in ensuring the victory of a neoliberal school of thought over the Keynesian school in the 1970s.

Malinowski (1884–1942) and Keynes (1883–1946) were age mates and neighbors in Bloomsbury in the early 1910s. Malinowski was not part of the Bloomsbury set, but they knew each other. Keynes, in his capacity as joint editor of *The Economic Journal,* commissioned Malinowski to write his 1921 article on the economics of the Trobriand Islanders (Young 2004: 154, 156). While we know little about their interactions, it is clear that they shared fundamental assumptions about the problems with the orthodox economic theory of their day.

Whereas Knight (1885–1972) was also an age mate, Firth (1901–2002) was an intellectual generation below this trio. He was schooled in the Marshallian tradition of the neoclassical orthodoxy. Alfred Marshall (1842–1924), Keynes's senior at Cambridge, synthesized and developed the work of the neoclassical pioneers in a textbook that set the agenda over the period from the 1890s to the 1920s (Marshall 2013). The Keynesian revolution erupted in the late 1930s, well after Firth had completed his economics training. There is no evidence that Firth revised his thinking about the neoclassical orthodoxy in the light of Keynes's theory. His 1957 article, for example, contains no reference to Keynes or to uncertainty.

Against this background, a revaluation of Malinowski's place in the history of economic thought is in order. To grasp the specificity of Malinowski's contribution, we need to bear in mind that the neoclassical revolution in economic theory occurred during the era of European imperialism. From 1870 to 1914 Britain, Germany, and other European nations were involved in the scramble for territory in Africa and the Pacific. Keynes, Malinowski, and Knight were all the children of this era of imperialism. In 1884, the year of Malinowski's birth, Britain colonized Papua, and the Germans colonized

New Guinea (until ousted by the British during World War I). This created the conditions in which Malinowski could conduct his ahistorical functionalist analysis of an Austronesian yam, fishing, and Kula economy, and argue that magical rituals were a consequence of economic uncertainty. Keynes was concerned with the implications of economic uncertainty for the functioning of the European industrial economy, one whose gold standard—the basis of its monetary system—was severely disrupted by war. For both theorists, "participant observation" was crucial. For Keynes, this involved work in London, sometimes as a financial investor and sometimes as an adviser to governments. Their common intellectual legacy is not a set of prescriptions for what is to be done, but rather a way to think critically about dominant ideas and an invitation to ponder the existential fact of economic uncertainty for understanding the human condition in radically different sociopolitical settings.

I turn now to illustrate this argument by means of a comparative examination of the approaches of Malinowski and Keynes to economic analysis in general and the problem of uncertainty in particular.

Keynes, Malinowski, and the Critique of Neoclassical Economic Thought

The neoclassical revolution in economic thought is based on the assumption that we *Homo sapiens* "economize" as we go about the task of acquiring the food, clothing, and shelter that will enable us to survive and reproduce our species. If "economize" is understood as the "principle of least effort," then this argument is hard to gainsay. Generally speaking, people prefer more for less in their quest for food, clothing, and shelter. The evidence for such a proposition is overwhelming. When engaging in acts of consumption, production, distribution, or exchange people everywhere, be they merchants, hunters and gatherers, or swidden cultivators, tend to act sensibly and economize in this sense. If given the choice between spending $100 on one's weekly grocery needs at Store A or $200 at neighboring Store B for exactly the same goods, a reasonable shopper will buy from Store A. The principle of least effort also applies if the measure is labor time. A swidden cultivator faced with the choice between spending ten hours to clear a plot of land using a stone axe or two hours to clear the same plot using a steel axe prefers to do the latter. Again, much ethnographic evidence can be assembled to demonstrate this proposition (Salisbury 1962).

Apparent exceptions to these general propositions often turn out to prove them. In monsoon Asia, for example, we find two quite distinct methods of rice production. In southern China the labor-intensive transplantation method of production is used. On the plains of eastern India, in contrast, the labor-saving method of broadcast sowing is used. The Chinese system is more productive in the sense that the yield per unit of labor is twice as high as the Indian system. However, the Indian system persists because it is more economical given the ecological conditions found there. The transplantation system requires secure water supplies, which the intermontane valleys and weirs of China provide. Farmers on the plains of India, by contrast, must rely on the uncertain monsoon rains for their irrigation requirements. They have found through long experience that it is simply not economical for them to expend the extra time needed to practice the transplantation method, because delays in the arrival of the monsoon often result in crop failure and wasted labor.

The principle of least effort, then, is an economic principle of great generality. We *Homo sapiens* are "rational economic actors" in this sense. Indeed, because the principle is so "obvious" it verges on being axiomatic. When it is not obvious, as the rice production example shows, the problem may be with the reasoning of the ill-informed observer rather than with the alleged "irrational" actions of the observed. Whatever, it behooves the ethnographer to grasp the values that inform the actions of a worker: Benthamite utilitarian values, as Malinowski (1922: 60) rightly notes, are not universal; the work ethic of the Trobriand yam farmer makes no sense from this perspective.

While grasping the obviousness of the workings of the principle of least effort is a relatively simple task, giving the principle a generalized theoretical expression is quite another. This is because it poses the hoary question of value: the notions of "more" and "less" presuppose a common comparator. Jevons used Bentham's notion of "utilitarian" values and the subjective conceptions of "pleasure and pain" it presupposed. Using this theory of value, the idea of "more for less" can be expressed as "maximize pleasure, minimize pain." Mathematically trained economists like Jevons, Walras, Marshall, and others in the nineteenth-century neoclassical tradition adapted the work of mathematicians like Lagrange (1736–1832) and Hamilton (1805–65) on the calculus of the max-min principle to provide a rigorous method for exploring the logical implications of the economizing principle of least effort. This is why the theory of marginal utility emerged as the independent invention of Jevons, Menger, and Walras at almost the same time. The idea of the "margin" in differential calculus was attractive because the idea of marginal utility it implied made obvious economic sense. One gets pleasure from eating an ice cream or maybe even two; but the third and fourth will bring less satisfaction as the marginal utility of the last ice cream eaten falls toward zero.

The mathematical formulation of the marginal utility theory of value had the effect of universalizing Bentham's theory of utility and giving it a more abstract formulation. The expression "maximize pleasure, minimize pain" became "maximize utility subject to constraints." This reformulation of the principle was in fact a radical transformation of it. Firstly, the empirically generalizable obviousness of the principle of least effort was reformulated as an axiom, which meant that a general principle that admitted exceptions became a *universal* principle that admitted none. Secondly, the concrete study of people located in specific geographical places at specific historical times became the abstract study of individuals located in an abstract spatiotemporal world.

Such was the textbook version of neoclassical economic theory available to Malinowski and Keynes when they began their postgraduate studies. These universal individuals, the neoclassical theorist assumed, had perfect knowledge and perfect foresight. For Malinowski and Keynes, however, uncertainty was an existential fact of the human condition whose implications had far-reaching consequences for understanding the thoughts and actions of *Homo sapiens*. Human knowledge of the future is imperfect and to assume the contrary is to ignore the most fundamental of all human challenges.

From his studies of Ernst Mach's use of the principle of the "economy of thought," Malinowski (1993: 89–90) was well aware of the history of European philosophical and mathematical thinking about the "principle of least effort." He understood the influence of this history on the thinking of neoclassical economists. For Malinowski, economic theories based on the assumption of perfect knowledge were complete nonsense. He dismissed them out of hand in a much-quoted paragraph:

> Another notion which must be exploded, once and for ever, is that of the Primitive Economic Man of some current economic text books. This fanciful, dummy creature, who has been very tenacious of existence in popular and semi-popular economic literature, and whose shadow haunts even the minds of competent anthropologists, blighting their outlook with a pre- conceived idea, is an imaginary, primitive man, or savage, prompted in all his actions by a rationalistic conception of self-interest, and achieving his aims directly and with the minimum of effort. Even one well established instance should show how preposterous is this assumption that man, and especially man on a low level of culture, should be actuated by pure economic motives of enlightened self-interest. The primitive Trobriander furnishes us with such an instance, contradicting this fallacious theory. He works prompted by motives of a highly complex, social and traditional nature, and towards aims which are certainly not directed towards the satisfaction of present wants, or to the direct achievement of utilitarian purposes. (Malinowski 1922: 60)

Keynes was much more measured and considerate in his critique. His goal was to modify and develop mainstream economic thought about the functioning of European industrial economies rather than to develop novel theories of non-European tribal economies.[2] Keynes believed that realistic assumptions matter. For Keynes, a theory of economic uncertainty that began by assuming that economic agents have perfect foresight was problematic, but of interest because it posed anew the question of time. He noted that the "explicit introduction of the element of Time as a factor in economic analysis is mainly due to Marshall" (Keynes 1924: 351). Having outlined Marshall's pathbreaking ideas on time, "which no one who wants to think clearly can do without," Keynes adds that "this is the quarter in which, in my opinion, the Marshall analysis is least complete and satisfactory, and where there remains most to do. As Marshall says himself in the Preface to the first edition of the *Principles*, the element of time 'is the center of the chief difficulty of almost every economic problem'" (ibid.).

Time in the sense of "tomorrow" was a central problem because the emergence of the idea that profit is the "reward for waiting" made it so. Early nineteenth-century classical political economists did not pose this problem because they were concerned with the principles that governed the distribution of the previous year's surplus product between worker and capitalist. When Smith (1723–90) and Ricardo (1772–1823) were writing, agricultural production still dominated. Come the end of winter, farmers in Europe harvested and threshed the wheat. They piled up the newly threshed grain and physically divided it between the different classes entitled to a share, be they landlord, tenant, or worker. Ritual distributions of this kind survive until this day in many parts of the world (as I have witnessed myself in my fieldwork in rural India).

The new theory of profit, which took the entrepreneur's rather than the workers' point of view, was concerned with tomorrow's prices and profits, not with the distribution of yesterday's profits (Sraffa 1960). Keynes rejects the neo-Ricardian theory of Piero Sraffa and instead develops Marshall's theory of profit and time by highlighting the importance of expectations about tomorrow.

> All production is for the purpose of ultimately satisfying a consumer. Time usually elapses, however, and sometimes much time, between the incurring of costs by the producer (with the consumer in view) and the purchase of the output by the ultimate consumer. Meanwhile the entrepreneur (including both the producer and the investor in this description) has to form the best expectations he can as to what the consumers will be prepared to pay when he is ready to supply them (directly or indirectly) after the elapse of what may be a lengthy period; and he has no choice but to be guided by these expectations, if he is to produce at all by processes which occupy time. (Keynes 1967: 46)

What followed from this insight was a new theory of the functioning, or rather malfunctioning, of capitalism. The argumentation in Keynes's theory is notoriously difficult to follow, but the conclusion is as clear as the reasoning is complex: the free market system if left to itself is liable to malfunction and lead to chronic unemployment. Government intervention through fiscal and monetary policies can avert crises such as the Great Depression of the 1930s.

One of Keynes's most influential critics was Frank Knight, who defended the assumptions of the neoclassical revolutionaries against all comers. This included anthropologists and others who shared Malinowski's view about the "fanciful dummy figure" in the economist's textbooks.

> The principles of economy are known intuitively; it is not possible to discriminate the economic character of behavior by sense observation; and the anthropologist, sociologist, or historian seeking to discover or validate economic laws by inductive investigation has embarked on a 'wild goose chase.' (Knight 1941: 254)

What is at stake here is the epistemological status of the principle of least effort. For Knight the principle is known intuitively because it is a *universal* truth that transcends all places and times and admits of no exceptions; in other words, it is not a mere *generalization* that admits of exceptions in some historically specific places and times. The "more for less" principle is intuitive for Knight because it is axiomatic; so too are the logical implications that flow from this assumption, as the max-min mathematics developed by Lagrange and Hamilton illustrates.

Knight's argument has attracted much criticism, but also some influential defenders. They include Knight's student Milton Friedman (1912–2006), whose monetarist theories earned him the Sveriges Riksbank Prize in Economic Sciences in Memory of Alfred Nobel. In an essay in *The Methodology of Positive Economics* Friedman (1953) argued that the realism of assumptions was irrelevant to the assessment of a scientific theory. He went further: to be important, "a hypothesis must be descriptively false in its assumptions" (ibid.: 14). Even Raymond Firth, a dispassionate scholar and by no means a neoliberal ideologue, saw merit in arguments of this kind:

> When economists used primitive man as an example, as they sometimes did, they could argue that like Robinson Crusoe their creation was fiction. But there still remained the idea that, like Crusoe again, fiction had a basis in fact. Even now it is sometimes necessary for economists to explain that in assuming rationality all they mean is that they tend to find people behaving in ways which would be identical with those eventuating if people did conform to principles of rational action. (Firth 1957: 217)

Ultimately it is a question of the explanatory adequacy of competing theories, all of which involve assumptions of some kind. The works of Keynes and Malinowski are not free of problematic assumptions. While Keynes and Malinowski were united in their rejection of the assumptions that informed Knight's approach to economics, all three scholars were concerned with the problem of uncertainty in economic life, and all three made pioneering contributions that have set the terms of debate. Their conceptions of economic uncertainty were basically the same, but their analyses of its implications varied dramatically. The following sections will outline these different implications in order to pinpoint where Malinowski's contribution to the history of economic thought lies.

Keynes on Economic Uncertainty

Uncertainty, as an existential fact of the human condition, raises two questions. The first is philosophical: How do students of the human condition conceive of uncertainty in general and economic uncertainty in particular? The second is pragmatic: How do foragers, hunters, farmers, fishers, entrepreneurs, investors, and other economic agents cope with the problem as they go about their everyday tasks of reproducing themselves and the societies of which they are part?

Malinowski and Keynes addressed both questions, but in different ways that reflect the differences in the economies they studied. The thoughts and actions of entrepreneurs and investors in the City of London could hardly differ more from the thoughts and actions of the yam farmers, fisherman, and Kula transactions of Trobriand Islanders. However, radical economic uncertainty is a great equalizer. Behind the obvious differences between the theories of Malinowski and Keynes lies a common problem: the limits of human knowledge of the world and the necessity of having to act on the basis of uncertain knowledge or even complete ignorance.

Keynes's answer to the philosophical question about uncertainty is found in his *A Treatise on Probability* of 1921. This book is not, as its title might suggest, a manual on the mathematics of games of chance, but a theory of knowledge in a world where thinking people have imperfect knowledge and foresight. People are confronted with the fact that there are some things about the future that they know well, many things about which they have partial knowledge, and much that they simply do not know and never will know. This is a world in which economic decision-makers find themselves located in a present that is betwixt a past about which they have some knowledge and a future about which they have differing expectations and predictions. Keynes's starting point was axiomatic reasoning, the logic that enables us to infer a certain conclusion from a given premise. This mode of reasoning, Keynes noted, has enabled mathematicians and physicists to make great advances in our understanding of the physical world and to make stunning predictions. His concern, however, was with the limits of axiomatic thought and hence with the limits of certain knowledge; with the world of uncertain knowledge where reasoning can lead to sensible conclusions about which there is always some doubt. His innovation was to develop a new conceptual framework for dealing with all the problems that arise.

Keynes's first move was to oppose axiomatic thought as a form of possible knowledge of a *certain* kind to nonaxiomatic thought as possible knowledge of an *uncertain* kind, to create a continuum of possibility from certainty at one extreme to total uncertainty at the other. His second move was to distinguish between uncertain knowledge that was *probable* and uncertain knowledge that was *improbable* but still possible. The logic of probable knowledge was his primary concern. Probable knowledge can be subdivided into calculable probable knowledge and incalculable probable knowledge, the latter being more uncertain. Calculable probable can be further subdivided into knowledge that can be expressed in numeric terms and knowledge that can only be expressed in nonnumeric qualitative terms, the latter being more uncertain. Of particular interest to Keynes was calculable probable knowledge of the nonnumeric kind, with verbal propositions of the kind "more likely to" and "less likely to." This conceptual framework underpinned Keynes's anti-utilitarian philosophy and his critique of neoclassical economics. How do capitalist entrepreneurs make big investment decisions with far-reaching consequences in the face of economic uncertainty? These decisions "cannot depend on strict mathematical expectation, since the basis for making such calculations does not exist; . . . it is our innate urge to activity which makes the wheels go round, our rational selves choosing between the alternatives as best we are able, calculating where we can, but often falling back for our motive on whim or sentiment or chance" (Keynes 1967: 62–63).

For Keynes, it was neoclassical economists like Knight seeking to discover economic laws using the certainty of axiomatic reasoning who were embarked on a wild goose chase, not the anthropologist, sociologist, or historian. Keynes spelled out this position in his reply to critics where he clarifies what he means by "uncertainty":

> By "uncertain" knowledge, let me explain, I do not mean merely to distinguish what is known for certain from what is only probable. The game of roulette is not subject, in this sense, to uncertainty; nor is the prospect of a Victory bond being drawn. Or, again, the expectation of life is only slightly uncertain. Even the weather is only moderately uncertain. The sense in which I am using the term is that in which the prospect of a European war is uncertain, or the price of copper and the rate of interest twenty years hence, or the obsolescence of a new invention, or the position of

private wealth-owners in the social system in 1970. About these matters there is *no scientific* basis on which to form any calculable probability whatever. We simply do not know. Nevertheless, the necessity for action and for decision compels us as practical men to do our best to overlook this awkward fact and to behave exactly as we should if we had behind us a good Benthamite calculation of a series of prospective advantages and disadvantages, each multiplied by its appropriate probability, waiting to be summed. (Keynes 1937: 213–14)

These examples can be arrayed along a continuum of degrees of certainty and predictability. At one extreme lie the games of chance: roulette and lottery. These games have *measurable* probabilities that can be given a precise *numerical* number. These measures are based on axiomatic reasoning of a mathematical kind that is universal in the sense that the propositions transcend the specificities of geography, history, and culture. A tossed coin always and everywhere has a 50 percent chance of coming down heads, no matter who throws it, when they throw it, or where it is thrown. Cheating aside, numerical predictions of this kind have a degree of certainty his other cases lack.

Next come expectations of life and weather forecasts, which are slightly or moderately uncertain. Knowledge of this kind consists in empirical generalizations based on robust statistical analyses of historical data. The efficient causes of uncertainty of this kind are what the insurance companies call "acts of God." The probability of economic risks of this kind is calculable and can be insured against. This is because they are predictable with relatively high degrees of confidence.

At the other extreme come the cases that are completely unpredictable: wars, future prices, new technologies, the future position of private wealth holders, and so on. The efficient cause of uncertainty of this kind is, among other things, the actions and unpredictable reactions of people located in specific times and places. Competitions between people, be it in the sporting arena or the marketplace, are the classic examples of uncertainty of this extreme type. British colonization ended the wars between competing groups in the Trobriand Islands, but not the disputes. Human disputation is one of the main causes of politico-economic uncertainty. We fight these disputes with sticks, stones, and words, all of which have the power to break our bones—especially the last, when they are part of the official discourse of power. But words also have the power to heal. People interact in ways that depend upon the particular circumstances of time, place, and person. Not all such interaction is completely unpredictable. Keynes distinguished between short-run and long-run expectations in order to capture this fact. His primary concern was with long-run expectations affecting the decisions taken by a reasonable entrepreneur.

The reasonable casino owner, well versed in the mathematical theory of probability, adjusts the workings of his poker machines and other games such that, in the medium to long run, the odds are in his favor; but not excessively so, since that would discourage customers. Insurance companies charge premiums that reflect long-term variations in life expectancy and weather patterns. When people begin to live longer than expected, or the weather becomes more unpredictable, the prudent company adjusts its premium to protect its rate of return. Again, the premium must be competitive to attract customers and ensure a profit.

Uncertainty of the completely unpredictable kind raises intractable problems. How do finance companies on Wall Street or in the City of London cope with the fact that they must often make big investment decisions for which there is no scientific basis on which to form any calculable probability whatever? Keynes's answer—"that the necessity for action and for decision compels us as practical men to do our best to overlook this awkward fact and to behave exactly as we should if we had behind us a good Benthamite calculation"—reveals a paradox at the center of capitalism with far-reaching implications, especially in the era of financialization. Keynes, and the Bloomsbury set to which he belonged, were implacably opposed to the values that informed Benthamite calculation (Mini 1991). Many of the most important things in life are *unmeasurable*.[3]

Malinowski on Economic Uncertainty

The word "uncertainty" is rare in Malinowski's texts. One could be forgiven for supposing that this author has no theory of uncertainty at all. However, a close reading of those passages where the word appears reveals that a concern with the distinction between relatively certain knowledge and relatively uncertain knowledge is a central preoccupation of all his work on the Trobriand Islands. Take, for example, his essay on *Magic, Science and Religion*, in which the word "uncertainty" occurs just three times. Here is one instance:

> It is most significant that in the Lagoon fishing, where man can rely completely upon his knowledge and skill, magic does not exist, while in the open-sea fishing, full of danger and uncertainty, there is extensive magical ritual to secure safety and good results. (Malinowski 1974: 14)

Here we find the central proposition that informs his whole theory of the tribal economy of the Trobriand Islands: magic begins where practical knowledge ends. It flourishes where knowledge of a future outcome is unknowable and unpredictable. This quotation presents his theory in its most general form. It defines the two endpoints of a continuum between certain and uncertain knowledge that resonates with Keynes's theory. History has taught the Trobrianders that fishing in the lagoon is safe and the yield abundant at certain times of the year. It has also taught them that fishing in the open sea is chancy, risky, and uncertain, but a risk worth taking for the different varieties of fish it yields.

In his earlier essay on fishing, Malinowski (1918: 21) outlined the intermediate cases and distinguished five techniques of fishing. First was poisoning, which was carried out in the lagoon. An abundant yield was highly likely and few, if any, magic rites were performed. Net casting from a canoe was also carried out in the lagoon. Some risk and uncertainty were associated with this activity, and some simple magical rites were performed. Third came long net fishing in shallow water in the reef to the east and south. As in the case of net casting with a canoe, some risk and uncertainty were involved, along with some magic. The fourth type of fishing was netting mullet at spawning time and the fifth was shark fishing. Both of these activities were performed in the open sea on the northern reef, where conditions were very risky and highly uncertain. Fishing magic finds its most highly developed form here.[4]

Yam cultivation is another economic activity in which magic flourishes. The rational economic Trobriander is guided in his activities by a profound knowledge of weather and seasons, plants and pests, soils and tuber. The acquisition of such practical knowledge enables him to achieve "more for less" as the economic principle of least effort would predict. However, as every farmer around the world knows from experience, efforts may be thwarted by bad luck in the form of drought, flooding, a swarm of insect pests, or other problems beyond the control of even the very best farmers. To control these factors, the Trobrianders employ magic. As Malinowski notes, "wherever there is an important human activity, which is at the same time dangerous, subject to chance and not completely mastered by technical means, there is always for the Trobriander a magical system, a body of rites and spells, to compensate for the uncertainty of chance and to forearm against bad luck" (1966, vol. 2: 217).

The ideas that inform this argument are as simple as they are profound. Malinowski's innovation is to accord fortune and misfortune a central place alongside forethought and practical knowledge in his conception of economic uncertainty. When a farmer finds that his annual production is lower than expected, the reason may be bad luck or bad economic management or a combination of the two. The problem of bad management can be tackled by improving one's techniques of production through application of knowledge and skillful work. To the extent that the lower output is due to bad luck, the farmer is up against the existential fact of misfortune:

the negative subfield of that "domain of the unaccountable and adverse influences" that also includes good luck, the "great unearned increment of fortunate coincidence" (Malinowski 1974: 12). It follows that, when a farmer finds that his annual production is much higher than expected, the reason may be due to good luck, or good management, or a combination of both. Fortune is, like economic uncertainty, an existential fact of the human condition, a universal fact of life. It is upon this foundation that Malinowski justifies his controversial methodology of generalizing from a single case, that of the Trobriand Islands:

> I have given my reasons why in this argument I had to rely principally on the material collected in the classical land of magic, Melanesia. But the facts discussed are so fundamental, the conclusions drawn of such a general nature, that it will be easy to check them on any modern detailed ethnographic record. Comparing agricultural work and magic, the building of canoes, the art of healing by magic and by natural remedies, the ideas about the causes of death in other regions, the universal validity of what has been established here could easily be proved. Only, since no observations have methodically been made with reference to the problem of primitive knowledge, the data from other writers could be gleaned only piecemeal and their testimony though clear would be indirect. (Malinowski 1974: 15–16)

This is a big claim, but it is a hypothesis, a general theory in need of verification in the light of comparative and historical evidence. What is at stake here is not his claim that magic spells are a means of coping with fortune, but the generality of the theory of fortune this presupposes. The fundamental question that a theory of economic uncertainty poses concerns how people in different geographical and historical settings conceive of (mis)fortune and cope with it. Malinowski broaches this question up front, whereas Keynes barely recognizes it, and Knight not at all.

The word *fortune* refers, first and foremost, to wealth of a "spiritual" kind, as the *Oxford English Dictionary* (1921) makes clear. Fortune is "chance, hap, or luck, regarded as a cause of events and changes in men's affairs." Fortune is often, in accordance with its Latin etymology, personified as a goddess. This is Fortune (with a capital F), "the power supposed to distribute the lots of life according to her own humor." These "lots of life" define fortune (lowercase f) in its material form as wealth. Thus, for many people, fortune, considered as invisible, mysterious, fickle power, is the efficient cause of *fortune* considered as visible material possessions. In other words, Fortune personified is the cause, fortune materialized is the effect.[5] The causes of the wealth of nations were the central preoccupation of classical European economic thought. By the late nineteenth century, the work of the economic theorist was to exorcize the role of Fortune and replace her with scientific theories of the operations of the free market. By raising the question of economic uncertainty in the 1920s, Keynes and

Knight invited Fortune back to have her say. They did so by developing a radically new conception of the "man of fortune," the capitalist entrepreneur who, as investment decision-maker, was not afraid to confront Fortune in her guise of radical economic uncertainty. The wealth of the man of fortune in pre-1700 Europe was grounded in agricultural land.[6] By the time Keynes and Knight were writing in the 1920s, the great transformation in the material form of wealth of the European man of fortune was over. The type of economic uncertainty facing the industrial capitalist was of a kind unique in human history. Never before in human history have the investment decisions of a few had such consequences for the many. Knight and Keynes were all agreed on this point, but drew different conclusions from it.[7] For Frank Knight it was not man in general who was compelled to face the sober senses of his real conditions of life, but specifically the capitalist entrepreneur. While accepting that uncertainty "is one of the fundamental facts of life," and that it "is as ineradicable from business decisions as from those in any other field," Knight notes that it can be reduced in several ways. These include the progress of scientific research and the accumulation of data, and "the clubbing of uncertainties through large-scale organization of various forms." "Finally," he notes, "uncertainty might be further reduced almost indefinitely by slowing up the march of progress, which, of course, involves a direct sacrifice in addition to both the forms of cost already noticed" (Knight 1921: 347). This latter argument is a restatement of his theory of profit in a different form. For Knight, an economy characterized by zero investment and growth where all risk is measurable is one without "Knightian uncertainty," without progress, and without Knightian profit. The human cause of uncertainty in this world is the entrepreneurial spirit of the capitalist who braves "true uncertainty" in the pursuit of progress. No entrepreneur means no progress and no progress means no "true" economic uncertainty of the "we simply do not know" kind. Good fortune brings profit, misfortune brings losses, but Fortune is no match for the efficient entrepreneur ever ready to learn from his mistakes, whose reasonable forethought conquers the whims of an unknowable future by creating a brave new world for the brave entrepreneur.

For Keynes, magic has its origins in the fact that people live in a world where uncertainty prevails. Entrepreneurs who make investment decisions are located in a present that is betwixt and between a past they have lived and a future that is uncertain. The instrument of their thoughts and actions is not the utterance of a magical spell, but money that enables them to create a bridge between yesterday and tomorrow:

> Money in its significant attributes is, above all, a subtle device for linking the present to the future; and we cannot even begin to discuss the effect of changing expectations on current activities except in monetary terms. We cannot get rid of money

even by abolishing gold and silver and legal tender instruments. So long as there exists any durable asset, it is capable of possessing monetary attributes and, therefore, of giving rise to the characteristic problems of a monetary economy. (Keynes 1967: 293)

Gold, as every student of economic history of money knows, has performed this bridging function since the beginning of commercial time. It was doing so a century ago as the world shifted from a British gold standard to an American dollar-gold standard. It still does today, despite efforts to demonetize gold. Those familiar with the historical geography of world gold production may question the rationality of an economic system that sends African miners three miles underground to unearth a yellow metal in order to ship it across the world and rebury it in carefully guarded vaults at Fort Knox. Keynes (1971: 258–59) diagnosed this as irrationality, as proof that the "magical properties, with which the Egyptian anciently imbued the yellow metal, [have never been] altogether lost."

Herein lies the significance of Malinowski's contribution to the history of economic thought: his conception of "tribal economy" provides us with a comparative perspective on how people cope with radical economic uncertainty, with how they act when confronted by the real conditions of their economic life. The Austronesian tribal economy did not use the gold standard or any other monetary bridge between today and tomorrow. In place of a numerical standard of calculation, "we find a state of affairs where production, exchange and consumption are socially organized and regulated by custom, and where *a special system of traditional economic values* governs their activities and spurs them on to efforts" (Malinowski 1921: 16, emphasis added). Malinowski's books elaborate this "special system of traditional economic values" in great detail, the essence of which is a nonnumerical qualitative value system that ranks people and things ordinally rather than cardinally. The measure of the Eurasian man of fortune was his weight in gold while the measure of the Austronesian man of fortune was the quality of shell valuables whose transaction history identified men of renown; in both cases their measure of their future fortune was subject to the mysterious workings of Misfortune, who they tried to keep at bay with concocted mathematical calculations and meaningless magical chants respectively.

Numericality, Verbality, and the Pragmatic Consequences of Economic Uncertainty

As noted above, Keynes signals his deviation from Knight with the phrase "Benthamite calculation." "Benthamite calculation" has been through four incarnations. Jeremy Bentham's original utilitarian theory of pleasure and pain (Bentham 1780) was followed a century later by Jevons's reformulation in terms of the marginal utility theory of value (Jevons 1970). Frank Knight's 1921 reformulation of Jevons in terms of a theory of profit as reward for facing radical economic uncertainty was the third incarnation. The fourth came in 1973 when Fischer Black and Myron Scholes developed a formula to explain the value of derivatives, a newly invented form of financial commodity that enables investors to make speculative profits by buying cheap tomorrow and selling dear today (and vice versa) in futures markets (Black 1989).[8]

Keynes had moral philosophical as well as economic objections to Benthamite calculation in all its forms. When asked by an editor if he would like to reply to Knight's critique of his *General Theory*, his reply to the editor was as follows (Keynes 1979: 217-218):

> I am grateful for your letter of March 1st about Professor Knight's review of my book. I read his Passionate expiring cries, but, controversial-minded though I am, I could not discover any concrete criticism to reply to. In fact, I really felt that there was nothing at all to be said. Indeed, with Professor Knight's two main conclusions, namely, that my book had caused him intense irritation, and that he had had great difficulty in understanding it, I am in agreement. So perhaps you will excuse me if I leave the article alone. In a sense I should, I suppose, feel relieved that so able a critic should find so little definite to say. But I cannot really comfort myself in that way, for the truth is, I feel sure, that our minds have not met, and that there is scarcely a single particular in which he has seen what I was driving at. So if I were to write, I could do no more than ask him forgiveness for having been so obscure and so irritating.

What was it that Knight failed to see? Clearly, the unpalatable fact that Keynes's theory of the knowability of the unknowable reveals a paradox that lies at the heart of mainstream theory of entrepreneurial decision-making, namely, that the necessity for action in the face of incalculable economic uncertainty leads to the paradox of having to measure the unmeasurable in situations where, as Keynes (1937: 213–14) noted, "we simply do not know." I call this paradox the numericality paradox.

Numericality is not a word one finds in the *Oxford English Dictionary* (*OED*). Dr. Google, however, leads to a helpful clue: "Numericality isn't a word. Numerically means to solve something by coming up with an actual number, skipping any algebraic solution."[9] To grasp numericality, we must compare it with the word *verbality*, which does exist in the *OED*. It is a word that Malinowski helped to define. The *OED* defines *verbality* as the art of being "long-winded, verbose, or lacking in meaning, substance, value, a basis in reality" (OED, verbality, 2023). One of the illustrative examples the *OED* uses comes from Malinowski: "The fact that the community are aware of the spell and know its wording is the most important clue to the appreciation of the verbalities of magic" (Malinowski 1966, vol. 2: 246). Verbality, then, is the specialist product of wordsmiths, be they priests or scholars. In the Trobriand Islands it is the specialist art of the *towosi*, which Malinowski translates as "garden magician," noting that the etymology of the word suggests "chanter" from *to*, "man," and *wosi*, "to chant." As the chanter of esoteric sacred mantras, the Trobriand *towosi* is a specific cultural form of priestly economic labor found the world over. He invokes ancestral spirits, makes sacrificial offerings to them, communicates with them, and performs exorcism rituals to rid the fields of insect pests and so on.

In central India, for example, the "garden magician" is called a *gainta*, a non-Brahmin priest whose specialist concern is Mother Earth (*mati*, *jagarani*). Villagers say that "nothing can be done without the *gainta*." As in the Trobriand Islands, the *gainta*'s work begins with the first striking of the soil and punctuates every stage of the production process of rice up until the harvest and the storage of the threshed grain. The rice economy of the Halbi-speaking people of central India differs in many ways from the yam economy of the Trobriand Islands, but like the producers of staple food the world over, rice farmers in central India must make consequential decisions today with implications for tomorrow in the face of incalculable uncertainty. Verbality is their reasoned response to this existential fact of human existence, a response made in awareness of the unknowability of the unknowable. Their magnificent verbality takes the form of thirty-thousand-line epic poems sung by priestesses called *gurumai* about the goddess Lakshmi, the deified personification of Wealth and Fortune, and her jealous senior co-wife Alakshmi, the deified personification of Poverty and Misfortune, here symbolized by rice and millet respectively. This awareness of one's own verbality, as the *OED* quotation from Malinowski reminds us, is the most important clue not only to the appreciation of the verbalities of Trobriand magic but to the understanding of political and economic theology in general.

Malinowski devotes the second volume of *Coral Gardens and Their Magic* to the paradox that *verbality* presents: "the puzzle of translating untranslatable words," which soon becomes the paradoxical problem of understanding "the meaning of meaningless words." The final section, entitled "An Ethnographic Theory of the Magical Word," presents his conclusions. Keynes's paradox of the *measures of the unmeasurable* in Benthamite calculation finds its complement in Malinowski's paradox of the *meaning of meaningless words* in Trobriand magical chants. If *verbality* is the word that names the manifest form of the Malinowskian paradox, then *numericality* is the word we need to name the historical manifestation of the Keynesian paradox.

Trobriand wordsmiths and their counterparts in India and elsewhere are conscious that the mysterious workings of Fortune and Misfortune test the limits of their knowledge. But are the Nobel Prize-winning economists who make Benthamite calculations aware of the paradoxes of their own *numericality*? When they reduce the workings of fortune and misfortune in the marketplace to statistical measures based on a misuse of probability theory, are they aware that this is false science in the sense that Keynes argued in his works on probability theory and economic uncertainty? To belittle the work of the Benthamite calculator by rendering it as "magic" is to resort to pejorative understanding of magic as "false science" and thereby denigrate the thoughts and actions of the sacred poets and chanters of mantras who, unlike the Benthamite calculator, are fully aware that the mysterious working of fortune and misfortune is the force to be reckoned with.

The formula concocted by Black, Scholes, and Merton is an example of *numericality* in its highest and most dangerous form. The growth of speculative derivatives has become the "single biggest influence on human life in the twenty-first century" (Hawkes 2019: 66). The *OED* entry for *derivatives* traces the word back to 1985 and defines it as a financial instrument whose value derives from an underlying variable asset. They emerged as a supposed hedge against risk and uncertainty, but they have ended up creating more uncertainty, such that "The market in derivatives, which barters against the changing value of anything from coal to currencies, is now so fast, so intermeshed and the packages traded so complex that the risks attached to a deal may not be at all obvious" (*OED*, derivatives, 2023).

This would be no surprise to Keynes, but no one wants to hear his message that "we simply do not know." Keynes has noticed the *numericality* paradox at the heart of Benthamite calculation but has not named it. Malinowski went three steps further than Keynes: he named his version of the paradox, posed it as a question to be analyzed, and produced a detailed analysis of it in its linguistic (1966, vol. 2) and sociological (1922, 1974) forms and functions. The paradox of *verbality* serves important sociological and political functions for the macroeconomy as well as important psychological functions for the individual. One can question the adequacy of Malinowski's functionalist answers, but not the legitimacy of his functionalist questions. They suggest the complementary question: What is the function of *numericality*? Mainstream economists are yet to discover the language in which to pose this question, let alone answer it. However, for so long as the neoclassical economist perceives the world from the perspective of a universalist theory of the economy, rather than from the perspective of a generalist theory grounded in cultural geography and political history, then the question will forever escape them.

Acknowledgments

In addition to fellow participants at the Centenary Workshop at the London School of Economics in July 2022, I would like to thank Don Gardner and Michael Young for their insightful comments on an earlier draft of this chapter.

Chris Gregory is Emeritus Professor of Anthropology at the Australian National University. He has been attached to the ANU since 1984 and has held visiting positions in the UK, Germany, Japan, and the USA. He has lived and worked for extended periods in Papua New Guinea, India, and Fiji. His fieldwork in these countries has resulted in many publications in the fields of kinship, economy, and culture.

Notes

1. One measure of this is the number of times his 1921 article has been cited in economics journals over the last hundred years. My search revealed just one hit, which was to an article of mine in the *Cambridge Journal of Economics* (Gregory 1981).
2. Another factor here was Keynes's personal relationship to Alfred Marshall. Keynes held Marshall in high regard: his critique sought to refine and develop Marshall's ideas, not to dismiss them.
3. Measuring the unmeasurable nowadays goes by the name of the "astrology of finance" ("Why Investors are Reaching for the Astrology of Finance" 2022).
4. Mosko, this volume, reports that, according to the fishers he interviewed, successful lagoon fishing involves complex magico-religious practices analogous to those employed in shark and mullet fishing, gardening, Kula, and the like. This report, if true, poses the question of "radical disparity" with Malinowski's report. Is this because Malinowski was wrong or because of the political, economic, and cultural changes in the Trobriand Islands over the past hundred years?
5. Samuel Johnson's famous 1755 dictionary defines fortune as "The power supposed to distribute the lots of life according to her own humour" (Johnson's Dictionary Online n.d.). This is illustrated by a quotation from King Lear:
    Fortune, that arrant whore,
    Ne'er turns the key to th' poor.
   Giovanni da Col and Caroline Humphrey have edited a special double issue of *Social Analysis* (56, no. 1–2) that looks at "the ways in which fortune, luck, and chance are conceived of in different societies and how the concepts are employed to negotiate the contingencies and uncertainties of everyday life" (2012: v).
6. In Britain, for example, agricultural land constituted 71 percent of total wealth in 1700. This fell to 42 percent by 1800, and 28 percent in 1900. Today agricultural land accounts for less than 5 percent of total wealth (Piketty 2014: Table 3.1).

7. So too was Marx. *Capital*, vol. 1 has just one reference to uncertainty:

    The bourgeoisie cannot exist without continually revolutionizing the instruments of production, and thereby the relations of production and all the social relations. Conservation, in an unaltered form, of the old modes of production was on the contrary the first condition of existence for all earlier industrial classes. Constant revolution in production, uninterrupted disturbance of all social conditions, everlasting uncertainty and agitation, distinguish the bourgeois epoch from all earlier ones. All fixed, fast-frozen relations, with their train of ancient and venerable prejudices and opinions, are swept away, all new formed ones become antiquated before they can ossify. All that is solid melts into air, all that is holy is profaned, and man is at last compelled to face with sober senses his real conditions of life, and his relations with his kind. (Marx 1867: 352n226)

8. After Black's death, Scholes worked with Robert C. Merton to develop the formula, for which they were awarded the Nobel Prize for Economics in 1997 ("Press Release" 1997). Scholes and Merton put their formula to an empirical test in Wall Street by becoming participant observers. In 1994, they became directors of a hedge fund called Long Term Capital Management (LTCM). The firm made spectacular returns over the next three years: from a 21 percent annualized return in 1994, their profits rose to 43 percent in 1995 and 41 percent in 1996. In absolute money terms, these percentages translated into billions. Come 1997 they received their Nobel Prize, but the profits of the firm were looking shaky, having dropped to 17 percent. Thereafter disaster struck. Their formula, a measure of the unmeasurable, was unable to resolve the paradox on which it was based, and a huge loss of USD 4.6 billion was the result. Their losses were socialized by the US Federal Reserve who gave them a USD 3.6 billion bailout. The company was wound up in 2000, but Merton and Scholes kept their Nobel Prize.

9. jdorje, "Numericality isn't a word," Reddit comment, 27 November 2019, retrieved 2 November 2023 from https://www.reddit.com/r/learnmath/comments/e2aptr/comment/f8uk1ej/?utm_source=share&utm_medium=web2x&context=3.

References

Bentham, Jeremy. 1780. *An Introduction to the Principles of Morals and Legislation*. Wikisource. Retrieved 2 November 2023 from https://en.wikisource.org/wiki/An_Introduction_to_the_Principles_of_Morals_and_Legislation.

Black, Fischer. 1989. "How We Came Up with the Option Formula." *Journal of Portfolio Management* 15(2): 4–8.

da Col, Giovanni, and Caroline Humphrey. 2012. "Preface." *Social Analysis: The International Journal of Social and Cultural Practice* 56(1): v–vi.

Faulkner, Phil, et al. 2021. "F. H. Knight's *Risk, Uncertainty, and Profit* and J. M. Keynes' *Treatise on Probability* after 100 Years." *Cambridge Journal of Economics* 45(5): 857–82.

Firth, Raymond. 1957. "The Place of Malinowski in the History of Economic Anthropology." In *Man and Culture: An Evaluation of the Work of Bronislaw Malinowski*, ed. Raymond Firth, 209–28. London: Routledge & Kegan Paul.

Friedman, Milton. 1953. *Essays in Positive Economics*. Chicago: University of Chicago Press.

Geertz, Clifford. 1978. "The Bazaar Economy: Information and Search in Peasant Marketing." *American Economic Review* 68(2): 28–32.

Gregory, C. A. 1981. "A Conceptual Analysis of a Non-Capitalist Gift Economy with Particular Reference to PNG." *Cambridge Journal of Economics* 5: 119–35.

———. 2021. "On the Spirit of the Gift That is 'Stone Age Economics.'" *Annals of the Fondazione Luigi Einaudi* 55(1): 11–34.

Hawkes, D. 2019. "Against Financial Derivatives: Towards an Ethics of Representation." *Journal of Interdisciplinary Economics* 31(2): 165–82.

Jevons, W. Stanley. 1970 [1871]. *The Theory of Political Economy*. Harmondsworth: Penguin.

Johnson's Dictionary Online. n.d. "Fortune." Retrieved 2 November 2023 from https://johnsonsdictionaryonline.com/views/search.php?term=fortune.

Keynes, John Maynard. 1921. *A Treatise on Probability*. London: Macmillan.

———. 1924. "Alfred Marshall: 1842–1924." *The Economic Journal* 34(135): 311–72.

———. 1871 [1930]. "A Treatise on Money: Vol. 2. The Applied Theory of Money." In *The Collected Writings of John Maynard Keynes: Vol. VI*. Cambridge: Royal Economic Society.

———. 1937. "The General Theory of Employment." *Quarterly Journal of Economics* 51(2): 209–23.

———. 1967 [1936]. *The General Theory of Employment, Interest and Money*. London: Macmillan.

———. 1979 [1937]. "Letter to Bladen." In *The Collected Writings of John Maynard Keynes, XXIX. The General Theory and After: A Supplement*, (pp. 217–218). ed. Donald Moggridge. London: Royal Economic Society.

Knight, Frank H. 1921. *Risk, Uncertainty, and Profit*. Boston, MA: Houghton Mifflin.

———. 1941. "Anthropology and Economics." *Journal of Political Economy* 49(2): 247–68.

Malinowski, Bronislaw. 1918. "Fishing in the Trobriand Islands." *Man* 18: 87–92.

———. 1921. "The Primitive Economics of the Trobriand Islanders." *The Economic Journal* 31: 1–16.

———. 1922. *Argonauts of the Western Pacific: An Account of Native Enterprise and Adventure in the Archipelagoes of Melanesian New Guinea*. London: Routledge & Kegan Paul.

———. 1966 [1935]. *Coral Gardens and Their Magic: A Study of the Methods of Tilling the Soil and of Agricultural Rites in the Trobriand Islands*. 2 vols. London: George Allen & Unwin.

———. 1974 [1925]. *Magic, Science, Religion and Other Essays*. London: Souvenir Press.

———. 1993. "On the Principle of the Economy of Thought (1906)." In *The Early Writings of Bronislaw Malinowski*, ed. Robert J. Thornton and Peter Skalník, 89–115. Cambridge: Cambridge University Press.

Marshall, Alfred. 2013 [1890]. *Principles of Economics*. London: Palgrave Macmillan.

Marx, Karl. 1867. *Capital. Vol. I: A Critical Analysis of Capitalist Production*. Moscow: Progress.

Menger, Carl. 2007 [1871]. *Principles of Economics*. Auburn, AL: Ludwig von Mises Institute.

Mini, P. V. 1991. "The Anti-Benthamism of J. M. Keynes: Implications for the General Theory." *American Journal of Economics and Sociology* 50(4): 453–68.

OED, derivatives, 2023. "derivative, adj. & n.". Oxford English Dictionary, Oxford University Press, September 2023, <https://doi.org/10.1093/OED/1007901444>

OED verbality, 2023. "verbality, n.". Oxford English Dictionary, Oxford University Press, July 2023, <https://doi.org/10.1093/OED/2814237248>

Packard, M. D., P. L. Bylund, and B. B. Clark. 2021. "Keynes and Knight on Uncertainty: Peas in a Pod or Chalk and Cheese?" *Cambridge Journal of Economics* 45: 1099–1125.

Piketty, Thomas. 2014. *Capital in the Twenty-First Century*. Cambridge, MA: Harvard University Press.

"Press Release." 1997. Nobel Prize website, 14 October. Retrieved 2 November 2023 from https://www.nobelprize.org/prizes/economic-sciences/1997/press-release/.

Salisbury, Richard. F. 1962. *From Stone to Steel: Economic Consequences of a Technological Change in New Guinea*. Melbourne: Melbourne University Press.

Sraffa, Pierro. 1960. *Production of Commodities by Means of Commodities: Prelude to a Critique of Economic Theory*. Cambridge: Cambridge University Press.

Thornton, Robert J., and Peter Skalník. 1993. "Introduction: Malinowski's Reading, Writing, 1904–1914." In *The Early Writings of Bronislaw Malinowski*, ed. Robert J. Thornton and Peter Skalník, 1–64. Cambridge: Cambridge University Press.

Walras, Léon. 1874. *Elements of Pure Economics, or, The Theory of Social Wealth*. London: Routledge.

"Why Investors Are Reaching for the Astrology of Finance." *Economist*, 1 September. Retrieved 2 November 2023 from https://www.economist.com/finance-and-economics/2022/09/01/why-investors-are-reaching-for-the-astrology-of-finance.

Young, Michael W. 2004. *Malinowski: Odyssey of an Anthropologist, 1884–1920*. New Haven: Yale.

8

Can Economic Anthropology Escape from Primitive Economics?
Thinking Ethnographically from the Brazilian Oikos

Benoît de L'Estoile

One year before *Argonauts of the Western Pacific*, Bronisław Malinowski published "The Primitive Economics of the Trobriand Islanders" in *The Economic Journal*. My argument in the opening section of this chapter is that this 1921 article simultaneously opened up new horizons for anthropology and set us on the wrong track, trapping economic anthropology in primitive economics. In subsequent sections, in conversation with Aristotle and contemporary interlocutors in former sugarcane plantations in the northeast region of Brazil and in a Rio de Janeiro *favela*, I outline an alternative framework, *oikonomia*, that might help us to imagine new modes of description and explanation.

From Primitive Economics to Other Economies

Malinowski's 1921 article was both an outline of a research program for anthropology and an offer to cooperate with a well-established discipline, economics. It had a strategic dimension, as Malinowski was then hoping to gain a foothold at the London School of Economics (LSE), where he had studied in 1910–11 before sailing to Australia (Young 2004: 171). The article is presented as a *résumé* of a course of lectures he gave at LSE in the summer term of 1920, shortly after returning to London.

Stating that "primitive economics are not by any means the simple matter we are generally led to suppose," Malinowski (1921: 15) used a trope he would appeal to regularly: (1) The topic is an essential one for scholars in other fields, but (2) we lack empirical data; (3) this is because of the inadequacy of existing theories; therefore (4) it is the anthropologist's task to devise a theoretical framework as a basis for research and subsequently provide the data to nourish new theoretical advances.

As would become habitual, he depicted the Trobrianders he had lived with as paradigmatic "savages," offering an ideal-typical mirror image of modern Western society. Malinowski affirmed the pervasiveness of economic activities and concerns among Trobriand Islanders:

> This *constant economic undertow to all public and private activities*—this materialistic streak which runs through all their doings—gives a special and unexpected color to the existence of the natives, and shows *the immense importance to them of the economic aspect of everything*. (Malinowski 1921: 8, my emphasis)

Malinowski took here for granted the congruence of "material" and "economic." In his holistic approach, he concluded that "Economic elements enter into tribal life in all its aspects—social, customary, legal and magico-religious—and are in turn controlled by these" (ibid.: 15). Malinowski structured his account of "Trobriand economy" using familiar economic categories: production, work, consumption, division of labor, exchange, and so on. At the same time, he displayed great sensitivity to the question of difference, and to conditions for using Western concepts, such as the notion of *ownership*.

> The main difficulty in this ... lies in our giving *our own meaning* of "ownership" to the corresponding *native word*. In doing this we overlook the fact that *to the natives* the word "ownership" not only has a different significance, but that *they* use one word to denote several legal and economic relationships, between which it is absolutely necessary *for us* to distinguish. (Ibid.: 3, my emphasis)

Thus, Malinowski stressed the need to pay attention to native words, but justified the use of Western economic terms for analytical purposes. Western distinctions between "legal and economic relationships" were seen as grounded in objectivity, that is ontologically universal.

Malinowski singled out as a foil the evolutionist three-stage model of German economic historian Karl Bücher, whose lectures he had attended in Leipzig in 1908. Bücher classified "savages," like the ancient Greeks, as being at a "pre-economic" stage of "closed household economy."[1] Rejecting "Buecher's assumption that the only alternative [to modern economy] is a pre-economic stage, where an individual person or a single household satisfy their primary wants as best they can, without any more elaborate mechanism than division of labor according to sex, and an occasional spasmodic bit of barter," Malinowski (1921: 15) insisted on the existence of "distinct forms of economic organization," both equivalent to and different from that of the modern West. Reversing Bücher's focus on the household, Malinowski prioritized "the public economy of the tribe" (ibid.: 8).[2] He concluded:

> In savage societies *national economy* certainly does not exist, if we mean by the term a system of free competitive exchange of goods and services, with the interplay of supply and demand determining value and regulating all economic life. . . . [but] we find a state of affairs where production, exchange and consumption are socially organized and regulated by custom, and where a special system of traditional economic values governs their activities and spurs them on to efforts. This state of affairs might be called—as a new conception requires a new term—Tribal Economy. (Ibid.: 15)

Just as the nation-centric notion of "society" has been extended to non-Western situations, so the "national economy" serves here explicitly as a model to order a series of practices into an interrelated whole, which Malinowski proposes to call "Tribal Economy." The analogy allowed him to bring into focus a new set of phenomena, framed as 'economic'. While economics is the apposite science to analyze (Western) "national economies," he argued it was anthropology's task to develop a new branch of knowledge, Primitive Economics, to study Tribal Economy.[3] A few years later, he reaffirmed in *Nature* that among the subjects that the "new anthropology" had to tackle, "primitive economics has been perhaps most neglected, in Great Britain at least" (Malinowski 1925: 917).

Malinowski fleshed out his program for Primitive Economics in *Argonauts* (1922) and in *Coral Gardens* (1935) (where he used as synonyms "tribal" or "native economics"), as well as in his teaching (Scott and Young 2016). In lecture notes dated September 1932, he stressed that any attempt at analytical ordering in the field implied relying on a theoretical framework:

> Start with a problem: what are the questions which need investigating if you were suddenly dropped in a native tribe in Africa or otherwise, and had to inquire into their economic organization? Show, starting from this problem, that any intelligent plan which you would have to evolve in a hurry would have to be based on some economic theory. What sort of economic theories were there developed in anthropology?
> Books to be read:
> (a) Taussig, Cassel, Marshall
> (b) Max Schmidt, Thurnwald, Bücher, R. Firth.[4]

There is an implicit syllogism here, which can be formulated as follows: any inquiry into "*economic* organization" in unfamiliar (non-Western) settings has to be based on "some *economic* theory." Ergo, anthropologists need to engage with the various "economic theories" available and adapt them to their needs. Malinowski's syllogism makes apparent the intrinsically derivative character of anthropological inquiries on economic issues, as they imply a previous *economic framing*. His bibliography included two kinds of authors: on the one hand, the then hegemonic economics textbooks;[5] on the other, economists of the German historical school dealing with tribal economies, such as Bücher and Max Schmidt (1920), and the emerging anthropological literature on Primitive Economics by Richard Thurnwald (1932) and by his own pupil Raymond Firth (1929).

Throughout his long career, Firth actively contributed to the expansion of Primitive Economics into "economic anthropology" (Foks 2020), always insisting on interlocution with economics and economists. He had studied economics in New Zealand, came to the LSE intending to obtain a PhD in that field, but ended up shifting discipline. When I met him in 1991, he proudly indicated that he had been a Fellow of the Royal Economic Society for seventy years and that "the LSE's prime reputation had been based on economics and must remain so."[6] Firth's initial title for the book version of his doctoral thesis, defended in 1927, was *Wealth and Work of the Maori* (Firth 1927: 312). He finally settled on *Primitive Economics of the New Zealand Maori* (1929), taking up Malinowski's phrasing, which he had also used in a review essay on "the study of primitive economics," published in *Economica*, the LSE house journal (1927). In 1995, he agreed that he had "imported some of [his] interests as an economist into anthropology," but gently chided me for suggesting that his position had been close to that taken by the formalists in the famous controversy of the 1960s:

> The fundamental economic factors, or principles, are common . . . : resources everywhere have a certain scarcity, and demands or wants have an almost indefinite character. Therefore the problem in any society is: how to match these scarce resources against the various demands that are made? But the point I was making all along, to the economists (when I could reach them, which is very rarely) and to the anthropologists, was that the framework within which the economic element works is very different from one society to another; therefore the kind of assumptions that the economist makes, [adapted to] present-day capitalist society, were inadequate for any universal principles, and that for any kind of universal economics, they would have to take account of the social factors in each kind of society, for example a non-monetary society [with] the significance of gift-exchange; and this [point] I made again and again and again.

Firth stressed his fundamental orientation toward a dialogue with the economists and lamented his failure to attract their attention. In 1964, engaging with the then burgeoning field of development economics in a collection on "capital, saving and credit in peasant societies," he outlined "a view point from economic anthropology." Claiming that anthropologists were in a position to "answer . . . fundamental questions posed by economists," he defined the task of this emerging subdiscipline as expanding and adapting economics to nonstandard (non-Western) economic settings, in "primitive," "peasant," or "developing" societies. This depended on finding ways to apply economic categories to non-market situations. Anthropologists were equipped to recognize universal economic realities—such as "capital," "credit," "commodities," "labor," and "consumption"—hidden under a variety of cultural forms. For instance, Firth (1964: 22, my emphasis) described how, in the Highlands of New Guinea or Aboriginal Australia, "some men emerge as entrepreneurs by controlling the flow of capital goods between groups, and taking a profit either in material items, or in that intangible good, reputation." Thus, for Firth (ibid.: 26), "it is possible to conceive of an economic system in which the items of productivity, of concern in maximization, are status tokens and symbolic ties."[7] In effect, he was extending Malinowski's conception of Tribal Economy to the "peasant economies" of a later era.

Economic anthropology as it developed from the 1940s onward has privileged non-market settings, or at any rate settings where standard "laws of the market" are somehow suspended, euphemized, or diluted (Hann and Hart 2011).[8] Alongside Tribal Economy, claimed by Malinowski as the preserve of Primitive Economics, other "qualified economies" (e.g., "indigenous," "peasant," "domestic," "informal," or "gift economy") were identified, offering new fields to an expanding subdiscipline. These "strange economies" (Gudeman 2016: 10) were located not only in non-Western contexts (which of course in the meantime have been increasingly integrated into market capitalism) but also as "pockets" within modern Western societies or at the "periphery" of the capitalist market.[9]

The work of Pierre Bourdieu provides a fascinating illustration. While Firth advocated a translation of economics into anthropology, Bourdieu pursued a compelling critique of the reductionism of economics (what he dubbed "economicism") and of the paradigm of *Homo economicus* (Bourdieu 2017). Instead he put forward an ambitious alternative project of "generalized political economy."[10] For him, the economists' account is not so much erroneous as incomplete, in so far as it fails to include social agents' perceptions. Its full adequacy is limited to certain spheres, especially in modern capitalist society, which enjoys the epistemic privilege of being transparent to itself:

> Everything happens as if the *economy as economy* were the product of a kind of collective self-confession of society, by which it acknowledges it is what it is. In other words, society takes the objective truth of its exchanges as its subjective truth, saying: "even exchanges of gifts are tit for tat." (Bourdieu 2017: 67, my translation and emphasis)

By contrast, in "precapitalist" societies, such as Kabyle "traditional society," as well as in specific fields in the modern Western world that are (or were) at least partially autonomous from the market, especially in the arts, literature, and the academia, "the economy as we know it" fails to provide an adequate model for understanding social agents. Bourdieu therefore spoke of an "economy of symbolic goods, marked by the existence of specific forms of capital (I call it 'symbolic capital'), specific forms of profit (I call it 'symbolic profit'), [and] specific forms of symbolic intentions (generous dispositions)" (ibid.: 44). An essential feature of this "paradoxical economy" (ibid.: 47) is that it is based on a *denegation* of its real (i.e., economic) character, which he dubs "a collective bad faith, a lie to oneself" (ibid.: 55). Thus, while Bourdieu claims to recover the phenomenological dimension left out of "scientific" accounts of economic phenomena, he does so only as a subordinate perception of reality, discounted as "illusion" while "objective truth" remains the "economy as economy."

The dualist model of a sphere dominated by economic rationality and another by "non-economic" factors has been highly persistent in economic anthropology. In a suggestive synthesis, Stephen Gudeman (2016: 10) dismisses the commonly held view that "economy means market and that theories about markets are theories about the economy" as a "50 percent view," because it omits many aspects of economic action. He contends that anthropology, starting from "material life in the house," offers a more complete vision. Again, the claim here is not that the economists' account is wrongheaded, but rather that it is partial. Similarly, James Carrier (2018) endeavors to give more substance to the notion of "moral economy." Following Mauss, he characterizes "moral economic activity" as that associated with "relationships in which the transactors have become obligated to each other because of their past transactions" (ibid.: 13). For Carrier, while there is indeed a realm of "purely economic relationships," such as the capitalist market, "some parts of the economy seem to be predominantly moral," such as the household, or family and friendship links. In other words, the "moral economy" is a residual form found in pockets outside the "pure economy."

As Timothy Mitchell has pointed out, such a research program consists in studying the "rest," what is beyond, outside of, or deviating from the market (associated with the "purely economic"), which, however, remains the main reference point:

> The goal of economic sociology is to show that this world of market rationality is restrained or compromised by the ties of friendship, affection, altruism, morality, control, culture or other apparently non-economic relations that market practices depend upon or cannot completely escape. From this perspective, economic calculation (or the market, or the economy) always already exists, as the expression of some sort of pure self-interest. (Mitchell 2008: 1117–18)

When Narotzky and Besnier (2014) articulate a cogent critique of hegemonic (neoliberal) views of the economy in postcrisis contexts, they rightly call for ethnographic attention to the diversity of ways of making a living and to "grassroots" points of view in order to "rethink the economy." However, they too stop short of questioning the existence of "the economy" itself. Their invocation of a "new political economy" remains rooted in Western native ontological beliefs and categories.

The paradox is that these critical approaches generally embrace some version of Karl Polanyi's (1944) hypothesis of embeddedness. They challenge the practical value of boundaries between the economic and the social and cultural, but ultimately reaffirm their analytical validity. The importance of paying attention to those aspects we call economic is for many social scientists grounded in their association with the *material* basis of life, subsistence, or livelihood. This was explicit in Polanyi's redefinition of "economic" as "bearing reference to the process of satisfying material wants," so that "to study human livelihood is to study the economy in this substantive sense of the term" (Polanyi 1977: 20).[11] However, as Louis Dumont (1983: xvi) pointed out in his foreword to the French translation of *The Great Transformation*, "having criticized the economy as an idea, he conserved it as a thing, and ended up proposing to use general concepts, among them reciprocity. But this is just slightly less ethnocentric than [the concept of] production." Polanyi failed to question the economic framing because he too was committed to an ontological belief in "the economy."

"The House is Mine, I Am the One Who Rules Here": Oikonomia in Rural Pernambuco

"Peasant households" have offered privileged terrains to economic anthropologists in search of "non-market pockets."[12] Thus Gudeman and Hann (2015) contrast *oikos* with markets, stressing the resilience of the Aristotelian ideal of *autarkeia* in postsocialist European rural contexts, and suggesting that the "economy of the house" abides by its own rules. Various analytical constructs such as "domestic economy" (Weber and Tenedos 2006), "householding" (Polanyi), or "house economy" (Gudeman 2016), while avowedly aiming to move beyond standard economics paradigms by showing that "economic" and "social" phenomena are entangled, still take for granted (more or less explicitly) an analytical and ontological divide between "the economy" and the rest. This is partly the result of a (repeatedly frustrated) longing to demonstrate to economists and policymakers the "relevance" of our trade. However, the economic framing impacts negatively on the potential heuristic contribution of ethnography, because it shapes the kind of questions we can raise while excluding others.

In the early 1970s, a group of anthropologists from the Museu Nacional in Rio de Janeiro espousing a Marxian version of economic anthropology established the anthropology of peasantry in Brazil, largely based on fieldwork in the sugarcane region of northeastern Brazil (Sigaud 2008).[13] They also drew on A. V. Chayanov (1966)'s non-Marxist insights into the centrality of family labor in peasant economy. Afrânio Garcia, Jr. (1982: 15) thus aimed "to start from the ethnographic analysis of the representations and behavioral models of small producers about their economic practice, to try to reconstruct the economy of the small producer," while Beatriz Heredia (1979) studied the house as a "unit of production and consumption." Both stressed the paramount role of the male head of the *casa* (a term that in Portuguese encompasses both the house and its inhabitants, the family). Despite the richness of these ethnographies, notions such as "domestic economy" or "peasant economy" acted as straitjackets: observers did pay close attention to local categories, especially concerning authority within the house, but these were not allowed to challenge the analytical frame itself.

While my own work has developed in sustained dialogue with these researchers (e.g. de L'Estoile and Sigaud 2006), I refrain from marking out a set of practices as "economic," preferring to start from the ways that my interlocutors in the field describe their own life and concerns.[14] "The house is mine, I do as I want!" exclaimed Dona Maria, a *beneficiária* (allottee) of the land reform program in the sugarcane area of Pernambuco, as I sat in her kitchen.[15] Later that night, she repeated to Dona Lourdes, a neighbor and *beneficiária*: "The house is mine, I am the one who rules (*manda*) here." Lourdes echoed: "I am the one who rules in my house." We discussed these statements repeatedly during the following days, for instance as I drove Maria, who was then president of Bonito settlement's association, and Lourdes to the regional headquarters of INCRA in Recife, in order to formalize the latter's status as sole *beneficiária* of the plot after her husband had left her to live with another woman.[16] Following Malinowski's (1921: 3) advice not to give our own meaning of "ownership" to "native words," let us point out that when Maria said "the house is mine," she was not claiming legal *ownership*. She was well aware that the owner of her house, as of the whole *assentamento* (rural settlement project), was the Brazilian state, which had expropriated the plantation and remained formally in charge through INCRA. The immediate context of her statement was somewhat trivial: she explained why, coming back home after a long day out at the Assembly of God, she had prepared dinner without cleaning up her house, departing from her usual practice. Each time I arrived at Dona Maria's place, she would list all the household chores she had accomplished since dawn, thereby demonstrating her excellence as a *dona de casa* and validating herself as a worthy person. Growing flowers on her front porch conveyed her care of the house and sense of aesthetics. Conversely, she decried one of her neighbors for neglecting her house and failing to take proper care of her children and grandchildren, who were suffering physical and moral ailments. She implied an equivalence between morality and cleanliness. As a widow, Maria was the sole *beneficiária* of her plot (*parcela*); her adult sons helped her to "sustain the house."

While taking care of her house, her grandchildren, and her cooking involved material operations, analyzing such practices as "domestic economy" would miss the ways in which these women experience and make sense of their lives. Taking pride in the care of her *casa*, Maria repeated, "I do what I want at the time I want" in order to stress that she was the one who was in control. This claim to what might be called temporal autonomy contrasted with other moments in her life, in which other persons had been in control of her time: the boss when she was working on sugarcane plantations, a husband expecting a meal when he came back from work, or, when she was "working in a family house" (as a domestic worker), the chores imposed by the housewife. Her self-description as a "free woman" referred particularly to independence from men (she had her six children with different fathers, pointing out that she was always the one who left her partners). Women, especially when they are *donas* (masters) of the *casa* (because they have no male companion, or because they are the official *beneficiária*), use the language of rule (*mandar*). This widespread insistence on "freedom," and on "ruling" oneself and one's own house, had particular resonance in a setting like rural Pernambuco, historically marked by slavery and later by the personal domination of the "mill masters" (*senhores de engenho)* in the plantation system.

The reference to *mandar* (ruling/commanding) and being a *dono* or *dona* (master) turned up in many discourses and practices I encountered in Pernambuco, both in the context of the *casa* and of the *assentamento*. This concern should be the cornerstone of our analysis. One possible path would have been to use *mandar* as an organizing notion; it is, however, too grounded in a specific region and language to be suitable as a transversal analytic concept. We need a more general framework, sufficiently encompassing to make comparison meaningful, and yet flexible enough to be operationalized in quite different settings. It needs to be a conceptualization that respects the formulations and everyday practices of our interlocutors from their own perspective. I suggest we can achieve this by the reappropriation of the ancient Greek words *oikonomia* (the etymological root of economy) and *politikè*.

Oikos (οἶκος) has a wide semantic range in ancient Greek: it denotes the house as a building, but also the family, the home, or the estate; *oikos* is thus closer to the Iberic notion of *casa* than to "house" or *maison*. *Oikos* in fact provided the paradigm for Bücher's "closed household economy" stage. *Oikonomia* is often translated as "domestic economy" (a tautology inasmuch as *domus* (house/household) is the standard Latin translation of *oikos*), or as "management of the household." Polanyi (1944: 55) turned *oikonomia* into his "principle of householding," which he defined as "production for one's own use"—although he abandoned it in later works (Gregory 2009). Such translations pull the notion of *oikonomia* toward an economic discussion. In other words, modern economic framing is projected back onto other worlds. However, *oikonomia* in ancient Greece was primarily about government. Thus in *Politics*, Aristotle (n.d.: 1255b) described *oikonomikè* and *politikè* as exemplifying two forms of rule or government (*arkhè*): one, in the context of the *oikos*, the domestic community, is exercised in a monarchic manner by the house-master over his dependents; the other, in the context of the *polis*, the political community, by the city magistrate over the citizens who are equals.[17] Foucault (1986: 153) characterized *Oikonomikos*, Xenophon's treaty on the care of the house, in a similar way as essentially "an art of ruling."[18] *Oikonomia* is composed of two roots, *oikos* and *nemein*: the latter verb has various meanings, including to distribute, pasture, order, manage, rule, and govern. I draw on this last meaning to translate it as "government of the house," or "domestic government."

Aristotle (n.d.: 1256a) draws a further distinction between *oikonomikè* and what he calls *khrematistikè*. *Khrematistikè* refers to the set of practices providing the *khrèmata*, the "things indispensable to live, primarily through production, and secondarily, exchange."[19] For Aristotle, this art (*tekhnè*) of provision—which is quite similar to what Polanyi later called "substantive economy"—is vital insofar as it guarantees the self-sufficiency (*autarkeia*) of the *oikos*. Supplying the *oikos* with the necessaries of life (*khrematistikè*) is, however, subordinated to *oikonomia*, which is ultimately concerned with the government of humans rather than with the management of things.[20] Polanyi was well aware of this specificity of *oikonomia*:

> The economy—as the root or the word shows, a matter of the domestic household or *oikos*—concerns directly the relationship of the persons who make up the natural institution of the household. Not possessions, but parents, offspring and slaves constitute it. (Polanyi 1957: 81)[21]

A central feature of *oikonomia* is that it highlights the importance of the ideal of "autonomy"—the capacity to define one's own rules, to give orders rather than obeying—as an organizing concern in domestic practices. *Oikonomia* involves the government both of oneself and of others. Its intrinsic political and moral dimension, excluded in economic framing, is thus central. Claiming back the term *oikonomia* does not entail an anachronistic return to Aristotle's focus on the perspective of the male master of the *oikos*, nor to the "household stage" theory. Rather, appropriating the ancient Greek terms in a creative manner opens up the possibility of an alternative to the conventional economic paradigm. The *oikonomia* perspective foregrounds the articulation between four interrelated concerns in domestic government:

(a) everyday domestic practices aimed at supplying the "necessities of life" (*khrematistikè*), either by production, by exchange in the market, or by mobilizing networks of reciprocity and mutuality, so as to ensure the autonomy of the house.
(b) the ability to govern oneself, one's own house, and one's own land (autonomy), and the whole question of power relations within the house.[22]
(c) the domestic community (*oikos*) as a privileged place for realizing a local version of the ideal of a worthy or "good life,"[23] both materially and morally; it implies achieving control of oneself and of one's house, and being recognized by one's peers as a "proper person."
(d) a specific form of orientation to the future and of dealing with uncertainty.

Oikonomia is an ideal-typical construction that allowed me to offer an alternative description of the frames of reference that shape the expectations of my interlocutors in Pernambuco (de L'Estoile 2014). These expectations developed within a specific configuration of uncertainty and a given field of opportunities and constraints that defined the "conditions for life" for individuals and communities—what Max Weber (1968: 927) called "life chances" (*Lebenschancen*).

Complementarily, I use the term *politikè* to point to concerns and practices regarding the government of the political community, which structure and define the fields of opportunities and constraints for the actors. In the case of land reform settlements, *politikè* involves three distinct (but interrelated) sets of relations, corresponding to different scales:

(a) at a micro-local level, it refers to relationships of power within the settlement project (*assentamento*), and within the beneficiaries' association, which formally governs it;
(b) at the municipal level, it involves local politicians (mayors, candidates, municipal representatives), local policies, and patronage;
(c) finally, it refers to the more "vertical" relationships of beneficiaries (both individually and collectively) with the state agencies and

NGOs governing the land reform, implementing the policies of the federal government, and supervising the settlements through a form of indirect rule. (de L'Estoile 2015)[24]

I use these Greek terms because, although both *oikonomia* and *politikè* are obviously related etymologically to our notions of economic and political, their archaic ring alerts us to the fact that they actually subvert our modern distinctions. The use of *oikonomia* and *politikè* foregrounds a process of "decentering." This ideal-typical pair refers not to different "spheres" or "domains," but rather to points of view from which questions can be posed. The boundary between *oikonomia* and *politikè* and the nature of the relationship between them are left open, not fixed a priori. The acid test for this heuristic framework is its capacity to illuminate the lived reality of our interlocutors better than the economic framing.

Market, Economic Calculation, and "Worthy Life": Seu Zé Joaquim

It is important to stress that *oikonomia* is not some kind of "survival" of a precapitalist economic system, a form of Primitive Economics. On the contrary, it can illuminate situations where people are fully inserted in the market, such as that of Seu Zé Joaquim, a lean 62-year-old man with an astute smile who received a plot in Pedra Azul, another *assentamento*. He was considered to be one of the few successful producers in the land reform settlements in Coqueiros. He and his wife sold their own fruit and vegetable production in three local marketplaces, supplemented by products bought in the wholesale market in Recife. Although he resided in the nearby small town, Zé Joaquim worked daily on his plot.

When I visited him in November 2015, Seu Zé Joaquim took me around what he called his *sítio*, proudly showing the improvements since my previous visit two years earlier. A *sítio* refers in this area to a housing and agricultural unit usually composed of a house surrounded by fruit trees and a garden or tract of land for cultivating food crops. Traditional *sítios* were either autonomous houses within a plantation, usually in isolated areas, or independent plots in lands that had little agricultural value. In the former *engenho* (sugarcane plantation), gaining access to land to cultivate was usually dependent on being granted *morada*, a dwelling place, as any *morador* (worker living on the plantation) could grow annual crops for his family; the ultimate ideal was, however, to be granted a *sitio* and the right to plant fruit trees, thereby enabling the *casa* to attain relative autonomy and security (Palmeira 1977). For rural workers living on the periphery of small towns, a major attraction of the land reform program in the mid-1990s was the opportunity to realize the "dream of the *sítio*." Gaining permanent access to some land to "sustain the house" was the harbinger of *liberdade* (freedom), meaning the possibility to rule as a *dono* (master) over one's house and piece of land.[25]

Zé Joaquim led me to an orange tree loaded with fruit, explaining that he had recently discovered a water source and set up an irrigation system by gravity. His excitement stemmed from the protection it would afford from climatic uncertainty. Nearby, a middle-aged woman was watering patches of maize with a hose. As we approached, Zé Joaquim told me he had already spent a lot of money on the crop that year (with several months still to go before harvest time), but he expressed his doubts as to the final result. From an outlay of roughly thirty-thousand *reais*, he hoped to make at most five or six thousand. He had had to take money out of what he called his "wage,"[26] sometimes "one week" (i.e., a quarter of his monthly allowance), to pay the woman who helped him (as his wife was now too tired to help him with tilling). He concluded: "This crop does not bring profit." Zé Joaquim proceeded to give a detailed account of his expenses, including the quantities of fertilizer and weed killer he had had to buy, and the car he had rented to take his products to the market. He added: "It was Seu Carlos who taught me this: 'Write down all your expenses in a notebook, even the food you eat when you go to work. Then you'll be able to know if you incurred a loss or a profit.'" Ultimately, he concluded, his *sitio* would be "saved" that year by oranges. As I listened to Seu Zé Joaquim, I was fascinated by his tale of the transmission of bookkeeping practices and "economic reasoning" from Seu Carlos, the former boss of the economically profitable Pedra Azul sugarcane plantation, to his former worker. However, here again an economic account proves insufficient. When I asked him why he insisted on planting maize if he was making a loss, he replied, gesturing toward his neighbors' uncultivated plots: "I don't like leaving my plot naked [*descuberta*]." Those who consider themselves to be proper peasants describe as "ugly" plots that are "left for the bush to take care of," thereby stigmatizing their *donos* as "lazy." This is a striking reminder of Malinowski's (1935: 10) non-utilitarian characterization of the Trobriand valuation of agricultural work as merging ethics and aesthetics: "the Trobriander is above all a gardener, who digs with pleasure and collects with pride, to whom accumulated food gives the sense of safety and pleasure in achievement, to whom the rich foliage of yam-vines or taro leaves is a direct expression of beauty." Zé Joaquim claims recognition as a "good agriculturalist," and also, implicitly, states that he is actually working the land, thus performing possession, which in Brazilian law is a form of entitlement known as *posse*.

Zé Joaquim has a long-standing interest in matters of *politikè*. A dedicated member of the local Rural Workers' Union, he has been a member of various delegations to Brasília, the federal capital. In his opinion, land reform had been badly administered: the beneficiaries, having been provided with a tract of land, had been abandoned by the government after a few failed development projects; the promised electrification arrived too late and inadequately, impeding irrigation projects. Zé Joaquim imagined alternative ways of governing the *assentamento*: beneficiaries should be asked which crops they wish to produce and given the necessary means to do so. After two years, state inspectors should visit the plots and evaluate the performance. Those who have been efficient would receive further help, but those with uncultivated land would be sanctioned. "If you have twenty *beneficiários* working, those who do nothing feel ashamed: either they [start to] work to have a worthy life [*vida digna*], or they leave!" In effect, he advocated a form of mutual emulation based on reputation, under benevolent government supervision. This, however, was not happening. Zé Joaquim railed against the inaction of "the race of politicians," responsible for "the cultivator being called a lazy bum." He lamented that "the government has no interest in the little nation" (meaning "little people" like him). Here again, political considerations cannot be disentangled from moral ones.

I had heard Seu Zé Joaquim mention *vida digna* the previous Saturday at the marketplace, when he had stated that his aim was not to become "rich," but rather to lead a "worthy life." When I asked what he meant, he paused before replying: "To be honest and serious . . . This is with myself," and then: "A worthy life is not to depend on anyone." A "worthy life" was associated with a certain level of material security, without which one would be dependent on others. But for Zé Joaquim a *vida digna* was above all associated with moral worth and with personal freedom, that is with the ability and possibility to govern himself.

Three years later, Zé Joaquim insisted: "I want to have a good life, eat the food I want, wear the clothes I want. But I don't have this ambition of greed [*ganância*], of money. Because after I die, I won't take anything with me!" While he strove for material security, his orientation to the future was rooted in a Christian vision of the afterlife. His complaints about his difficulty in accessing credit, the cost of transporting products to the market, or the incompetence of "technicians" sent to implement agricultural development projects are interwoven with moral considerations about work, laziness, or the failings of politicians. In other words, while Seu Zé Joaquim is fully integrated into the market and practices a form of "economic calculation," this remains subordinated to other concerns: having enough money to be sheltered from uncertainty to lead a *vida digna*, and be recognized as a proper person. These *oikonomia* concerns in turn shape his relation to *politikè*: his frustration with the government that fails to provide him with the opportunities to "grow in life."

"My House is of Paper": Survival, Life, and Proper Life in a Rio de Janeiro Favela

I developed the *oikonomia* framework to account for the ways that my interlocutors in rural Pernambuco ordered and made sense of their world. Later, I realized it also illuminated the concerns expressed in conversations in a poor urban neighborhood in Rio de Janeiro. One Sunday in June 2016, I visited my long-time friend Vânia in her small brick house, in one of the numerous *favelas* of the Santa Tereza hills, located in the Northern Zone of Rio de Janeiro, where she has been living for more than forty years.[27] While most of her neighbors have expanded their houses horizontally and vertically, following a common pattern in Rio *favelas* (Cavalcanti 2009; Motta 2014), Vânia's house is still basically the one I knew in 1994, made up of one bedroom, a small living room (used at night as a sleeping space), and a tiny kitchen and bathroom. Back then, Vânia said: "This is not what I wanted, but . . . my hope is that one day my house will become better." Twenty-two years later, she commented with her characteristic laugh: "I don't change! My house doesn't change. Not for lack of will . . . but it is impossible! You have to think like this: either I eat or I decorate my house."

Over the years, Vânia, by 2016 a widowed mother of three grown-up children, has worked in a number of occupations, formal and informal, among them domestic cleaner, telephone operator, and caregiver for old people. She has sometimes combined jobs to make ends meet, while also experiencing periods of unemployment and illness. For the five years before 2016, she had been earning the minimum wage as a general auxiliary in a private nursery for middle-class children in Rio's Southern Zone. While she complained that the "minimum wage" she earned did not correspond to the amount and quality of work she provided, she stressed that she "needed" to work in order to "pay the bills." In 2012 she had suffered a work accident, whose effects were still painfully evident four years later because she had not received treatment in the public hospital system and lacked the means to access the private one. Her physical ailments impaired her ability to do her own household chores: "Either I clean at work, or I clean at home." In fact, she had no choice, because at work she was constantly under pressure from her bosses, so that "suffering or not, ailing or not, I have to do it." As a result, she was unable to take proper care of her own house.

In this context of justifying what she saw as her failure to "improve" her house, Vânia vividly recalled that fateful day when the police had searched the *favela*. Her son, who had been associated with drug dealers, was lying in bed with fever, unable to escape. Vânia recounted how the police had searched her house, failed to find anything, but planted evidence and then arrested her son, who was later sentenced to a five-year prison term. This has been a turning point in Vânia's life, generating a deep sense of insecurity and uncertainty, and making it hard for her to feel "at home" in her own house:

> This was in 2009, when they invaded . . . they tore my house apart. Since then I can't make it to arrange my house, I can't. I think this was an effect of trauma. Especially here in the room [gesturing toward her bedroom]. I try to organize, everything, but here, . . . when I enter the room, this image comes to me . . . I see the image of what they did in my room. They threw all my clothes to the floor, my ID papers, the clothes of my grandchild, they threw out everything that was in the drawers, stamped . . . on it. A horrible thing they did here in our houses, really horrible.

The invasion of her home by the police, the arrest of her son, and the violation of her privacy and intimacy were experienced by Vânia as a "trauma," dramatically changing her relationship toward her own house, over which she felt she had lost control. Her capacity to project herself into the future was compromised in this moment. Daily routine in the *favela* is normally quiet, but violence can occur at any moment, brutally disrupting life. Vânia told me about hours of gunfire between the police and gang members the day before my visit, with the inhabitants caught in the crossfire. A young man further down the hill had been killed by a stray bullet.

> This week, there were two days of shooting. I didn't know where to run. I kept running from kitchen to bathroom, from bathroom to kitchen. One can't stay in the living room, because my house is [made] of paper. The walls [made of cheap bricks] can't withstand rifle bullets, things like that. We are not safe within the house, we are not! Sometimes, if you see there will be a shooting, it's better to go to the street, if you can. You don't feel protected in your house.

Vânia described her fear, worrying whether the bullets would "get her" when she took cover on the kitchen floor. Uncertainty here takes an extreme form. This is an inversion of the usual Brazilian cultural logic, where the house (*casa*) offers protection, however precarious and temporary, as opposed to "the street" (Da Matta 1987) and "the world" (Dumans Guedes 2017). Twenty years earlier, Vânia had described how she felt "rich" by virtue of having a house, in comparison with those who were living "under the bridges." In 2016, however, she stressed the fragility of the very same house. She literally had to risk her life in order to make a living. While her adult children urged her to stay at home, Vânia could not afford to listen to them, as missing one day at work would result in her losing forty *reais*.

To help me grasp what it meant to her, she mentioned the price of a gas canister: seventy *reais*. She chose an item belonging to the category that Aristotle called *khrèmata*, the necessities for life indispensable for cooking food, that is, for securing subsistence. On the face of it, an analysis in terms of "survival strategies" in severe economic conditions—be it in a neoclassical, marginalist frame (pondering Vânia's preferences for existential safety versus food or bettering her house) or a political economy one (stressing her need to sell her labor on the market to reproduce her family)—would seem appropriate. However, such framings fail to account for her own experience of the situation. Vânia vividly told me on numerous occasions about how difficult it was for a *favela* mother to make a living, maintain her house, protect her children, and cope with her physical and moral pain. Terms such as money, salary, minimum wage, costs, and prices cropped up constantly in her conversation. When we hear them, we code them as "economic." However, Vânia was not just talking about "economic" realities. She resented the constant menace of a police intrusion, as it impinged on the government of daily life. She mentioned the "privations" of leisure imposed by the police: with the new policy of "pacification" (this *favela* had officially been "pacified" since 2012 through the establishment of a police station at its heart), she and her family had stopped having parties in the space beyond the house, for fear of police intrusion. When she exclaimed: "I am in my house, I have the right to have fun," she was making a claim to autonomy and a "good life" in her own home.

Like most *favela* inhabitants, Vânia has to live in a specific configuration of high uncertainty that is largely shaped by *politikè*. Conflicting agencies of government constrain her mobility and her autonomy: local drug gangs, the police, and the state (however precarious and intermittent it appears from the perspective of the poor). She juggles with various allies and the resources to which she has access (family relatives, neighbors, employers, a precarious public health service, etc.). Vânia's account of the entanglement of concerns for surviving, making a living, and leading a worthy life makes apparent the truncated character of a notion such as *"favela* economy." A formulation in terms of field of opportunities, configurations of uncertainty, and *oikonomia* provides a more adequate ground to understand her efforts to govern her own life, trying to reconcile her need for protection with her aspiration to autonomy.

Concluding Remarks: Entering New Conversations

A century after the publication of *Argonauts*, I contend that economic anthropology is still trapped in Malinowski's Primitive Economics. This framing allowed him to identify a new set of "economic" phenomena for inquiry, thus opening up an original field of research. At the same time however, this initial gesture established it as derivative, largely as a result of the wish to be heard by economists. Variously qualified as "tribal," "household," "moral," and so on, the "strange economies" it has privileged as its objects all derive from similar definitions of "economy." It is unsurprising that a field calling itself "economic anthropology" should be characterized by economic framing! In fact, the plurality of "economic framings" was made apparent by the formalist versus substantivist controversy in economic anthropology in the 1960s, as the very definition of the field and of its central questions were dependent on the meanings given to "economic" and "economy." The crux of the problem, as I have argued, lies not with these various definitions but in these very terms.

When we hear our interlocutors in the field use words such as "market," "profit," or "consumption," we rashly conclude that they are talking about "economic questions" because the economic framing is hegemonic for us, as inhabitants of the modern ontology and as social scientists. When they seek to secure food, shelter, health care, material items, or transportation, we classify all these as "economic practices," because they relate to what Karl Polanyi called *provisioning*, that is, securing the material means to live, which represents for any human a fundamental concern and source of uncertainty. The material dimension Malinowski associated with the economy is, of course, essential: a structural lack of means severely constrains the possibilities of autonomy, as is made clear by the examples of Dona Maria, Seu Zé Joaquim, and Vânia. However, I argue that these material aspects, corresponding to what Aristotle calls *khrematistikè*, while necessary for life, are subordinate to the real concerns of *oikonomia*: the government of the *casa* (house/family) is intimately related to government of the self and the government of uncertainty. It is striking to contrast Maria, who asserts her right and capacity to govern her *casa* and take care of it, with Vânia's despair about the frailty of her house and her inability to do likewise. However, considering such words and practices as "economic" carries the risk of imposing meanings that may be alien—at least in part—to their *lived* experience.

Malinowski's syllogism was to the point: if we set out to "inquire into . . . *economic*" phenomena, even with a critical intent, we are bound to rely, explicitly or not, on "some *economic* theory," and thus reproduce an "*economic* framing," be it of a formalist, Marxist, substantivist, Bourdieusian, or other hue. If, however, we are looking not for phenomena predefined as "economic," but for something else, our point of departure should rather be the ways that our interlocutors frame their own experience. Instead of insisting on maintaining a one-sided conversation with economists, we should privilege the dialogue with our interlocutors in the field.[28]

The challenge I suggest then is a moratorium on the routine use of economic language (both of economics as a discipline and of "the economy") in our descriptions and explanations of social practices and processes. "Economic" terms should figure in our accounts only as *native* categories within the world we study, not as analytical notions. For the latter task, we need to imagine new frameworks and descriptive repertoires. I have put forward the heuristic pair *oikonomia* and *politikè* as a way to escape from the legacy of primitive economics and instead to foreground (a) people's own experiential frames; (b) their concern with what makes life and "good life" possible; (c) their ways of dealing with uncertainty; and (d) their relationships with each other and with various forms of government, at different scales. In this way, *oikonomia* and *politikè* may help us to foreground the political and moral dimensions left out by economic framing. While this framework cannot dispel our ontological belief in the reality of "the economy," it helps to open up alternative modes of describing and making sense of daily practices of "surviving," "making a living," and trying to "lead a good life" in conditions of uncertainty.

Acknowledgments

This research has been financed by the CNRS, the Tepsis Research Fund project "Oikonomia: Une anthropologie politique de la maison," and the Capes-Cofecub project "Modes of Government and Ordinary Economic Practices." Former versions of this chapter have been presented at the Real Economy conference in Rio de Janeiro in 2016, the Cambridge University Senior Anthropological Seminar in 2019, and the LSE *Argonauts* workshop in July 2022. I thank the participants in these encounters for their stimulating comments, especially Sian Lazar, Rebecca Empson, Adam Kuper, and Jonathan Parry, as well as the students participating in my seminars at the École Normale Supérieure and the EHESS.

Benoît de L'Estoile is Research Professor at the Centre National de la Recherche Scientifique (CNRS), Centre Maurice Halbwachs, Paris. He has worked on the emergence of British social anthropology, colonial legacies, and museums, and pursues fieldwork in Brazil. Coeditor of *Empires, Nations and Natives: Anthropology and State Making* (Duke University Press, 2005), he is currently codirecting a comparative project on the government of uncertainty.

Notes

1. "Buecher comes to the conclusion that the savages . . . have no economic organisation" (Malinowski 1921: 1). Malinowski quoted Bücher (1901), whose original title referred to the genesis of (national) economy (*Volkswirtschaft*).
2. It is ironic that *Argonauts* was devoted to what Malinowski describes here as a "side issue": "Whenever the native moves—to a feast, to an expedition, or in warfare—he will have to deal with the problems of giving and counter-giving. The detailed analysis of this state of affairs would lead us to interesting results, but it would be a side issue from our main theme—the public economy of the tribe" (1921: 8).
3. Pearson's (2000) historical account of "primitive economics" starts way before Malinowski, but does not provide evidence of anterior uses of the term.
4. Lecture notes, dated September 1932, Bronislaw Malinowski Papers, LSE library. See also Foks, this volume.
5. Probably referring to books by F. W. Taussig (1911), Alfred Marshall (1890–1920), and Gustav Cassel (1923).
6. Notes, author's interview with Sir Raymond Firth, 16 June 1991.
7. This is precisely the basic tenet of the formalist position he later denied espousing.
8. It must however be pointed out that Malinowski himself undertook in 1940–41 a pioneering (but largely forgotten) study of the "system of markets in the Oaxaca valley" in Mexico (Malinowski and de la Fuente 1982).
9. For the sake of the argument, I am leaving aside a number of fascinating ethnographies of capitalist markets, some of which specifically analyze "the Work of Economics" (Mitchell 2005); see for instance the "ethnographies of economy/ics" in Brazil by Motta et al. (2014).
10. For a synthetic (and sympathetic) appraisal, see Garcia-Parpet (2014). Bourdieu followed Max Weber in borrowing a number of economic terms, such as capital, market, investment, conversion rate, etc., to describe and explain the social world.
11. Polanyi drew heavily on Malinowski and Richard Thurnwald to elaborate his principles of redistribution and reciprocity (see especially Polanyi 1944: Chapter 4).
12. For an early critique of "household" as an analytic category in African anthropology, see Guyer (1981).
13. Another group conducted parallel inquiries among Amazonian peasant communities.
14. In fact, I am here following Malinowski's own advice: "If we were to use our criterion of economic relevance to the exclusion of other considerations, . . . we would do violence to the native point of view, which no anthropologist can afford to do" (1965: 335).
15. I have been conducting fieldwork since 1997 in three land reform settlement projects (*projetos de assentamento*) on former sugarcane plantations (*engenhos*), in the district I call Coqueiros, in the Zona da Mata of southern Pernambuco. See de L'Estoile (in press).
16. INCRA (National Institute for Colonization and Land Reform) is the official federal agency in charge of managing the Brazilian Land Reform policy. Its regional headquarters are located in Recife, the capital of Pernambuco.

17. The parallel between these modes of rule underpins Foucault's play on the polysemy of "government," when, inspired by Aristotle and Xenophon, he proposes to analyze "governmental technologies" (1997: 300). Among the various formulations of governmentality by Foucault, I find "contact between the technologies of domination of others and those of the self" (ibid.: 18) the most stimulating.
18. Foucault (1986: 153) sums up Xenophon's approach of *oikonomia* as follows: "the domestic skill is of the same nature than political or military skills, in so far as it is about governing the other."
19. Polanyi (1957: 92) points out that *"Chrematistiké* was deliberately employed by Aristotle in the literal sense of providing for the necessaries of life, instead of its usual meaning of money-making." He suggests it refers to "the art of supply, i.e. procuring the necessaries of life in kind."
20. Aristotle (n.d.: 1259b) underlines that *"oikonomia* involves more care for humans that for the acquisition of things, more for the quality of humans than of things, more for free men than for slaves."
21. However, Polanyi's interest in countering the "market model" in economics led him to enlist Aristotle as a pioneer of the substantivist position (1957: 82).
22. For the ethnographic productivity of looking at the house from the point of view of its government, see de L'Estoile and Neiburg (2020).
23. In *Politics*, Book 3, Aristotle (n.d.: 1278b) states that the end of the political community (*polis*) is not only to insure life (*zein*), but good life (*kalôs zein*). Here I stretch Aristotle's reasoning by suggesting that this works also for the *oikos*. My concern is not exegetic (being faithful to the letter of Aristotle), but rather heuristic (pursuing a conversation involving ancient Greeks and my contemporary interlocutors).
24. In the Trobriand case, *politiké* would include the power relationships with the chiefs, but also the colonial context mostly left out of Malinowski's account.
25. In this region, land reform program beneficiaries received plots which usually varied from 7 to 12 ha.
26. Having reached 60, Zé Joaquim is entitled to receive a "rural pension," the value of which is equivalent to the minimum wage.
27. I have been visiting the place as a friend since 1993. Over the years, I have shared numerous activities, celebrations, and conversations with Vânia, her family, and her neighbors.
28. While a similar point could be made about other fields, such as political or moral anthropology, economic anthropology is unique in its long-standing dependence on another discipline.

References

Aristotle. n.d. "Politics (Politika)." Perseus Digital Library Project. Retrieved 3 November 2023 from https://www.perseus.tufts.edu/hopper/text.jsp?doc=Perseus:text:1999.01.0057.

Bourdieu, Pierre. 2017. *Anthropologie économique, Fondements sociaux de l'action économique. Cours au Collège de France 1992–1993*. Paris: Seuil.

Bücher, Karl. 1901 [1893]. *Industrial Evolution*. New York: H. Holt.
Carrier, James. 2018. "Moral Economy: What's In a Name." *Anthropological Theory* 18(1): 18–35.
Cassel, Gustav. 1923. *The Theory of Social Economy*. London: T. Fisher Unwin.
Cavalcanti, Mariana. 2009. "Do barraco à casa: Tempo, espaço e valor(es) em uma favela Consolidada." *Revista Brasileira de Ciências Sociais* 24(69): 69–81.
Chayanov, A. V. 1966. *On the Theory of Peasant Economy*. Homewood, IL: Richard Irwin.
Cook, Scott, and Michael W. Young, 2016. "Malinowski, Herskovits, and the Controversy over Economics in Anthropology." *History of Political Economy* 48(4): 657–79.
Da Matta, Roberto. 1987. *A casa e a rua*. Rio de Janeiro: Guanabara.
De L'Estoile, Benoît. 2014. "'Money Is Good, but a Friend Is Better': Uncertainty, Orientation to the Future, and 'the Economy.'" *Current Anthropology* 55(9): 62–73.
———. 2015. "La réunion comme outil et rituel de gouvernement." *Genèses* 98(1): 7–27.
———. In press. "Economy, Oikonomia, Governing Everyday Practices (Brazil)." In *Oxford Research Encyclopaedia* (online). Oxford: Oxford University Press.
De L'Estoile, Benoît, and Federico Neiburg, eds. 2020. "Governing the House." Special issue. *Etnografica* 24(3).
De L'Estoile, Benoît, and Lygia Sigaud. 2006. *Ocupações de terra e transformações sociais: Uma experiência de etnografia coletiva*. Rio de Janeiro: Editora da Fundaçao Getulio Vargas.
Dumont, Louis. 1983. "Preface." In Karl Polanyi, *La grande transformation: Aux origines politiques et économiques de notre temps*, i–xix. Paris: Gallimard.
Dumans Guedes, André. 2017. "Construindo e Estabilizando: Cidades, Casas e Pessoas." *Mana—Estudos de Antropologia Social* 23(3): 403–35.
Firth, Raymond. 1927. "The Study of Primitive Economics." *Economica* 21: 312–35.
———. 1929. *Primitive Economics of the New Zealand Maori*. New York: E.P. Dutton.
———. 1964. "Capital, Saving and Credit in Peasant Societies: A Viewpoint from Economic Anthropology." In *Capital, Saving and Credit in Peasant Societies: Studies from Asia, Oceania, the Caribbean and Middle America*, ed. Raymond Firth and Basil Yamey, 15–34. Chicago: Aldine.
Foks, Freddy. 2020. "Raymond Firth, between Economics and Anthropology." In *Bérose—Encyclopédie internationale des histoires de l'anthropologie*. Paris. Retrieved 3 November 2023 from https://www.berose.fr/article1926.html?lang=fr.
Foucault, Michel. 1986. *The History of Sexuality (Vol. 2): The Use of Pleasure*. London: Penguin.
———.1988. "Technologies of the Self." In *Technologies of the Self: A Seminar with Michel Foucault*, ed. Luther H. Martin, Huck Gutman, and Patrick H. Hutton, 16–49. Amherst: University of Massachusetts Press.
———. 1997. [1984]. "The Ethics of the Concern of the Self as a Practice of Freedom." In *Ethics: Subjectivity and Truth*, 281–301. New York: New Press.
Garcia, Afrânio, Jr. 1983. *Terra de trabalho: Trabalho familiar de pequenos produtores*. Rio de Janeiro: Paz e Terra.
Garcia-Parpet, Marie-France. 2014. "Marché, rationalité et faits sociaux totaux: Pierre Bourdieu et l'économie." *Revue Française de Socio-Économie* 13: 107–27.

Gregory, Chris. 2009. "Whatever Happened to Householding?" In *Market and Society: The Great Transformation Today*, ed. Chris Hann and Keith Hart, 133–59. Cambridge: Cambridge University Press.

Gudeman, Stephen. 2016. *Anthropology and Economy*. Cambridge: Cambridge University Press.

Gudeman, Stephen, and Chris Hann, eds. 2015. *Oikos and Market: Explorations in Self-Sufficiency after Socialism*. New York: Berghahn.

Guyer, Jane. 1981. "Household and Community in African Studies." *African Studies Review* 24: 87–138.

Hann, Chris, and Keith Hart. 2011. *Economic Anthropology: History, Ethnography, Critique*. Cambridge: Polity.

Heredia, Beatriz. 1979. *Morada da vida*. Rio de Janeiro: Paz e Terra.

Malinowski, Bronisław. 1921. "The Primitive Economics of the Trobriand Islanders." *The Economic Journal* 31(121): 1–16.

———. 1922. *Argonauts of the Western Pacific: An Account of Native Enterprise and Adventure in the Archipelagoes of Melanesian New Guinea*. London: Routledge & Kegan Paul.

———. 1925. "Labour and Primitive Economics." *Nature* 116: 926–30.

———. 1965 [1935]. *Coral Gardens and Their Magic*. 2 vols. Bloomington: Indiana University Press.

Malinowski, Bronisław, and Julio de la Fuente. 1982. *Malinowski in Mexico: The Economics of a Mexican Market System*, ed. Susan Drucker-Brown. London: Routledge & Kegan Paul.

Marshall, Alfred. 1890–1920. *Principles of Economics*. London: Palgrave Macmillan.

Mitchell, Timothy. 2005. "The Work of Economics: How a Discipline Makes Its World." *European Journal of Sociology* 46(2): 297–320.

———. 2008. "Rethinking Economy." *Geoforum* 39(3): 1116–21.

Motta, Eugênia. 2014. "Houses and Economy in the Favela." *Vibrant—Virtual Brazilian Anthropology* 11(1): 118–58.

Motta, Eugênia, Federico Neiburg, Fernando Rabossi, and Lúcia Müller, eds. 2014. "Ethnographies of Economy/ics." *Vibrant—Virtual Brazilian Anthropology* 11(1).

Narotzky, Susana, and Niko Besnier. 2014. "Crisis, Value, and Hope: Rethinking the Economy." *Current Anthropology* 55(9): 4–16.

Palmeira, Moacir. 1977. "Casa e trabalho: notas sobre as relações sociais na plantation tradicional." *Contraponto*, 2: 103–14.

Pearson, Heath. 2000. "Homo Economicus Goes Native, 1859–1945: The Rise and Fall of Primitive Economics." *History of Political Economy* 32(4): 933–89.

Polanyi, Karl. 1944. *The Great Transformation*. New York: Farrar & Rinehart.

———. 1957. "Aristotle Discovers the Economy." In *Trade and Market in the Early Empires: Economies in History and Theory*, ed. Karl Polanyi, Conrad M. Arensberg, and Harry W. Pearson, 64–94. Glencoe, IL: Free Press.

———. 1977. *The Livelihood of Man*. New York: Academic Press.

Schmidt, Max. 1920. *Grundriss der ethnologischen Volkswirtschatslehre*. Stuttgart: Enke.

Sigaud, Lygia. 2008. "A Collective Ethnographer: Fieldwork Experience in the Brazilian Northeast." *Social Science Information* 47: 71–97.

Taussig, F. W. 1911. *Principles of Economics*. New York: Macmillan.

Thurnwald, Richard. 1932. *Economics in Primitive Communities*. Oxford: Oxford University Press.

Xenophon. n.d. *The Economist: A Treatise on the Science of the Household in the Form of a Dialogue*. Project Gutenberg. Retrieved 3 November 2023 from https://www.gutenberg.org/files/1173/1173-h/1173-h.htm.

Young, Michael W. 2004. *Malinowski: Odyssey of an Anthropologist, 1884–1920*. New Haven, CT: Yale University Press.

Weber, Florence, and Julien Ténédos. 2006. *L'économie domestique: Entretien avec Florence Weber*. Paris. Aux Lieux d'être.

Weber, Max. 1968 [1922]. *Economy and Society*, ed. Guenther Roth and Claus Wittich. New York: Bedminster.

Part III

Cosmology, History, and Social Organization

9

Baloma

The Spirits of the Kula in the Trobriand Islands

MARK S. MOSKO

> In general the spirits do not influence human beings very much, for better or worse.
> —Bronisław Malinowski, *Argonauts of the Western Pacific*

> As it turns out, the ancestors are indispensable agents in all varieties of human endeavor, risky or not.
> —Marshall Sahlins, *The New Science of the Enchanted Universe*

Few works in anthropology rival the influence of Bronisław Malinowski's *Argonauts of the Western Pacific* (1922). Its publication established the modern standards for ethnographic research, launched the subfield of economic anthropology, reshaped the discipline's early grasp of premodern societies generally, and, supplemented by later works, enshrined the Trobriand Islands as emblematic of Melanesia as a culture area.

In this chapter, grounded on fieldwork conducted over sixteen years from 2006 at Omarakana where Malinowski initiated his pathbreaking studies, I reexamine certain ethnographic anomalies and misinterpretations of Indigenous Trobriand magico-religious practices as reported in *Argonauts* that have resulted in an impoverished view of the scope of economics as conceptualized by subsequent generations of scholars within and beyond anthropology. First, I challenge Malinowski's conclusion that, in islanders' understanding, *baloma* spirits of the dead do not play the principal agentive role in the Kula-associated magical spells (*megwa, yopu*) in which they are invoked. Second, I argue that this dismissal of spirits' participation in magic mistakenly restricted the scope of Massim Kula practice to relations between living people and between them and the material "things" physically exchanged or otherwise utilized in facilitating such exchanges (e.g., transacted shell valuables, canoes, and items of bodily decoration and hospitality). Third, I offer a new, ethnographically based interpretation of Trobrianders' Kula magic as instances of sacrificial reciprocity, termed *bwekasa*, between living people and spirits of the dead. Fourth, from that vantage I reanalyze certain long-standing anomalous comparative distinctions between the Trobriand Islands and other Massim societies: chieftainship versus egalitarian leadership; differential ranking of Kula magical spells, shell valuables, and exchange "roads"; variations in Kula players' access to *vaigua* ("wealth") and *butula* ("fame"); discrepant ideologies of procreation and the afterlife (i.e., spirit immortality versus reincarnation); and variations in players' motivations for entering the Kula. Finally, fifth, I examine critically Marcel Mauss's (2016) analytical reduction of precapitalist economics to the three classic obligations (i.e., giving, receiving, and returning) as an unwarranted consequence of his acceptance of Malinowski's pragmatic view of Kula magic.

The Magical Agency of Spirits

In Chapter 17 of *Argonauts* (1922: 392–427), Malinowski analyzed the magical spells and successive rites of Kula: canoe manufacture, sailing and captaincy, weather control, protection from witch attack and shipwreck, the courting of trading partners, the elicitation of valuables, and, upon arrival at home, their ceremonial distribution. Despite highly equivocal evidence, he concluded that the "magical force" of Kula *megwa* spells resided in the enunciated words themselves rather than with the agency of the ancestral *baloma* spirits invoked in them.

> [W]e see that the spirits act as advisors and helpers. They fill the role of guardian of the traditions when they get angry because of a bad performance, or as associates and sympathizers when they share the magician's [payment for services]. But they are not agencies which get to work directly. In the Trobriand demonology, the magician does not command the spirits to go and set to work. The work is done by the agency of the spell, assisted by the accompanying ritual, and performed by the proper magician. The spirits stand in the same relation, as the performer does, to the magical force, which alone is active. They can help him to wield it properly, but they can never become his instruments. (Ibid.: 423)[1]

Malinowski's theoretical pragmatism here followed directly from James Frazer's (1922) categorical distinction between "magic," which is basically mechanistic, and "religion," which relies on interventions of transcendental supernatural beings. Subsequent ethnographers of the Massim have mostly confined their investigations of Kula magic, and thus Kula itself, to the Frazerian parameters accepted by Malinowski.[2]

My recent consultations with the Omarakana Tabalu Paramount Chief, Pulayasi Daniel, and other acknowledged ritual authorities across northern Kiriwina, supplemented by archival study, point to the exact opposite conclusion. *Megwa* spells are a type of sacrificial gift reciprocity (*bwekasa*) between living people inhabiting the visible, material world (Boyowa) and ancestral *baloma* residing in the immaterial, invisible spirit world of the dead (Tuma). Thus, as Marshall Sahlins (2017: 54; 2022: 18–19, 63–66, 94) recently noted, the failure to address ancestral *baloma* participation in Kula and other Indigenous "magic" has excluded the very agents deemed critical by native practitioners. This omission has reduced anthropologists' grasp of economics to acts of production, exchange, and consumption *between strictly living people.*

In *Argonauts*, Malinowski makes passing reference to several examples of *bwekasa* using different rubrics. During the concluding ceremonies of *milamala* harvest ceremonies, community members' current hoard of Kula valuables and other permanent wealth (axe blades, body ornaments and decorations) are formally presented (*yolova*) to departing ancestral *baloma*, who extract from them their inner "shadows" (*kekwabu*) to carry back to the underworld, Tuma. Of these, the Kula shells "represent the most effective offering to be given to the spirits, through which they can be put into a pleasant state of mind" (Malinowski 1922: 512).[3] Also during *milamala*, neighboring households exchange bowls of cooked food that have been "ceremoniously exposed in houses for the use of the spirits, after these have consumed the spiritual substance" (ibid.: 184; see below). *Pokala* "solicitory offerings" to "mythical" (i.e., spiritual) persons, "Kultur-heroes," and ancestral spirits are given to elicit their benefits and blessings (ibid.: 332–34, 378). Malinowski uses the same term, *pokala*, when describing the solicitory gifts and offerings presented by Kula players to their exchange partners when seeking to obtain a specific shell valuable from them (ibid.: 99, 205, 354–55, 360). He mentions *yolova* presentations of crewmen's acquired shells to accompanying spirits as "sacrifices" in *tanarere* ceremonies performed at the conclusion of Kula voyages (ibid.: 512). Receiving these gifts, *baloma* perform their own *tanerere* ceremonies on the beach of Tuma Island (ibid.: 374, 375, 391, 512) and thereafter engage in Kula exchanges of their own. Both of those activities, as *bwekasa*, reinvigorate the shells and fame of the spirits and their descendants.[4]

Trobrianders are not alone in formally seeking to elicit benefits and blessings from *baloma* through the offering of *bwekasa*-like sacrifices. Upon return from voyaging to Sinaketa and Vakua, Dobuans staged *tanarere* offerings of collectively acquired Kula wealth to the assisting ancestral spirits who had been invited to accompany them (Malinowski 1922: 375, 393). My Omarakana interlocutors insist that sacrificial practices like *bwekasa* are performed in all Kula communities, wherever magical spells are addressed to local spirits.

Bwekasa: Sacrificial Reciprocity

The labors involved in the production, exchange, and consumption of daily family meals usefully illustrate the intimate link between human–human "exchange" and human–spirit *bwekasa* sacrifice that is characteristic of Kula and other transactional contexts. Cutting and boiling raw plant and meat staples "kills" them, rendering them "dirty" and inimical to or disharmonious with villager life and thereby "sacred" or "tabooed" (*bomaboma*). Once cooked, the food is placed in bowls and briefly set aside while family members reflect upon all the "blessings" (*bobwelila*) they have received from their ancestors, including the meal set before them. During these moments, the spirits consume the food's inner shadows, depositing invisible bits of their watery "saliva" (*bubwalua*) that miraculously transform the dead meal into a taboo-free, "open," "harmonious," "clean," and, therefore, life-giving state for family members to eat.[5] Additional bowls of desanctified food are often prepared for reciprocal exchange between related households (and not just during *milamala* festivities, as claimed by Malinowski).

The term *bubwalua* is used to denote all fluids (*sopi*, "water") of the body, particularly when expelled, not just as saliva, but as "sweat" (*kapwe'isi*), "blood" (*buyai*), and genital secretions (*momona*). The examples given above, where Malinowski alluded to several instances of essentially *bwekasa* offerings as "*bubwalua*," affirm *baloma* spirits' sacrificially transformative nature and powers.

In their initial raw state, food staples are ambiguously inedible to both human and spirit persons since they embody the "dead" and "dirty" "sweat" excreted by the parties that worked jointly in their production. The killing effect of cooking converts food further to being unambiguously dead as far as living people are concerned, but unambiguously open, clean, harmonious, and supportive of the spiritual being of deceased *baloma* spirits. Analogously, the spirits' potent excreted saliva, which is dead and thus dirty and inimical to their Tuman life, is clean, open, harmonious, and life-giving to people of Boyowa. Omarakanans maintain that if they ate their foods raw or even cooked but untransformed by spirits' saliva, they would starve. And in the absence of *bwekasa* offerings of food, spirits in Tuma would be deprived of the sustenance required for their spirit lives.

Through these and analogous *bwekasa* reciprocities, humans and spirits provision each other with "life" (*momova*).[6] They can do this because the refracted human Boyowa and spirit Tuma realms both mirror and invert each other. What is dead to the dead is living to the living, and what is living to the dead is dead to the living.

The bodily and magical exertions collaboratively undertaken by people and ancestral spirits during all phases of food production and distribution (Malinowski 1935a, 1935b) and in other culturally sanctioned enterprises (fishing, house building, canoe and artifact carving, dancing, feasting, copulation, Kula exchange and hospitalities, sorcery, etc.) are classified as instances of *paisewa* ("labor" or "work"). In other words, goal-directed "mental activity" or "thought" (*nano*) qualifies as transactable mind-to-mind *paisewa* labor no less than skin-to-skin physical effort. Indeed, peoples' thoughts are frequently referred to as *sopi*, the generic term for water, in view of the manner in which thoughts are experienced as flowing through one's mind.[7] Accordingly, products generated through human agency incorporate both the liquid physical and the fluid mental *bubwalua* sweat of their respective creators' persons. In this way, the bodily and mental *kekwabu* images of a working person are transferred to the items created through those efforts or to the person(s) to whom they are directed (or both). Virtually all types of exchange in Trobriand sociality consist of transactions involving personal tokens of *bubwalua*. Parents wishing to instill in their children an appreciation of the life they have received, for example, commonly refer to the "sweat" that they have bestowed upon them.

A particular dynamic of "life" (*momova*) and "death" (*kaliga*) is central to the link between *paisewa* labor and *bwekasa* sacrifice.[8] Any act of work is understood to engender in the laborer the feeling of "pain" (*gidageda*) that is construed as a kind or expression of death. The experiences of "pleasure" or "happiness" (*mwasila*) in the absence of work and pain are indicative of or consonant with life. Even so, villagers view labor as essential for life's sustenance. Garden labor, for example, while painful and deathlike, is a necessity for the provision of the foods required for human (and spirit) existence. By the same token, for human beings to be capable of deathlike laboring, they must be alive. Additionally, the hot *bubwalua* sweat of laboring humans, transferred to the skins of co-laboring spirits, enables the latter to cool and revive their spirit bodies so that they can return to deathlike labors; and reciprocally the sweat resulting from *baloma* labor revivifies people at rest sufficiently for them eventually to resume their exertions. In this way, humans and spirits enable each other to undertake and complete arduous projects without killing themselves, which would be the result if they endeavored to labor ceaselessly. This explains how and why *bubwalua* excretions that are dead and dirty to one party in contexts of *bwekasa* sacrifice are clean and life-giving to the other. *Bwekasa* labors conducted for the life of others incur death to oneself. Death is a prerequisite to life, just as life is to death. Accordingly, ancestral *baloma* are mythically the "source" or "origin" (*u'ula*) of living Trobrianders' lives, just as living people's death-like labors are necessary for the continuance of their deceased ancestors' Tuman existence. Through *bwekasa*, the living and dead provide life to each other.

These new data illustrate the radical disparity between Trobrianders' ritualistic cosmology and Malinowski's pragmatic perspective on the formal meaning of "labor" and his untenable dichotomization of the "economic" versus the "non-economic." Recall, for example, Malinowski's (1918: 89; 1921; 1935a: 17, 435; 1992b: 30–31: 1992c: 139) accounts of villagers' felt needs for magical support in high-risk, dangerous or highly uncertain shark and mullet (*kalala*) fishing and the absence of any need for magic in the supposedly low-risk, safe, and predictable fishing on reefs of the shallow lagoon. In fact, according to fishers I have interviewed, successful lagoon fishing involves complex magico-religious *bwekasa*-type transactions of labor-sweat with spirit beings analogous to those employed in shark and mullet fishing, gardening, canoe carving, sorcery, curing, and Kula, whether in the form of traditional *megwa* or, nowadays, introduced Christian prayers (Mosko 2017: 397–411; cf. Gregory, this volume).[9]

Just how the verbal utterance of a *megwa* magical spell in Kula or other contexts qualifies as *bubwalua* sweat- or saliva-generating labor (or both) analogous to other physical *paisewa* exertions, as outlined above, requires additional explication. First, the recital of *megwa* spells is regarded as "hot" (*gasisi, yuviyavi*) or effective in producing the magician's desired result, like every other type of labor. The mere voicing of spells thus involves the oral discharge of dead, dirty saliva and breath containing the images or shadows referenced by the words of the spell, which ordinarily, once learned by the magician, are dispersed throughout their body (*wowola*) and mind (*nanola*).[10] The externalized complex of images that *is* the spell is thus a *bwekasa* offering to the magician's invisibly-attending *baloma* predecessors who, during their material Boyowan lifetimes, also embodied and vocalized it. The acting magician and associated spirits thus amount to a single "person" (*tomota*). Once invoked, through the invisible transference of the magician's oral *bubwalua*, his allied spirits invisibly affect the changes stipulated in the spell so as to transform the target's or patient's previous dispositions to align with the magician's desires (e.g., light to heavy, slow to fast, repulsive to attractive, dirty to clean, greedy to generous, living to dead, and so on, or the reverse of these), just as they had accomplished during their earlier Boyowan careers.

Kula Exchange as *Bwekasa*

Via *bubwalua* transfers of sweat and saliva between persons (living and deceased) implicated in the manufacture, handling, exchange, and magical treatment of armshells (*mwali*) and necklaces (*soulava*), Kula valuables come to incorporate the detached *kekwabu*, personal images, of their current and previous possessors. This is a clear ethnographic illustration of Marilyn Strathern's (1988, 2018) basic model of Melanesian dividuality, which expands the concept of personhood to encompass the kinds of material "objects" routinely transacted by people in systems of elicitive gift exchange epitomized by Kula. However, the Trobriand view of *baloma* spirits' participation in sacrificial *bwekasa* reciprocities (including Kula) broadens this idea of the dividual or partible person to include the sorts of nonhuman spiritual or sacred beings—"*divine* dividuals"—with whom Melanesians and other peoples commonly interact in accord with the econo-magico-religious contexts of their cosmologies and cultures.[11]

That Kula consists in life–death *bwekasa* conversions for inhabitants of both Boyowa and Tuma is exemplified when, in presenting an armshell or necklace to his partner, the host forcefully throws it (i.e., an act of vigorous, laboriously generated sweat) to the ground. This is effectively to kill and sacrifice his relation to it, which his affiliated ancestors, being dead, experience as *bubwalua* that gives them new Kula life.[12] While momentarily resting there, the giver's *baloma* allies simultaneously coordinate their labors with his so as to deposit their sweat on the armshell or necklace, thereby reinvigorating it for attachment to, and to the benefit of, the new owners—the receiving partner and his *baloma* allies. When the object is next sacrificed by that first recipient to his partner, the original giver and his ancestors are revived as the sweat of that transaction is communicated to them via the images of their persons still attached to the shell. Through these embodiments and disembodiments of the shadowy images of participating *baloma* spirits, the roads of Kula exchange that Malinowski described as circulating through Boyowa are invisibly extended to and duplicated across Tuma. When living people transact Kula, ancestral *baloma* are thereby equipped to engage in shell exchanges of their own (see below).

Anomalies

Recognition that *baloma* and other spirits are traditionally recognized as the crucial agents of Trobriand Kula magic presents an opportunity for reexamining certain long-recognized contrasts between the Trobriand Islands and most other Massim societies, which till now have been either poorly explained or left as anomalous. These include variations in leadership patterns; the ranking of Kula spells, shells, and roads; the factors underpinning the achievement of "fame" and "renown" (*butula*); and understandings of the afterlife and procreative process. The last of these have triggered some of the most animated disputes of modern anthropology's history.

The Trobriand system of hierarchically ranked, hereditary "chiefs" (*guyau*) has been recognized as distinct from more "egalitarian" Massim polities (approximating the Melanesian "big men" model) since before Malinowski's time (cf. Liang, Steinmüller, this volume). On the basis of hereditary succession and traditional entitlement, certain high-ranking Tabalu and other official chiefs of the Trobriands have monopolized the shells that flow through the archipelago. These men have enjoyed near absolute access to the highest-ranked (*tukwa*) shells circulating on the highest-ranked Kula roads. As items of durable wealth, such shells and roads are regarded as effectively permanent or eternal, immune to the possibilities of shell loss or road corruption. Lower-ranking "commoner" (*tokay*) Trobrianders who serve as their chiefly captains' crewmen are limited to the trade of fewer and lower-ranked (*sosewa*) shells flowing on lower-ranked roads, which are much more vulnerable to rerouting, theft, loss, and disappearance.

Such hereditary disparities in social standing and access to Kula valuables and renown are largely absent elsewhere in the Massim. Although some local leaders may be accorded the title of *guyau*, they realize and hold their positions on mostly performative criteria that are nominally open to others—notably the achievement of Kula renown. The competition for large numbers of shells and for high-ranking ones is thus relatively open to all competent adult men, with the support of industrious wives.

The inherent temporal durability and spatial transportability of Kula shell valuables distinguishes them from other items of material wealth traditionally encountered in the economies of the societies of the Kula ring (Malinowski 1922: 357–58). As such, Kula shells serve as unique imperishable vehicles for the achievement of widespread, lasting personal fame for Kula participants. However, those capacities are not uniform for the differently ranked shells that travel along differently ranked *keda* roads. Personal histories of the manufacturing, possession, and exchange of armshells and necklaces serve as matchless indices of players' fame (but see below). Compared with neighboring regions, these capacities play out differently in the Trobriands. The chiefs' heritable monopoly of the most renowned shells and the most stable roads on which they travel effectively guarantees that their fame will resound in perpetuity, or as long as Kula continues to function. Few Kula masters elsewhere in the Massim can match this control over the highest-ranked shells and roads. The fame of commoner Trobrianders, however, is curbed because their participation in Kula is limited to lower-ranking *sosewa* shells associated with comparatively mobile *sosewa* magical spells and roads.

The *megwa* spells of Trobriand magic in Kula and other contexts, which function as *bwekasa* sacrifice, as outlined above, are also culturally distinguished as *tukwa* or *sosewa*. In *Argonauts*, Malinowski glossed these terms as "systematic" and "independent," respectively.

> The [independent, *sosewa*] incantation is a free, individual act, which may be performed and is performed in any of the circumstances which require it. It is quite another matter with the spells belonging to what I have called here *systematic magic*. Such magic consists of a connected and consecutive body of incantation and concomitant rites, not one of which can be torn out of its sequence and performed by itself . . . *in this book almost all the rites and spells described belong to this* [tukwa] *class*. (1922: 413, emphasis added)

Tukwa spells are tied to specific *dala* matrilineages. They require the correct invocation by name of the ancestral *baloma* who previously possessed them and who are identified as their agents. When a *tukwa* magician dies, his name is added to the list of spirits to be invoked by his successors. *Tukwa* spells are thus inherited within the *dala*, and to that extent they and the names and fame of their possessors are perpetual and only members are qualified to recite and use them effectively.[13] *Tukwa* spells typically target whole groups of people rather than single persons (i.e., hamlets, villages, gardening parties, canoe crews, etc.) as patients or beneficiaries. By that measure, *tukwa* are considerably more powerful than *sosewa* spells. Most of the Kula magic described is *Argonauts* is *tukwa*, as Malinowski noted. While *tolivalu* headmen of commoner *dala* and villages transact heritable *tukwa* spells transacted along *tukwa* roads, those spells tend to be collectively subsidiary or tied to the *tukwa* spells and powers of the locally preeminent chief's *dala*.[14] In the Trobriands, the *tukwa* spells pertaining to Kula are overwhelmingly chiefly possessions.

In contrast, there is no requirement to invoke by name a spell's previous possessors in the case of the less powerful independent spells deployed by Kula traders in seeking to elicit specific low-ranking shells from their partners. However, *sosewa* too rely on *baloma* agency insofar as *sosewa* magicians identify personally with their predecessors through the strict observance of the "taboos" (*kikila*) that they in their lifetimes had observed. *Sosewa* spells are not associated with particular *dalas* and are transmitted through diverse relations and exchange processes. Thus, the magical knowledge of most commoner Kula players in the Trobriands consists of *sosewa* spells that typically mark singular persons as patients, such as one's Kula partner. Insofar as the names of the previous owners of *sosewa* spells are *not* voiced, the spatio-temporal quotient of their possessors' fame is considerably less than that attributed to the possessors of *tukwa* spells, past and present.

Analogues of both *tukwa* and *sosewa* spells appear to exist in the magical repertoires of non-Trobriand Kula communities of the Massim. Given the more open big-man styles of leadership encountered throughout the region, active Kula players there are not categorically denied access to the most powerful spells because of birthright discriminations.

The achievement of personal fame or renown (*butula*) is, of course, the prime motivating factor for all participating men in Kula and their wives in lending support. As argued by Munn, Damon, and others, Massim fame consists in the extent to which a person's name is spread spatially and temporally: that is, detached from his person and incorporated in the knowledge tied to the inalienable material tokens (i.e., *vaigua* shells) that he has formally transacted through exchange. By receiving and giving away a specific shell, a Kula player includes his name in its lore as far and as long as it circulates along its appointed road. The cumulative extent of a man's (and wife's) Kula fame thus correlates with the overall volume of the shells transacted over his career; the rank of shells transacted, whether *tukwa* or *sosewa*; the rank of the magic, *tukwa* or *sosewa*, identified with his person and the potency of the spirits included in it; and the extent of hospitality that they as a couple are known to have extended to the man's Kula partners.

On the basis of these criteria, Trobriand chiefs active in the Kula nominally enjoy perpetual fame and renown on a scale vastly exceeding that of the men and women of their local commoner followings. Historically there have been Kula masters elsewhere in the Kula ring whose fame has rivaled or even exceeded that of Trobriand chiefs, but no analogous categorical impediment blocks other Massim players in the way that *tokai* Trobrianders are unable to rival their chiefs. Returning from Kula expeditions with significantly more renowned and greater numbers of shells received from their more numerous trade partners, Trobriand chiefs are equipped to sponsor the most generous and impressive *yolova* (i.e., *bwekasa*) "offering" to spirits "of what is most valued by the living" (Malinowski 1922: 512) at key moments of the Kiriwinan calendar (for example, at the conclusion of *milamala* festivities noted above, when *baloma* spirits upon departure for Tuma are formally presented Kula shells). Similarly, the wives of Kula-active chiefs have greater access than other women to a wider range of other wealth items through *valova* exchange and are thereby in privileged positions for accumulating large quantities of *doba* bundles and skirts to distribute at sacrificial *lisaladabu* mortuary distributions (Lepani 2012: 91). This is a distinctive Trobriand practice and key source of the inflated "fame" of chiefs' wives.[15]

Trobriand chiefs' advantages in generating Kula fame are amplified through their role in staging consolidated offerings of shell valuables (*tanarere*) acquired on overseas *uvalaku* voyages. As Malinowski (1922: 375) described, upon landing the shells obtained by the men of a given canoe are grouped together and sacrificially displayed in the name of their "captain" (*toliwaga*), typically one of the local chiefs. But the shells of all the canoes comprising the whole flotilla are also presented simultaneously in the name of the one "fleet master" (*toli'uvalaku*) who, throughout Omarakana history, has always been the Tabalu Paramount Chief. Thus his name becomes attached to each shell included in the fleet's entire hoard, and his fame is magnified proportionately. According to Malinowski (ibid.: 374–75, 512), these displays were *yolova* offerings to the *baloma* who had joined the voyage. My Omarakana sources affirm that *tanarere*, like *yolova* at the conclusion of *milamala* festivities, qualify as *bwekasa* obligations, but of a greatly enhanced order. Given that Kula fame is achieved largely through the number and quality of shells transacted by each Kula player, the name and recognition of Trobriand chiefs in the Kula system is greatly magnified by comparison with that of their commoner followings.[16] The postmortem dividend of Kula fame achievable by commoner men and women is comparatively limited; their renown, unlikely to be transmitted to future generations, will eventually be forgotten.

Kula and the Afterlife: Spirit Reincarnation versus Immortality

Throughout the Massim, among various competitive activities (gardening, fishing, canoe carving, *doba* mortuary distribution, dancing, singing, sorcery, etc.), Kula is by far the most effective means for the spreading of a person's *butula*. The fact that fame, once achieved, can and often does resound long after a person's death confirms that *butula*, by its very nature, possesses distinctive eschatological properties that transcend the gulf between Boyowa (in the Trobriand case) and the Tuman afterworld.

Nonetheless, visions of the hereafter across the Massim are far from uniform. As reported by Malinowski (1932: 145–52; 1992a) and affirmed by nearly all subsequent investigators, Trobriand notions of spirit reincarnation (*no'isi*) are unique. At death, the *baloma* leaves the body and ventures to Tuma where it enjoys a blissful existence as a *baloma* spirit undergoing a series of cyclical agings and rejuvenations—sloughing off old skin, teeth, and hair and donning a new youthful body. Eventually, however, the *baloma* tires, weakens, or becomes bored with its repetitive spirit lifestyle, especially when distant descendants neglect to acknowledge it in *bwekasa* offerings. At this point the *baloma* dies as a spirit, shedding its aged spirit body to become a *waiwaia* ("foetus" or "spirit child"). Following transportation to the womb of a Boyowan woman of the same matrilineal *dala* identity, the *waiwaia* conceives a human infant, consistent with Trobrianders' supposed "ignorance of physiological paternity."[17]

Analogous notions of spirit rebirth, however, are absent in other Kula-participating societies. There, upon dying, deceased people's souls pass to locally recognized Tuma-like realms to remain forever as immortal ancestral spirits.

What can explain this difference? The above outline of the differential scopes of Trobriand chiefly and commoner participation in sacrificial Kula exchange and magic offers a plausible answer. Given the distinctive heritable durability of chiefly *tukwa* shells, spells, and roads and the near certainty that chiefs' names will be indefinitely recalled through magical invocations and other modes of life-giving *bwekasa* offerings, Trobriand chiefs' local domination of Kula effectively guarantees that they will not reincarnate. Their fame will resound forever, just as the fame of major Kula players does elsewhere, or at least as long as the Kula system itself persists.

Commoner Trobrianders, however, are effectively denied the prospect of *baloma* immortality that is potentially available to virtually all of the adult male residents of neighboring egalitarian Massim communities. However, this does not necessarily deter *tokai* Trobrianders from participating enthusiastically in Kula or seeking fame in other contexts. On the contrary, it motivates them all the more stridently. Despite the limited durability and longevity of *sosewa*-classified shells, spells, and roads, compared with other, more mundane spheres of competition, even limited Kula success offers the most effective road or pathway for prolonging Tuma's posthumous pleasures.

The diversity of Massim views of the afterlife was recognized in the "Virgin Birth" debate of the 1960s and 1970s, but that and subsequent discussions tended to focus primarily on Indigenous ideas about procreation, while details concerning the afterlife itself attracted less interest.[18]

The controversy was recently reopened in a colloquium in the journal *Hau*. Based on survey research, Jarillo et al. (2020a, 2020b) contend that Malinowski and others who have documented Trobriand beliefs in reincarnation have been wrong; that once *baloma* pass from Boyowa to Tuma, they stay there forever in accord with the views elsewhere in the Massim. The lead authors claim that they were led to question the doctrine of reincarnation because of a fatal contradiction they perceived in my own recent treatment of Trobriand magic and kinship (Mosko 2017): "Any *baloma* brought back to life [through reincarnation] would be unavailable when called for help through magic" (Jarillo et al. 2020a: 368–69; see also MacCarthy 2020). In my published response (Mosko 2020: 401), I noted that, if people lovingly celebrate a specific *baloma* through *bwekasa* offerings—*megwa*, food, tobacco, labor, *yolova, pokala, tanerere*, etc.—that ancestor's Tuman life will be sustained, potentially forever. Over generations, as the names and exploits of other *baloma* are eventually forgotten, they will die as spirits and reincarnate.

More recently, I came across Jerry Leach's and Shirley Campbell's report of an early-1970s study where some twenty Trobriand Islanders, after reading *Argonauts*, voiced a common criticism: missing from Malinowski's account was the understanding "that men whose names are preserved by the [Kula] system break out of the cycle of reincarnation through Tuma, to live above ground forever" (Leach 1983: 12); that is, as celestial stars, as Campbell (1983: 204–5) and Scoditti (1983: 272) separately reported.[19]

I take these data to confirm my account of there being two traditional roads to the Trobriand afterlife, with Kula participation as a key determining factor: reincarnation for those *baloma* spirits whose *butula* fame among the living of Boyowa is relatively limited; and celestial immortality for those spirits whose earthly fame is effectively everlasting.

This finding is directly relevant to questions in Massim prehistory and history: namely, whether Trobriand chiefly inequality is an "evolutionary" product of early European influences upon a previously egalitarian population, or whether the larger region's egalitarian polities are the consequence of "devolution" from previously hierarchical systems (see e.g., Macintyre 1994; Young 1994; Bickler 2006; cf. Steinmüller, this volume). The correspondence of Trobriand chiefly immortality with Massim eschatologies elsewhere would seem to support the latter hypothesis. And if that is the case, it could be argued that the cultural anomaly that Trobriand society presents for the wider region is not so much the presence of ranked *guyau* chieftainship but that of *tokai* commonership.

Malinowski, *Megwa*, and Mauss

By way of conclusion, I suggest that Malinowski's dismissal of *baloma* spirits' agentive participations in Trobriand magic and Kula has had a misleading influence upon economic anthropology because of Marcel Mauss's (2016) appropriation of Malinowski's account of Kula.[20] As Jane Guyer (2016: 5) recently noted, for Mauss, "the '*spiritual* character' of exchange" (my emphasis) was a "fundamental point of the whole argument of *The Gift*," well exemplified by Mauss's two other major illustrations of total prestation.[21] For Mauss (2016: 62, 79, 116–17n141, 119–20n152), northwest American potlatches highlighted the "worship of the great gods, totems, or the collective or individual ancestors of the clan" and the sacrifices directed toward them. With respect to the Maori notion of *hau*, he argued that "the most important amongst these *spiritual* mechanisms is evidently that which obliges the return on the present received" (ibid.: 64, emphasis added).²²

Mauss was considerably more circumspect when drawing upon Malinowski's materials, cautiously eliding personified spirits' analogous participation in Kula and other contexts of Trobriand gifting. This has served to differentiate the economies of the Massim and Melanesia generally from premodern societies elsewhere, at least on this score. While dealing with *baloma* spirits' supposed lack of magical agency, Mauss noted that Kula contained

> its mythical, religious, and magical aspect ... It is not possible to say that [Kula valuables] are really the objects of a cult, *since the Trobrianders are positivists in their own way*. But it is impossible not to recognize their eminent and sacred nature. Contact alone is enough to transfer their virtues. . . .
>
> But there is more. The contract itself is affected by this nature of the *vaygu'a*. Not only the armshells and the necklaces, but all the goods, decorations, and weapons as well, everything that belongs to the partner is thus *animated, by sentiment at least, if not by a personal soul*, so that they themselves take part in the contract. (Mauss 2016: 94–95, emphases added, footnotes deleted)

It would seem that Mauss was warily weighing factors that inhibited any direct calling out of Malinowski on his disclaimers of *baloma* magical agency. No doubt *Argonauts* justifiably steered Mauss toward his formulation of the three core obligations: to give, to receive, and to return (Mauss 2016: 73–76). But, as Maurice Godelier (1999: 29–31) has reminded us, Mauss also noted a fourth obligation, missing from the well-known trilogy, namely, "the gift (*cadeau*) made to men, in sight of the gods and of nature ... The exchanges of gifts (*cadeaux*) between men, 'namesakes,' homonyms of the spirits, incite the spirits of the dead, the gods, things, animals, nature to be 'generous towards them'" (Mauss 2016: 76–77)—that is, to offer sacrifices in the expectation that the sacred recipients will reciprocate with blessings of their own.

Mauss flagged his reservations pertaining to Malinowski's disenchanted view of Trobriand magic with these words:

> *We have not conducted the general study necessary to bring out the importance of [the obligation to sacrifice]*. Moreover, the facts available do not all relate to those areas to which we have limited ourselves. Finally, *the mythological element, which we still understand poorly, is too strong on this point for us to omit it*. So we limit ourselves to a few remarks. (2016: 76, emphasis added)

This seems absurd. As early as 1899, Mauss and Henri Hubert had published *Sacrifice* (Hubert and Mauss 1964)—the foundation text for virtually all later anthropological treatments of the subject—specifically to document the cross-cultural imbrication of religion and magic, and the widespread attribution of *magical* efficacy to spirit-like beings (ibid.: 7–10). In their subsequent *A General Theory of Magic* (Mauss and Hubert 1972), they roundly demolished Frazer's differentiation of "magic" from "religion," upon which Malinowski premised his claims regarding magical agency.

Mauss's caution is all the stranger because he does in fact distil from *Argonauts* several unambiguous instances of Trobriand sacrificial practice (those that Malinowski termed "bubwalu'a," as noted above) in which Kula valuables are proffered to *baloma* to "render their spirits good" (Mauss 2016: 80). He gently chides Malinowski's (1922: 513) claim near the end of *Argonauts* that "in several respects, the Kula presents to us a new type of phenomenon." He remarks, "Malinowski exaggerates a little. . . , the novelty of these facts which are identical to those of the Tlingit potlatch and the Haida potlatch" (Mauss 2016: 80).

Additionally, Mauss certainly knew that prior to undertaking fieldwork in the Trobriands, Malinowski (1913) had reviewed Durkheim's *Elementary Forms of the Religious Life* (1912) in highly critical terms—flatly rejecting the author's methodology and core ideas concerning the universality of the sacred versus profane opposition and religion's base in society and collective representations. In opening that review, Malinowski (1913: 525) had offered thanks to Mauss and Hubert for their essays on sacrifice and magic; yet ironically, their work on those topics is entirely overlooked in *Argonauts*.

I can only surmise that Mauss chose to temper these and possibly other qualms for fear that denting Malinowski's authority on this point might undercut his use of Malinowski's ethnographic material in theorizing gift exchange more generally. After all, Malinowski's strident denials of *baloma* magical agency, based on the authority of his unprecedented field experience, left few grounds on which Mauss could confidently test him.[23]

Finally, it is perhaps worthwhile to reflect upon the effect that Mauss's reticence in critiquing Malinowski's pragmatism has had on economic anthropology more generally. How might the subdiscipline have developed had Mauss formulated precapitalist gift exchange in terms of four rather than three canonical obligations?

Acknowledgments

I am greatly indebted to key members of my Omarakana collaborators—Tabalu Pulayasi Daniel, Molubabeba Daniel, Pakalaki Tokulupai, and Yogaru Vincent—and many other northern Kiriwina elders for so generously sharing their knowledge of Indigenous traditions. The Australian Research

Council and the Wenner-Gren Foundation liberally funded my field and archival investigations. I have benefited particularly from Allan Darrah's sharing of the DEPTH database of Massim ethnography. Discussions with Marilyn Strathern, Fred Damon, and Cassandra Mosko have added greatly to the arguments, both theoretical and substantive, underpinning this chapter. I take responsibility for all errors and omissions.

Mark S. Mosko is Emeritus Professor of Anthropology at the Australian National University. He has published widely on anthropological theory based on his research of the cultures of North Mekeo and Trobriand peoples. His research collaboration at Omarakana village with locally acknowledged cultural authorities (*Ways of Baloma*, 2017) has resulted in a major reinterpretation of the Trobriand ethnographic corpus developed by Malinowski and the many ethnographers who followed in his wake.

Notes

1. See also Malinowski (1922: 407–8; 1935b: 213–50; 1992a: 201; 1992b: 73, 79, 85, 89–90).
2. See Uberoi (1962); Darrah (1972); Powell (1978); Leach and Leach (1983); Perrson (1992); Tambiah (1968, 1990). See also Mosko (2017: 109–218) for discussion of post-Malinowski ethnographers' views of *baloma* participation in further contexts.
3. Malinowski had earlier referred to *yolova* offerings (1992a: 280) as *ioiova*, which I transcribed as *yoyova* (Mosko 2017: 202). According to Hutchins (1980: 35, 140) and affirmed by my Trobriand interlocutors, the correct term is *yolova*. It connotes the general idea of payment or compensation for "care," especially "health care," previously rendered.
4. See below and Malinowski (1925: 44; 1992a: 181–82, 512). Elsewhere, Malinowski discusses additional categories of sacrificial spirit offering: *ula'ula* and *bubwalua*; see Mosko (2017).
5. In these terms, Trobriand *bwekasa* corresponds closely with Polynesian conversions between *tapu*, "sacred, prohibited, restricted" and *noa*, "non-sacred, unrestricted, open" (Hocart 1952, 1970; Shore 1989; Valeri 1985; Panoff 2018).
6. Hocart (1952, 1970) has given the classic statement of this Oceanic logic. Valeri (1985) and Panoff (2018) are elaborations.
7. The directionality of *sopi* water's "flowing" is generally downward or outward (Hutchins and Hutchins n.d.).
8. See Damon (2016); Strathern (2022); Mosko (2022).
9. The principal dangers of lagoon fishing include shark attack and sudden violent storms that can sink fishers' boats or blow them so far out to sea that they and their crews are lost forever.
10. See Mosko (2009, 2017: 144–50) for additional details of these processes.

11. I have elaborated upon this expansion of Strathernian partibility in terms of "divine dividuals" through synthesis with Lucien Lévy-Bruhl's (1973) notion of "participation" in numerous discussions of Mekeo, Polynesian, Christian, and Trobriand ritual and sociality (Mosko 1992, 1995, 2009, 2010, 2012, 2014, 2015, 2017, 2022). Michael Young's (1983) account of Kalauna (Goodenough Island) creation-spirit-impersonating magicians; Nancy Munn's (1983, 1986) discussions of *butula* "fame"; and Fred Damon's (1983, 2002, 2005, 2016, 2021) treatments of *ked* "roads" and Kula players' rank, renown, and experience of shell exchange have helped guide me to the path that I am here treading. Marshall Sahlins's theorizing of the comparative significance of "metapersons" in precapitalist societies converges with my notion of divine dividuality (Sahlins 2017: 54; 2022: 57; Graeber and Sahlins 2017: 3).
12. Despite the absence of ancestral *baloma* spirits as relevant actors in his analysis, Damon must be credited for discerning the basically sacrificial nature of the Kula exchange process when he describes how a player's name, and thus his fame, rises and falls as the valuables he transacts pass through the hands of himself, his partners, and other transactors on the same *ked* road (Damon 2005: 80–81; see also Damon 2016: 60; 2021: 291).
13. Magicians customarily pass *tukwa* spells to their sons as a temporary expedient before they are returned to the legitimate matrilineal heirs (*veyalela*). However, the concept of *dala* is inclusive of the male and female children of matrilineally affiliated male members (*litulela*) (see Mosko 2017: 355–68; see also Liang, this volume).
14. For example, the gardening spells of the various commoner *dala*s residing in Omarakana's village cluster are subsidiary to those of Tabalu *dala* insofar as the Paramount Chief is regarded as the community's *tama* "father."
15. Traditionally, the marriages of chiefly men and women to persons of similar *dala* rank were strongly preferred over unions with persons of commoner status (see Mosko 2017: Chapter 8).
16. This leadership opportunity is open, at least in theory, to all competent adult men in Kula communities other than the Trobriands.
17. For an updated discussion of the controversy surrounding this topic, see Mosko (2017: 152–58, passim; 2020, 2022).
18. The main protagonists in the Virgin Birth debate are listed in Mosko (2017: 13n11). See also Mosko (1995, 1998, 2005, 2017: Chapter 4; 2022).
19. Despite Malinowski's (1922: 322–26) view of reincarnation as the dominant Trobriand understanding, many of the main characters in foundation myths of the Kula, there and elsewhere in the Massim, are stated to exist as stars and constellations. The long-time missionary-linguist Ralph Lawton (1999: 99) also recorded beliefs that "the old Tabalu chiefs . . . controlled the rising and setting of the sun and movements of the moon and stars."
20. Stanley Tambiah's uncritical acceptance of Malinowski's disenchanted view of Trobriand magic (Tambiah 1968) has had a similar effect upon the anthropology of magic: see Mosko 2017: 92-96.
21. Guyer (2016: 17) proceeds to note that "*don* as a noun is mainly used [by Mauss] in contexts where *la force* (the forces *in the spiritual* [my emphasis] and social world) and/or the ancient quality of the practices are explicitly mentioned."

22. Namely, "magical, religious, and spiritual force," *"spiritual* power," "the spirit things," and *"mana* . . . reserved for men and spirits" (Mauss 2016: 69–75).
23 There is just one unrelated passing reference: "The conception of mana, discovered in a small Melanesian community has, by the work of Hubert and Mauss and others, been proved of fundamental importance" (Malinowski 1922: 514).

References

Bickler, Simon. 2006. "Prehistoric Stone Monuments in the Northern Region of the Kula Ring." *Antiquity* 80 (307): 38–51.

Campbell, Shirley. 1983. "Kula in Vakuta: The Mechanics of Keda." In *The Kula*, eds. Jerry Leach and Edmund Leach, 201-28. Cambridge: Cambridge University Press.

Damon, Fred. 1983. "What Moves the Kula: Opening and Closing Gifts on Woodlark Island." In *The Kula. New Perspectives on Massim Exchange*, eds. Jerry W. Leach and Edmund Leach, 309–42. Cambridge: Cambridge University Press.

———. 2002. "Kula Valuables: The Problem of Value and the Production of Names." *L'Homme* 162: 107–36.

———. 2005. "'Pity' and 'Ecstasy': The Problem of Order and Differentiated Difference across Kula Societies." In *On the Order of Chaos*, ed. Mark Mosko and Fred Damon, 79–107. Oxford: Berghahn.

———. 2016. "The Good, the Bad, and the Dead: The Place of Destruction in the Organization of Social Life, Which Means Hierarchy." *Social Analysis* 60(4): 58–75.

———. 2021. "On the Word Ked: The 'Way' of Being and Becoming in Muyuw." In *Austronesian Paths and Journeys*, ed. James Fox, 275–301. Canberra: Australian National University Press.

Darrah, Allan. N.d. "Ancestors in Trobriand Ritual." Unpublished paper, DEP Project, Department of Anthropology, California State University at Sacramento.

Frazer, James. 1922. *The Golden Bough*, vol. 1, abridged edn. New York: Macmillan.

Godelier, Maurice. 1999. *The Enigma of the Gift*. Chicago: University of Chicago Press.

Graeber, David, and Marshall Sahlins. 2017. "Theses on Kingship." In *On Kings*, 1–22. Chicago: University of Chicago Press.

Guyer, Jane. 2016. "The Gift That Keeps on Giving." In Marcel Mauss, *The Gift*, ed. and trans. Jane Guyer, expanded edn., 1–25. Chicago: Hau Books.

Hocart, A. M. 1952. *The Life-Giving Myth and Other Essays*. London: Methuen.

———. 1970 [1936]. *Kings and Councillors*. Chicago: University of Chicago Press.

Hubert, Henri, and Marcel Mauss. 1964 [1899]. *Sacrifice: Its Nature and Functions*. Chicago: University of Chicago Press.

Hutchins, Edwin. 1980. *Culture and Inference: A Trobriand Case Study*. Cambridge, MA: Harvard University Press.

Hutchins, Edwin, and Dona Hutchins. n.d. *Kilivila–English Dictionary*. Retrieved from https://hci.ucsd.edu/hutchins.dict/dictionary.htm.

Jarillo, Sergio, et al. 2020a. "Where Are Our Ancestors? Rethinking Trobriand Cosmology." *Hau* 10(2): 367–91.

———. 2020b. "Believing the Unbelievable: Reincarnation, Cultural Authority, and Politics in the Trobriand Islands." *Hau* 10(2): 409–19.

Lawton, Ralph. 1999. "The Chiefs of Kiriwina." *Records of the South Australian Museum* 32(1): 91–118.

Leach, Jerry W. 1983. "Introduction." In *The Kula. New Perspectives on Massim Exchange*, eds. Jerry W. Leach and Edmund Leach, 1–26. Cambridge: Cambridge University Press.

Leach, Jerry, and Edmund Leach. 1983, eds. *The Kula. New Perspectives on Massim Exchange*. Cambridge: Cambridge University Press.

Lepani, Katherine. 2012. *Islands of Love, Islands of Risk: Culture and HIV in the Trobriands*. Nashville, TN: Vanderbilt University Press.

Lévy-Bruhl, Lucien. 1973 [1949]. *Notebooks on Primitive Mentality*. Oxford: Basil Blackwell.

MacCarthy, Michelle. 2020. "The Rebirth of an Old Question: A Comment on 'Where Are Our Ancestors? Rethinking Trobriand Cosmology.'" *Hau* 10(2): 395–98.

Macintyre, Martha. 1994. "Too Many Chiefs? Leadership in the Massim in the Colonial Era." In *Transformations of Hierarchy: Structure, History and Horizon in the Austronesian World*, eds. Margaret Jolly and Mark Mosko. *History and Anthropology* (special issue) 7(1–4): 241–62.

Malinowski, Bronisław. 1913. "Review of *Les forms élémentaires de la vie religieuse* by Émile Durkheim." *Folklore* 24(4): 525–31.

———. 1918. "Fishing in the Trobriand Islands." *Man* 53: 87–92.

———. 1921. "The Primitive Economics of the Trobriand Islanders." *Economic Journal* 31: 1–16.

———. 1922. *Argonauts of the Western Pacific: An Account of Native Enterprise and Adventure in the Archipelagoes of Melanesian New Guinea*. London: Routledge & Kegan Paul.

———. 1932. *The Sexual Life of Savages*, 3rd edn. London: Routledge & Kegan Paul.

———. 1935a. *Coral Gardens and Their Magic*, vol. 1. New York: American Book Company.

———. 1935b. *Coral Gardens and Their Magic*, vol. 2. New York: American Book Company.

———. 1992a [1916]. "Baloma: The Spirits of the Dead in the Trobriand Islands." In *Magic, Science and Religion, and Other Essays*, 149–274. Prospect Heights, IL: Waveland Press.

———. 1992b [1925]. "Magic, Science and Religion." In *Magic, Science and Religion and Other Essays*, 17–92. Prospect Heights, IL: Waveland Press.

———. 1992c [1926], "Myth in Primitive Psychology." In *Magic, Science and Religion and Other Essays*, 93–148. Prospect Heights, IL: Waveland Press.

Mauss, Marcel. 2016 [1925]. *The Gift* expanded edn., trans. Jane Guyer. Chicago: Hau Books.

Mauss, Marcel, and Henri Hubert. 1972 [1902–3]. *A General Theory of Magic*, trans. Robert Brain. New York: Norton.

Merlan, Francesca. 2020. "Malinowski as Ancestor." *Hau* 10(2): 392–94.

Mosko, Mark S. 1992. "Motherless Sons: 'Divine Heroes' and 'Partible Persons' in Melanesia and Polynesia." *Man* 27(4): 697–717.

———. 1995. "Rethinking Trobriand Chieftainship." *Journal of the Royal Anthropological Institute* 1(4): 763–85.

———. 1998. "'Virgin Birth,' Comparability and Anthropological Method." *Current Anthropology* 35: 685–87.
———. 2005. "Sex, Procreation, and Menstruation: North Mekeo and the Trobriands." In *A Polymath Anthropologist: Essays in Honour of Ann Chowning*, eds. Claudia Gross, Harriet Lyons, and Dorothy Counts, 55–61. Auckland: Department of Anthropology: University of Auckland.
———. 2009. "The Fractal Yam: Botanical Imagery and Human Agency in the Trobriands." *Journal of the Royal Anthropological Institute* 15(4): 679–700.
———. 2010. "Partible Penitents: Dividual Personhood and Christian Practice in Melanesia and the West." *Journal of the Royal Anthropological Institute* 16(2): 215–40.
———. 2012. "*Laki* charms: 'Luck' and Personal Agency in North Mekeo Social Change." *Social Analysis* (special issue) 56(2): 19–38.
———. 2014. "Cards on Kiriwina: Magic, Cosmology, and the 'Divine Dividual' in Trobriand Gambling." In "Melanesian Gambling as Analytic," special issue, *Oceania* 84: 239–55.
———. 2015. "Unbecoming Individuals: The Partible Character of the Christian Person." *Hau* 5(1): 361–93.
———. 2020. "Reincarnation Redux." *Hau* 10(2): 399–408.
———. 2022. "The Sacrifice of the Yams: Tubers, Human Procreation, and Chiefly Hierarchy in the Trobriands." Paper presented at workshop, "Tuberous Collectivities: Interdisciplinary Explorations into Human-Tuber Companionship across Histories." Convenors David Nally and Olivia Angé, Jesus College, Cambridge, 14–15 March.
Mosko, Mark S. (with Tabalu Daniel Pulayasi, Daniel Molubabeba, Pakalaki Tokulupai, and Vincent Yogaru). 2017. *Ways of Baloma: Rethinking Magic and Kinship from the Trobriands.* Chicago: Hau Books.
Munn, Nancy. 1983. "Gawan Kula: Spatiotemporal Control and the Symbolism of Influence." In *The Kula. New Perspectives on Massim Exchange*, eds. Jerry W. Leach and Edmund Leach, 277–308. Cambridge: Cambridge University Press.
———. 1986. *The Fame of Gawa.* Cambridge: Cambridge University Press.
Panoff, Françoise. 2018 [1972]. *Maenge Gardens.* Marseille: Pacific-CREDO.
Perrson, Johnny. 1999. *Sagali and the Kula.* Lund: Department of Sociology, Lund University.
Powell, Harry. 1978. "The Kula in Trobriand Politics or Why Did Some of the Kiriwinians Have Semi-Hereditary Big Men but Apparently Not Hereditary Chiefs?" Unpublished paper for Kula and Massim Exchange Conference, King's College, Cambridge, July 1978.
Sahlins, Marshall. 2013. *What Kinship Is . . . and Is Not.* Chicago: University of Chicago Press.
———. 2017. "The Original Political Society." In David Graeber and Marshall Sahlins, *On Kings*, 23–64. Chicago: Hau Books.
———. 2022. *The New Science of the Enchanted Universe.* Princeton, NJ: Princeton University Press.
Scoditti, Giancarlo (with Jerry W. Leach). 1983. "Kula on Kitava." In *The Kula. New Perspectives on Massim Exchange*, eds. Jerry Leach and Edmund Leach, 249–76. Cambridge: Cambridge University Press.

Shore, Brad. 1989. "Mana and Tapu." In *Developments in Polynesian Ethnography*, eds. Alan Howard and Robert Borofsky, 137–73. Honolulu: University of Hawai'i Press.

Strathern, Marilyn. 1988. *The Gender of the Gift*. Berkeley: University of California Press.

———. 2018. "Persons and Partible Persons." In *Schools and Styles of Anthropological Theory*, ed. Matei Candea, 236–46. London: Routledge.

———. 2022. "A Question of Life and Death: Imagining Tropical Tubers." Paper presented at workshop, "Tuberous Collectivities: Interdisciplinary Explorations into Human-Tuber Companionship across Histories." Convenors: David Nally and Olivia Angé. Jesus College, Cambridge, 14 March 2022.

Tambiah, Stanley. 1968. "The Magical Power of Words." *Man* 3(2): 175–208.

———. 1990. "Malinowski's Demarcations and His Exposition of the Magical Act." In *Magic, Science, Religion and the Scope of Rationality*, eds. Russell T. McCutcheon and Graham Harvey, 65–83. Cambridge: Cambridge University Press.

Uberoi, J. P. Singh. 1962. *Politics of the Kula Ring*. Manchester: Manchester University Press.

Valeri, Valerio. 1985. *Kinship and Sacrifice: Ritual and Society in Ancient Hawaii*. Chicago: University of Chicago Press.

Weiner, Annette. 1992. *Inalienable Possessions: The Paradox of Keeping while Giving*. Berkeley: University of California Press.

Young, Michael. 1983. *Magicians of Manumanua*. Berkeley: University of California Press.

———. 1994. "From Riches to Rags: Dismantling Hierarchy in Kalauna." In *Transformations of Hierarchy: Structure, History and Horizon in the Austronesian World*, eds. Margaret Jolly and Mark Mosko. *History and Anthropology* (special issue) 7(1–4): 263–78.

10

 The Archaeology of the Kula and Malinowski's Notion of Economy

Hans Steinmüller

Malinowski was keenly aware that the societies of the Kula ring had changed a lot in the two generations before his arrival. The characteristic subjunctive present that Malinowski uses in the first three chapters of the *Argonauts* to take the reader on a round trip of the Kula islands ("imagine yourself") sometimes switches into the past, to speculate on what might have happened earlier. For instance, passing the islands of the Southern Massim, immediately east of the New Guinea mainland, Malinowski writes:

> In olden days, before the advent of white men, these pleasant, apparently effete people were inveterate cannibals and head-hunters, and in their large war-canoes they carried on treacherous, cruel raids, falling upon sleeping villages, killing man, woman and child, and feasting on their bodies. The attractive stone circles in their villages were associated with their cannibal feasts. (1922: 37)

Malinowski, however, was not interested in head-hunting and cannibalism. Neither did he write much about those stone circles. What is more, the Southern Massim, where cannibal warfare had occurred not so long ago, became something of a mirror image in contrast to which the Trobrianders emerged, with clarity and reason, as the true *Argonauts*.

Malinowski did his research during World War I and published his monograph soon afterward. Against this background, he emphasized the peaceful and reasonable nature of "native" custom. What seemed superficially to resemble war was actually trade. The warfare that had occurred on the Trobriands as recently as 1899, Malinowski emphasized, was anything but senseless aggression. Hostilities never included surprise raids, and always followed established rules, like an aristocratic duel (Malinowski

1920). While acknowledging that "the romance of danger had gone from native life" (Malinowski 1922: 45), Malinowski downplayed the difference that warfare might have made to the Kula in the precontact era. Rather than a functionalist "peace of the market," the Kula he observed was the historical result of colonial pacification. Once the colonial authorities had banished war, entry into the Kula became easier; valuables previously used for ransom and peacemaking were instead directed into it. At the same time, steel tools raised production in gardens, and burial practices were simplified following missionary interventions.

Malinowski did not see the inflationary effect these changes had on the Kula and he was not interested in historical speculation of the Frazerian kind. Had he been, the stone monuments of the Massim would have offered plenty of "evidence" for diffusionist guesswork (Riesenfeld 1950). But Malinowski preferred to emphasize how culture corresponded to the needs of human nature and to a specific local context (Malinowski 1927). His *Argonauts* became the exemplar of the new functionalist ethnography that explained how "culture" worked at a particular point in time. To be fair, the archaeological data available on the Massim at the time was scant. But a century later, it is instructive to reexamine the Kula in light of what we know today about its history, from its emergence ca. 600 BP to the colonial interventions of the nineteenth century.

A particular focus of my reexamination in what follows is how Malinowski and subsequent anthropologists understood the gift logic of primitive economies. This understanding required some strategic ignorance: the anthropologist wishing to emphasize rational rule-following was obliged to downplay violence and creativity. Let me illustrate the problem with the metaphor of play that both Massim Islanders and foreign anthropologists have commonly used to describe the Kula.[1] Commenting on the proceedings of the 1978 Cambridge Kula conference, Edmund Leach used a chess metaphor to argue that historical explanation was pointless. If one asks oneself, "why is chess played like that?",

> The only possible answer is historical: the modern game of chess evolved a long time ago out of other somewhat chess-like games, not because it was especially efficient for any particular purpose but because people found it was fun to play. (1983: 530)

Similarly, Leach points out, it doesn't make any sense to ask "why the various Massim islanders play the game of kula as they do and keep on inventing new variations" (ibid.: 531). Instead, anthropologists should focus on the difference that particular moves make within the wider system, that is, they should try to understand the beautiful structure of the Kula, which coincidentally approximated the generalized exchange of Kachin marriage rules. The thought sequences of the structuralist that reduce social action to its most fundamental logical elements, zeroes and ones, accomplish theoretically what in historical reality is achieved by human violence and creativity. If in theory the Kula is like a game of chess, in historical reality the pieces were carved once for the first time—and it is possible to say more about this moment than just that it was fun. And again, we may wish to excuse the anthropologist for disregarding the long-term history of the Kula, because in 1983 the archaeological data were still very inadequate.

But in the 2020s the situation is very different. It is now possible to say much more about the origins of the Kula—where the pawns and the kings came from, and why it was fun to play. On the basis of a brief review of recent archaeological literature, I suggest that the Kula began as a creative response to a time of great upheaval. New foodstuffs, new possibilities for exchange, and new burial practices appeared at about the same time, possibly as a consequence of climatic changes related to the El Niño phenomenon. By carving shells, assembling bracelets and armshells into new valuables, and then offering them to others ceremonially, people established lasting value. But making Kula valuables was only one response among many possible alternatives, one of them being the building of stone monuments. The archaeological findings suggest that the Kula cannot be understood as a rational game of reciprocity. This leads me to a reappraisal of the concept of the gift, and in particular its links to violence and creativity.

Colonial Pacification

Before reviewing the new archaeological contributions, it is worth considering the Kula at the time of "first contact." There can be no doubt that the impact of colonial pacification was massive. Malinowski's emphasis on the custom and rules of an elite game suggested that the Kula was a noble substitute for war (Uberoi 1962), or alternatively a ceremonial "umbrella" for trade in ordinary goods (Fortune 1932: 209ff.). In this way, anthropologists could make sense of everything that happened in the "heat of the battle," the deceit that was so common in Kula exchanges, the fear of sorcery, and the aggression with which trade partners are met. But the containment of potential aggression had as much to do with colonial pacification as it did with functionalist theorizing.

Michael Young, Martha Macintyre, and others have challenged the "peace of the market" idea on two basic grounds. First, the Kula trade did not guarantee peaceful relations, but often resulted in hostilities. Second, Kula valuables were never purely ceremonial luxuries: they were also used for marriage and death rituals, and to make war payments (Young 1983: 8). Prior to pacification, for the Bwanabwana of Tubetube, for instance, all relations between islands were either *kune* (kula) or *kalea* (war). All inter-island trade—no matter whether the ceremonial exchange of great valuables, the provision of food, or the supply of tools—was called "kune" (= kula). The most important valuables, called *kitomwa*, are "signs of human lives," and represent a person's *wasana*, "renown," and *saugana*, "time" or "life." They were used in trade, but also to pay ransom, in preparation for war, and to make peace (Macintyre 1983: 21). Each transaction—no matter whether a "friendly" offer to a Kula partner, a homicide payment to the relatives of a victim, or the ransom exacted from a powerful sorcerer—added to the power and force of the valuable exchanged. Each matrilineage (*susu*) needed such valuables to wage war and for peace ceremonies, and thus "the suppression of warfare must therefore have released large numbers of valuables into the kune exchange system and contributed to the processes of democratization and inflation observed by older informants" (ibid.: 22). Another historical possibility was to replace open warfare with secret witchcraft: strong continuities in witchcraft accusations were noted on the island of Dobu (Fortune 1932); they appear to have intensified under colonial rule in Vanatinai (Lepowsky 1991) and Molima (Chowning 1987).

The end of warfare, then, meant that more people could participate in the Kula (not only successful warriors as before), and that valuables previously reserved for ransom and homicide payments and peacemaking ceremonies could be used in the Kula instead (Young 1983: 8–9; MacIntyre 1983). The prohibition of war was accompanied by other thoroughgoing changes in production and in politics that created a new context for the Kula.

Whalers had been visiting the Northern Massim for several decades when permanent trade stores were established around 1870. Tool production in the stone quarries of Soloug on Woodlark ceased soon after, since iron axes and blades were readily available in those stores. In 1890, when two European traders were killed in Woodlark, the colonial administrator of British New Guinea, William MacGregor, sent a punitive expedition and had one man hanged. After this episode, the population of Woodlark fell from about 2,500 in 1904 to a mere seven hundred in 1915, remaining at this level until World War II (Damon 1983a: 39). At the same time, many of the crafts necessary for the Kula also changed substantially. On Woodlark, Kweyakwoya, the village that had specialized in canoe carving, dispersed and dwindled before disappearing altogether by about 1920. In the same generation, "yam production became generally diffused through the culture," while the powerful villages of Kaulay and Dikwayas began to decline (ibid.: 56).

By the time Malinowski arrived in the nearby Trobriands, trade stores existed on most major islands, supplying metal tools, tobacco, salt, and many other goods. Tobacco in particular became a crucial exchange item. Malinowski (1922: 46) mentions that he enticed Trobrianders with a "generous promise of tobacco." Traders and colonial officials also used tobacco in exchange for valuable items (such as pearls), or to encourage cash cropping. In 1912, the British magistrate Raynor Bellamy banned the eating of coconuts (Young 2004: 386) and ended the chiefs' monopoly on the crop in the Trobriands (ibid.: 499). Instead, the magistrate promoted coconut plantations, and had people jailed when they refused to participate. While coconut became an important cash crop, yam was the staple. Both could be planted more easily and harvested more quickly using the new metal tools provided by the trade stores. The production and exchange of important staples thus changed greatly in the course of a generation. It seems likely that the practice of *gimwali*—the utilitarian barter that Malinowski contrasted with the ceremonial exchange of the Kula (Malinowski 1922: 189ff.)—originated in the trade store selling tobacco and metal tools.[2]

Throughout the Massim, colonial administration and missionaries prohibited polygyny and secondary burial. Malinowski (1922: 465) saw the prohibition of polygyny as the main reason for the declining powers of the chief of Omarakana. Later scholars have argued to the contrary that colonialism induced the emergence of "big men" in the Massim (Macintyre 1994). Their "limited authority, building support through generosity and reputation from feasting, was what was left when colonial rule had outlawed the use of violence and missions had undermined earlier indigenous ritual beliefs and practices" (Liep 2009: 20; cf. also Liep 1996). It is possible that something similar occurred when missionaries outlawed secondary burial (Young and de Vera 1980). Islanders throughout the Massim had long reopened graves and reburied the bones in jars, often hidden in caves and rocks. Ending this custom simplified funerary ceremonies and thereby freed even more goods and gifts for alternative use. Colonialism and missionization thus brought radical changes in terms of war, production, and politics. While offering rich empirical descriptions and stressing "creative originality" in his theorizing, Malinowski insisted on simplifying the material though a parsimonious theory of social complexity. Behind the messiness of social reality, he uncovered very specific "limitations and regularities" (Malinowski 1922: 91) in exchange: rules of "law" and "custom," according to which Kula valuables were ceremonial objects similar to the "crown jewels" (ibid.: 88). Yet some of these rules—for instance, those governing participation in Kula exchanges and the valuables to be exchanged—had been set only fairly recently, concomitantly with the inflation in yam production.

While he emphasized the unity of the Kula ring, Malinowski was clearly aware that seafaring expeditions and shell valuables were important to various neighbors who did not directly participate in Kula exchanges with Trobrianders. Shells produced on Rossel Island reached the Motu of Port Moresby through *lakatoi* trade expeditions, whence they entered the Kula; yet neither of these peoples participated in the Kula. Many villages within the Trobriands never participated either. It should also be remembered that Kiriwina, where Malinowski's fieldwork was conducted, was exceptional in two respects: the power of the chief of Omarakana, where Malinowski pitched his tent, and the absence of cannibalism.

Malinowski was wise to refrain from speculation about the origins of such regional differences, and about the history of Kula shells. The great importance of *Argonauts* was to find an underlying logic in what appeared bizarre to the outsider, and to show this logic *at one point in time*. What had happened "in olden days" was irrelevant to this picture. But in historical reality, the Kula only resembled an elegant schematic ring during a brief period of time. The rules of the Kula were not eternal. Rather, they were created by violent interventions at the end of the nineteenth century. The ceremonial nature of the exchanges and the guiding principle of reciprocity emphasized by Malinowski need to be seen in the context of colonial policies, the end of local warfare, the arrival of manufactured goods, and the commodification of local economies. This "context" did not appear out of nothing but was violently imposed by the colonial authorities on pain of penalties.

This does not imply, however, that Kula exchanges did not exist at all before European traders, missionaries, and officials arrived on the Massim. Until recently, the origins of the Kula were practically unknown. This has changed thanks to a new generation of archaeologists' excavations across the Massim. On the basis of their data, it is now possible to identify a historical sequence for the emergence of the Kula. A great transformation occurred ca. 800–600 BP. Stone monuments in the Northern Massim were abandoned, shell money was adopted throughout the territory, and war, trade, and death ritual all changed substantially. I turn now to review this transformation.

The Great Transformation, 600 BP

Apart from the sporadic observations of anthropologists and colonial officials, no systematic excavations took place on the Massim before the 1970s.[3] Since then, archaeological work on these islands has resulted in a consensus that a specific sequence of historical changes gave rise to the emergence of the Kula in about 800–600 BP.[4] In this period, earlier trade links with mainland New Guinea weakened and inter-island trade intensified (Egloff 1978). Subregional integration is implied by the increasing unity of art styles, as well as the appearance of Southern Massim pottery on Woodlark island in the north (Shaw 2016: 118–19). The islands to the north had already shared another feature several centuries earlier: Megalithic complexes had been constructed on Woodlark, Kiriwina, and neighboring islands since about 1200 BP. These monuments were much larger than the stone circles referred to casually by Malinowski. Although he and other ethnographers could not help noticing the ruins of the large megalithic arrangements, the stones were overgrown and their uses forgotten by local inhabitants. Researchers could only hazard a guess as to their past meanings: as sacred stones, boundary markers, or burial places. The monuments range from single stone slabs of about 1.5 m height, to wider enclosures marking rectangles, to large complexes of small and large stones (up to 3 m high), usually arranged to cover multiple internal "rooms." Most stones are either coral or sandstone; the former was available nearby in the bush. The latter, however, had to be transported over long distances, in some cases between islands. Stones from Woodlark, for instance, were used in Liluta village on Kiriwina, some 200 kilometers away by canoe (Bickler 2006: 45). Modern excavations have confirmed that most of the larger stone arrangements were used for primary burial; the skeletons found there were carefully placed in particular positions and orientations. All monuments were eventually abandoned. Some of the monuments contained bone-jars presumably placed there for secondary burial by later generations after the monuments had been abandoned.

Archaeologists agree that the megaliths indicate a shared regional landscape and intra-island hierarchy with clusters around central villages (Bickler 1998, 2006; Bickler and Ivuyo 2002). They also agree on a timeline: The stone monuments were abandoned ca. 800–600 BP, when secondary pot burial (sometimes in caves, sometimes in the abandoned stone monuments, but always removed from places of settlement) became common. Pottery found in the secondary burial sites is markedly different from that found in the vicinity of the megalithic structures (Burenhult 2002). The transition from primary to secondary burials on Trobriand and Woodlark was not immediate. Both forms coexisted for several generations, as radiocarbon dating has confirmed (Shaw 2016: 119). The first carved shells similar to those used in the modern Kula date from 750 BP (Ambrose et al. 2012). Many of these early shell valuables were not initially exchanged between islands; in this sense they resemble the famously complicated shell money of Russel Island that was also invented in the same period (Shaw and Langley 2017).

So why did the inhabitants of the Northern Massim let their stone monuments fall into disrepair, and start to trade in shell valuables? Was it a "devolution" from a hierarchical society that built megaliths to an egalitarian society that traded in Kula shells (as suggested by Liang 2022)? This narrative is strangely reminiscent of earlier diffusionist accounts, for instance that of Alphonse Riesenfeld (1950), who argued that stone monuments throughout Melanesia and the wider Pacific bore the traces of Polynesian invaders, fair-skinned people who dominated the more dark-skinned natives and then moved on to occupy other islands. This was precisely the kind of speculation that Malinowski opposed, both in theory and in his ethnographic practice. Anthropologists have been careful to avoid the pitfalls of diffusionism ever since: perhaps sometimes too careful, to the extent that they have ignored historical questions altogether.

In Kula ethnography, Fred Damon has proposed new historical perspectives, specifically to do with the megalithic structures on Muyuw (Woodlark). In several publications (1979, 1983b), he remarked on their similarities, in orientation and symbolism, to those objects and practices concerned with gardening, seafaring, and war. Simon Bickler, the archaeologist who led the excavations on Muyuw, concluded that the megaliths "were used to provide a regional framework for the settlement of new communities perhaps led by some form of organized elite" (Bickler 2006: 49). They might well have functioned as a "store of value," not unlike the carved shells that replaced them:

> It is clear that megalithic building necessitated a spatially concentrated set of activities, resulting in a highly visible marker of relatively permanent regional relationships. Burying one's relatives inside a stone arrangement at the center of one's village served as a potent reminder of these relationships. The rituals which had their origins in the secondary burial practices that followed dispersed these ancient relationships, both in moving the dead to the periphery, such as caves, and by producing potentially less enduring monuments. Their purpose was to pass productive resources from one to the next. . . .
> It is shell valuables of the kula which now extend relations through time, and by doing so, now interrelate varied productive processes through space. . . .
> Perhaps these carved shells are stores of value like the stone of the arrangements. They may also point to new ways Massim peoples located themselves in time and space. In the modern Kula, swapping shells moves the names of the living, thereby negotiating the precarious regional interdependencies of well-established Massim communities. (Bickler 2006: 48–49)

To argue that something of the reverence shown to Kula valuables had once been directed at stones becomes more plausible when we look at the ways that people dealt with different kinds of stone more recently. Malinowski (1922: 44, 333) himself mentions the worship of "two men turned into stone" on the beach of Sarubwoyna, which included the Kula "offering gift" of *pokala*. He also mentions various sacred sites, and stones used for storehouses and as garden markers (Malinowski 1935: 221). The stone circles of the Southern Massim, mentioned in the quotation at the beginning of this chapter, were widely reported (Seligman 1910: 463–66, 556–57; Armstrong 1928: 13, 113–14; Young 1971: 22; Liep 2009: 100). The assumption that they were used to butcher humans has been confirmed by archaeologists (Shaw and Coxe 2021).

While there are some obvious differences between these stone circles, the natural stones of Sarubwoyna beach, garden markers on Trobriand, and the megalithic arrangements of the past, what they share is that stones can mark the permanence and singularity of a social relation. The possibility of attaching such values to stones was still apparent in the practice of secondary burial, where bones were unearthed and then placed into the abandoned stone monuments (and later into caves, cliffs, and rocks). As mentioned above, colonial officials and missionaries interdicted secondary burial; but the practice was still recalled in the second half of the twentieth century on Goodenough (Young and de Vera 1980). Even though secondary burial had ended by the time of her fieldwork, Martha Macintyre found that the transformation from "something black and stinking into a bundle of pure white bones" (that is what secondary burial achieved) was central to the meaning of funerals on Tubetube: ultimately, this is the reconstitution of the *susu* matrilineage as a "corporate whole," "the lineage's triumph over death" (Macintyre 1989: 138).

The resurrection of the lineage in the form of dry bones is but one of myriad forms of death ritual on the Massim islands. Anthropologists have described a general sequence that seems common across the region (Damon and Wagner 1989). On Tubetube, as well as Muyuw, the valuables presented at funerary rituals are basically the same "inalienable possessions" (*kitoum/kitomwa*) that are presented in inter-island Kula. Thus the mortuary cycles on these islands possibly had a strong "pulsing" effect on the Kula, "damming the circulation of armshells and necklaces, and then suddenly releasing them in waves that travel around the ring" (Wagner 1989: 270). In his overview of funerary rites on the Massim, Roy Wagner points to two further differences between western and eastern islands: whereas in the western part (Bwaidoka, Molima, Normanby, Kaduwage, and Vakuta), perishable goods such as yams and pigs feature prominently in the exchanges, this is not the case in the east (Tubetube, Muyuw, Vanatinai, and Rossel), where the items exchanged are primarily nonperishable objects such as shell money, axes, and blades (ibid.: 269).[5] The second major difference is that, in the west, "the mourning relic . . . makes an object out of parts of a person, whereas the mortuary prestations on Sabarl and Vanatinai [make] a 'person' out of objects" (ibid.). If the "western personification corresponds to the essentially binary and limited exchange of perishable wealth," the "tendency of mourning objectification in the eastern area is congruent with the movement of imperishable wealth objects" (ibid.: 270). This distinction between "personification" and "objectification" in funerary rites may not be falsifiable, and it may not correspond exactly to an east–west axis of cultural difference. But the concrete contrast between perishables and imperishables does seem clear: imperishable goods such as axes and shell money are more common, and indeed central in funerary exchanges, the further to the east one goes.

This east–west continuum crisscrosses the islands participating in the Kula. In theory, there would be four ways to combine the use of primary goods at funerals (perishable–imperishable) with participation in the Kula: (1) perishable goods without Kula, (2) perishable goods and Kula, (3) nonperishable goods with Kula, and (4) nonperishable goods without Kula. The summaries provided by Damon and Wagner suggest that (2) and (3) largely coincide, that is, both perishable and imperishable goods are important in the death rituals of societies that participate in the Kula. Category (1) is illustrated by Goodenough and Normanby in the west, while category (4) is well documented in the more easterly islands of Sabarl, Vanatinai, and Rossel. Wagner (1989: 273) goes on to suggest that the displays of wealth at funerals in societies outside the Kula is a substitute for the Kula—maybe even an "equivalent statement of value."

Thus the shell money of Rossel Island is perhaps best viewed as an inland alternative to inter-island Kula. Somewhat similar to the "internal Kula" in the Trobriands and elsewhere, the shells of Rossel Island are classified into twenty categories of single shells (*ndap*) and fifteen categories of perforated and stringed discs (*kê*). While the phenomenon was known to Seligman, and noted in an ethnography published in the 1920s (Armstrong 1928), the first comprehensive description and analysis of the shell money only appeared recently (Liep 2009). The most valuable shells, *ndap*, were used in war payments, funerals, and ceremonial exchanges between senior men (members of a "Papuan plutocracy," as Liep terms them). The same shells that might become *ndap* could also became *bagi* (Malinowski's "*soulava*") when they entered the Kula exchanges of neighboring islands. This fact— that the same shells could mean completely different things in different places—should give us pause. The third possibility is not to use shell money at all, as in the western islands (Young 1971), and on mainland PNG, where funerary exchanges center on perishable food (category 1 above). Goodenough and Rossel represented contrasting possibilities in regard to exchange, but they resemble each other in that no megalithic complexes were ever erected on these islands. However, the smaller stone circles mentioned earlier continued to be used for much longer than was the case on the islands of the Kula.

All these distinctions between funerary practices, shell money, and stone monuments and circles are made on shaky ground, given the lack of ethnographic evidence. What matters is that historical changes occurred, as we know from the archaeologists, and that local actors in the Massim are well aware of at least some of the differences discussed so far, including which islands participate in the Kula and which do not. Given that the stone monuments in the Northern Massim were abandoned at the time when the Kula emerged, when secondary burial spread, and when shell money was adopted on Rossel Island, and given that all these changes happened gradually, it seems likely that the first Kula players had a choice between using stone, shells, or food. That is, they could choose between the "inalienable wealth" of a stone arrangement, the "inalienable possession" of a shell necklace, and the more ephemeral "gift" of food.[6] The social creativity that ensued in this distant era has its parallels in recent generations. Jerry Leach (1983b: 11ff.) documented how the Kula could become a platform for election campaigns and social movements. Kula valuables can be transported "in a rice bag on a motor vessel" (MacIntyre 1989: 151), and they can be baptized Taleypun ("telephone") (Damon 1983a: 38), Waialesi ("wireless") (Kuehling 2017: 285), Plaplowes ("flowers"), and Long Talosis ("long trousers") (Damon 2002: 124). Each name reflects something noteworthy that happened to the maker of the shell valuable, who was near a new telephone station, found the shell in a coral reef shaped like flowers, or simply happened to wear long trousers when carving this particular shell. More commonly, a valuable simply carries the name of its maker and is ranked according to age, size, and fame, just like humans are (Damon 2002: 125). The names of Kula valuables emphasize a coincidence of place and subject, and likely so did the names of shells and stones before the Kula existed, thus uniting the dead and the living with their kin groups, and the places where they were buried with the places where they had lived.

Conclusion

Malinowski emphasized the rationality and peaceful nature of gift-giving in the Kula for good reasons. His own background and upbringing in Austria-Hungary, the serendipities of ending up in the Trobriands (rather than Dobu or Rossel Island), and the global environment of World War I all helped to shape *Argonauts*. The emphasis on rational action and rule-following and the overlooking of historical change proved to be enormously inspiring and productive for social anthropology. The method of participant observation was to be the basis on which "Ethnology ... might become one of the most deeply philosophic, enlightening and elevating disciplines of scientific research" (Malinowski 1922: 518). For Malinowski at the time, this was the scientific corrective to "hunting after curios." But the evidence available today allows us to do better.

What emerges from the ethnographic and archaeological record is that the ethnographic Kula is a relatively recent invention, and that its prehistory is intimately tied in with changes in ecology, warfare, and memory (Damon 2016). This undermines the functionalist postulates of Malinowski: the Kula ring was not stable, lacked historical depth, and did not operate according to the principle of "give and take." This last assumption—that "the social code of rules, with regard to give and take" (Malinowski 1922: 96), lay at the heart of Kula exchanges—has constrained the ways in which anthropologists went on to conceptualize the gift, and the economy in general. Malinowski's neglect of history, violence, and creativity became shared dogma when "the economy" was defined by the rationality of reciprocity. The rules of the game (say, the social conventions governing particular local economies) were thus assumed to be transparent and stable, ignoring that (a) rules sometimes had to be enforced and (b) rules could change.

The problem is most obvious in relation to the gift. What distinguishes a gift from share and plunder are the intentions of the people involved: the victim of plunder doesn't want to let go, and the person who shares doesn't expect anything in return. Only the gift requires reciprocity: the reparation for the victim of plunder and the reward for the one who shares are of a different kind. The error lies in the assumption that the same kind of reciprocity, the lowest common denominator accessible to rational analysis, underlies these very different intentions. What happens in reality is usually a mix of all kinds of intentions. But Mauss, building on Malinowski, found the idea of the gift to be the most "economical" way to reduce the complexity. Despite Mauss's eloquent articulation of multidimensional "total social facts," and a specific recognition that rituals and supernatural agents needed to be integrated into analysis of the human economy (see Mosko, this volume), Mauss and Malinowski together caused generations of anthropologists to find reciprocity everywhere, even in war and in history.[7] The result was the proliferation of arguments about "rational war" and the "peace of the market" similar to those of Fortune and Uberoi referred to above.

Anthropologists thus ignored the ways that the equivalences necessary for reciprocity were created, sometimes violently.[8] Instead of retracing actual physical violence, they engaged themselves in the kind of "violent abstraction" that is perhaps the defining feature of capitalist modernity (Sayer 1987). Concretely this meant, for instance, accepting the rules of barter as a given, when they had in fact been established only a few years earlier in the new trade stores on the Massim islands. The main purpose of such abstraction was the imposition of equivalence by the observer, via "the principle of the economy of thought" (Malinowski 1993 [1906]; see Thornton and Skalník 1993; Staley, this volume). Even though Malinowski was keenly aware of the complexity of "primitive economics," the positivist parsimony that had been the topic of his doctoral dissertation in Kraków later became Occam's razor in anthropology. Students and successors sought to cut reality down to the simplest possible element, which was the axiom that give and take must be equal. The limiting effect of this thought operation can be seen clearly when we apply it back to history, and specifically to war and to the stone monuments.

Both the "peace of the market" and "rational war" theories are based on the imposition of reciprocity, and thus fail to capture the actual physical violence necessary to create equivalence. In historical fact, this violence was exercised by the colonial officials who ended local warfare just before Malinowski arrived in the Trobriands. Rather than some underlying principle of reciprocity, it was impending sanctions and punishment that prevented warfare. Consequently, less time and effort had to be invested in feuding and funerals and more was freed for Kula expeditions. Additionally, metal tools became available and were used in planting and carving, and the barter in manufactured goods became a foil for the ceremonial exchanges of the Kula.

The imposition of reciprocity also led anthropologists to downplay social creativity. It is as if we assumed the chess pieces were always made of the same material, and the same rules always applied. But Kula valuables did not exist before the great transformation of 600 BP, and the rules of the game were up for debate for at least two centuries or longer. Between 800 and 600 BP, stone monuments and Kula valuables coexisted. Individuals must have chosen between them: some using both, some rejecting both and confining their rituals to exchanges of perishables, and some working out novel combinations. Recent archaeological discoveries force us to rethink the part that social creativity played in this epoch that was constitutive for the Kula.

Malinowski's notion of economy, which has played such an influential role in twentieth century anthropology, needs to be revised. History and archaeology show that the Kula thrived not because of some nebulous force of reciprocity, but because of violence and creativity. Rather than a theoretical equivalent of war, the Kula was its practical replacement. And the first offer of Kula was a creative act, not a rational choice.

Acknowledgments

This chapter builds on the work of numerous ethnographers and archaeologists of the Kula. It is also a response to ideas first proposed by Liang Yongjia, Fred Damon, and David Graeber. I am grateful to Yongjia for drawing my attention to the stone monuments of the Northern Massim, to Fred for Chinese perspectives on the Kula, and to David for continuing inspiration. Special thanks to Rémi Hadad for his generous comments on the last draft.

Hans Steinmüller is an associate professor in the Department of Anthropology at the London School of Economics. Based on long-term fieldwork in Hubei province (central China) and in the Wa hills of the China–Burma border, he writes about irony, ritual, and sovereignty. He is the author of *Communities of Complicity* (Berghahn, 2013), and has edited (with Natalia Buitron) *The Ends of Egalitarianism* (L'Homme, 2020).

Notes

1. Major figures in the ring today are called "Kula players" in pidgin (Kuehling 2017).
2. At least this is how Trobriand intellectuals today understand the origins of *gimwali*; Mark Mosko, personal communication, July 2022.
3. The forerunners included Austen (1939); Riesenfeld (1950) and Ollier and Holdsworth (1968); Ollier, Holdsworth, and Heers (1970a, 1970b, 1971a, 1971b, 1973); Ollier and Pain (1978a, 1978b).
4. For overviews see Kirch (1991), Irwin (1991), and Shaw (2016). Especially the work of Geoff Irwin on Mailu and in the Trobriands (Irwin 1978, 1983; Irwin, Shaw, and Mcalister 2019), Fred Damon (1979, 1983b) and Simon Bickler (1998, 1999, 2006; Bickler and Ivuyo 2002; Bickler, Ivuyo, and Kewibu 1997; Ambrose et al. 2012) on Woodlark, and Ben Shaw on Rossel Island (Shaw 2017; Shaw and Coxe 2021; Shaw and Langley 2017) have radically changed what we know about the longer history of the region.
5. Even if the general opposition of perishables in the west and nonperishables in the east holds, Wagner is not quite correct on all the details, and sometimes plainly wrong. In Muyuw, for instance, perishable products (*sagal*, and specifically *anagin tavalam*) dominate the largest and most common exchanges (Fred Damon, personal communication, June 2023).
6. Mauss proposed the term of "inalienable wealth" (*immeuble*) to describe goods that were restricted in circulation. The notion was extended and generalized as "inalienable possessions" by Annette Weiner (1985, 1992). I use the distinction proposed by Kockelman (2007: 364ff.) between sociological wealth and linguistic possession (but unlike him, I am interested in sociology rather than linguistics).
7. In other words, allowing the modality of "exchange" to be governed by the principle of reciprocity led us to ignore the baseline communism that doesn't expect

anything back and is central to most everyday interaction (Graeber 2011: Chapter 5).
8. Annette Weiner makes the point forcefully in her classic argument about the paradox of "keeping while giving": "It is . . . not the hoary idea of a return gift that generates the thrust of exchange, but the radiating power of keeping inalienable possessions out of exchange" (1992: 150). This kind of radiation, I argue, must be related to the historical forces of violence and creativity.

References

Ambrose, Wal, Fiona Petchey, Pamela Swadling, et al. 2012. "Engraved Prehistoric Conus Shell Valuables from Southeastern Papua New Guinea: Their Antiquity, Motifs and Distribution." *Archaeology in Oceania* 47(3): 113–32.
Armstrong, Wallace E. 1928. *Rossel Island: An Ethnological Study*. Cambridge: Cambridge University Press.
Austen, Leo. 1939. "Megalithic Structures in the Trobriand Islands." *Oceania* 10(1): 30–53.
Bickler, Simon H. 1998. "Eating Stone and Dying: Archaeological Survey on Woodlark Island, Milne Bay Province, Papua New Guinea." PhD dissertation. Charlottesville: University of Virginia.
———. 1999. "Secondary Burial Practices in the Northern Kula Ring." In *The Entangled Past: Integrating History and Archaeology*, ed. M. Boyd, J. C. Erwin, and M. Hendrickson, 98–107. Calgary: University of Calgary Press.
———. 2006. "Prehistoric Stone Monuments in the Northern Region of the Kula Ring." *Antiquity* 80(307): 38–51.
Bickler, Simon H., Baiva Ivuyo, and V. Kewibu. 1997. "Archaeology at the Suloga Stone Tool Manufacturing Sites, Woodlark Island, Milne Bay Province, PNG." *Archaeology in New Zealand* 40: 204–19.
Bickler, Simon H., and Baiva Ivuyo. 2002. "Megaliths of Muyuw (Woodlark Island), Milne Bay Province, PNG." *Archaeology in Oceania* 37(1): 22–36.
Burenhult, G. 2002. *The Archaeology of the Trobriand Islands, Milne Bay Province, Papua New Guinea: Excavation Season 1999*. Oxford: Archaeopress.
Chowning, Ann. 1987. "Sorcery and the Social Order in Kove." In *Sorcerer and Witch in Melanesia*, ed. Michelle Stephen, 149–82. Melbourne: Melbourne University Press.
Damon, Frederick H. 1979. "Woodlark Island Megalithic Structures and Trenches: Towards an Interpretation." *Archaeology and Physical Anthropology in Oceania* 14: 195–226.
———. 1983a. "On the Transformation of Muyuw into Woodlark Island: Two Minutes in December, 1974." *Journal of Pacific History* 18(1): 35–56.
———. 1983b. "Further Notes on Woodlark Megaliths and Trenches." *Bulletin of the Indo-Pacific Prehistory Association* 4: 100–13.
———. 2002. "Kula Valuables." *L'Homme* 162(2): 107–36.
———. 2016. "Deep Historical Ecology: The Kula Ring as a Representative Moral System from the Indo-Pacific." *World Archaeology* 48(4): 544–62.
Damon, Frederick H., and Roy Wagner, eds. 1989. *Death Rituals and Life in the Societies of the Kula Ring*. DeKalb, IL: Northern Illinois University Press.

Egloff, Brian J. 1978. "The Kula before Malinowski: A Changing Configuration." *Mankind* 11(3): 429–35.

Fortune, Reo F. 1932. *Sorcerers of Dobu: The Social Anthropology of the Dobu Islanders of the Western Pacific*. London: George Routledge & Sons.

Graeber, David. 2011. *Debt: The First 5,000 Years*. New York: Melville House.

Irwin, Geoffrey. 1978. "The Development of Mailu as a Specialized Trading and Manufacturing Centre in Papuan Prehistory: The Causes and Implications." *Mankind* 11: 406–15.

———. 1983. "Chieftainship, Kula, and Trade in Massim Prehistory." In *The Kula: New Perspectives on Massim Exchange*, ed. Jerry W. Leach and Edmund R. Leach, 29–72. Cambridge: Cambridge University Press.

———. 1991. "Themes in the Prehistory of Coastal Papua and the Massim." In *Man and a Half: Essays in Pacific Anthropology and Ethnobiology in Honour of Ralph Bulmer*, ed. E. Pawley, 503–10. Auckland: Polynesian Society.

Irwin, Geoffrey, Ben Shaw, and Andrew McAlister. 2019. "The Origins of the Kula Ring: Archaeological and Maritime Perspectives from the Southern Massim and Mailu Areas of Papua New Guinea." *Archaeology in Oceania* 54(1): 1–16.

Kirch, Patrick. 1991. "Prehistoric Exchange in Western Melanesia." *Annual Review of Anthropology* 20: 141–65.

Kockelman, Paul. 2007. "Inalienable Possession and Personhood in a Q'eqchi'-Mayan Community." *Language in Society* 36(3): 343–69.

Kuehling, Susanne. 2017. "'We Die for Kula'—An Object-Centred View of Motivations and Strategies in Gift Exchange." *Journal of the Polynesian Society* 126(2): 181–208.

Leach, Edmund. 1983. "The Kula: An Alternative View." In *The Kula: New Perspectives on Massim Exchange*, ed. Jerry W. Leach and Edmund Leach, 529–38. Cambridge: Cambridge University Press.

Leach, Jerry W. 1983a. "Trobriand Territorial Categories and the Problem of Who is Not in the Kula." In *The Kula: New Perspectives on Massim Exchange*, ed. Jerry W. Leach and Edmund Leach, 121–46. Cambridge: Cambridge University Press.

———. 1983b. "Introduction." In *The Kula: New Perspectives on Massim Exchange*, ed. Jerry W. Leach and Edmund Leach, 1–27. Cambridge: Cambridge University Press.

Lepowsky, Maria. 1991. "The Way of the Ancestors: Custom, Innovation, and Resistance." *Ethnology* 30(3): 217–35.

Liang, Yongjia. 2022. "Esteeming Goods for Non-Accumulation, Small Realms with Few People: Interpreting Kula with Laozi." *American Anthropologist* 124(3): 456–66.

Liep, John. 1996. "The Bigmanisation Process: Theoretical and Historical Secularisation of Power in Melanesia." In *Melanesian Modernities*, ed. J. Friedman and J. G. Carrier, 121–41. Lund: Lund University Press.

———. 2009. *A Papuan Plutocracy: Ranked Exchange on Rossel Island*. Aarhus: Aarhus University Press.

MacIntyre, Martha. 1983. "Warfare and the Changing Context of 'Kune' on Tubetube." *Journal of Pacific History* 18(1): 11–34.

———. 1989. "The Triumph of Susu: Mortuary Exchanges on Tubetube." In *Death Rituals and Life in the Societies of the Kula Ring*, ed. Frederick H. Damon and Roy Wagner, 133–52. DeKalb, IL: Northern Illinois University Press.

———. 1994. "Too Many Chiefs? Leadership in the Massim in the Colonial Era." *History and Anthropology* 7(1–4): 241–62.
Malinowski, Bronisław. 1920. "War and Weapons among the Natives of the Trobriand Islands." *Man* 20: 10–12.
———. 1922. *Argonauts of the Western Pacific: An Account of Native Enterprise and Adventure in the Archipelagoes of Melanesian New Guinea*. London: Routledge & Kegan Paul.
———. 1927. "The Life of Culture." In *Culture: The Diffusion Controversy*, ed. Grafton Elliot Smith, Bronisław Malinowski, Herbert J. Spinden, and Alexander Goldenweiser, 26–46. New York: W.W. Norton.
———. 1935. *Coral Gardens and Their Magic*. London: Allen & Unwin.
———. 1993 [1906]. "On the Principle of the Economy of Thought." In *The Early Writings of Bronislaw Malinowski*, ed. Robert J. Thornton and Peter Skalník, 89–116. Cambridge: Cambridge University Press.
Ollier, Clifford D., and David K. Holdsworth. 1968. "A Survey of a Megalithic Structure in the Trobriand Islands, Papua." *Archaeology and Physical Anthropology in Oceania* 3(2): 156–58.
Ollier, Clifford D., David K. Holdsworth, and Gilbert Heers. 1970a. "Megaliths at Wagura, Vakuta, Trobriand Islands." *Archaeology and Physical Anthropology in Oceania* 5: 24–26.
———. 1970b. "Megaliths of Kitava, Trobriand Islands." *Records of the Papua New Guinea Museum* 1: 5–15.
———. 1971a. "Inakebu Cave Art at Kitava in the Trobriand Islands." *Archaeology* 24: 22–27.
———. 1971b. "Further Caves of Kitava, Trobriand Islands, Papua." *Helicite* 9: 61–70.
———. 1973. "Megaliths, Stones and Bwala on Kitava, Trobriand Islands." *Archaeology and Physical Anthropology in Oceania* 8: 41–50.
Ollier, Clifford D., and Colin F. Pain. 1978a. "Caves of Woodlark Island, Papua New Guinea." *Helicite* 16: 64–78.
———. 1978b. "Some Megaliths and Cave Burials: Woodlark Island (Murua), Papua New Guinea." *Archaeology and Physical Anthropology in Oceania* 13: 10–18.
Riesenfeld, Alphonse. 1950. *Megalithic Culture of Melanesia*. Leiden: Brill.
Sayer, Derek. 1987. *The Violence of Abstraction: The Analytic Foundations of Historical Materialism*. Oxford: Blackwell.
Seligman, Charles. 1910. *The Melanesians of British New Guinea*. Cambridge: Cambridge University Press.
Shaw, Ben. 2016. "The Massim Region of Papua New Guinea: A Review and Proposed Chronology." *Journal of Pacific Archaeology* 7(1): 106–25.
———. 2017. "Late Pleistocene Colonisation of the Eastern New Guinea Islands? The Potential Implications of Robust Waisted Stone Tool Finds from Rossel Island on the Long Term Settlement Dynamics in the Massim Region." *Journal of Pacific Archaeology* 8(2): 1–16.
Shaw, Ben, and Simon Coxe. 2021. "Cannibalism and Developments to Socio-Political Systems from 540 BP in the Massim Islands of South-East Papua New Guinea." *Technical Reports of the Australian Museum Online* 34: 47–60.

Shaw, Ben, and Michelle Langley. 2017. "Investigating the Development of Prehistoric Cultural Practices in the Massim Region of Eastern Papua New Guinea: Insights from the Manufacture and Use of Shell Objects in the Louisiade Archipelago." *Journal of Anthropological Archaeology* 48: 149–65.

Thornton, Robert J., and Peter Skalník. 1993. "Introduction: Malinowski's Reading, Writing, 1904–1914." In *The Early Writings of Bronislaw Malinowski*, ed. Robert J. Thornton and Peter Skalník, 1–66. Cambridge: Cambridge University Press.

Uberoi, J. P. Singh. 1962. *The Politics of the Kula Ring: An Analysis of the Findings of Bronislaw Malinowski*. Manchester: Manchester University Press.

Wagner, Roy. 1989. "Conclusion: The Exchange Context of the Kula." In *Death Rituals and Life in the Societies of the Kula Ring*, ed. Frederick H. Damon and Roy Wagner, 254–74. DeKalb, IL: Northern Illinois University Press.

Weiner, Annette B. 1985. "Inalienable Wealth." *American Ethnologist* 12(2): 210–27.

———. 1992. *Inalienable Possessions*. Berkeley: University of California Press.

Young, Michael, and Maribelle de Vera. 1980. "Secondary Burial on Goodenough Island: Some Archaeological and Ethnographic Observations." In *Occasional Papers in Anthropology 10*, 229–48. Queensland: Anthropology Museum, University of Queensland.

Young, Michael W. 1971. *Fighting with Food: Leadership, Values and Social Control in a Massim Society*. Cambridge: Cambridge University Press.

———. 1983. "The Massim: An Introduction." *Journal of Pacific History* 18(1): 4–10.

———. 2004. *Malinowski: Odyssey of an Anthropologist, 1884–1920*. New Haven, CT: Yale University Press.

11

 Using Laozi to Interpret the Kula Ring

Rethinking the Dual Chieftainship in Kiriwina

YONGJIA LIANG

From the 1940s to the 1990s, Bronisław Malinowski was the best-known anthropologist in China (Guldin 1994). This was largely due to his pupil Fei Xiaotong (or Fei Hsiao-tung, 1910–2005). Fei played a pivotal role in pioneering Chinese anthropology in the 1940s and leading its revival in the 1980s. Rooted in traditional Chinese literati values, Fei proposed a "cross-civilizational understanding" (*wenming jiejian*) that was influenced by Malinowski's version of functionalism, resting on the fundamental dichotomy of human biology and culture. It can be said that Malinowski sowed the seeds of cross-civilizational understanding in Fei by recognizing his doctoral work as the endeavor of a committed scholar from a different civilization.

Fei's perspective on cross-civilizational understanding is encapsulated in the phrase "appreciating what others appreciate" (*mei ren zhi mei*). He believed that "there is eternal, brilliant, unprecedented, and unrepeatable wisdom" in any great civilization (Fei 2003: 14). Thus, it was necessary for Chinese scholars to understand different human societies with ancient Chinese thought in mind. If Malinowski's interpretation of the Trobriand Islanders was shaped by his own civilizational context, can a Chinese anthropologist make use of a different lens when viewing the same culture? As Fei's pupil, I draw inspiration from his insights and employ the ideas of the ancient Chinese thinker Laozi to examine the ethnographies of the Kula ring, offering an alternative interpretation to honor the anthropological legacy of both Malinowski and Fei.

As I have elaborated elsewhere (Liang 2022), Laozi holds a place in Chinese philosophy akin to that of Plato in the Western tradition. His eponymous work is often compared to the *Republic*. He is regarded as the founding figure of Daoism, a prominent school of thought second only to Confucianism in its influence. Functioning as both a historian and diviner attuned to the underlying patterns of enduring transformations, Laozi was a thinker who sought a unifying principle capable of generating the complexity of existence, known as "all ten thousand things" (*wanwu*). This unifying force is commonly referred to as Dao, or the Way.

To make use of a six-century-BCE classic from China to understand a classic of twentieth-century non-Western ethnography is an unusual undertaking. However, it is epistemically unoriginal, in the sense that I too engage in implicit comparison between the world of the anthropologists and that of their others. The only difference is that I shift the lens from what I call the Greco-Roman episteme to a Chinese one. Elaborating on my earlier work (Liang 2022), I shall first explain how Laozi illuminates the spatial-temporal field of the Kula as explored by Bronisław Malinowski. Then, engaging in particular with the recent work of Mark Mosko (2017), I shall apply Laozi's notion of the "intellects" (a pejorative word in his vocabulary) to interpret political disputes in Kiriwina, the principal island of the Trobriands. I argue that Laozi not only helps us understand how Kula avoids the accumulation of shells and fame, but also sheds light on how matrilineal dual chieftainship may provide room for "the intellects ... to act," allowing for attempts to transition from a dispersed political order to an accumulative one.

This chapter focuses on the concept of "accumulation," which is essential to Laozi and to the economic anthropology that was established by Malinowski in his groundbreaking study. The goal of exchanging valuables is to accumulate shells and fame, but this accumulation did not result in the consolidation of significant "political units." Although Kula exchanges often take place between political or cultural units, their success does not necessarily correspond to the prestige of the chiefs or the Paramount Chief. This results in an "incongruency" that was largely neglected by Marcel Mauss, who believed that the Kula trade was "reserved for the chiefs, who are simultaneously the leaders of the fleets and canoes, the traders, and who are the recipients of the gifts" (Mauss 2016: 90). Malinowski (1922: 69) acknowledges this political-economic incongruency and emphasizes the importance of understanding the political to comprehend the economic:

> It has been necessary to give a somewhat detailed description of chieftainship and political divisions, as a firm grasp of the main political institutions is essential to the understanding of the Kula. All departments of tribal life, religion, magic, and economics are interwoven, but the social organization of the tribe lies at the foundation of everything else.

My focus is on political dynamics and their implications for historical change. Comparisons with patriliny in China illuminate the evolutionary significance of the distinctive form of matrilineal kinship organization found on the Trobriands, which forms an obstacle to the consolidation of "civilization." My usage of the term "civilization" is inspired by Lévi-Strauss's distinction between "hot" and "cold" societies, where the former are characterized by state-formation and class, while complex social structures are precluded in the latter (Lévi-Strauss 1974: 286–97). Arnason (2018) notes that Lévi-Strauss's work bridged Weberian and Maussian approaches to civilizational studies. Clastres (2011) documented how seemingly simple societies actively avoided state formation and central power through the emphasis they placed on leisure, prestige, and generosity. "Hot" and "cold" societies are not static but are in constant flux, with the possibility of shifting from one to the other. Godelier (2007) observed a diversity of non-civilizational societies in the Pacific islands, from New Guinean tribes to the more complex Polynesian islands, which he sought to explain historically. In the Kula ring, societies have devolved from stratified to egalitarian, but a tentative return to civilization may have been underway before Western colonial impact. I argue in this chapter that this is to be seen in the instability of the dual chieftainship.

The Greco-Roman Episteme

Paradigm shifts in social anthropology, as in other branches of science, are almost always achieved through reviving different lines of thought within Western philosophy, with ultimate roots in ancient Greece. This means that ethnographic data from every corner of the world is interpreted with some reference to Western antiquity. I call this metanarrative the "Greco-Roman episteme." I use "episteme" in the Foucauldian sense to refer to knowledge production and its conditions of possibility. Many social theorists have taken pride in returning to ancient roots, signaling their intention by using words of Greek or Latin origin in their titles and texts.

The perennial problem is how to describe other empirical worlds in time and space, without the freight of Greco-Roman vocabulary. Grand theories of natural law, social contract, and, above all, "human nature" have all been inspired by Greek philosophy. Western social science is based not only on the "Western illusion of human nature" (Sahlins 2008) but also on the most insightful, liberal regime of knowledge humans have ever achieved. There is nothing wrong with this "Greco-Roman episteme"; indeed, it seems inevitable that one should analyze the empirical world on the basis of the canon of this civilization as it developed in the

Axial Age. Without such a universalist anchor, social science is simply impossible.

A theory, according to Leigh Jenco (2016: 4), is "a generalization in which conditions in one place or at one time, or both, are articulated in such a way to apply to other places or times. Put differently, a theory is the deterritorialization of ideas to produce new and broader insight into social and political conditions elsewhere." In this sense, it is counterproductive to try, as some influential postcolonialists or decolonialists have done, to "provincialize" Europe or "the West," because doing so fails to *deterritorialize* ideas in the way that the Greco-Roman episteme has done in the epoch we know as modernity. To complement theories produced in the Greco-Roman episteme, non-Western anthropologists should try the reverse. They need to deterritorialize their own civilizational conundrums to their others. While numerous influential anthropologists have emphasized a hermeneutic relativism and cultural translation, in practice, even the most radical have been concerned with building bridges across social universes by means of a recourse to the Greco-Roman episteme.

I propose to pursue the agenda of "cultural translation" from a Sinic perspective by deterritorializing thoughts proposed in Chinese antiquity. It is common sense among philosophers (Martin Heidegger, for example) that concepts and ideas proposed by ancient philosophers like Laozi find no equivalence in their Western counterparts (Nelson 2022). If a social scientist can capture just 2 percent of the social world, half of what physicists claim they can do with the physical world, it is important to inquire into what can be revealed through the lens of another Axial Age civilization. The civilizations of that era were ontologically different from one another, though they made equally strong universalizing claims. This opens up the potential for deterritorialization. China would not be an exception if its classical philosophers theorized the world universally from their particular perspectives (Elvin 1986). The goal of Sinic perspectivism is not to replace the Greco-Roman episteme. Rather, it seeks to add interpretive density by "recognizing the universalism of the other worlds" (Wang 2011: 116).

The Laozi was consolidated in an age of concentration of resources for warfare among hegemons in a constellation of city-states (Zhao 2015). Observing that all deeds would eventually fail, Laozi discourages excessive accumulation and the stratification necessary to create larger and stronger states. Such trends would go against "the self-momentum of the Way" (*daofa ziran*). An ideal world is a world of "small realms" (*xiaobang*) in which "Neighboring states view each other. They hear the cries of chicken and dog, yet people reach old age without meeting each other" (Laozi 2008: 165). A ruler should follow "the sage" and practice "doing nothing" (*wuwei*), which means "under-acting," "under-governing," "laying no claim," "not striving," and "pursuing no end" (Laozi 2001: 31–32). Excessive taxation and regulation of the population are bad. So are excessive rituals, virtues, codes, pleasures, desires, and ambitions. All run against the natural cause of the Way, and they will inevitably lead to failure, loss, danger, betrayal, or disintegration. In addition to *wuwei*, the tenets are also generated from Laozi's other central concept: *ziran*, meaning spontaneity and self-becoming. In laying out his political philosophy, Laozi has nothing to say about "human nature." Rather, the universe is not anthropocentric, and humans are depicted as rather ordinary beings with an inglorious capacity to betray the Way.

Laozi's depiction of an ideal world is composed not just of "ideals" but of a series of practical concepts that together prevent the system from reaching the tipping point of an irreversible breakthrough that would irretrievably undermine human self-momentum. Contrary to the common dismissal that Laozi is nothing but a utopian construct, his immense impact on Chinese political thought leads one to wonder if its manifestations might be realized in practice, at least partially, in "small realms" such as those of the Kula ring—illiterate, "uncivilized," and "cold" in the terminology of Lévi-Strauss. The precepts of Laozi, combining "esteeming goods" with "non-accumulation" in the context of a "small realm with few people," have the potential for deterritorialization. This is why it makes sense to read Kula through the lens of Laozi.

Kula through the Lens of Laozi?

In the lucid mottos of Laozi, the Kula is a system of "non-accumulation" featuring delicate ways of avoiding the concentration of crucial resources through constant doing and undoing. Unlike Laozi, who proposes that "non-accumulation" could be achieved only through *not* esteeming "goods hard to obtain," Kula maintains a small realm in the opposite way, by esteeming goods (Liang 2022).

Laozi mentioned his objections to "esteeming goods" twice. Stanza 3 says: "Promote not the worthy, then the people will not compete. *Esteem not goods* hard to obtain, then the people will not be thieves. Display not what is desirable, then the people's hearts will not be turbid." Stanza 12 reads, "*Goods hard to obtain* cause a man's progress to halt" (Laozi 2008: 27). Laozi opposes "esteeming goods" because valuable goods generate the excessive desire to possess and disturb orderly life: "The Sage does not accumulate: Having done all for others, he has yet still more; Having given all to others, he has yet made more." Accumulation encumbers possessions through theft, deception, taxation, or exploitation, ruining the spontaneous order of society. As he argues in Stanza 19: "Cut off knavery, get rid of profiteering, thieves and robbers are no more" (Laozi 2008: 41).

Things are different in the Kula, where "valuables" (*vagu'a*) are precious because they are hard to make. Size matters (Damon 2002: 114), and so does a valuable's transaction history (Kuehling 2006: 212). However, neither Kula shells nor Kula fame can be accumulated. The longer one keeps a shell, the more one is exposed to collective efforts to make one give it up, through delicate management to channel the "spouse" of a famous artifact, sweetening "opening gifts," or even sorcery. Contrary to capitalist wealth, which is measured through the relation between "men and things" (Dumont 1977: 5–6) that can come about through immediate alienation (purchase), systematic exploitation, and even robbery, Kula fame depends on partners' voluntary relinquishment (Damon 1983: 327). *Kitoum*, a "responsibility-free kula" ready for broader circulation, makes fame accumulation even harder (Macintyre 1983: 373). When a *kitoum* is given away, the giver keeps it until an equivalent shell is returned, implying that the fame must be repaid with little "marginal gain" generated along the transaction chain.

The Kula is esteemed but hard to accumulate because its goods require "voluntary" relinquishment and near zero-sum transactions. When a Kula valuable is transferred, the fame of the giver will fall, while the fame of the recipient and the giver once removed (*murimuri*) will rise. However, the overall fame produced is near zero because each transaction creates "winners and losers" in terms of Kula fame and shells (Damon 2002). Kula moving among partners is like a heavy ball moving around on a soft plate, constantly creating an uneven terrace that is flattened automatically afterward. In other words, the partners collectively participate in a noncooperative game. The collective "noncooperation" through which fame is dispersed is far from the noble and total exchange suggested by Mauss, but close to Laozi's "spontaneous order" (*ziran*). Through constant doing and undoing, esteem in the Kula leads to entropy, that is, "non-accumulation" is achieved by "esteeming goods."

Fame, the goal to accumulate Kula transactions, dissipates quickly after an elder's death. The elder usually gives the "kula path" (*ked*, his partner) to his nephew, the "legal" heir, and the shell to his son. Nevertheless, his fame is inheritable because, upon his death, his partners automatically recalibrate their strategies against his fame by soliciting shells from his heir, like a bank run. "Cashing" too many shells often causes an inexperienced heir to quickly lose stocks inherited from his uncle. This is particularly so when the deceased elder is a well-known Kula tycoon. The perishable fame makes Kula non-accumulative at a profound level, impossible to institutionalize.

Laozi and Kula differ in the exemplars they uphold. For Laozi, the ideal order depends on a ruler who follows the exemplary "sage" (*shengren*) while, in the Kula, the exemplary figure is the aged player who accumulates fame and survives sorcery. However, collective coordination prevents this elder from transmitting fame to his heir after death. Therefore, unlike the early Chinese polity, the Kula ring is populated by ordinary players who cannot hold on to the partners they inherit from their maternal uncles. Again, we see Laozi and Kula achieving the same goal in different ways. In the *Laozi*, "esteem no goods" and "non-accumulate" apply to none but "the sage" (Stanza 81). Laozi mentions "the sage" thirty-two times in a work of merely five thousand words. The Sage constitutes "an exemplary figure of the world" (Liu 2006: 560–61), toward which the ruler should strive. To deserve the name, a sage must practice "inaction" (*wuwei*) through non-accumulation. In Kula, most participants are commoners whose "excessive action" is no threat to anyone. Laozi nowhere opposes action on the part of the commoners.

Active elders propel an egalitarian society without accumulation. According to Fred Damon (2002: 127), "every male wanted to be an 'elder,' someone who achieved a stature like the highest-ranked valuables—'known' and talked about everywhere." The goal is temporary possession of "consumable" goods, not the ownership of inheritable "real estate." This ties in with Laozi's counsel of "esteeming the body": "The ruling of the Sage is by the belly, not by the eyes" (Stanza 12). "The government of the Sage is thus: He empties his mind, fills his belly; Weakens his will, strengthens his bones" (Stanza 3). The Kula, too, generally discourages intergenerational, physical bodily trust.

We can generalize that both Laozi and Kula transcend the ethics of large-scale, historical societies. The Sage enables commoners to remain free from exploitation by being inactive and achieving a spontaneous order. In "hot" societies, by contrast, a man may be expected to sacrifice his life for the benefit of his descendants or any "public good." In Kula, the name of a deceased person, whether successful or not, should not be mentioned. The taboo maintains a deliberate "amnesia," revealing Kula's purpose: one spends one's life striving to accumulate but has nothing in the end. The Kula fulfills Laozi's injunction to "Keep the realm small, its people few." Laozi's distaste for technologies, mobilities, weapons, administration, and writing can be construed as anti-civilizational (Lévi-Strauss 1974: 286–97). Technologies need large-scale cooperation that is bound to result in massive exploitation, leading the society either to disintegration or to an irreversible stratification, both undesirable to Laozi.

The Kula system can be approached as a devolution from a competitive, hierarchical social system. The megalithic works widely found in the northern part of the Kula ring must have been built by societies starkly different from the system in which the Kula could later flourish (Egloff 1978; see

Steinmüller, this volume). While Laozi depicts a hypothetical devolution pathway, the archaeologists have shown us its form in this concrete case. Kula was a creative and economical way to create a more peaceful, sustainable society and to keep value flowing. It is a chain of "small realms with few people." Political and kinship organizations, language groups, and regimes of time are confined to one island or even one section of an island. Matrilineal kinship allows big men to create clienteles, but they are easy to reorganize. Matrilineal kin can easily become enemies (Kuehling 2017: 186). Lineage consolidation of the kind found in "civilizational" societies such as China and India was thus avoided.

Though some Kula participants travel frequently, most visit only neighboring islands. They do not measure their products with precision (Damon 2010). The oppositional flow of *mwali* and *bagi* seems designed to prevent calculation and render the Marxist theory of labor value irrelevant. For a *mwali*, the larger the conus shell, the more labor it implies; for a *bagi*, the labor is congealed in grinding shell pieces to small diameters. People expect equivalence, but they "did not, however, count hours, so there was a point at which the specific application of our measures was, or seemed to be, an unwarranted imposition" (Damon 2002: 116). This leads to endless complaints about whether a counter-gift is really equivalent, but were it not for this lack of precision there would have been no gossip, argument, tact, magic, or sorcery: in short, no Kula at all.

Regimes of space and time demonstrate how different islands or parts of an island orient differently with incoherent calendars. Damon (2017: 23) argues that this is a deliberate arrangement designed to mitigate the uncertainties of drought by harvesting at different times. By suppressing the standardization of kinship organization, livelihood, calendars, and language across the archipelago, the devolved arrangements are more viable than their megalithic predecessors.

The Kula system is a world in which, as Laozi proclaims, "Shield and blade best not to show" (Laozi 2001: 186). Violence is seldom involved in the case of minor altercations. The pacification policy of the Australian colonial government after World War II (Young 1971: 16) was highly successful, enabling former renegades to be drawn into the transactions of the Kula (Thune 1983: 352). Kula transactions are completed through complex negotiations involving visits, verbal exchange, coaxing, sex, and magic. As a Dobuan said, "greasing for 'kune' [Kula] is like greasing for sex" (Kuehling 2006: 210). Kula valuables could conceivably be accumulated by force, but that would ruin a man's reputation. Instead, violence takes the form of witchcraft (*welabana*) and sorcery (*balau*), which result from envy or anger and can cause sudden death or a series of deaths. However, such metaphorical explanation remains secret, sensitive, and shameful (Munn 1986: 234–65).

The Kula constrained political and military organization both between and within islands. As Sahlins (2017: 281, emphasis in original) pointed out, "in the absence of external guarantees, as of a Sovereign Power, peace must be otherwise secured: by extension of sociable relations to foreigners—thus, the trade-friendship or trade-kinship—and, most significantly, *by the terms of exchange itself.*" Archaeological evidence suggests that the Kula ring was developed as Massim became differentiated from the Papua New Guinea mainland in the seventeenth century (Irwin et al. 2019: 11). Kula and warfare were mutually exclusive. People competed intensively, but the competition did not escalate into political subordination or military raids. This approximates the dream of Laozi, who believes that military actions are sinister and do not conform to the Way: "Weapons of war are omens of doom, to be loathed by every living thing and shunned by those who keep the Way . . . [they should] not be used unless compelled. Above all, with mind and heart unstirred. To arms give no glory: For to glory in arms is to sing and rejoice in the slaughter of men" (Laozi 2001: 93).

Laozi offers a Sinic reading of the Kula. Laozi's "esteeming goods," "non-accumulation," and "small realms with few people," together with a variety of other interrelated, motto-like concepts, help us understand an array of neglected, "paradoxical" aspects of Kula: the most esteemed goods and the fame generated through them can hardly be accumulated, though this activity consumes more energy than anything else. The system remains small in terms of technology, calendar, and organization. People toil in fierce competition, but the overall effect is egalitarian, small realms conducive to nonviolence.

Dual Chieftainship in Kiriwina

I turn now to apply *Laozi* to the case of the "intellects." I have long been intrigued by the institution of dual chieftainship in Omarakana, the village where Malinowski stayed for much of his fieldwork. Mark Mosko (2017: 370) notes that "it will come as a surprise to many anthropologists of Melanesia, Oceania, and elsewhere to learn that there is a dual chieftainship at Omarakana which predates the establishment of colonial domination." Mosko hints at comparisons with Polynesian societies and divine chiefdoms and kingdoms elsewhere, as described by Hocart, Valeri, and Sahlins. Omarakana dual chieftainship refers to the transmission of the title of Paramount Chief through the alliance of the Tabalu and Osapola-Bwaydaga (OB), two of the most high-ranking matrilineal descent groups (*dala*) in the northern part of Kiriwina. The Paramount Chief succeeds his mother's brother. This exclusive marriage arrangement sustains a monopoly over the most potent and dangerous corpus of magic (*megwa*) that mediates crucial phenomena (such as weather and epidemics).

While the Paramount Chief was a Tabalu, the brothers of his "major wife," who must be an OB, formed a council headed by Katayuvisa, a man known as "Mother of Kiriwina," who assumed the administrative duties of the realm as "Oratory Chief." Taking charge of the council, he mediates between the people and the Tabalu chief, who is considered the living form of Baloma (an ancestral spirit). As such, the Paramount Chief has to observe rigorous dietary restrictions and lead a secluded lifestyle, since his magic is dangerous. This inactivity is antithetical to his intense engagements with the sacred beings of the spiritual worlds (Tuma) on behalf of the people. Mosko (2017: 377) observes that this dual chieftainship "approximates the distinction between the sacred (*bomaboma*) and the relative profane (*itugwali*)," the form of paramountcy found in several other parts of the Trobriands and even in Samoa.

A Paramount Chief usually learns the spells from his maternal uncle's son, to whom he presents gifts (*pokala*) in return. Alternatively, he may learn them from his uncle and give *pokala* to him, as if his uncle were his adopted father. This implies being a Tabalu and an OB at the same time, a contradiction. The practice of adoption into one's maternal uncle's father's *dala* to form a classificatory father–son relationship with that uncle is widespread. Another arrangement is that when a man becomes a head (*guyau*) of the *dala* in his mother's natal village, he relocates to that village and becomes the "father" (*tama*) of that *dala*. Now the "father" of his mother's *dala*, he has switched identity.

Mosko (2017: 13) refers to these tangled links as "quasi-incest." In Figure 11.1, the alliance between A and B is between the father's sister's son and the mother's brother's daughter, as well as between the mother's brother's son and the father's sister's daughter, both expressing the preferred cross-cousin marriage. However, the marriage is also brother–sister incest because A marries the classificatory sister by being adopted by his maternal uncle C, and father–daughter incest because A becomes the *tama* father of his *dala*, the women of which become his "daughters." Sexual congress of brother and sister (*luta*) or father and daughter is precisely the intensely forbidden Baloma taboo, called *suvasova*. This is an ambiguous situation: the chiefly alliance is incestuous and non-incestuous at once.

The dual chieftainship familiar to me as a native of China is the patrilineal Dali kingship that existed in southwest China between the tenth and twelfth centuries. The title of emperor was transmitted through the royal house of the Duan, who intermarried with the house of Gao, which provided many aristocratic ministers who administered the kingdom's secular affairs. The emperor was largely confined to his palace at the center of the

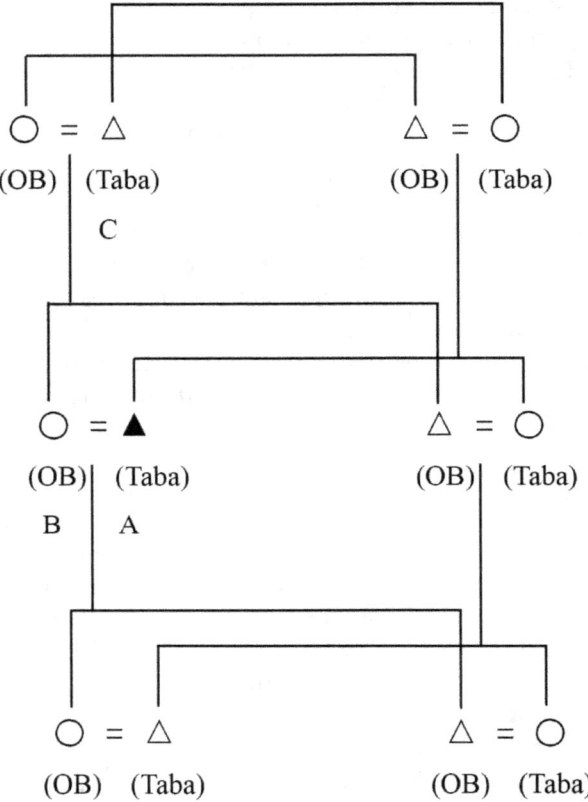

Figure 11.1. Tabalu–OB alliance.

kingdom. He was supposed to live in seclusion and practice esoteric Buddhism as a cosmos-ruler of the world (Lian 2007). He usually ended his this-worldly life by abdicating from the throne and being ordained into the royal monastery, corresponding to his Chakravarti identity, which permitted him to rule the world one last time before subliming into Buddhaship (Liang 2011). The ministers of the Gao house complemented the emperor: they practiced Zen Buddhism, were well-versed in the Confucian art of governance, and had no special access to the other world.

The dual chieftainships in southwest Dali and Kiriwina resemble each other in the opposition between this-worldliness and otherworldliness. However, there is a major difference: while in Dali kingship, the "familiar type" to world history, a father passes his throne to his son, in Omarakara kingship, an uncle passes his position to his sister's son, even when this is constructed to look like a father–son succession.

Mosko provides a detailed analysis of how and why dual chieftainship has to remain paradoxical regarding incest. The arrangement avoids *suvasova* incest and endogamy by being "quasi-incestuous or quasi-endogamous, and thereby to that extent *bomaboma* or sacred in character" (Mosko 2017: 382). The chiefly magic "intended for inheritance ... within a *dala* must be first passed to a relation *beyond it* before the magic can reenter, but he who first receives it is a partial *dala* affiliate ... in any case." As Mosko (ibid.) further explains:

> This is a consequence of the joint transmission of *both* parents' maternally identified *dala* images and powers to their children. The marriages of a Tabalu man to an Osapola-Bwaydaga woman or a Tabalu woman to an Osapola-Bwaydaga man produce children whose *kekwabu* images and *peu'ula* powers are duplicated or compounded. This would amount to sibling incest, *except* that the redoubled personal components of each child are conceived as not being the result of intra-*dala* transmission along the matrilineal lines of connections. Inverse pedigrees have acquired them. What one child has taken from its mother, the other has received from its father, and vice versa. The resulting relations between the marital couple in either *tabu-tabu* or *tama-latu* regarding sexual intimacy and marriage thus mirror *suvasova* while at the same time avoiding it—an arrangement not structurally dissimilar to that between Boyowa and Tuma.

If dual chieftainship is confined to just two *dalas*, it seems unnecessary to add these complicated refinements. Why bother to ensure that the inheritance "must be first passed to a relation *beyond it* before the magic can re-enter"? Why does a legitimate alliance have to take on the allure of incest?

I argue that this is so because the Paramount Chief is on his way to creating a transcendent kingship, implying a monopoly over both land and magic, which inevitably leaves much room for *kobala* ("usurpation" or "subversion"). In order to accumulate and monopolize what Michael Mann (1986) called "ideological powers," the Chief cannot share his magic with another *dala*. Were he to do so, both would "sink" as the knowledge passed through space and time (cf. Geertz 1980 on "sinking status" in Bali). A monopoly means that the "throne" has to be accessed by a single *dala*, as was the case with the Dali Chakravarti king. Familiar, patrilineal kingship is the source of the absolutist state that has dominated world history.

The Trobriand alternative is expressed in the system of land tenure. If the chief is expected to take wives from every landowning *dala*, he is a "glorified brother-in-law" to the village and the entire chiefdom (Malinowski 1935: 192). Mosko (2017: 344) observes:

> The men of each affinally connected *dala* are, therefore, collectively responsible for subsidizing the marriage of their *dala* sister or niece with annual prestations of

urigubu garden "tribute." A chiefly wife's father would also contribute substantially to his daughter's *urigubu* payments. It is expected that the summary payment accompanying a single chiefly wife would be at least four times that of the annual gift given by another man to his sister's husband. Thus a chief with numerous wives is regularly provided with considerable amounts of wealth with which he could underwrite a wide range of collective activities in the validation of his rank and influence.

This is a familiar form of "accumulation" in the world of patrilineal kingship, exemplified by "thigh-eating chiefs" among the Kachin (Leach 1954: 93). Accumulating garden products requires control of the land, but the combination of matrilineal descent with virilocal residence inhibits differentiation of the sort found, for example, in African patrilineal societies. Incest, or its metaphorical representation, resolves the tension between land-based resource extracting and the instability of fluctuating *dala* identities.

In ancient China, the rise of patrilineal-cum-patriarchal kingdoms commonly involved monarchs practicing cross-generational incest to establish transcendent kingship (Granet 1932). This was also the case in the medieval Dali kingdom when the legitimacy of the supreme ruler experienced a major shift. He was first depicted as a "barbarian" outsider who annexed the local polity through a royal alliance with the indigenous princess. By establishing transcendent kingship, the ruler was represented as Avalokiteśvara, descended from the extramundane world. In other words, it was an ideological construct that the "stranger-king" (Sahlins 2008) shifted from the affines of the indigenous people to being their consanguine in order to establish a cosmocracy (Liang 2011). I agree with Leach (1961: 19–24) that a fundamental ideological opposition characterizes the Trobriands. It is not an opposition between "incorporation" (kinship) and "mystical influence" (affinity and magic), but rather one between kinship-based exchange and land-based administration. The entangled symbiosis of matriliny dilutes the potential for monopoly by allowing for alternative social orders (cf. Graeber and Wengrow 2021). The alternating regimes constitute a world with irreducible internal tensions.

The Intellects Dare to Act

The alternating arrangement makes altercations possible and politics increasingly relevant in the realm. A politicized world is an unstable one. When Malinowski was in Kiriwina, a dramatic event occurred between Namwanaguyau (Nam, an OB), who was the favored son of the Paramount Chief To'uluwa (To'u, a Tabalu), and Mitakata (Mit, a Tabalu) who was To'u's sister's son and the legal heir to his position. Nam accused Mit of

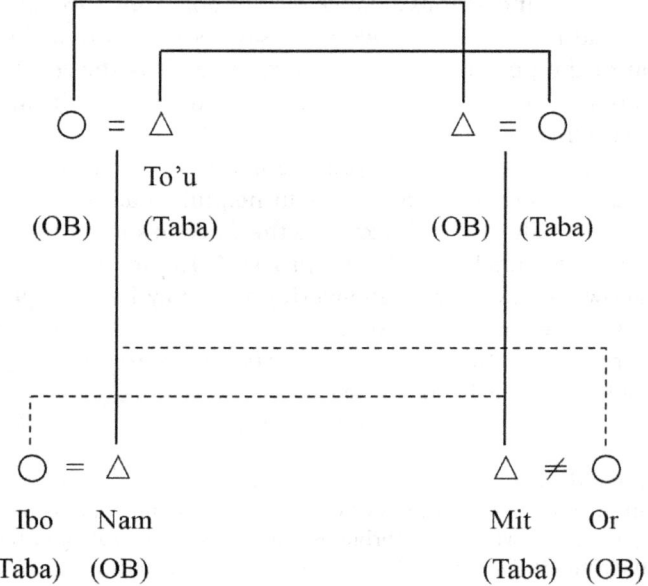

Figure 11.2. Nam–Mit dispute.

committing incestuous adultery with his wife, Ibomala (Ibo), a Tabalu woman raised in Omarakana and thus Mit's "sister." Mit was brought by Nam to the white magistrate and jailed. In revenge, Mit's Tabalu brothers banished Nam from Omarakana.

The political consequences were profound, as Baldwin (cited in Mosko 2017: 374) recorded in 1949: "Obviously it was no less a political question then than it is now." This event was still recalled when Mosko conducted his fieldwork a century later. Malinowski provides an explanation based on psychology, arguing that a father's natural affection for his son may operate against the rules of a matrilineal society if his son grew up with him while his legal heir, his sister's son, was raised somewhere else and is therefore less close to him. Mosko provides a more sophisticated explanation by arguing that it is inadequate to characterize a *dala* as "matrilineal." Neither *dala* nor its extension (*kumila*) is a matrilineal group in substance due to subtle practices of adoption, fostering, flexibility in residence, and the practice of *suvasova* (incest). He argues that caste-like, exclusive alliances involving "quasi-incest" are "positively enjoined" for the chiefly rank and legitimated in myth (Mosko 2017: 15). *Suvasova* incest does not apply to the transmission of chiefly magic because, in the precolonial epoch, the act of creation was consolidated into the magics respectively owned by different *dalas*. The act itself was a result of incest between brother and sister. The fact that the quasi-incestuous alliance of the Tabalu and OB does not bring about personal ill-health or collective disasters proves that the exclusive possession of the powerful spells (*tukwa*) created by the *tosunapula* sibling ancestors is powerful in itself. This is how dual chieftainship works in northern Kiriwina.

Both Malinowski and Mosko provide instructive observations, but for a more satisfying explanation it is again helpful to adopt the lens of the *Laozi* and view duality in Omarakana as the dawn of something that has yet to become an irreversible "civilizing process." The matrilineal dual chieftainship allows for political maneuvering that may become permanently contentious. I offer my explanation here. At issue is the rise of what Laozi called the action of "the intellects" (*zhizhe*), who are antithetical to the spontaneous order idealized by the rule of the Sage.

In Stanza 3, Laozi (2008: 9) famously said:

> Promote not the worthy, then the people will not compete. Esteem not goods hard to obtain, then the people will not be thieves. Display not what is desirable, then the people's hearts will not be turbid. For this reason, the ruling of the Sage is to empty their minds, fill their bellies; weaken their wills, and strengthen their bones. He keeps the folk from knowing and craving and *the intellects from daring to act*. Underacting makes nothing ungovernable. (My emphasis)

The injunction to "promote not the worthy" is justified by the proposition that this avoids creating any incentive to "the intellects" to rebel and instigate turbulence among people who "know" and "crave" excessively. Any modern, enlightened scholar would immediately accuse Laozi of "obscurantism," as the Neo-Confucian master Zhu Xi (1130–1200), sometimes referred to as the Chinese Thomas Aquinas, did. However, contextualizing the stanza in the larger work, what Laozi means is not to keep the people ignorant for the purposes of efficient exploitation, but rather to keep them innocent and not have them demand more than their earthly needs. The "intellects" would then have no reason to take the initiative to change the spontaneous order people already have. If, on the other hand, a ruler "promotes the worthy" (*shangxian*) by rewarding those who excel, the people would compete over who is virtuous and capable. To Laozi, the "intellect" pejoratively refers to any cunning, astute member of the elite who seeks to mobilize the people ostensibly for lofty, noble reasons but in reality to fulfil their own selfish ambitions. An ideal, Way-abiding order needs neither "the intellect" nor "lofty," "noble" virtues, as proclaimed in Stanza 19: "Refuse the intellects and dismiss debates, the folk will reap a hundredfold; Refuse devotion and loyalty, the folk again will love as child and parent."

These mottos from the *Laozi* help us to interpret the Nam–Mit event from another perspective—an attempt by an "intellect" to manipulate an ambiguous rule. The event has lingered in the collective memory for a century because of the ambition of To'u and Nam, which endangered the established matrilineal succession principle and the dual chieftainship. Nam was a charismatic leader who calculated that he could get away with it, as indicated by the testimony of the missionary Baldwin in 1949. His father To'u taught him alone (not his legal heir) all the chiefly spells. It was probably of great importance that Nam was aware that the "great world" outside the Trobriands practiced father–son succession. He seems to have assumed he would enjoy the white magistrate's support to override the local rule. On this basis, he publicly announced that he would not teach Mit or Mit's Tabalu brothers the crucial spells learned from his father when To'u died, even though he was obliged to do so if Mit offered the payment of *pokala*.

In the event, the magistrate did not disinherit Mit, though he upheld Nam's accusation that Mit was guilty of incestuous relations with his wife. The reasoning was consistent with the ethos of what came to be known as colonial indirect rule (see Foks, this volume). Mit succeeded To'u and held the position of Paramount Chief until his death ten years later. His intentional adultery with Nam's wife was politically astute since it eventually led to Nam's banishment. Despite his lack of personal charisma, Mit succeeded because he had the support of other "intellects," especially in the person of his own OB father, who was To'u's "political or orator chief" or "chiefly advisor." We see a long lineup of the intellects here—Nam, Mit, To'u, and Mit's father, all reflexive, astute figures who dared to act.

This political contestation was common enough in precolonial times to warrant a name, *kobala*, which might be translated as "usurpation" or "subversion," referring to commoners rising to chiefly status in terms of their "politico-ritual rank through the forceful 'big-head' (*keveka nona*, literally 'determined mind') defense of claims to ritual proficiency to which they are not hereditarily entitled" (Mosko 2017: 321). The pre-Kula era was a time of intensive competition and wars (Macintyre 1983; Steinmüller, this volume). In the specific setting of Omarakana, the OB were a strong rival of the Tabalu, who "domesticated" the OB. The Tabalu's monopoly of the Paramount Chieftainship in northern Kiriwina was also a result of precolonial *kobala* through displacing the local leadership of Kasanai and Omarakana. During the reign of To'u's predecessor Namakala, another *kobala* took place, leading to the burning down of Omarakana at war against the *toliwaga* leaders. Namakala was defeated in his failed attempt to "secure wives and agricultural surpluses from the *toliwaga* leaders of Otilawa villages where he did not have traditional claims" (Mosko 2017: 321). The *toliwaga* leader who defeated him was another example of *kobala* because of his commoner rank. He proved to be a great military master. When a successor of Mit turned out to be a weak leader, he was challenged both by his nephew, whose father was a commoner, and by potentially eligible Tabalu rivals (ibid.: 381).

The recurrence of *kobala* in Kiriwina society suggests that matrilineal dual chieftainship is in constant crisis, to the point that Nam attempted to remove it entirely, while other intellects too seized opportunities and dared to challenge the existing order. Godelier (2007), drawing on extensive fieldwork in Papua New Guinea, proposes that larger societies emerge when a territory is appropriated and requires ideologically justified authority to defend it. This trend parallels the recurrence of *kobala*, as accumulating land resources for redistribution creates centralized power that becomes a target for usurpation. In this light, Laozi's ideas on "the intellects" anticipate the relationship between accumulation and instability. As accumulating political power becomes a target, options become increasingly available to the intellects to take advantage of the room left for political maneuvering in the principle of matrilineal succession.

Conclusion

What if To'u and his son Nam had succeeded in their act of *kobala*? Would these "intellects" have been able to rearrange society permanently along patrilineal lines? I am not suggesting that a patrilineal chieftainship is more stable than a matrilineal one. Rather, the former entails the mass mobilization of human capital for objectives beyond earthly needs: megalithic works, wars, taxation, and endless bloodshed related to succession. A civilizational society is characterized by the rise and fall of royal houses, but "rise or fall, it is always the people who suffer," exclaimed Zhang Yanghao (1270–1329), the Chinese poet who explained suffering with reference to the malicious cycle of empires that accumulate beyond human needs. This is also what Laozi had warned against.

It is not my intention, either, to propose a linear evolution from matriliny to patriliny. The dynamic movement between "hot" and "cold" societies, as observed by scholars like Maurice Godelier (2007) and Pierre Clastres (2011), indicates that human social organizations are both evolutionary and devolutionary, before they eventually become "stuck" in monotonous, civilizational forms (Graeber and Wengrow 2021: 112). While the transition to civilization is typically examined in terms of material and infrastructural factors, it is also crucial to consider the cognitive possibilities. As Chris Hann (2018: 350) notes, this requires striking "a balance between on the one hand, the idealist bias that characterizes much of the sociological literature (not to mention the new 'anthropology of ethics'), and on the other the 'vulgar materialist' bias of most Marxist and neo-Marxist paradigms."

Laozi's notion of "the intellects daring to act" aims at maintaining such a balance. It suggests that ethics and infrastructures are deeply intertwined as one process, and the conditions for their coevolution. When a society "esteems goods" and "promotes the worthy," the intellects begin to accumulate political powers and act to create their imagined communities. Therefore, an ideal ruler should "rule by the belly not by the eyes" (Laozi 2008: 27, Stanza 12). He cannot maintain order when the people "know" and "crave." He himself should not know or crave either. As Stanza 48 has it, instead he needs "to pursue learning, learn more day by day; to pursue the Way, unlearn it day by day: unlearn and unlearn again, until there is nothing to pursue" (Laozi 2001: 128).

There is abundant evidence to illustrate how "the intellects dare to act" when a society not only "esteems goods" but also "promotes the worthy." In the Greco-Roman episteme, such ambition is often considered innate to "human nature." Since Darwin, some social scientists have biologized the hunger for power. *Kobala* might then be interpreted as a stage along the evolutionary road whereby humans have gradually refined their societies, both corporate and competitive, like monkeys with ideologies (Mann 1986). However, Laozi's warning concerning "the intellects" allows us to consider matrilineal dual chieftainship from another angle. Tracing descent in "quasi-incestuous" ways hinders the political emergence of transcendent kingship with its entrenched hierarchical monopoly of territory and magic.

In spite of all its theoretical turns, global anthropology has largely remained a story of how the West looks at the rest. Anthropologists of the Global South seem content with coming up with "more correct versions" of their home societies, while remaining within the Greco-Roman episteme and its assumptions concerning human nature. When Malinowski laid the foundation for economic anthropology through his groundbreaking ethnographic works, he consistently conveyed the message that "economy" should be a more encompassing concept than the narrow definition that emphasizes scarce resources, rational choice, or profit maximization. As aptly summarized by Marshall Sahlins (2017: xx), "The traditional economic terms of Fijians were not what our economic science would recognize as such." Malinowski recognized this when he noted that his student Fei Xiaotong's studies were not limited to the economic aspects of a village, but rather explored the whole of "peasant life in China" (Malinowski 1938, 1939). Drawing inspiration from Fei's proposal of "appreciating what others appreciate," this chapter has applied the insights of Laozi to the ethnography of the Trobriands, offering an alternative means of honoring Malinowski's legacy.

Acknowledgments

Thanks to Hans Steinmüller, Zhang Yahui, Elizabeth Chin, and Frederick Damon for their help with this challenging work.

Yongjia Liang is Qiushi Distinguished Professor of Anthropology and Director of the Institute of Anthropology at Zhejiang University, China. He has published extensively in English and Chinese on religion, ethnicity, and the political philosophy of ancient and contemporary China. His ongoing research involves applying Chinese thinking in the Axial Age to ethnographic materials outside the Sinosphere.

References

Arnason, Johann. 2018. "Making Contact and Mapping the Terrain." In *Anthropology and Civilizational Analysis*, ed. Johann Arnason and Chris Hann, i–xlii. Albany: State University of New York Press.
Clastres, Pierre. 2011. *Society Against the State: Essays on Political Anthropology*, trans. Robert Hurley and Abe Stein. London: Zone.
Damon, Frederick. 1983. "What Moves the Kula: Opening and Closing Gifts on Woodlark Island." In *The Kula: New Perspectives on Massim Exchange*, ed. Jerry Leach and Edmund Leach, 309–42. Cambridge: Cambridge University Press.
———. 2002. "Kula Valuables: The Problem of Value and the Production of Names." *L'Homme* 162: 107–36.
———. 2010. "Kula." In *Routledge Encyclopedia of Social and Cultural Anthropology*, ed. Alan Barnard and Jonathan Spencer, 404–6. London: Routledge.
———. 2017. *Trees, Knots, and Outriggers: Environmental Knowledge in the Northeast Kula Ring*. New York: Berghahn.
Dumont, Louis. 1977. *From Mandeville to Marx: The Genesis and Triumph of Economic Ideology*. Chicago: University of Chicago Press.
Egloff, B. J. 1978. "The Kula before Malinowski: A Changing Configuration." *Mankind* 11: 429–35.
Elvin, Mark. 1986. "Was There a Transcendental Breakthrough in China?" In *The Origins and Diversity of Axial Age Civilizations*, ed. S. N. Eisenstadt, 325–59. Albany: State University of New York Press.
Fei, Xiaotong. 2003. "Shitan Kuozhan Shehuixue de Chuantong Jiexian" [On expanding traditional borders of sociology]. *Beijing Daxue Xuebao* 3: 5–16.
Geertz, Clifford. 1980. *Negara: The Theatre-State in Nineteenth-Century Bali*. Princeton, NJ: Princeton University Press.
Godelier, Maurice. 2007. *Au fondement des sociétés humaines: Ce que nous apprend l'anthropologie*. Paris: Albin Michel.
Graeber, David. 2015. *The Utopia of Rules*. Melville House.

Graeber, David, and David Wengrow. 2021. *The Dawn of Everything*. London: Penguin.
Granet, Marcel. 1932. *Festivals and Songs of Ancient China*, trans. E. D. Edwards. London: Routledge & Sons.
Guldin, Gregory. 1994. *The Saga of Anthropology in China: From Malinowski to Moscow to Mao*. Armonk, NY: M. E. Sharpe.
Hann, Chris. 2018. "Afterword: Anthropology, Eurasia, and Global History." In *Anthropology and Civilizational Analysis*, ed. Johann Arnason and Chris Hann, 339–50. Albany: State University of New York Press.
Irwin, Geoffrey, Ben Shaw, and Andrew Mcalister. 2019. "The Origins of the Kula Ring." *Archaeology in Oceania* 54(1): 1–16.
Jenco, Leigh, ed. 2016. *Chinese Thought as Global Theory: Diversifying Knowledge Production in the Social Sciences and Humanities*. Albany: State University of New York Press.
Kuehling, Susanne. 2006. *Dobu: Ethics of Exchange on a Massim Island, Papua New Guinea*. Honolulu: University of Hawai'i Press.
———. 2017. "We Die for Kula—An Object-Centered View of Motivations and Strategies in Gift Exchange." *Journal of the Polynesian Society* 126(2): 181–208.
Laozi. 2001. *Dao De Jing: The Book of the Way*, trans. Moss Roberts. Berkeley: University of California Press.
———. 2008. *Dao De Jing*, trans. Edmund Ryden. Oxford: Oxford University Press.
Leach, Edmund. 1954. *Political Systems of Highland Burma*. Cambridge: Cambridge University Press.
———. 1961. "Rethinking Anthropology." In *Rethinking Anthropology*, 1–27. London: Athlone.
Lévi-Strauss, Claude. 1967. *The Scope of Anthropology*. London: Jonathan Cape.
———. 1974 [1955]. *Tristes Tropiques*, trans. D. Weightman. New York: Atheneum.
Lian, Ruizhi. 2007. *Yincang de Zuxian: Nanzhao Miaoxiangguo de Chuanshuo yu Shehui* [The hidden ancestors: The Gandahar legend and society of Nanzhao]. Beijing: Sanlian Shudian.
Liang, Yongjia. 2011. "Stranger-Kingship and Cosmocracy; Or, Sahlins in Southwest China." *Asia Pacific Journal of Anthropology* 12(3): 236–54.
———. 2022. "Esteeming Goods for Non-Accumulation, Small Realms with Few People: Interpreting Kula with Laozi." *American Anthropologist* 124: 456–66.
Liu, Xiaogan. 2006. *Laozi Gujin* [Laozi now and then]. Beijing: Zhongguo Shehui Kexue Chubanshe.
Macintyre, Martha. 1983. "Kune on Tubetube and in the Bwanabwana Region of the Southern Massim." In *The Kula: New Perspectives on Massim Exchange*, ed. Jerry Leach and Edmund Leach, 369–82. Cambridge: Cambridge University Press.
Malinowski, Bronisław. 1922. *Argonauts of the Western Pacific. An Account of Native Enterprise and Adventure in the Archipelagoes of Melanesian New Guinea*. London: Routledge and Kegan Paul.
———. 1935. *Coral Gardens and their Magic*. New York: American Book Company.
———. 1938. "Letter to Hsiao-tung Fei." Bolzano, Italy, 6 September. Yale University Library, courtesy of Professor Michael Young.
———. 1939. "Preface," in Hsiao-tung Fei, *Peasant Life in China: A Field Study of Country Life in the Yangtze Valley*, xix–xxvi. London: Routledge & Kegan Paul.

Mann, Michael. 1986. *The Sources of Social Power*, vol. 1. Cambridge: Cambridge University Press.
Mauss, Marcel. 2016. *The Gift*, ed. and trans. Jane I. Guyer. Chicago: Hau Books.
Mosko, Mark. 2017. *Ways of Baloma*. Chicago: Hau Books.
Munn, Nancy. 1986. *The Fame of Gawa*. Chicago: University of Chicago Press.
Nelson, Eric. 2022. "Thing and World in Laozi and Heidegger." In *Daoist Resonances in Heidegger: Exploring a Forgotten Debt*, ed. David Chai, 141–62. London: Bloomsbury.
Sahlins, Marshall. 2008. *The Western Illusion of Human Nature*. Chicago: Prickly Paradigm Press.
———. 2017 [1972]. *Stone Age Economics*. Chicago: University of Chicago Press.
Thune, Carl. 1983. "Kula Traders and Lineage Members." In *The Kula: New Perspectives on Massim Exchange*, ed. Jerry Leach and Edmund Leach, 345–68. Cambridge: Cambridge University Press.
Wang, Mingming. 2011. "Suowei Haiwai Minzuzhi" [On so-called overseas ethnography]. *Xibei Minzu Yanjiu* 69(2): 116–29.
Young, Michael. 1971. *Fighting with Food*. Cambridge: Cambridge University Press.
Zhao, Dingxin. 2015. *The Confucian-Legalist State: A New Theory of Chinese History*. Oxford: Oxford University Press.

Part IV

Adaptations in Space and Time

12

 Passing On, Passing Around, and Passing Through

Urban Inheritance in South Africa as Circulation

MAXIM BOLT

Introduction

Bronisław Malinowski's *Argonauts of the Western Pacific* (1922) presented the Kula ring as an unusually literal case of value circulation. Anthropologists' subsequent engagement with it expanded on the complex dynamics underlying its pattern. Together, Malinowski's ethnography and later writings that built on it offer a provocation. They invite examination of what exactly we mean by circulation, how it might be composed of interacting forms and patterns, and with what effects.

While Malinowski described the Kula ring evocatively, later anthropologists developed his analysis and augmented the ethnographic richness. They challenged Kula's apparent orderliness, probed the sources of contradictions lying within it, and injected greater dynamism. While Kula traces an enormous circle, actors attend to those positioned before and after them. Participation in defined and irreversible object pathways is therefore essentially linear. Around those linear paths are other, more locally palpable circulatory flows, which are less prescribed or institutionalized. Kula, then, illuminates the different degrees to which distinct "paths" are defined and insisted upon. They interact as people mobilize value, put it into circulation, or withdraw and withhold it as inalienable.

In this chapter, taking *Argonauts* as a provocation, I explore these kinds of movement in a very different ethnographic context: the state-administered inheritance of homes in Johannesburg's townships. Such dynamics can be usefully brought into dialogue with what, after all, are flows across generations. One kind I describe as *passing on*, in which wealth moves in irreversible paths. This is inheritance as wealth transfer, the paths prescribed in official legal terms or (less straightforwardly) in one restrictive rendering of patrilineal succession. A contrasting dynamic is *passing around*: messier circulation in which rules and plans give way to negotiated accommodations. The latter depends on withholding wealth from linear paths. That withdrawal is enabled by a third dynamic, widely defended as customary. Rather than being transferred, wealth is *passed through*: it endures beyond the generations that come and go, as a shared "site" materializing kinship itself.

Disputes over the inheritance of homes throw the interaction between passing on, passing around, and passing through into relief. Delineation sharpens disagreements because it makes individual entitlements and exclusions explicit. A looser field of circulation offers a livable alternative. In a fractious context, emphasizing enduring family patrimony removes the home from questions of who gets what, creating a space for ongoing informal circulation. There is continual struggle between allowing property to be transferred irreversibly as alienable, and withholding it from those pathways to keep it inalienably available to a wider kin group. That shared availability produces its own exclusions, as surviving spouses especially are sidelined. Resorting to state process offers another way to protect interests—one premised on linear paths, whose restrictive bureaucratic processes introduce one-way thresholds that mean ceding control and risking new dangers.

Debates in the wake of *Argonauts* draw attention to intersecting circulatory dynamics, and the tensions between them. These elements are configured differently in different settings. What follows examines a context of dispute, where passing on jostles with passing through, which leaves space for passing around. Breaking down these dynamics and considering how they relate to one another challenges a common assumption: that circulation reproduces order and routinely fosters social and economic integration. I argue that, to the contrary, circulatory patterns may be accommodations to social fragmentation, and that they may reproduce that fragmentation.

Circulation in Argonauts and Beyond

Argonauts is rightly remembered as Malinowski's early ethnographic challenge to market thinking in economics. The Massim was a region connected by the movement and distribution of wealth—*mwali* (armshells) and *soulava* (necklaces)—and items of everyday use. Kula participants acquired and passed on prestige objects as gifts through high-profile voyages, and the objects' biographies enhanced the renown of their transitory holders. Here was an economic system driven by values and understandings far from those of capitalist markets (see also Malinowski 1921). The regional integration of the Kula ring provided the political umbrella that enabled other negotiated circuits of movement of items like food (see Hart 1986: 647–48).

By focusing on distinguishable and storied objects, Malinowski traced circulation in a starkly literal sense. At the most obvious level, he took as his object of analysis a geographically distributed ring that involved periodic maritime travel. Necklaces and armshells traveled in opposite directions around this ring. Ethnography meant "studying the concrete data of economic transactions, in order to trace the history of a valuable object, and to gauge the nature of its circulation" (Malinowski 1922: 12). In the case of Kula, it meant "follow[ing] the ring of the Kula, noticing its commercial side tracks" (ibid.: 521), and also how *mwali* and *soulava* entered and left it (ibid.: Chapter 21).

Malinowski's ethnography sharpens a critical approach to circulation precisely because the Kula ring forms such a clear, explicit pattern. But the pattern's significance, in his writing and in relation to economic practice, is not straightforward. On the one hand, Malinowski had a "highly realistic view of the anthropologist's subject matter," as opposed to the preoccupations with idealized schemas of social structure that followed in British social anthropology (Bloch 1977: 278). Malinowski was less interested in the formal rules, the institutionalized and prescriptive aspects of social life, than he was in the messier arrangements that lay around these, and indeed made them possible (see Young, Kuper, this volume).

At the same time, Malinowski also abstracted from complexity. He produced an account of correct practice that emphasized economic and social integration; reappraisal by later anthropologists would place more emphasis on improvisation and contestation. In a seminal collection that reconsidered Kula circulation over half a century later, Edmund Leach (1983) questioned the way "the Kula" had been reified. Anthropologists risked mistaking a model constructed from intricate and multivalent activity, including divergent and competing perspectives on how to categorize objects and how they should circulate, for the concrete reality.

Recently, Anthony Pickles (2020) has suggested that the dangers of reification be addressed by dissolving circulation into more basic elements. Typologies of exchange have narrowed anthropological approaches to economic life. Kula has become paradigmatic of delayed reciprocity, which is commonly reduced to gift exchange, which in turn is contrasted with market transactions. Pickles proposes examining individual one-way transfers and the way people combine them into socially recognized forms of "transaction" such as repertoires of exchange (or the failure to achieve such aggregations in practice). This approach self-consciously trains attention on form and composition: transfers "can be used to delimit components" (ibid.: 11). But, while Pickles announces circulation as his object of critique, his analysis is largely confined to forms of exchange. This chapter extends his approach by "delimiting components" of larger-scale circulatory patterns, but without entirely dissolving them into discrete elements, as a means to understand degrees of prescription and institutionalization.

Anthropologists engaging more directly with Kula have pointed the way to dissecting the dynamics of circulation itself—focusing on patterns of flow rather than zooming in to individual transfers. Damon (1980) emphasized the insertion of manufactured valuables into circulation, and hence the vulnerability of Kula to the withdrawal of objects by the people who had made them. Applying Lévi-Strauss's abstract model of circulation as a thought experiment, Damon showed that asymmetrical exchange between gift-giver and gift-receiver shaped wider circulation (in contrast to the restricted reciprocity of dyadic exchanges). In Kula, hierarchically arranged opening and closing gifts did indeed maintain a ring. But tension came from production: the fact that objects continued to be owned by the people who had made them, and could be taken back.

Weiner (1992) brought still more complexity and dynamism to the analysis: she took withdrawal from circulation in a different direction, while emphasizing distinct but overlaid circulatory patterns. While many valuables were indeed owned by their makers, the most important—the ones on which Kula reputations were built—had become detached from those histories and were seen in terms of their long and famous histories of circulation. High-prestige shells followed clearly defined, normatively framed paths. Indeed, high-prestige objects were, in practice, *not* experienced as part of a ring. The salient term for participants was *ked*, "path" (see also Damon 1980). Other *kitomu* shells of lower prestige circulated in the penumbra of the main *keda*—as stopgaps in sustaining Kula partnerships, and within kin groups—but in a more improvisatory manner without the sense of established and protected pathways. These rapid and more fluid forms of circulation compensated for the fact that the most prestigious Kula objects were frequently withheld by their possessors for as long as possible. Their reputational benefits could be prolonged for decades, though they would have to circulate again eventually. So linear and messier flows coexisted, punctuated and connected by forms of withdrawal.

Kula, then, is not settled and structural, but has to be constantly made and remade through the interplay between delineated paths and fluid circulation. That interplay is shaped by the withholding of objects, on the one hand, and by the extent to which prescribed circulation is irreversible, on the other. Conventional approaches to circulation and inheritance do not capture this diversity. The distinction between delineation and fluidity—the more or less formalized, institutionalized, and explicitly articulated versus the more or less openly negotiable—offers a more illuminating approach.

Channels of Circulation?

When Malinowski wrote, circulation was already a long-established idea in political economy. Attention to velocity of circulation emerged with a focus on currency in the mid-1600s. The context was a synthetic view of systems inseparable from a concern to manage them. It coincided with a similar systemic view of circulation of blood in the body, which was also informed by attempts to intervene (see Weston 2013). But unlike blood, and setting the tone for later economic understandings, circulation of money was meant more loosely. It was a systemic aggregation and abstraction rendered in graspable concrete terms. William Petty, the first political economist explicitly to address circulation, mused about whether the money supply sufficed for trade:

> I answer yes; for the expence being 40 Millions, if the revolutions were in such short Circles, viz. weekly, as happens among poorer artizans and labourers, who receive and pay every Saturday, then 40/52 parts of 1 Million would answer those ends: But if the Circles be quarterly, according to our Custom of paying rent, and gathering Taxes, then 10 Millions were requisite. Wherefore supposing payments in general to be of a mixed Circle between One week and 13, then add 10 Millions to 40/52, the half of the which will be 5 ½, so as if we have 5 ½ Millions we have enough. (Petty 1664 cited in Holtrop 1929: 503; spelling as in the original)

Here was aggregation in service of mathematical estimates—no one was tracing the circuits of particular coins. The goal may, of course, be more concretely object-oriented: central banks and mints today monitor estimates of banknote and coin circulation because different denominations pass through hands more or less quickly and degrade at different rates. But the methodological problem remains.

This view of circulation also persists in important critiques of influential perspectives on capitalist markets. For Viviana Zelizer, an economic sociologist, circuits offer a starting point for getting under the skin of capitalism. Her approach is motivated by frustration with an implausibly thin view of markets contrasted with society. There is an enduring tendency, she contends, to accept the idea that markets erode all distinctions, make everything saleable, and invade intimate spheres with which they are fundamentally incompatible. But market societies are comprised not simply of atomized transactions. Distinct forms of value are transferred among participants who are connected through shared meaning, bridging the intimate and the impersonal. A core problem is grasping "the mechanisms and processes that generate bounded media and transfers" (Zelizer 2010: 316). Circuits show us how bridging actually works:

> they consist of dynamic, meaningful, incessantly negotiated interactions among the sites—be those sites individuals, households, organizations, or other social entities. Second, in addition to dynamic relations, they include distinctive media (for example, legal tender or localized tokens) and an array of organized, differentiated transfers (for example, gifts or compensation) between sites. Commercial circuits also differ from communities as conceived of in the *Gemeinschaft-Gesellschaft* tradition. They do not consist of spatially and socially segregated rounds of life; although circuits sometimes exist *within* encompassing communities, they ordinarily cut across multiple social settings, coordinating only certain kinds of activities and social relations within each setting. (Zelizer 2010: 315)

Here too, circulation is deployed loosely. Circuits are distinguished from mere networks by the media that change hands and the density of meaningful transactions. Revealing the limits of generalized exchange, circuits are demarcated. But they are not tracked. Similarly, and also emerging from a critique of generalized exchange, anthropologists have contributed the concept of spheres of exchange (Bohannan 1955; Parry and Bloch 1989). A sphere delineates a field of integration: circulation within it is fluid and often relatively improvisational, whereas conversions between spheres must follow defined pathways. Yet established spheres risk emphasizing demarcation at the expense of tracing how pathways are dynamically made or sustained in practice.

In contrast to these approaches, other anthropologists have addressed the creation of specific channels. Connections are restricted, identifiable chains emerge, and networks are cut (Strathern 1996). Appadurai's (1986) "social life of things" offered a seminal perspective on the courses charted by material objects. Taking the Kula ring as a paradigmatic example, Appadurai explored the constant tussle between pathways and diversions from them. Object circulation depends on diligently maintained connections, entangled with the making of people and memory, within their institutional and power-laden contexts. Appadurai's social lives were ultimately linear, emphasizing iterative phases. That biographical lens inspired an approach to writing ethnographically about particular material objects (e.g., Long and Villarreal 1998).

There are thus substantial bodies of scholarship illuminating circulation without pathways, and also pathways with more or less strongly institutionalized channels. A small number of anthropologists have mapped more complex circulatory patterns, dwelling on pragmatics and on barriers to exchange. In Barth's (1967) mapping of flows of resources between spheres of exchange in Darfur, a barrier to conversion might simply be a lack of buyers rather than moral prohibition. Ferguson's (1992) "topography of wealth" in Lesotho included houses that were unsaleable because only the bricks were owned, not the land. More recently, a rubric of "itinerant objects" (Bauer 2019) has opened the way to still more complex trajectories: ramifying entanglements in which the material characteristics and affordances of objects shape the relations they forge.

Yet how more prescriptive and explicitly articulated flows relate to other, less institutionalized flows is a topic that has not been examined sufficiently closely. The same is true of the scholarship on inheritance, which is usefully recast through the perspectives on circulation that I have outlined. Ethnographic scholarship on inheritance offers crucial insight regarding circulation, which I introduce in the next section. But again, the bias in the anthropological literature is toward ordered arrangements that are socially integrative.

In the empirical sections of this chapter that follow, I describe how people move between delineation and fluidity in navigating uncertainty and dissensus in urban South African inheritance. People selectively assert ownership of homes in family disputes, in legal and customary registers, thereby placing value within sanctioned linear paths. Indeed, once property has entered channels formalized by the state, it passes thresholds of irreversibility, with the advantages and risks of relinquishing control over its circulation. Aware of this, many people withhold and withdraw houses from prescribed linear trajectories. Asserting that homes stand beyond other flows of value, and transcend generations of occupants, they thereby also create spaces for other messier forms of kin-based circulation that deflect disagreement.

Inheritance: As It Should Be?

My ethnographic case concerns the process of formal, state-administered inheritance in urban South Africa. In Johannesburg's historically Black township areas, homes are generally families' biggest assets. Inheritance appears a quintessentially delineated and one-way flow: rules set out who gets what. Yet circulation invites a layered and complex view of inheritance at the center of formal "deceased estates" (the legal term). While, in official terms, houses passed on in deceased estates are considered to be assets tracing a one-way journey, I shall argue that inherited homes are also both objects and sites of more complex circulation. As linear transfers of property stall, homes pass between kin, and kin move through them in ad hoc ways. This occurs in a context characterized by fracture, bitter dispute among claimants, a broader lack of moral consensus, substantial confusion concerning a complicated and burdensome system, and obstacles to navigating its institutional avenues for redress.

One aspect of this variegated picture resonates with Jack Goody's (1962) seminal study of inheritance. He distinguishes both exchange and unreciprocated property donations from inheritance, strictly speaking, because the former are transfers that imply some alienation of property rights. By contrast, inheritance in Goody's West African context means the retention of property in a corporate body—not its transfer, testation, or exclusive ownership. Where Weiner (1992) emphasized the importance of withdrawing from the Kula its items of enduring value, Goody underlines that collective wealth may not be an object of transfer at all, but instead a "site" through which generations pass—it outlives the people who come and go and materializes a group.

Yet in Johannesburg there are fundamental contestations over whether and how property can be passed on, passed through, or passed around. These do not square with inheritance as it appears in seminal anthropological writing. Goody places property alongside the transfer of rights and offices in the overall framework of an "inheritance system." He emphasizes moral prescriptions and their consequences and conundrums, such as which sex inherits, the rights of particular kin members, how these determine property's consolidation or dispersal, and how they shape cross-generational tensions. Systems are composed of rules, which can be compared in cross-regional analysis (Goody 1976; see also Hann 2008).

More recently, Shipton (2007) has approached inheritance under the rubric of "entrustment": among the Luo of Kenya, the transfer of value at death is one component of flows between and within generations. Material goods and even kin pass around and pass along, in dense and layered webs of obligations that lie between and complicate notions of property ownership, gift exchange, and loans. Entrustment produces chains, and inheritance is largely a negotiation of one-way obligation: one receives from the deceased, and one passes on in turn at one's own death (although offerings to ancestors create loops of obligation).

Like Goody, Shipton (2007: 184) recognizes the conundrums: "inheritance is a tricky thing . . . a game of navigating conflicting principles." Moreover, as with circulation more generally, one dimension of negotiated inheritance is an interplay between specified, delineated pathways and messier fields of circulation. Shipton is keen to emphasize that "inheritance is plastic; each generation can change its form" (ibid.: 185–86). What constitutes a delineated path may itself depend on how actions are justified. An important lesson from Shipton is that, in circumstances that are materially constrained and with rules that are in practice elastic, "to play the game" means convincing others that a chain of entrustment has been perpetuated—"it is to enter the flow" (ibid.: 186).

Yet, as with Goody, here is a moral economy ultimately described through its rules—"the Luo order of things" (Shipton 2007: 176)—however complicated and manipulable. As with circulation, then, anthropological scholarship on inheritance privileges integrated systems, how things *should* be, even if "the system" may allow for or even encourage variation. How should we approach inheritance ethnographically where arrangements are fundamentally contested? The approach to circulation I have proposed—exploring how delineation and fluidity are negotiated—is instructive. Avoiding specifying a pathway may be important. Shared patrimony as a site through which kin pass may represent less a consolidative rule than a provisional space in which other kinds of material access can be negotiated. Linear *passing on* may be asserted, but a less linear *passing around* is key to reaching accommodations, and property available for *passing through* may facilitate that.

Postapartheid South Africa's township houses offer a distinct vantage point. Racially organized townships had been conceived of as dormitories for Black labor in a white city. Homes were rentals from state authorities, because Black people were not allowed to own land. Known as "family houses," they were passed on by applying to register the next, generally male, householder on an official permit that listed the house's occupants. From the late 1970s, though, leaseholds were offered as a means to consolidate a Black middle class. As apartheid restrictions began to give way further in the 1980s, householders could buy their houses. Soon they received them free of charge, as the state shed assets it could not maintain and gave them to sitting tenants in the spirit of racial redress. This represented a massive wave of redistribution, which put a large amount of property into circulation.

What kind of redistribution it was, however, remains unclear. Family houses had come to approximate a customary idea of collective entitlement, a view also legitimated by the apartheid-era permits with their listed occupants. Many believed that family tenure was now being formalized and strengthened. When the authorities invited individuals to come to tribunals for titling, kin thought they were sending a representative—a "custodian" of group interests. Yet typically, those individuals became exclusive owners, unbeknown to their kin or even sometimes themselves. In Johannesburg, as part of Gauteng province, tribunals did write up agreements to define the representative as custodian, and to recognize other family members' residence rights as members of a kin group. But it later emerged that they had insufficient legal weight to limit the freehold. The "custodian," who had become a titleholder, was still able to sell, and it was from that individual alone that the property was transferred in inheritance.[1]

When it comes to houses, Johannesburg's township residents disagree fundamentally about rules and consequences. One source of contestation is that between formal law and customary norms about who inherits. Intestate succession law (for those without a will) has property passing to surviving spouses first, shared with all biological and legally adopted children equally over a defined value threshold. In the absence of surviving spouses and children, the parents of the deceased inherit. If they are dead, their own children inherit their entitlements—these are the deceased's siblings, far down the queue. By contrast, patrilineal succession, defended in a customary register, has the deceased's paternal siblings enjoying entitlement to what was originally their father's home. Preeminent access and responsibility may be claimed by the oldest or youngest brother. Spouses (and even their children) are routinely sidelined as lacking proper membership in the patriline.

But these are not just competing models of transfer—the dissensus goes further still. In intestate succession, the inheriting spouse may remarry and transfer exclusive rights to their new partner, and thereby out of the patrilineal group. By contrast, "family houses" have "custodians," not owners, who enjoy primary access but accept primary responsibility. Disputes are therefore not only about who gets what, but also about whether property is transferred at all. Inheritance is composed of ongoing flows of entrustment, and equally of attempts to withhold the house. In a highly contested and fractious context, attempts to avoid an explicit articulation of "flow" or pathway are common. Homes are removed from linear devolution: people themselves circulate through them, which also means they can move in an ad hoc manner within generations.

Such flexible circulation is defended in a customary register. But this opens up more uncertainty. The stakes of disagreement are sharpened by a context of acute housing shortage and the fact that a house is often a kin group's only significant asset. Bitter disputes arise from the exclusion of more distant or precarious categories of kin, even as kin groups expand and people risk having nowhere else to go. The depth of dissensus leads some to approach the state in an attempt to insert the dwelling into an officially delineated path of transfer. As residents struggle between the legal path and patrilineal claims that themselves bleed into a wider range of attempts to retain access, circulatory dynamics are not societally and economically integrative as the literature tends to suggest. Nor are they easily depicted in terms of behavioral norms.

Passing On, Passing Around, and Passing Through in Johannesburg

Until apartheid's gradual demise in the 1980s, inheritance among Black residents of the city operated substantially outside the state's formal system. Rather than the inheritance-dedicated legal bureaucracy—in an institution called the Master of the High Court—Black estates were channeled into a separate system under generalist magistrates. The Black Administration Act that required this separation removed the Black population from intestate succession law, and placed it under administratively determined regulations crudely approximating an idea of African custom. In any case, as already explained, Black urbanites were not permitted to own land. They were thus unlikely to have assets that made it worth working through a state system of inheritance. All that changed when municipally owned "family houses," leading up to and following the democratic transition, were transferred en masse to their inhabitants. The size of these assets drew families to formalize inheritance for the first time.

In this confusing and rapidly changing environment, some try to delineate a flow of inherited wealth down the generations. Humphrey and Daisy, married residents of Soweto, are a good example. Aged 78 at the time of research,[2] Humphrey had been a courier for a parastatal company,[3] and he was first the tenant then the owner of his house. Daisy, 60, worked for a diamond cutter before she was sacked without compensation. They have five children and twelve grandchildren. Only one daughter is fully employed, as a nurse; two further daughters draw stipends as NGO volunteers; two sons are unemployed. All are divorced or separated. All have new "RDP houses"—part of a postapartheid state program of housing provision but transferred into their names as property—except one daughter. A peer educator on a health program, she lives with Humphrey and Daisy, along with her own two children, and the household of five largely live off two state pensions.

This house is the family's prime asset, and Humphrey and Daisy are clear about its role. It should pass to the children and grandchildren, providing security, while its ultimate fate will be a matter of collective choice. A casual threat by one of their sons to expropriate their daughter after their deaths led Humphrey to write a will. Daisy's and then their daughter's rights to live in the house will be protected—via an explicitly delimited channel of de facto circulation. Beyond that protection, though, they decided to name all of their five children as beneficiaries. Humphrey and Daisy anticipate that after their daughter's death the house will be monetized and the heirs—which by then would include their daughter's children, as her heirs—will have to decide whether to sell or rent out the property. Unlike Humphrey's rural house, which is unsaleable because of its remoteness and its location on communal land, the Soweto one could fetch as much as ZAR 400,000 (around GBP 24,000 at the time of fieldwork). More sustainably, rent would generate an income for a family short on jobs.

Humphrey and Daisy have attempted to carve out economic security for their immediate family. When I asked about the role of "uncles"—senior male relatives—in future inheritance discussions, Humphrey was clear: "I said, no, they [my children] mustn't give anybody a chance to destroy them or to say, 'no, we'll take over here and here.' No, not that." Uncles tend to support potential claims from broader kin groups. There are other threats: estranged husbands, and community organizations that offer advice but are "just coming to check and see who's weak in the minds . . . There's no good Samaritans now; there's only hyenas."

Wills are rare in Soweto. However, those who now own a house often have a strong wish to pass it on to their children, in linear fashion—at least in the immediate term. The implications of such a transfer become increasingly complicated over time. It may therefore be liquidated—put into another kind of circulation—and the proceeds divided. Humphrey's and Daisy's insistence on the downward flow of wealth aligns with the state perspective. As noted above, in the official view, inheritance is a matter of one-way transmission grounded in a transfer of legal title—first to a surviving spouse and then equally to all biological and legally adopted children.

In practice, the officials of the inheritance bureaucracy are petitioned by families in endless disputes. In one archetypal scenario, a group of siblings decide on the new custodian on behalf of a collective entitlement following the death of an elder brother. However, the deceased's surviving spouse, whom the petitioners would like to sideline, is now the sole legal owner. She is the heir of the individual who had been named by the family as custodian but by the state as titleholder back in the 1990s. The fight revolves around a legal version of inheritance that passes assets along a chain of kin ordered according to a nuclear family model, and that is rendered irreversible as it is formalized and documented by state authorities. This leaves little room for a version of succession in which a group of people pass through a materialized site of kinship.

Houses circulate between family members independently of persons dying. A schoolteacher in Soweto explained to me that, while his own immediate household would benefit from his father's house for the foreseeable future, it should remain available to 'rotate among members of the family' (in reference to his brothers). Kin considered to be deserving are seldom turned away, and so in some instances people constantly circulate through. A nurse explained the contingent status of her role as custodian of the house: undergirded by the authority of "the uncles," it represents a stable point for kin to return to whenever domestic relationships fall apart or life becomes precarious. It is also a first port of call for rural relatives establishing a foothold in the city. Her rural cousin, who was sleeping on the sofa while he sought work, mapped out on paper for me the house's place in a wide kin network spanning Johannesburg and town and village settings in KwaZulu Natal. A crucial dimension of this circulation is the informal code by which women are assumed to have a natal home to return to—in instances of widowhood, but also after domestic separation. The death of a custodian or owner may change the loose, improvised character of these cycles, depending on who takes over the primary responsibility. The prospect of irreversible (or hard-to-reverse) change pulls powerfully against stark decisions and delineation and toward a more complex workable consensus.

Yet, when conflicts cannot be resolved by "the uncles," complainants approach the state. A sole legal heir may assert the rights of one part of the family against the de facto residence of an expanding kin group, or a marginalized individual may seek intervention against eviction. Houses are then inserted into an officially delineated path of transfer. Such formalized paths—and the hard-to-reverse effects of legal registration—may interrupt circulation within a kin group in dramatic fashion. This can be seen in court judgments (in rare cases where matters reach the courts). In a High Court case adjudicated in 2017, a woman had been invited in 1995 to apply for ownership of her house as the rental permit holder.[4] She died in 1996 before hearing the outcome, which would have put her in a situation like that of Humphrey and Daisy. Her daughter had been living with her. Her son had moved away when he married, but he and his wife had in the meantime returned to the family home. They were put on the lodgers' permit—because the house was still at the time a rental property—but, inexplicably, the sister was not. After their mother died, the estate of the deceased was never wound up, but the married couple were registered as owners when the application came through. The brother appears not to have applied for the registration or known about it. Even so, his circulation back to the house had been formalized and would later become the basis for a delineated path. Two decades later, during divorce proceedings, the brother's wife claimed her share of the house in community of property. In the wife's version, her mother-in-law had suggested that she and her husband return to the house, and that invitation to return demonstrated her wish that they should take over ownership; she argued that her sister-in-law (the daughter of the original tenant) had been allocated another house in a small town elsewhere in the country. The judge, finding this implausible, ordered the title deed canceled. Circulation through a house should not, here, have translated into the deviation of property into a new linear path—a view shared by the brother (and son of the original tenant), who was supporting his sister against his wife.

Given these bewildering and fraught instances, it is unsurprising that where conflicts do not exist—or where they do not erupt—many houses are not formally transferred at death. Doing so sharpens the division between entitlement and non-entitlement. Leaving a house in the name of the deceased resonates with the sense that a house belongs to a lineage, and they to it. The house is not passing on, but is potentially available for future kin members to circulate through, and for ancestors to return to. This also means that many estates are reported long after the legally stipulated time of two weeks. At the time of my research, the backlog of Black deceased estates in Johannesburg's Central Magistrate's Court dated back to the 1970s.

Away from the law, a chosen successor and collective access need not stand as starkly opposed alternatives. The nurse's rural cousin who was sleeping on the sofa was keen to tell me how inheritance should work, and to emphasize the entitlement of the eldest son as a successor who keeps most of the estate intact. Yet his life was more complicated, partly because he had been born out of wedlock (although with his father's name after the latter's payment of "damages"[5] to his mother's family). He relied on family homes remaining as fluid nodes of belonging, in such a way as to "combine the advantages of non-partible inheritance, by which the property remains undivided and devolves to a single heir, with those of its partible variant, which gives all children an equal stake in their parents' property" (James 2015: 191).

Often, this tension refracts into generational differences, dividing people according to when they acquired their houses. The original householders on the tenancy permits when homes were allocated, like Humphrey, were able to become unambiguous owners. For them, the moment of redistribution anchored their families in property, and it offered an unprecedented opportunity to pass this on—enabling the linear flow of a single asset. But for their children, family entitlement requires more intricate navigation, as they figure out how to live with the legacy of that redistribution. In some cases, the parents had already died when houses were allocated, leaving a group of siblings with an out-of-date permit to negotiate their respective entitlements to a single home. Nominating a custodian who would ensure everyone's right to stay put and to return was a workable answer. In other cases, the parents died later, but the effect was similar: claims to collective belonging must be articulated and negotiated between the children. It is here that more contained projects of property accumulation and inheritance diffuse as a result of claims by a sibling group whose members have their own growing families. The story of Humphrey and Daisy was unusual because so many of their children had secured alternative accommodation.

Frequently, descendants have few places to go, or at any rate too little security elsewhere to relinquish their foothold. The linear notion of passing the house on runs into the navigation-by-circulation of passing the house around and passing through the house.

The Thresholds of Formality

State involvement makes house transfer irreversible. Disputing parties, including individuals who have been excluded by kin groups, come to the Master's Office for a decision on inheritance. When they do so, they risk losing their own ability to control processes and become sucked into one-way trajectories (Merry 1990). In the official system, the question of delineated channels is sharpened from the outset. The system is undergirded by the possibility of division—of creating "side tracks" from a linear path of unitary property. A core part of deceased estates is "liquidation and distribution," liquidation being the ultimate mechanism for resolving competing claims. It is also the threat brought as a caution against warring family members. In cases where multiple relatives have a legal claim, the Master's official will ask whether the house should be sold. The question focuses minds, because it is usually the house and its circulation through the kin group, rather than its monetary value, that drives disagreement (although some do indeed wish to sell and thus alienate the house from kin-based circulation). It is not just delineation that distinguishes formal pathways here; it is the one-way character of thresholds in state process. Formal sale of the house—liquidation, alienation—entails a new registration that takes on its own official life.

The inheritance process is laid down as a one-way linear route that is safeguarded by information gathering and checks. But in practice, as property and people become entangled with documents and files (see Latour 2009; Hull 2012; Mathur 2015), the one-way directionality of formalization leaves people vulnerable.

A very large number of estates in South Africa are classified as small, valued at less than ZAR 250,000 (about GBP 15,000 at the time of fieldwork). They follow a simplified route with minimal oversight. The only point of control is when issuing a Letter—a completed, stamped, and signed Microsoft Word template authorizing one or more individuals to take control of assets in an estate and appropriate or distribute them. Once clerks have captured relevant basic information and documentary evidence, prospective beneficiaries appear before an official who assesses entitlement. As officials struggle to grasp complicated situations, the Letter narrows a great deal of informational uncertainty to a semblance of documentary clarity.

Unsurprisingly, given the power it confers, the Letter is highly sought after. Routinely, a later complainant will argue that a beneficiary was left out and is now being sidelined, or that the holder of a Letter has done nothing at all with the estate. Sometimes a Letter is procured by deliberate misinformation or identity fraud.[6] Information in the Home Affairs database may be erroneous or subject to criminal tampering. The prescribed safeguard is to recall and cancel the Letter by issuing a summons. However, the loop remains, in many cases, unclosed. New information comes too late: the house has been sold, marking the irreversible crossing of one threshold through a new registration. In other instances, the Letter is diverted. The principle of the Letter is one of "keeping-while-giving" (Weiner 1992) state authority: delegation is limited; authority is never irrevocably given away. Yet paperwork is known to operate as de facto entitlement to a family house. Like the many title deeds that circulate informally as emblems of ownership, despite displaying names other than their bearers', Letters reveal a system unable to control its various documents.

Where family members disagree with an official's determination, a different one-way threshold makes it hard to revisit cases. Once stamp and signature have been affixed, decisions cannot legally be overturned within the Master's Office, because supervisors and subordinates are legally equivalent manifestations of "the Master." The last-resort feedback loop is to take the case for review to the High Court, where a judge can cancel the document and send it back for reappraisal. But this option is cumbersome, expensive, intimidating, and unsurprisingly rare.

One-way thresholds shape the experience of would-be beneficiaries. Thresholds are official and unofficial. They include the lack of internal review of determinations, the irreversibility of sale, and the fact that canceled documentation remains persuasive beyond official purview.

From Thresholds to Reversals

Delineated bureaucratic pathways are defined, not only by such one-way thresholds, but also by criteria that in practice cause reversals. There are cases where it is extremely difficult to take estates matters forward. For example, if a beneficiary is missing—a brother whom no one has seen in ten years—then the usual requirement to bring everyone to the Master for a determination goes unmet. The interplay between such obstructive circumstances and the official system of one-way thresholds is illustrated in the following example. To pass on and to receive along linear paths, channels must be forged, asserted, or protected. Irreversible thresholds may be harnessed, but this is not straightforward.

A weekly legal advice clinic is run by a legal NGO in a wood-paneled boardroom in the Master's Office. Queues down the hallway show the extent of cases in which the devolution of houses is contested. On one occasion at the clinic, I was shadowing a young attorney who was wrestling with the intricacies of the matter in front of her. A young man, Sizwe, and his mother, Patience, sat across the table, visibly agitated. They had been trying to navigate the system since shortly after Sizwe's father died in 2004. Sizwe's mother and father had never married, so Patience had no claim on the estate. The Master's Office had agreed with Sizwe when he reported the estate: that he should split the property equally with the woman his father had married and then divorced late in life—he as sole heir, and she through her rights in community of property. But, however straightforward the rules, making anything happen had proven to be almost impossible. His father, a senior employee of the Department of Health, had done well in life, and accumulated two township houses. The estate was not claimed by many heirs. Yet Sizwe and Patience lacked purchase on the situation while Sizwe's stepmother, an employee of a major insurance company, had employed an international law firm to act on her behalf.

Sizwe had acquired an all-important Letter from the Master. Yet things unraveled after that. The attorney appointed by Sizwe to organize matters (required because this was not a small estate, thus involving executorship and greater official scrutiny) stalled on selling the houses. Sizwe and Patience reported him to the Law Society, after which he withdrew and recommended a liquidator. The first house was sold, but they never received the proceeds, and they suspected fraud on the part of the liquidator. The second house, where the deceased's ex-wife continued to live, was never included in the paperwork. In a further restart, Sizwe and Patience found another attorney, whom they instructed to take the matter to court. They hoped that a court order to split the estate would cut through the morass of inaction and unaccountability. But this attorney prepared the case inadequately, causing mother and son to withdraw it from the court roll for fear of being held responsible for misrepresenting their circumstances. They were back to square one. Patience and Sizwe each had a massive stack of paper, accumulated since they first came to the Master's Office in 2006, much legally irrelevant. Patience's carefully protected red file testified to the fact that she and her son had experienced not stasis, but ceaseless circulation through the system.

Sizwe and Patience's referral date at the legal assistance NGO came up five months later. As they sat down in a consultation room at the NGO, they embarked on a tirade against the attorney from the clinic and her superior at her firm, who had prevaricated about assisting before declining. Sitting down with the legal intern responsible for the referral program, they repeated their story. Now there was no optimism. When the intern explained that they would need to find an attorney willing to take up the matter, and that there was no obligation for anyone to do so, Patience snapped: "it's useless coming here then!" "It's fifty-fifty," Sizwe responded more cautiously. A week later, the intern would report to them by phone, in advance of their next meeting, that the liquidator had indeed perpetrated probable fraud and had disappeared—his number was out of order. Removing him would be a process in itself—it also appeared that his appointment was authorized by a court. Equally disturbing, the intern had called the Master's Office, and there was no record of the funds from the sale of the first house. Discouraged, Sizwe and Patience never returned for their next consultation.

The "referral" of the NGO's referral program took on a rather different meaning—being sent back more times than Sizwe and Patience could count, until they finally gave up. Theirs was a story of repeated restarts and reversals, punctuated by one-way thresholds that they were unable to challenge. The first house was sold. The liquidator, while fraudulent, had formal status and so could only be removed in an equally formal manner. Sizwe and Patience had hoped that formal determinations would work to their advantage. But, in processes that depend on fly-by-night lawyers, acquiring a Letter carries insufficient authority, and persuading a judge to issue a court order is difficult. New information, appeal, or even simple oversight came too late to prevent the sale of a house before others were able to dispute it—the ultimate irreversible flow. Forward-moving process was hurried along by those hoping to traverse thresholds before they became impassable, using criminal methods if necessary.

Conclusion

The Kula, as analyzed by Malinowski and subsequent generations of anthropologists, invites us to examine how institutionalized, linear, and irreversible paths (*passing on*) relate to and rely on messier and more openly negotiated circulatory flows (*passing around*). The anthropology of inheritance adds greater appreciation of collective property as a site rather than an object of circulation—to be *passed through*. This chapter extends analyses of the Kula to interrogate received ideas of inheritance and circulation, both of which are often depicted theoretically as ordered and integrating forces for economy and society.

Focusing on houses, in a context conspicuously lacking consensus and integration, I examined how linear paths are complemented by looser forms of circulation. Houses are withheld from defined channels of transfer, thus becoming sites of circulation. But this withdrawal is less the enactment of clear-cut rules or idealized systems than the negotiation of divergent interests and the avoidance of stark determinations of entitlement. At the same time, those excluded respond to disputes by placing themselves at the mercy of formal process, with its defined linear paths, its abrupt one-way thresholds, and its endless setbacks.

Negotiated circulation in Kula is not usually brought into dialogue with negotiated circulation across generations. But in both, the interaction of circulatory elements suggests a picture that is more dynamic and improvised, and less stable. It reveals the differences between idealized systems and the negotiated arrangements that underpin circulation—a distinction of the kind Malinowski was always keen to draw (Bloch 1977).

Acknowledgments

Many thanks to my interlocutors for their participation in the research. For helpful engagement with the chapter as it developed, I am grateful to Jessica Jacobson and Paulo Savaget; Chris Gregory and other participants of the *Argonauts of the Western Pacific* centenary symposium at LSE; and Kate Skinner, Simon Yarrow, Chris Wickham, and participants of the University of Birmingham workshop on "'Things Taken as Given': Economy, Governance, and Moral Ordering." Research was funded by ESRC Future Research Leaders grant ES/N003071/1.

Maxim Bolt is Associate Professor of Development Studies at the Oxford Department of International Development, University of Oxford, and Research Associate at the Wits Institute of Social and Economic Research, University of the Witwatersrand. He is the author of *Zimbabwe's Migrants and South Africa's Border Farms: The Roots of Impermanence* (Cambridge University Press, 2015). His current research explores inheritance in Johannesburg.

Notes

1. This was recently underlined in a landmark High Court judgment: Shomang vs. Matsose, 2022.
2. I carried out a year's ethnographic fieldwork in 2017, exploring the field of formal inheritance in Johannesburg. This involved shadowing and interviewing a range of actors including state officials, legal assistance professionals, wealth managers, and people navigating inheritance-related institutions and family disputes. It ramified out from a focus on wills, following people's views on what mattered.

3. Known elsewhere as a state-owned enterprise.
4. Maimela vs. Maimela, 2017.
5. Compensation in place of bridewealth, understood as affiliating a child to the father's family.
6. It was explained to me that the Master's Office was only relatively recently linked to the Home Affairs database to check information, and the unified system has limited time depth.

References

Appadurai, Arjun. 1986. "Introduction: Commodities and the Politics of Value." In *The Social Life of Things: Commodities in Cultural Perspective*, ed. Arjun Appadurai, 3–63. Cambridge: Cambridge University Press.
Barth, Fredrik. 1967. "Economic Spheres in Darfur." In *Themes in Economic Anthropology*, ed. Raymond Firth, 149–74. London: Tavistock.
Bauer, A. A. 2019. "Itinerant Objects." *Annual Review of Anthropology* 48: 335–52.
Bloch, Maurice. 1977. "The Past and the Present in the Present." *Man* 12(2): 278–92.
Bohannan, Paul. 1955. "Some Principles of Exchange and Investment among the Tiv." *American Anthropologist* 57(1): 60–70.
Bolt, Maxim. 2021. "Homeownership, Legal Administration, and the Uncertainties of Inheritance in South Africa's Townships: Apartheid's Legal Shadows." *African Affairs* 120(479): 219–41.
Damon, Frederick H. 1980. "The Kula and Generalised Exchange: Considering Some Unconsidered Aspects of *The Elementary Structures of Kinship*." *Man* 15(2): 267–92.
Ferguson, James. 1992. "The Cultural Topography of Wealth: Commodity Paths and the Structure of Property in Rural Lesotho." *American Anthropologist* 94(1): 55–73.
Goody, Jack. 1962. *Death, Property and the Ancestors: A Study of the Mortuary Customs of the LoDagaa of West Africa*. London: Tavistock.
———. 1976. *Production and Reproduction: A Comparative Study of the Domestic Domain*. Cambridge: Cambridge University Press
Hann, Chris. 2008. "Reproduction and Inheritance: Goody Revisited." *Annual Review of Anthropology* 37: 145–58.
Hart, Keith. 1986. "Heads or Tails? Two Sides of the Coin." *Man* 21(4): 637–56.
Holtrop, Marius W. 1929. "Theories of the Velocity of Circulation of Money in Earlier Economic Literature." *The Economic Journal* 39(S1): 503–24.
Hull, Matthew S. 2012. *Government of Paper: The Materiality of Bureaucracy in Urban Pakistan*. Berkeley, CA: University of California Press.
James, Deborah. 2015. *Money from Nothing: Indebtedness and Aspiration in South Africa*. Palo Alto, CA: Stanford University Press.
Latour, Bruno. 2009. *The Making of Law: An Ethnography of the Conseil d'Etat*. Cambridge: Polity.
Leach, Edmund R. 1983. "The Kula: An Alternative View." In *The Kula: New Perspectives on Massim Exchange*, ed. Jerry W. Leach and Edmund Leach, 529–38. Cambridge: Cambridge University Press.

Long, Norman, and Magdalena Villarreal. 1998. "Small Product, Big Issues: Value Contestations and Cultural Identities in Cross-Border Commodity Networks." *Development and Change* 29(4): 725–50.

Malinowski, Bronisław. 1921. "The Primitive Economics of the Trobriand Islanders." *The Economic Journal* 31(121): 1–16.

———. 1922. *Argonauts of the Western Pacific: An Account of Native Enterprise and Adventure in the Archipelagoes of Melanesian New Guinea.* London: Routledge & Kegan Paul.

Mathur, Nayanika. 2015. *Paper Tiger: Law, Bureaucracy and the Developmental State in Himalayan India.* Cambridge: Cambridge University Press.

Merry, Sally E. 1990. *Getting Justice and Getting Even: Legal Consciousness among Working-Class Americans.* Chicago, IL: University of Chicago Press.

Parry, Jonathan, and Maurice Bloch. 1989. "Introduction: Money and the Morality of Exchange." In *Money and the Morality of Exchange*, ed. Jonathan Parry and Maurice Bloch, 1–32. Cambridge: Cambridge University Press.

Pickles, Anthony J. 2020. "Transfers: A Deductive Approach to Gifts, Gambles, and Economy at Large." *Current Anthropology* 61(1): 11–21.

Shipton, Parker. 2007. *The Nature of Entrustment: Intimacy, Exchange, and the Sacred in Africa.* New Haven, CT: Yale University Press.

Strathern, Marilyn. 1996. "Cutting the Network." *Journal of the Royal Anthropological Institute* 2(3): 517–35.

Weiner, Annette B. 1992. *Inalienable Possessions: The Paradox of Keeping-while-Giving.* Berkeley, CA: University of California Press.

Weston, Kath. 2013. "Lifeblood, Liquidity, and Cash Transfusions: Beyond Metaphor in the Cultural Study of Finance." *Journal of the Royal Anthropological Institute* 19(S1): S24–S41.

Zelizer, Viviana A. 2010. "Circuits within Capitalism." In *Economic Lives: How Culture Shapes the Economy*, 311–43. Princeton, NJ: Princeton University Press.

13

 The Anthropological Turn in the Sociology of Money

ARIEL WILKIS

When (modern) economic anthropology was born, the nature of money was already a source of controversy. Marcel Mauss's (1925) criticism of Bronisław Malinowski's (1921, 1922) notion of money represents an important chapter in these initial debates. The controversy focused, first, on what defined the nature of money, and second on whether this definition applied only to *modern* monies. While Mauss defended a broader notion of money, Malinowski opted for a more limited view, arguing that as the sole objective measure of value, only modern money qualified as money. In Mauss's view, a subjective dimension of value was inherent—such as the association of money with a figure of authority. This made money as ubiquitous as the gift (Mauss 2016). Mauss thereby questioned the general fungibility of monies. If monies are not, by their very nature, subject to unrestricted exchange, it is possible to recognize them in a diverse range of societies and, in turn, to investigate these societies through the lens of their monetary exchanges. In his conclusion to *Argonauts*, Malinowski (1922) emphatically opposes this approach.

During the twentieth century, the breadth of money-related phenomena attracting the attention of anthropologists expanded greatly. Karl Polanyi (1957) entered the debate by distinguishing "all-purpose" money from "special-purpose" money. This was pursued in numerous investigations of "spheres of exchange" in what has been referred to as the "golden age" of economic anthropology (Hann and Hart 2011). Jonathan Parry and Maurice Bloch (1989) examined the plurality of money's meanings in non-Western societies by contrasting short-term calculation with long-term cycles of exchanges in which the moral component was uppermost. Keith

Hart (2000) delved into the way in which money always acts both personally and impersonally. Jane Guyer (2004) renewed this anthropological tradition by analyzing the rich plurality of money practices in West Africa as both a condition for and a result of economic transactions.

While economic anthropologists have disputed making universal fungibility a necessary and sufficient condition for money for over a century, sociologists began doing so only much later. Originally published in 1994 and by now translated into many languages, and republished in an updated edition in 2017, Viviana Zelizer's *The Social Meaning of Money* represents a true milestone in the field of economic sociology. After decades in which sociology had tended to overlook an object central to the understanding of capitalist societies, this work called into question the theoretical frameworks of classical sociologists. The process by which money was standardized and became a homogenizing force in the United States became the laboratory that enabled Zelizer to contest earlier theories. Issued by the federal government, the dollar was gradually adopted for use across the union, replacing all other currencies previously in circulation that people had used in multiple ways and constantly redefined. But these myriad uses and definitions, Zelizer (1994) argued, enabled new special monies.

Sociology and anthropology have taken very different paths in expressing their respective doubts regarding money's fungibility. Reservations about money's capacity to lubricate universal exchange came much later in sociology. Despite a shared skepticism concerning the preeminence of the fungibility criterion, synergies between the two subdisciplines have not emerged. In general, anthropologists have been more open to sociology than the other way around (Maurer 2006; Hann and Hart 2011; Ortiz 2021).[1]

In earlier work, after reviewing the paucity of collaboration between sociology and anthropology in academia in advanced capitalist countries, I examined the ways in which conditions for such scholarly exchange were somewhat more favorable in the institutional and intellectual milieu of economic sociology in the Southern Cone (Wilkis 2022). Malinowski's *Argonauts* has been a point of reference, either implicit or explicit, for a generation of Argentine scholars whose work draws on ethnographic research (Figueiro 2013; Wilkis 2017; Hornes 2020). My personal research evolved within this milieu and leveraged debates in both fields dating back to *Argonauts*.

In his analysis of how the sociology of money has moved away from classical sociology in recent decades, sociologist Nigel Dodd argues:

> Against this [a view of money as culturally corrosive], a strong literature has developed, mainly during the last quarter of the twentieth century, which advances the

view that money is richly embedded in and shaped by its social and cultural context. What is needed, according to this view, is a theory of money's *qualities*, not simply an account of its role as a *quantifier*. Such a theory needs to focus not only on how money is "marked" by cultural practices from the outside but also on a deeper level, on the way in which those practices shape money *from within*, for example, by defining its scales of value. (2014: 271)

In this chapter I lay out how my own research echoes these oscillations of the contemporary sociology of money, as pinpointed by Dodd. Specifically, I show how the ethnographic method, as outlined in *Argonauts*, reinterprets money through the lens of a monetary hierarchy that became the dominant tradition of economic anthropology (Bohannan 1955; Guyer 2004, 2016). Beginning with a description of some of the ways in which money circulates among the poor in Greater Buenos Aires (Argentina), I show how the ethnographic method led me to question Zelizer's (1994) notion of "types of money" and instead to explore the uses and moral meanings of money using "pieces of money" as a guide. The ethnography expands the conventional sociological framework of analysis and enables an understanding of how the hierarchical relationships between meanings and moral uses of money contribute to produce a microsocial order at family level. This is followed by a second section in which I focus on the role of the US dollar in a dual-currency economy such as that of Argentina. I do so via an ethnography of economic transactions surrounding Argentina's principal crop, the soybean, thereby illuminating the hierarchical relation between the dollar and the peso, and the functions of money that include the shaping of investments, savings, and profits, but also include political acts against state regulations and government decisions.

I chose the two cases because they illuminate monetary dynamics linked to polar social sectors (social groups located in poor urban areas and rich rural areas) and because they illuminate the plasticity of the concept of monetary hierarchy, which operates in contexts of a single national currency (in the first case) and of more than one national currency (in the second one).

In the first of these investigations, the notion of a monetary hierarchy allows me to interpret the multiple meanings of a single currency (the Argentine peso) that connects different spheres of life for those living on society's margins. In the second, this same notion allows the multiple meanings of multiple currencies to be interpreted when a national currency (the Argentine peso) and a global one (the US dollar) co-constitute regular economic transactions in the context of an exchange rate crisis. In both cases the ethnography led me to unpack power relations at different levels. In the first, gendered power relations emerge at the level of family and local political networks on the margins of society. In the second, monetary hierarchy is a means to understand class power exercised against the state by those seeking to expand the agrobusiness model. My conclusion is that the ethnographic method allows us to study money from the perspective of hierarchy and to connect it to the analysis of power relations, thereby pushing the contemporary sociology of money still further away from the theories of the classical sociologists.

Monetary Pluralism in the Life of the Urban Poor

When I first visited Villa Olimpia in Buenos Aires, I focused on a key topic among Argentine sociologists in the 1990s and 2000s: the political transformations brought about by neoliberalism and the role of political clientelism. An ethnographic approach, I believed, would enable the broadest perspective on people's lives. This meant taking account of collateral or "secondary" themes, including topics not previously marked as relevant in academic literature. Ethnographies allow room for innovation, giving researchers a chance to embark on an intellectual adventure.

I began with visits to the parish church to build my credentials in the community. Mary, a parishioner, asked me to her house and, during that first visit, in the first month of my fieldwork, I spent three hours listening to her life story. She was the first person I met who was actively involved in the network of Salcedo, a local political boss. During the time I spent with Mary at her home, and accompanying her on visits to other members of her network, I gained a comprehensive understanding of her household economy and realized that politics was only one dimension of the multiple social orders on which her survival depended. Moreover, once she began to speak openly with me about a range of topics, I learned that money was pertinent to almost every other aspect of everyday life—a life conditioned by constant financial stress. Our talks, originally guided by my interest in understanding power relations through involvement in political networks, left me determined to understand how money featured in these same relations. As a result, I shifted my focus and began, during talks with other informants, to explore the circulation of money. I also reflected back on how money had come up in the interviews I had conducted, even though it had not been my main focus at that point. It was gratifying to find abundant material: money was a constant preoccupation for the citizens of Villa Olimpia.

While continuing to frequent the parish church and to visit Mary, I gradually expanded my contacts to include persons such as shopkeepers in order to glean additional insight into monetary dynamics. Not all informants find mention in my book, yet the argument in the book (Wilkis

2017) was underpinned by their collective comments and insights. I sought out individuals whose everyday activities involved them in different social orders and required different pieces of money. I relied on snowball sampling (mainly through the church) and was grateful for people's readiness to open up their homes to me.

"En Villa Olimpia el dinero cae de los arboles!" (Money grows on trees here in Villa Olimpia!), Mary once said. This was a revelatory comment to me, given that the topic of how the poor use money had been virtually absent from Argentine sociology. In other works, I have focused on the reasons for this absence. Despite money's increasing prominence in social life, the tools required to interpret this process did not seem to exist. Most social scientists in Argentina took the view that money was "corrosive," that it undermined social life and fostered individualism. The very progressivism of these scholars made it hard for them to accept the idea that money might shed more variegated light on the social world. At best, they looked upon money as an "accessory" that people might or might not have, but not an institution capable of producing its own sui generis effects.

In the 1970s, Mexican anthropologist Larissa Lomnitz (1976) carried out an extraordinary study of how marginalized people get by. Her work set the agenda for investigations of poor families in the decades that followed, in both sociology and anthropology. Lomnitz's principal argument was that, given the inability of the state and the job market to provide them with the resources they needed, marginalized families of Latin America had to rely on reciprocal ties with friends, family, and neighbors to survive. This approach came back into fashion in the 1990s in the guise of a new concept, social capital: something akin to what Mary was getting at with her enigmatic remark about money growing on trees. The renewed focus on reciprocity and the social capital of poor families cast money as a sociological "accessory," but it was still far from becoming a substantive object of sociological research in its own right.

Meanwhile, the governments of most major countries in Latin America turned increasingly progressive. After the neoliberal wave of the 1990s, new left-leaning governments worked to increase real wages and stimulate consumption among the poor. An international climate favorable toward the commodities exported by these countries—like soybean in the case of Argentina—freed up fiscal resources that were used to introduce conditional cash transfers across the region. A consumer lending market opened up for low-income sectors and the use of credit cards multiplied. In this context, money became a tool for identifying differences between social orders and illuminating negotiations between them in a comprehensive approach to the world of the poor. Instead of analyzing only separate fragments of the lives of the poor—politics, religion, family, and so on—money was crucial because it connected them all. The ideas and feelings associated with money connected homes not only to shops and markets, but also to drug houses, political party offices, and parish churches.

This approach went against the grain of the social sciences. Considering the social life of the poor as intrinsically bound up with money, the task was to map the connections between the various components of this "total social fact" (Mauss 2016: 61). Jane Guyer's (2004) research into the economies of Atlantic Africa proved inspirational here. Although its monetary context—unlike Zelizer's or my own—was not that of single national currencies, it helped to address these other monetary configurations based on the multiplicity of meanings and uses of such currencies. Guyer's interest in the hierarchy of currencies opened up a field largely neglected by Zelizer: the interactions between domestic and non-domestic monies. Zelizer's notion of circuit, for example, can help us analyze the remittances migrants send home, but it blinds us to the other monies they use outside that circuit and which take priority. As a result, the impact of different forms of money on social life is unclear. In contrast, in her study, Guyer emphasizes that people relate to heterogeneous currencies with different values, establishing a hierarchy of payment methods. All monetary transactions express a social order (Guyer 2004: 82). I thus proposed to replace Zelizer's "kinds" with "pieces" of money.

Swapping "kinds" of money for "pieces" of money allowed monetary hierarchies and their systematic role in producing a social order to be incorporated into a bigger picture. As in a puzzle, pieces provide only a partial understanding when observed in isolation. The value of each piece depends on how it connects to the others. By classifying money as pieces, it is possible to understand how people are judged within a certain monetary hierarchy and how they build a moral reputation. Originating in the ethnography, this conceptual change from "kinds" to "pieces" required not only connecting social spheres but also establishing the hierarchies between them and seeing how people position themselves to reproduce or transform them through their use of money and the meanings they attribute to it, stabilizing or challenging power relations. Once this hypothesis is taken as a given, money can no longer be treated as an "accessory" to people's lives. It is an integral part of a unique social reality. This leads to a series of questions once the pieces have been identified. Are all the pieces worth the same? How are they organized? Is there a moral ranking?

The pieces of money are shaped by ideas and beliefs about morality, with each of these pieces differing from the others. When seen through the lives of Mary and her family, pieces of money are revealed to be diverse and multifaceted but also often entwined. They are used to create moral hierarchies. The dynamic of the pieces—a dynamic involving hierarchies, tensions, and contradictions—challenges the definition and the negotiation of people's status and power in specific social orders. To paraphrase Karl Marx, we can say that people negotiate their status and power within monetary hierarchies, but under circumstances not of their choosing. These hierarchies are embedded in institutional and macro-level social dynamics. Each specific sociohistorical context facilitates the emergence, expansion, and disappearance of certain pieces of money.

Mary's household income, for example, comprised heterogeneous pieces of money, including *political* money, money *earned,* money *lent,* and money *donated.* The family finances, managed by Mary, became an arena for negotiating economic goods and social status. The multiple pieces that comprised income had to be organized within the set of feelings and perspectives of *caregiving* money. The money her children *earned* became savings when she put it into a rainy-day fund, to manage the eventuality that something at home would need to be repaired or replaced. Money saved was *caregiving* money. This allowed Mary to objectify and quantify her sons' contributions to the household finances. Mary's power over her children was tied to these savings and it became evident in the household hierarchy that *caregiving* money ranked higher than the other pieces. Concessions and negotiations surrounded this piece of money, which was a source of both unity and conflict. As the piece of the money puzzle that held the household economy together with affective bonds, *caregiving money* defined the power and status of family members. While all pieces evoke both social hierarchies and hierarchies of money, *caregiving money* does so within the microsocial order of the family.

Mary bought her refrigerator in instalments from a traveling saleswoman. When Mary began explaining the payment options to me on a November afternoon in 2008, our conversation soon turned to how she made enough to get by and her sons' contribution to the household.

M. Antonio is quite the wise guy. Sometimes I'm afraid he'll never grow up.

A. Why's that?

M. His friends come over and then they all go out to play pool and drink beer. They're a little old for that, and granted, I'd rather have him drinking beer than doing drugs, but he still wastes his money there. One day I'm going to march in there and then he'll see. He also spends his money on clothes, on expensive tennis shoes. But he's slow when it comes to paying me.

A. What does he pay you for?

M. I put away the money the boys give me. I know how much my sons make every week. And don't they know that if something happens to me, all of this is going to belong to them? The other day Pato—my oldest—said to me, "I paid the cable bill—twenty pesos!" I paid the instalments on the fridge and when the television broke, I paid to have it fixed and used up my savings. Sure, I could ask Salcedo for it, he'd give it to me, but I don't always want to ask him.

A. And when they give you the money, how do you save?

M. I give the money I want to save to my daughter, the one who doesn't live here, because if I've got that money here, I'll spend it. With the merchandise I get I can wait to use the *tarjeta* [the government welfare card], Salcedo's money, what the boys give me. Some months are better than others, like when I sell my *yerbas medicinales* [medicinal herbs].

The money *earned* by her children was a frequent source of arguments. When they didn't deliver, Mary would get angry, like the time she had to yell at them to get them to work on a rainy day. "Yo tengo mi límite!" (I've reached my limit!), she shouted. They had to understand how important it was to earn money. The household finances were precarious. Starting that day, they agreed on a fixed amount of 50 pesos per week each.

Had Mary's sons not responded to her demands, she might have been forced to ask the leader of the political network for more money. Since Mary preferred not to depend on the feelings and perspectives associated with *political* money, she instead pressured her children as permitted within *caregiving* money. In addition, getting her sons to work was part of helping them assume their responsibilities as men: "Hasta su casamiento me deben dar la plata a mi!" (Until they get married, they have to give me their money!).

When her sons didn't pay, the tension in the household grew. When Mary called her youngest son immature, she did so from the perspective of *caregiving* money. The speed with which money was spent was a factor in her negative assessment of Pato, who wasted money going out with friends but was slow to hand over what he owed his mother. This temporal difference (quick to spend, slow to pay) revealed a lack of responsibility. Mary had to stay on her toes, remind him and even pressure him to hand over a percentage of his earnings. This tension increased when Pato reminded her that he had spent 20 pesos on the cable bill or when he tried to argue against giving her a portion of money *earned* doing an odd job for a neighbor. Mary also oversaw the money her children spent on other things. Her children made good "investments" when they used the money *earned* to buy shoes or clothing, unless of course they opted to buy expensive brand items. When it reached Mary's hands, the money *earned* by her children was transformed into *caregiving* money in a very specific form, namely, savings. As the poor are excluded from formal savings institutions in their daily economic life, the most common way for them to save money is to set it aside (*separ*), a practice that is part of the set of feelings and perspectives of *caregiving* money. Saving is a monetary practice that reveals the intensity of this type.

The money *earned* by Mary's children became savings when she took it to her daughter's house. This money was a rainy-day fund, for instance if a home appliance needed to be repaired or a new one purchased. Through savings, the sons' commitments and responsibilities in household finances were objectified and quantified. These savings thus indicated Mary's power over her children, while revealing how *caregiving* money ranked higher than other pieces on the household hierarchy of money.

Mary launched into a lengthy monologue that touched on the family economy and Pato's personal life:

> *Pato toma alcohol hasta por los codos!* [Pato drinks like a fish!] If he gets paid two hundred pesos on a Friday, he doesn't come home until Monday, drunk and broke. If he had looked after his money, he wouldn't be in the state he's in. When he was earning a good salary—living here with his wife and kids—I said to him, watch your money, save some money. But his wife got fed up with him disappearing for days at a time and told him she was done. And she's right. He says I'm on her side, but that's not it—I just don't approve of what he's doing.

Pato's excess weight symbolized his irresponsible use of money *earned*. For Mary, it was simple and painful: when Pato had had money, he had not looked after it—"He never saved." By saving, he would have set aside money for child support and preserved the family unit. His inability to transform one type of money (money *earned*) into another (*caregiving* money) had distanced Pato from his wife and children, and his body was a living indicator of this. Now he had to find a way to put things back together.

When Mary took sides with Pato's wife after the couple split up, Pato felt that his mother was betraying him. However, Mary also considered it fair to help him with money *lent*. "I feel bad for the kids," she would say, referring to her grandchildren. This piece circulated to make up for Pato's inability to adhere to the set of feelings and perspectives associated with *caregiving* money. By helping her son, Mary reasserted her position as the protector of the family unit and reaffirmed her ethical stance. With this monetary assistance, she was supporting her grandchildren and assisting her son.

Mary demanded that her younger sons go out and find work whenever she ran out of money, and she *lent* money to Pato. Both were part of the same economic socialization. The money *lent* to the eldest son was an attempt to salvage his masculine moral capital (based on the obligation to take care of one's family), while the youngest sons had to give their mother money to prepare them for the day when their own masculine honor would come into play, that is, when they had wives of their own. Mary's responsibility for supporting her children framed her relationship to money. She managed her earnings based on feelings and perspectives associated with *caregiving* money, treating all her income as mutual. Her children, however, could use the money they *earned* to purchase tennis shoes or alcohol, or use it for other things outside the realm of the household. When her eldest son spent money this way, Mary helped him out with *lent* money. By reconstructing these money dynamics, we see how power, gender relations, and solidarity are articulated to produce the social order of the family.

One of the monetary resources Mary considered in her household budget was *political* money. The link between *pieces* of money allows us to assess the connections between the household and the political realm. For Mary, the transformation of *political* money into *caregiving* money was one of her gender obligations within both her family and her political group. This meant that the money that circulated as a political salary sustained her hopes for her children's well-being, establishing her role as a mother who guaranteed the financial security of her household. That is why Salcedo's unfulfilled promises related to her household caused her more disappointment than the others. For the same reason, being low on the list of the leader's priorities was closely connected to her expectations of social continuity.

Monetary Pluralism in the Life of Wealthy Farmers

In the final months of 2011, just as President Cristina Fernandez started her second term, the Argentine banking system suffered a massive withdrawal of dollars (Luzzi and Wilkis 2023). As had occurred on numerous occasions since the 1950s, the run on the peso was a means for Argentine capital to pressure the national government into a devaluation that would make Argentine goods more competitive abroad, while reducing labor costs for exporters. At the end of October 2011, the state responded to this pressure by changing the requirements for the purchase and sale of foreign currency. The regulations and controls grew progressively stricter until July 2012, when the government prohibited the purchase of dollars or other foreign currencies for the purpose of savings. In January 2014, it again became possible to purchase dollars for savings, though certain restrictions continued until the new government under President Mauricio Macri eliminated them in December 2015.

The recent history of currency in Argentina—like that in Israel (Dominguez 1990), Ecuador (Nelms 2012), Nigeria (Guyer 2004), Russia (Lemon 1998), and El Salvador (Pedersen 2002)—can be narrated in terms of the interactions between a "hard," "healthy," or "real" currency (the US dollar) and a "soft," "ill," or "false" currency (in the case of Argentina, the peso). Such narratives buttress the status of the US dollar as a hegemonic store of value in vastly diverse territories characterized by monetary pluralism. But what happens when monetary regulations restrict people's access to and use of the "hard" currency? What is the impact of constraining access to foreign exchange markets on the hierarchical dynamic of currencies and monetary functions? The restrictions introduced in Argentina in 2011 and the monetary practices they engendered can help us answer these questions.

In Argentina, the US dollar has existed alongside various iterations of the national currency for over half a century. In certain markets, like that of real estate, the vast majority of transactions are carried out in US dollars. The foreign exchange restrictions introduced in 2011 forced citizens to find ways to get around the restrictions or to come up with new transactions altogether. Ethnographic reconstruction of these economic practices reveals how the monetary hierarchy structures economic transactions and political decisions and acts against the state (Luzzi and Wilkis 2018). Between 2014 and 2019 Mariana Luzzi and I conducted ethnographic and historical research on the social and cultural history of the US dollar in Argentine society. As part of that research, we did interviews with, shared moments of leisure with, and visited the farms of soybean farmers and their families from affluent areas of the province of Santa Fe, in the Argentine littoral.

"La soja es como el dólar" (The soybean is like the dollar), a farm owner from the province of Santa Fe told us. This was one of our first visits to this region, whose social, economic, and productive milieu had changed since the expansion of soybean planting at the end of the 1980s. The soybean boom was accompanied by a true technological revolution in the countryside thanks to the incorporation of genetically modified organisms (GMOs) and the direct sowing method (Hernández and Gras 2014). In the years since, the crop had transformed into a global commodity that contributed billions of dollars to the Argentine economy. According to the National Institute of Statistics and Censuses (INDEC), in 2014 almost 20 billion dollars from the export of soybean entered Argentina, which represented 30 percent of the foreign sales made by the country. It is no wonder then that an attempt by the national government in 2008 to increase the taxes on exporting soy farmers ignited one of the most severe political conflicts in the past decade. Farmers responded with a strike that lasted for months, leading the Minister of Economy to hand in his notice and dividing the government coalition.

Three years later, soy farmers were back on the front pages due to the exchange restriction policies. In conjunction with major trade companies, they were accused by the government of attempting to "destabilize" the Argentine peso. Farmers, claimed the government, were stockpiling soybeans instead of selling them on foreign markets, thus keeping much-needed dollars from entering the country and speculating with the peso's devaluation. Such practices had been common during the 1980s, a decade of strong currency instability and drastic fluctuations in exchange rates.

San Justo is a small town located north of Santa Fe, the capital city of the province of the same name in the middle of the country. An area of small and medium-sized farmers, Santa Fe has undergone a profound transformation in the past fifteen years that affected the entire fertile region of Argentina known as *la Pampa húmeda* (humid Pampas). Soybeans have gradually replaced other grains—and livestock—making this region almost monocultural. At the same time, this change has reduced the number of small farmers, who have increasingly rented out their lands to the large crop pools that have become more profitable than small-scale agriculture. In this way, although the structure of property ownership has remained more or less the same, the dynamics of production have changed entirely, as has the life of the rural towns in the region, where farmers went to make a new living after abandoning their trade altogether.

During our fieldwork, we found out more about the production and sales of this crop, which had been Argentina's number one export for over a decade. In San Justo, we talked with men and women from the countryside: old farmers who inherited the family farm and other new farmers who joined the bonanza of the past decade, employees of the cooperatives that stockpile crops, retailers selling agricultural machinery, and agricultural technicians working for large farms.

Abel was a third-generation farmer, whose grandfather had purchased the family farm after arriving as an Italian immigrant at the beginning of the twentieth century. Formerly dedicated to livestock, the farm had begun incorporating soybean at the beginning of the 1980s. By the 2010s his entire farm was dedicated to soybean production. Part of his crop was sold through a co-op with storage facilities and experience in dealing with exporters. Sometimes, however, Abel exported directly via Rosario, the largest city in the province. This eliminated the middlemen, but it only made sense if the harvest was good: "Solo tenes que llenar el camion!" (you have to fill the truck), as Abel explained. This accounts for the use of "truckloads" as a unit of measure.

For Abel's calculations, a key number is the price per 100 kg of soy, generally its Chicago market value (in June of 2015, USD 345.85 per ton). Abel's production costs are calculated in different currencies. While workforce salaries, fuel, agricultural machinery rentals, utilities, and transportation costs are calculated in pesos, the seeds and agrochemicals purchased from multinationals like Monsanto are in dollars, along with equipment costs. When a farmer rents another farmer's land, payment can be made in one of two ways: the landowner can be paid a percentage of what the renter earns in soy quintals or in an agreed quantity of soy quintals, regardless of the crop yield. In both cases, the final payment depends on the price of soybean at the time. When equipment is rented for the harvest, a similar agreement is struck with the contractor: the rental cost is based on soy quintals, as a percentage of the harvest (usually around 9 percent). Websites, cell phone apps, and cable TV channels keep farmers abreast of the international commodity markets and feed them numbers for their daily accounting. Industry journals provide essential information on the cost of the raw materials, helping farmers to calculate costs and earnings. Although certain costs are paid in pesos, the totals are always estimated in dollars, requiring conversions of everything paid in pesos, including taxes. Thus, while monetary pluralism persists, the dollar clearly takes precedence, although it is rarely used as a payment instrument. Soybean farmers tend to reinvest the pesos they earn, and to use this currency for most everyday transactions.

The most important currency in these transactions, however, is the soybean itself. As Abel said, it functions like the dollar, but soybeans are more accessible, and farmers are more accustomed to this currency. Once the soybean's worth has been calculated in dollars, it serves as a method of payment and a store of value. Farmers use the official exchange rate for their calculations, which is the rate they receive for their exports. However, they also rely on the soybean dollar, which is the official price minus a government withholding of approximately 35 percent as an extra tax for exportations. "Soybean is a common currency. I pick up the phone and I've made a sale," explained one farmer in reference to crops from his field being stored by a co-op. While a percentage of the crop is sold right after the harvest to cover land and machinery rental and production costs, what remains can be sold later at the farmer's behest. In practice, one or more "truckloads" are set aside for buying fuel, agrochemicals, or equipment when the sowing season comes around again. Silo co-ops play a key role in the soybean financial circuit, allowing this unit of currency (the soybean itself) to be stored, used as a payment method, and used for currency speculation—that is, a hedge against upcoming devaluations of the national currency.

Use of the soybean for currency speculation became prevalent when exchange rate restrictions were implemented in 2011. In the eyes of government officials, farmers were undermining the Argentine currency. Farmers, however, argued that they were waiting for a better exchange rate before exporting their crop. As they themselves put it, having more than one currency at their disposal enabled a whole range of transactions. In an economy in which access to US currency had become limited, the fact that soybeans were convertible in dollars placed farmers in an enviable position, allowing them to dollarize transactions without ever touching an actual dollar. When he takes inventory of his production costs, Abel mentions the question of the dispute between farmers and the government on grain export retentions, which are set at 35 percent of their sales abroad. *"El 35 percent es una locura!* [35 percent is madness!] Think about a hundred trucks [of grain]: they take thirty-five of those trucks: it's insanity! The taxes are unbelievable ... The government steals your money." For Abel and other farmers, keeping the earnings in soybean is a way to elude such taxes.

Monetary pluralism offered additional benefits to farmers, allowing them to increase profit margins, forgo middlemen, and take their time before making a sale. Here the question of when and how to "convert" soybean quintals into pesos, dollars into pesos, or pesos into dollars (or when and how to avoid these conversions) is the secret to conducting and understanding transactions. By maneuvering these currency conversions, farmers use the soybean to make time work in their favor, either in same-day sales or transactions in the near or distant future. Soybeans can be sold instantly if machinery needs to be rented, saved for transactions scheduled for later in the season, or stored in silos for many years. Farmers even contribute to their retirement "pension" by means of an account in the cooperative's soybean silos. In these transactions, producers treat the soybean the same way they would a state-backed legal currency.

In her analysis of how the dollar became hegemonic across the United States, Zelizer (1994) called into question the tenets of classical sociological theory by focusing on a single function of the US dollar: its role as a method of payment or exchange. Despite the homogenizing push of the dollar, there were limits to its circulation. These were mainly social (moral restrictions, ritualistic practices, etc.), though she also noted how the use of the dollar varied in different settings. Through her use of concepts like earmarking and multiple currencies, Zelizer's great accomplishment was to challenge the notion of fungibility that sociology (following political economy) had attributed to the analysis of modern currencies. In doing so, she undermined the idea that money was capable of configuring a society that was indifferent to interpersonal relations. However, when analyzing how the dollar became a global currency that circulates in territories with their own national currencies, this approach overlooks certain critical aspects.

The end of World War II, when the dollar became a global currency, ushered in a period—especially for countries outside the United States—very different from the epoch analyzed by Viviana Zelizer. Currency plurality stems, at least in part, from the personal creativity of those who deal in state-issued monies, establishing distinctions that allow them to organize their social relations. However, not all actors have access to these currencies; they are not equally known, or equally suited to particular transfers, making their conversions problematic. Such a multiplicity has been thoroughly investigated in Atlantic Africa (Guyer 1995, 2004). Eastern Europe provided further examples, both during and after socialism, with the US dollar quasi-hegemonic (but emulated in some countries by the deutschmark and later the euro). While most Western analysts considered such regions deviant or backward, since the 1990s the developed capitalist countries have themselves entered a new phase of multiple currencies (Guyer and Salami 2012: 212). The US dollar was consolidated not only as the currency used in foreign commerce globally, but also as a common account and exchange unit in numerous regional and national scenarios. Monetary functions are no longer embodied in a single national currency: while a local or national currency still serves as the primary medium of exchange, it is the US dollar that serves as a "harder" currency and thus as a more reliable store of value (Guyer 2011; Orléan 2009).

The sociology of money needs to come to terms with this plurality or multiplicity. At the same time, it needs to provide a more nuanced understanding of currency functions and hierarchies, moving away from the impact of money as a method of payment and exchange (Zelizer's main focus in *The Social Meaning of Money*) while also analyzing its role as a unit of account and store of value. This is particularly relevant when analyzing how the dollar gained a foothold as a currency in numerous territories outside the United States. The case of the soybean in Argentina provides insight into how dynamic currency pluralism enables agents to control the timing of transactions. The hierarchy of currencies and currency functions is embedded in cycles both long and short, but also in day-to-day calculations to increase profits. As we have shown, the soybean can function as a real currency, allowing farmers to plan and conduct transactions in the near or distant future, giving them room to maneuver, and helping them deal with (which may mean making the most of) economic uncertainties at any given time.

In our ethnography of soybean farmers, currencies and their functions are associated with the here and now (the peso), and the near or distant future (soybeans and US dollar). However, farmers have some leeway: they can "save" their soybeans for lengthy periods or use their harvest to cover immediate costs. Soybeans and dollars can both be considered "hard" currencies. Unlike the usual narrative, in which the US dollar tends to be treated as the sole "hard" currency, rather than distinguishing soft and hard currencies we prefer to outline the dynamics of a hierarchy. On one hand, monetary pluralism can only be understood by reconstructing cycles of transactions and the ways in which economic agents deal with the temporality associated with each of the currencies. And on the other hand, the temporalities of currencies give political meanings to soybean producers' decisions and actions against the state.

Regulations oriented toward limiting currency pluralism, like the restrictions implemented between 2011 and 2015 in Argentina, are attempts at domesticating practices and imaginaries sedimented over a long time. We have shown that the resistance to this domesticating corresponded to a plurality of currencies and monetary functions, with contingent and political properties. We have showed here how some economic agents in Argentine society find in currency pluralism a way of representing (and misrepresenting) their business activities. The case of the soybean producers allows us to understand the close relationship that exists between the ways in which currency pluralism is configured and the definition of imaginaries about the state, its capacities for regulation, and the resistances it encounters. When a producer complains about the quantity of truckloads the state withholds, he is monetizing political criticism. When producers define soy as a parallel banking system, they reveal the social and political power anchored in the multiple reality of money. In this way, how they imagine money affects how they imagine the state, based on a currency whose reality expands in parallel to their opposition to the state.

Conclusion

The authors of *Re-Imagining Economic Sociology* take stock of progress in recent decades while aiming to "reinvigorate the role of theory in economic sociology" (Aspers, Dodd, and Anderberg 2015: 1). Compared with earlier foundational handbooks (Smelser and Swedberg 1994; Granovetter and Swedberg 2001), Malinowski and *Argonauts* are cited in new terms. In their introduction, the editors write:

> First, economic sociologists *do not define the economy as a separate dimension of society*. One early scholar who deserves to be considered among the key figures of classical economic sociology was an anthropologist, Bronislaw Malinowski (1922). Malinowski referred to *Kula* ring as "Trobriand Economic Sociology." (Aspers, Dodd, and Anderberg, 2015: 4)

In this chapter, with ethnographic materials from Argentina, I have revisited debates about money that Malinowski helped to launch. Sociologists have belatedly followed anthropologists in questioning the fungibility of money and engaged instead with monetary plurality. Economic anthropology, a subdiscipline rooted in Malinowski's work, has been a source of inspiration for conceptual innovations in studies of money in the Southern Cone, transforming or expanding perspectives originating in Euro-American settings. Social ties, economic transactions, and political actions are configured by monetary hierarchies that organize and classify the uses, meanings, and functions of money. The ethnographic cases explored here show how the hierarchy of money's moral meanings and its interaction with power relations may be analyzed. Ultimately, a satisfactory sociology of money depends on understanding such hierarchies ethnographically, to analyze the monetary configuration of economic transactions, social order, and political conflict.

Acknowledgments

I would like to thank Horacio Ortiz for helping me to improve the argument developed here.

Ariel Wilkis holds a PhD in sociology (EHESS, Paris). He is a researcher at the National Council for Scientific and Technological Research (Argentina), full professor at the University of San Martin, and Dean of the Interdisciplinary School of Higher Social Studies at the same university. He is the author of *The Moral Power of Money: Morality and Economy in the Life of the Poor* (Stanford University Press, 2017) and coauthor of *The Dollar: How the US Dollar Became a Popular Currency in Argentina* (New Mexico University Press, 2023).

Notes

1. In addition to many individual contributions by Zelizer herself, Bandelj, Wherry, and Zelizer (2017) is a significant exception in the sociology camp.

References

Aspers, Patrik, Nigel Dodd, and Ellinor Anderberg. 2015. "Introduction." In *Re-Imagining Economic Sociology*, ed. Patrick Aspers and Nigel Dodd, 1–33. Oxford: Oxford University Press.
Bandelj, Nina, Frederick Wherry, and Viviana Zelizer, eds. 2017. *Money Talks: Explaining How Money Really Works*. New Jersey, NJ: Princeton University Press.
Bohannan, Paul. 1955. "Some Principles of Exchange and Investment among the Tiv." *American Anthropologist* 57(1): 60–70.
Dodd, Nigel. 2014. *The Social Life of Money*. New Jersey: Princeton University Press.
Dominguez, Virginia. 1990. "Representing Value and the Value of Representation: A Different Look at Money." *Cultural Anthropology* 5(1): 16–44.
Figueiro, Pablo. 2013. *Lógicas Sociales del Consumo: El Gasto Improductivo en un Asentamiento Bonaerense*. Buenos Aires: Unsam Edita.
Granovetter, Mark, and Richard Swedberg, eds. 2001. *The Sociology of Economic Life*. Boulder, CO: Westview.

Gras, Carla. 2009. "Changing Patterns in Family Farming: The Case of the Pampa Region, Argentina." *Journal of Agrarian Change* 9(3): 345–64.
Guyer, Jane. 1995. "Introduction: The Currency Interface and its Dynamics." In *Money Matters! Instability, Values and Social Payments in the Modern History of West African Communities*, ed. Jane Guyer, 1–33. Portsmouth, Heinemann.
———. 2004. *Marginal Gains: Monetary Transactions in Atlantic Africa*. Chicago: University of Chicago Press.
———. 2011. "Describing Urban 'No Man's Land' in Africa." *Africa* 81: 474–92.
———. 2016. *Legacies, Logics, Logistics: Essays in the Anthropology of the Platform Economy*. Chicago: University of Chicago Press.
Guyer, Jane, and Kabiru Salami. 2013. "Life Courses of Indebtedness in Rural Nigeria." In *Transitions and Transformations: Cultural Perspectives on Aging and the Life Course*, ed. Caitrin Lynch and Jason Danely, 206–17. Oxford: Berghahn.
Hann, Chris, and Keith Hart. 2011. *Economic Anthropology: History, Ethnography, Critique*. London: Polity Press.
Hart, Keith. 2000. *The Memory Bank: Money in an Unequal World*. London: Profile.
Hernández, Valeria, and Carla Gras. 2016. *Radiografía del Nuevo Campo Argentino: Del Terrateniente al Empresario Transnacional*. Buenos Aires: Siglo XXI Editores.
Hornes, Martín. 2020. *Las Tramas del Dinero Estatal: Saberes, Prácticas y Significados del Dinero en las Políticas Sociales Argentinas 2008–2015*. Buenos Aires: Teseopress.
Lemon, Alaina. 1998. "Your Eyes Are Green Like Dollars: Counterfeit Cash, National Substance, and Currency Apartheid in 1990s Russia." *Cultural Anthropology* 13(1): 22–55.
Lomnitz, Larissa. 1976. *Cómo Sobreviven los Marginados*. Mexico City: Siglo XXI Editores.
Luzzi, Mariana, and Ariel Wilkis. 2018. "Soybean, Bricks, Dollars and the Reality of Money: Multiple Monies during Currency Exchange Restrictions in Argentina (2011–2015)." *Hau: Journal of Ethnographic Theory* 8(1–2): 252–64.
———. 2023. *The Dollar: How the US Dollar Became a Popular Currency in Argentina*. Albuquerque: University of New Mexico Press.
Malinowski, Bronisław. 1921. "The Primitive Economics of the Trobriand Islanders." *The Economic Journal* 31(121): 1–16.
———. 1922. *Argonauts of the Western Pacific: An Account of Native Enterprise and Adventure in the Archipelagoes of Melanesian New Guinea*. London: Routledge & Kegan Paul.
Maurer, Bill. 2016. "The Anthropology of Money." *Annual Review of Anthropology* 35: 15–36.
Mauss, Marcel. 2016 [1925]. *The Gift: The Form and Reason for Exchange in Archaic Societies*. Chicago: Chicago University Press.
Nelms, Taylor. 2012. "The Zombie Bank and the Magic of Finance: Or: How to Write a History of Crisis." *Journal of Cultural Economy* 5(2): 231–46.
Orléan, André. 2009. *De l'euphorie à la panique: Penser la crise financière*. Paris: Éditions Rue d'Ulm.
Ortiz, Horacio. 2021. *The Everyday Practice of Valuation and Investment*. New York: Columbia University Press.

Parry, Jonathan, and Maurice Bloch. 1989. "Introduction." In *Money and the Morality of Exchange*, ed. Jonathan Parry and Maurice Bloch, 1–32. Cambridge: Cambridge University Press.

Pedersen, David. 2002. "The Storm We Call Dollars: Determining Value and Belief in El Salvador and the United States." *Cultural Anthropology* 17(3): 431–59.

Polanyi, Karl. 1957. "The Economy as Instituted Process." In *Trade and Market in the Early Empires*, ed. Karl Polanyi, Conrad Arensberg, and Harry Pearson, 243–70. New York: Free Press.

Smelser, Neil, and Richard Swedberg, eds. 1994. *The Handbook of Economic Sociology*. New York/Princeton, NJ: Russell Sage Foundation/Princeton University Press.

Wilkis, Ariel. 2017. *The Moral Power of Money: Morality and Economy in the Life of The Poor*. Stanford, CA: Stanford University Press.

———. 2022. "The Argonauts as a Classic of Sociology: Malinowski and the Recent History of New Economic Sociology." Unpublished manuscript.

Zelizer, Viviana. 1994. *The Social Meaning of Money: Pin Money, Paychecks, Poor Relief, and Other Currencies*. Princeton, NJ: Princeton University Press.

14

Digital Argonauts
From Kula Ring to Bush Internet in the Western Pacific

GEOFFREY HOBBIS AND
STEPHANIE KETTERER HOBBIS

The Argonauts of the Western Pacific are surfing the world wide web. And, as when they sail the Solomon, Bismarck, and Coral seas in their canoes and deep-sea vessels, they navigate the digital seas in the pursuit of enterprise and adventure. They steer through significant gulfs in information and communication technology and infrastructure and they do so with much precision and ingenuity, despite the many challenges they face. There are economic barriers. This region is, at least from the perspective of globally dominant measurement systems, one of the least developed on the planet (UNDP 2022). There are environmental barriers. The tropical climate "bedevils the permeance of all things" including the digital (Hobbis and Hobbis 2021: 750). And there are infrastructural challenges, owing to the geographic constraints of the tropical archipelago (Hobbis and Hobbis 2022a).

This chapter is part of a larger project that follows the Argonauts of the Western Pacific as they traverse their newly digitizing world (Hobbis and Hobbis 2021, 2022a, 2022b, 2023; Hobbis 2020). One aim of the project is to bring their experiences to bear on academic inquiries into digital transformation, which have, so far, barely considered this region as a worthwhile site of investigation. This chapter does so by arguing for a classic ethnographic approach to understanding Melanesia in the digital age, following in the footsteps of Bronisław Malinowski's 1922 classic, *Argonauts of the Western Pacific*. This monograph transformed sociocultural anthropology. Malinowski established long-term fieldwork in a *relationally* "exotic" locale involving rigorous participant observation and the aspiration to complete immersion in local life as the gold standard of anthropological research.

He also laid the foundation for a new subfield in the discipline, economic anthropology, and its critical engagement with prevailing orthodoxies in economic theory.

With precise detail and evocative, thickly described narrative, Malinowski laid out a rigorous, scientific case for the sophistication of what was, at the time, pejoratively conceptualized as "primitive economics." Specifically, he challenged Karl Bücher's argument that "the savages ... have no economic organization, and that they are in a pre-economic stage—the lowest in that of the individual search for food, the higher ones in the stage of self-sufficient household economy" (Malinowski 1921: 1). By focusing on economic organization holistically with a contextual emphasis on the Trobriands, Malinowski demonstrated how islanders engaged in an economic system that was "prompted by motives of a highly complex, social and traditional nature" (Malinowski 1922: 60).

Simultaneously, and perhaps most importantly, Malinowski demonstrated that this economic system was not about "buying cheap and selling dear" (Hart 2012: 169). Instead, he found it to be realized in a context where social reproduction was firmly grounded in networks of "giving and counter-giving" (Malinowski 1921: 8), a topic he himself considered, at the time, merely as a "side issue" (ibid.). With this insight, he empirically established the shortcomings of dominant economic theory, largely derived from armchair research, that postulated "Economic Man," driven by a "rationalistic conception of self-interest, and achieving his aims directly and with the minimum of effort" (Malinowski 1922: 60).

Malinowski's treatment of "Economic Man" has been frequently criticized for its simplified portrayal of both Trobriand Islanders and the economic theories of his time (Hann and Hart 2011). Still, *Argonauts* was foundational for a century of empirical and theoretical debate about the nature of economics and economies. Later taken up in the work, among many others, of Karl Polanyi (2001) and David Graeber (2011), Malinowski initiated a perspectival shift away from a focus on "the economy" toward an investigation of economies as "institutional processes through which people maintained social relations and upheld group-specific cultural values" (Strathern and Stewart 2012: 241).

In *this chapter*, we demonstrate how Malinowski's approach allows us to challenge the received wisdom of contemporary research on digital economies as they are embedded in sociocultural systems. Like Malinowski, we confront a preoccupation with the "average" in the dominant economic theory of the day. In the past, this was the "average," self-interested "Economic Man." With digital economics, it is commonly the "average" user and the self-interested "Economic Man" who produces digital technologies. Like Malinowski, we draw on longitudinal participant observation in Island

Melanesia. Also like Malinowski, we focus on exchanges of exceptional *and* seemingly everyday items at high costs and some risk over the open ocean that connects islands into economically and socially interwoven archipelagos. Finally, we embed this understanding in a holistic perspective on the *"imponderabilia of actual life and of typical behavior"* (Malinowski 1922: 20, emphasis in original).[1]

But we also depart from Malinowski in several ways. We draw on a century of methodological refinements and build on the tradition of married couples working side by side as research partners (Engelke 2004). This coupled approach brings out a gender perspective and more broadly a relational dimension that is missing in most earlier studies (Cupples and Kindon 2003). Rather than the Trobriand Islands of what was, at the time, northern New Guinea, our locations were roughly 1,000 km to the southeast, in the next closest significant archipelago, Solomon Islands. Specifically, we worked with the Lau speakers of Malaita in the eponymous Lau Lagoon and their (peri-)urban settlements in Malaita's provincial capital, Auki, and the national capital, Honiara (see Map 14.1).

Hence, while we draw on Malinowski's and subsequent scholarship on the Kula ring, we shall not be discussing the digital transformation of Kula itself (that would be another project—one that needs to be carried out as a matter of urgency). Instead, we engage with digital transformations in the context of a broader system of exchange as practiced in the northern cultural complex of Malaita Province. This system of exchange, connecting "bush" and "saltwater" peoples across the region, plays "an analogous structural role" (Ross 1978: 119) to the Kula in its focus on the creation, maintenance, and strengthening of networks across kinship and language divides. At the same time, this system of exchange also offers "an allegory of the world economy" with peoples "spread across many small islands, each incapable of providing a decent livelihood by itself, that rel[y] on an international trade mediated by the exchange of previous ornaments" (Hart 2012: 169). In the North Malaitan context, items such as ritually significant foods are substituted for Kula valuables. These similarities, we contend, allow us to follow Malinowski's example in challenging dominant economic theories.

Before diving into some of the details of our fieldwork in Solomon Islands,[2] we need to explain what we mean by a Malinowskian approach to digital research and how this approach challenges influential conceptualizations of "digital ethnography." While digital studies, including parts of digital anthropology but also disciplines such as media studies and data science, often suggest, if not celebrate, that they have transcended Malinowskian approaches, we argue that digital studies are still caught in a pre-Malinowskian moment. Digital studies are too often confined to a shallow

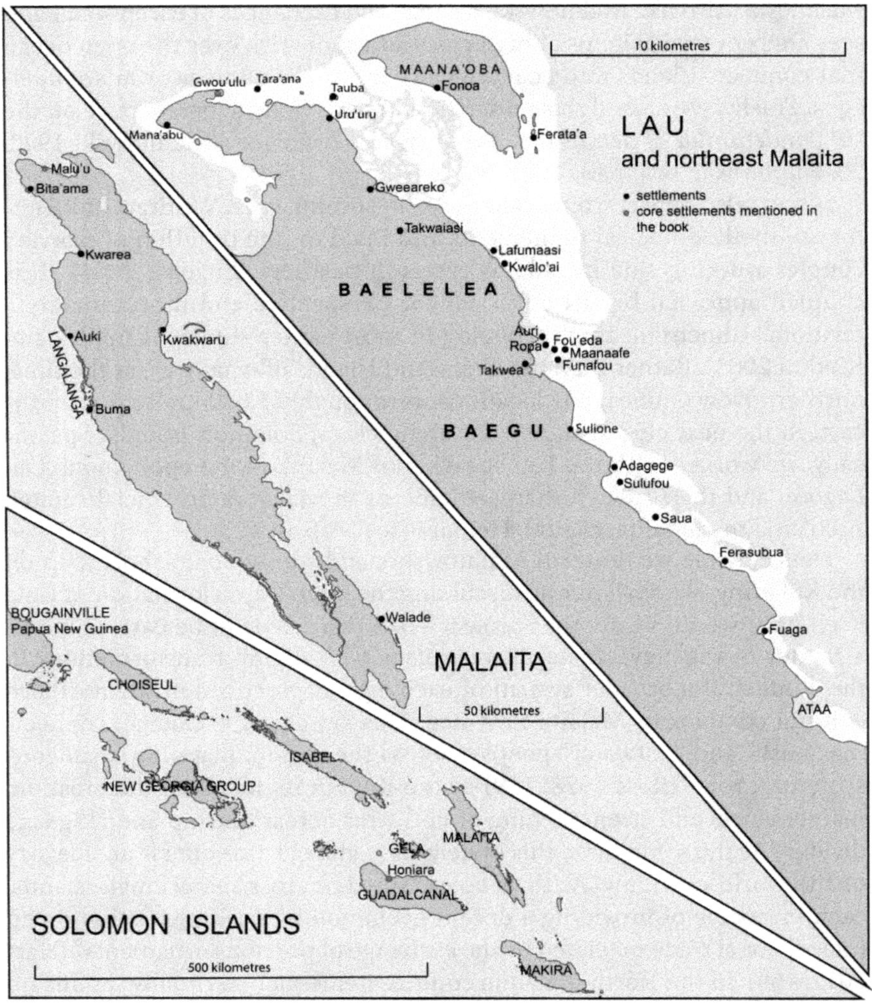

Map 14.1. Map of Solomon Islands, Malaita, and Lau Lagoon by Ben Burt; changes were made to the original map to highlight core settlements covered by our research.

empirical world comprised largely of armchair and desktop, aided, at best, by short trips to the field. The empirical focus tends to be on familiar, urban environments (cf. Hobbis et al. 2023) and sites dominated by industrial (usually capitalist) forms of production, consumption, and exchange (cf. Hobbis 2021). It is time to change that. It is time, in Malinowski's words, to leave the veranda (and unwieldy computer screens) and live cheek-by-jowl with the people whose lives now have a digital dimension, especially thanks to the smartphone.

Digital (Economic) Ethnography

We are by no means the first to bring anthropological perspectives to broader inter- and transdisciplinary debates on digital transformations. To find one of the earliest anthropological engagements with digital technology, we need look no further than the Lau Lagoon and our predecessor there, Pierre Maranda.³ From his early discussions of "Computers in the Bush" (Maranda 1967) to the creation and curation of oceanie.org as an attempt to move beyond linear, textual representations of Oceania in anthropology and beyond (Maranda 2010), Maranda pioneered the integration of local specificities into investigations of the transformations wrought by digital technologies and media (cf. Miller et al. 2016) and their embedding in "everyday routines, contingencies and accomplishments" (Pink et al. 2017: 1). Still, the relationship between anthropology and digital studies has also been a troubled one, with the touchstone issue in this meta-disciplinary discourse often being the methodological potential of "ethnography," and what it is, can, or should be—or should not be.

So what is "digital ethnography" (Murthy 2008; Pink et al. 2015; Varis 2016), or, as it is otherwise known, "netnography" (Kozinets 2009), "cyberethnography" (Robinson and Schultz 2009), "connective ethnography" (Hine 2007), or "internet ethnography" (Sade-Beck 2004)? The answer is not straightforward. The approaches proposed so far are as diverse as the names on offer, as they consider, for example, how digital technologies transform ethnographic recording, storing, and analysis, but also how digital media have opened up new spaces for research (Howard and Mawyer 2015). Still, existing debates about digital ethnography tend to agree that digital ethnography is *not* classically conceived Malinowskian ethnography, variously characterized as (1) physical, on-site, offline fieldwork that (2) lasts at least twelve months, (3) takes place in "exotic," usually rural, locations, and/or (4) is based on participant observation (and not just observation, lurking, or stalking).

So defined, Malinowskian ethnography has become the primary villain of digital ethnography; it is what digital ethnographers must perpetually defend themselves against. For example, Gabriele de Seta (2020: 78) notes that he feels pressured into defending his "self-labelling as a media anthropologist" because he did not complete twelve months of on-site fieldwork, instead working for six months on-site and six months online. Annette Markham (2014: 436) suggests that "for many young scholars, there is little room for flexible adaptation" as they "feel trapped by method," in this case the perceived need to be physically present—on location—for research to be recognized as ethnographic. In opposition to this "entrapment," Markham and others (e.g., Garcia et al. 2009; Ebo 1998) challenge the primacy of on-site research based on active, non-covert participant observation. They argue instead that digital ethnographers should be "often physically 'invisible' . . . as they 'read' web blogs, or . . . take on anonymous web 'avatars' in chat rooms or forums" (Murthy 2008: 840).

Similar examples, expressed both as a "defense" against Malinowskian ethnography and as necessary "transformations" of the approach to fit digital contexts, can be found throughout debates on digital ethnography. Scholars have helped untangle differences between "co-location" and "co-presence" (Beaulieu 2010) and more broadly the role of "place" and "space" in ethnographic research that seeks to transcend flimsy "virtual" versus "real" dichotomies in digital studies (Leander and McKim 2003). However, in the never-ending quest "to reform ethnographic research techniques" (Ritter 2022: 929), the question of what Malinowskian ethnography might have to offer to digital studies and its digital economics subfield is barely posed.

This question is central to our project. We wish to take seriously the contributions Malinowski made not only to anthropology and ethnography but also to broader interdisciplinary debates on economic systems and practices. We ask what happens to digital studies when we stop framing methodological value in terms of innovation and convenience and focus instead on rigor. In other words, our agenda is to interrogate key claims of digital studies from a classic Malinowskian point of view. This cannot be a step-by-step replication of Malinowski's work. That would contradict the core of his approach and deny a century of cumulative scientific progress. But we contend that to place classically conceived ethnography at the heart of investigations into digital transformations can be productive—and more fruitful than some fashionable alternatives.

Others have done some of this work already. Daniel Miller (2017: 28) has argued for the kind of "holistic contextualization" that Malinowski outlined when describing "the collecting of concrete data over a wide range of facts [as] one of the main points of field method" (Malinowski 1922: 13). Miller has sought to realize this vision through large-scale comparative investigations of the everyday dimensions of social media use, including one project that involved nine anthropologists conducting fifteen months of on-site (and online) ethnographic fieldwork in nine locations around the world (Miller et al. 2016). On a much smaller, individual scale, Julie Archambault's (2017) and Jenna Burrell's (2012) monographs on youths' adoption and adaptation of digital technologies in urban Mozambique and Ghana respectively are also based on long-term, on-site ethnographic fieldwork.

However, one of Malinowski's main recommendations to ethnographers is often missing from anthropological interventions in digital research. As Karen Sykes explains:

> The value of a good ethnography lies in its aim of destabilizing received common wisdom about human nature, by showing that people residing elsewhere—with fewer contrivances of modern living, and with different assumptions about what in their social life should be valued from day to day—do things differently and hold different beliefs about their own human nature. (Sykes 2005: 47)

Existing anthropological research on the digital has largely strayed from the relationally "exotic." Even in "foreign" locales, researchers have opted to remain in the "more" familiar, for example by focusing on urban or suburban environments, as the spaces most intensely embedded in dominant global political economic systems.[4] It is difficult to find dedicated, longitudinal ethnographic investigations of digital transformations in Island Melanesia.[5] The same is true of other economic systems, practices, and values that are, despite their increasing entanglements with industrialism and industrial capitalism, not dominated by them (Hobbis 2021). The digital studies literature has yet to engage with the critical insights that rigorous ethnographic research can bring to bear in sites where it is possible to empirically investigate the conceptual tensions between economies "where the creation and affirmation of relationships is the key goal of interaction, [and where] exchange is carried out precisely in order to foster mutual recognition" (Robbins 2008: 48) and those where the "enhancement of the self and its enterprises without regard for the other is what ideally motivates economic action" (ibid.).

Our research addresses this blind spot in digital studies and digital ethnography debates. Filling this gap has far-reaching implications. Digital research that has focused on platformization, the significance of Facebook, Google, Amazon, and even Uber, is increasingly presenting an argument about digital economics that closely resembles the evolutionary determinisms that Malinowski rejected. Under banners such as "platform capitalism" (Srnicek 2016), "surveillance capitalism" (Zuboff 2019), or "data colonialism" (Couldry and Mejias 2019), critical digital scholars have argued that platforms, by virtue of their design, necessarily "commodify *all* social relations by collecting, algorithmically processing, circulating, and selling user data" (de Kloet et al. 2019: 249, emphasis added). In other words, it is claimed that platforms, and digitization more broadly, by design promote and impose capitalist systems and values, irrespective of the extent to which end users and even producers may resist commodification. We suggest that all such claims need verification through extensive economic ethnographic fieldwork, comparable to Malinowski's own study of Kula.[6]

Active Methods of Digital Research

The ocean as a phenomenon merits serious consideration, though this is easy to forget because of its ubiquity in the archipelagic way-of-being. Like the digital, its navigation is dangerous, wrought with peril, but also teeming with potential for enterprise and adventure. It was also unavoidable, given that our ethnographies were based on a lagoon in a country with the word "island" in its name. And, clearly, these connections are deeply personal. From the moment we arrived on 12 February 2014 to our departure on 14 February 2015, our bodies, especially their sensory equipment, were employed in participation in and the observation of social and cultural life, immersed in geographic, political, and economic constraints. We certainly took breaks, but we did so as other people take breaks in this specific context. Not as solitary ethnographers, but as a married couple, we essentially followed Malinowski's advice "by camping right in . . . villages" and by having "a white man's compound . . . far enough away not to become a permanent milieu in which you live and from which you emerge at fixed hours only to 'do the village'" (Malinowski 1922: 6–7).

Taking detailed notes, audio recordings, and pictures daily, we followed the lives of the Lau of Malaita. While this was challenging, the yield is comprehensive insight into a year in the life of a village in the Lau Lagoon, including relatives living in the urban space of Honiara. We traveled with the Lau, and like the Lau, on dugout canoes, fiberglass boats with outboard motor engines, and various types of "ferries" connecting the Malaitan mainland with Guadalcanal island, where Honiara is located. On a day-to-day basis we learned how to garden. We participated in community work, not much different from the type described by Malinowski, but now largely organized by Christian churches. We went fishing and to markets, learned how to weave baskets and build houses. We also attended various exceptional events, large-scale reconciliations, baptisms, village feasts, and funeral rites, all while following gender-specific prescriptions and roles.

As recommended in classically conceived ethnographies (Malinowski 1922: 14), we started with a census and sought to map such features as "new" infrastructures, including water tanks and solar home systems. But, like Malinowski, we recognized the limitations of such activities as "dead material" (ibid.: 5). These initial data points were valuable as a starting point, as a way to make initial connections with villagers, before subsequently uncovering the complexities of shifting entanglements such as those involved in ownership claims. We did formal interviews here and there, often for the sake of what Malinowski described as "charts" or "the method of statistic documentation by concrete evidence" (ibid.: 17, emphasis removed) and what has since been developed in conversations with archaeology through the notion of the *chaîne opératoire*, operational sequences aimed at a detailed understanding of the steps taken to (for instance) create or use a particular technology (see Lemonnier 1976). The key elaboration in our process was the smartphone research schedule: one hundred semi-structured, object-centric interviews carried out on smartphones with the goal of investigating the relationships people have with and through them.[7]

For all the detailed information and insights generated by these more formal methods, the best interviews unfolded naturally, without any more of a prompt than what would happen in any conversation, over the course of the year of our participant observation. Just being in the everyday life of a village showed us what people think, without the artifice of a focus group or survey instrument, allowing for a more fine-tuned sense of the significance of digital transformations in everyday life. The advantage of being there for a year was the possibility to build a frame of reference that not only helped us better understand the content of our interviews, as well as other sources such as social media activity, but also acted as a net for intriguing content in its own right.

We sailed away from the experience in 2015 convinced that online-centric and particularly exclusively online digital ethnography misses a big part of the picture in Solomon Islands. The understanding one can gain of these people and this place from afar is less than adequate, and calls into the question the practice of online-only digital ethnography. We started engaging in online participant observation in 2012, around the time we decided to pursue doctoral projects with the Lau, and have continued for the decade since. The first impressions we developed were, frankly, nonsense, with a serious risk of cementing prejudice.[8] This is the key problem of online- only ethnography: the human subjects don't pass the Turing Test, they might be "bots." Only when one knows the person from extensive offline encounters does it become easier to pick up on that rapport and inside personal knowledge.

The problem is bigger than failing the Turing Test. The scary aspect of this is that online-centric and online-only digital ethnographers may never know they were mistaken. Consider this from a different angle. During our fieldwork, a foreign police officer asked Stephanie her opinion on two different public outreach brochures. Without opening either she pointed to the one in glossy print and said "that one, you can't use it for cigarette rolling paper": a clear, undeniable social fact to anyone who has spent time in the villages, but never seen by people living in the urban and expat bubbles, or what may be called echo chambers. Indeed, Malinowski cautioned against this when he exclaimed that

> Information which I received from some white residents in the district, valuable as it was in itself, was more discouraging than anything else with regard to my own work. Here were men who had lived for years in the place with constant opportunities of observing the natives and communicating with them, and who yet hardly knew one thing about them really well. (Malinowski 1922: 5)

The problems with the even greater distance of all forms of online ethnography are in a higher order of magnitude. These ethnographers are even more disadvantaged by geographical distance, even if (unlike the foreigners Malinowski critiqued) they are trained in scientific practices. This is why classically conceived ethnography is so important for digital studies, as we have shown in tracing the contours of Solomon Islands digital (economic) transformations and embedding them in the broader chaos of facts that we documented.

Facing a Chaos of Facts

The reason that Melanesia was a great place to disrupt primitive economics in the age of Malinowski is also the reason that it is so well positioned to disrupt digital economics today: Melanesian islanders continue to live economic lives that challenge commonsense assumptions developed from economic and broader social research in places with McDonalds outlets, be it metropolitan London or Trinidad. There is no better place to interrogate assumptions about average users and deterministic claims about digital economics than the Western Pacific. In one of his fieldnotes, Geoffrey put it like this:

> Based on my experiences traveling combined with my training in anthropology, I had this impression of globalization as being an unstoppable machine. Something similar to Anna Tsing's idea of a wheel rolling over terrain. After the heat, after the shock of the challenges of moving over the violent ocean and through the thick jungle, what struck me most about Solomon Islands was the sense that it often triumphs in the face of globalization. The truth of it is realized for me at one point on the North Road, the singular land-based route between the deep-sea port at Auki, the provincial capital, and our field site in the Lau Lagoon at the northwestern tip of Malaita. After passing one of the hundreds of sharp corners along this swampy route, just before one of its many treacherous passes and just after one of its long patches of meter-deep mud, there is a long stretch of beach with no one around. No communities, no visible homesteads, no one. Nothing, except for a rusting Caterpillar heavy machine engine excavator. The first time I saw it, I was struck; everything I have seen about the place crystallized in that iconic image of stranded globalization. It was like a forlorn mechanical Don Quixote in the face of a disinterested tropical truth.

Another way of saying this is that the reality in Solomon Islands was unexpected for both of us, in particular with regards to the continued dominance of "other" horticultural, hunter-gatherer economic systems and values despite the presence of various industrial-capitalist endeavors, from logging (cf. Minter and van der Ploeg 2023) to brick-and-mortar style retail businesses (cf. Hobbis and Hobbis 2023). Only a couple of years before we arrived, Solomon Islands had been promoted out of failed state status by their dominating and would-be hegemonic neighbor, Australia. Yet, unlike in other failed states, there was no modern history of mass famine here. The reason for this can be located in solid and sustainable traditions of horticultural and hunter-gatherer economics embedded in a socioeconomic system of reciprocal exchange: the epitome of the economic organization that inspired Polanyi's elaboration on earlier critiques of individualist "Economic Man" by Malinowski and others:

> As a rule, the individual in primitive society is not threatened by starvation unless the community as a whole is in a like predicament . . . It is the absence of the individual starvation which makes primitive society, in a sense more human than market economy. (Polanyi 2001: 171–72)

Rural Solomon Islanders garden using slash and burn techniques. When sufficient land is available, they rotate and leave some sites fallow; but nowadays land is increasingly scarce. Rather than storing or selling what they do not need, Solomon Islanders frequently redistribute the products of their garden work, and those of their fishing and other gathering techniques. In this tropical environment, storage is a challenge. Few things keep for long. Metal rusts, fabrics deteriorate, perishable foods perish rapidly. Few places have electricity, let alone fridges and freezers. Islanders could not accumulate much of what they produce or purchase in stores even if they wanted to. This context encourages redistribution. Our neighbor was skilled in night fishing. Every morning he would have more fish than his household needed, so he often shared with people who were less capable, notably us. He would shrug when we thanked him for his generosity. What else was he going to do with the fish? Well, we would respond, why not stop fishing when you have enough for your own household? Because I am good at it and I enjoy it, and I leave plenty. He would end the conversation with the mantra of village life: You do for me, I do for you.

This basic commitment to giving (and receiving) can be found throughout Lau socioeconomic lives. It is fundamentally embedded in a flexible, transient sense of ownership.[9] Let us take a step back and consider the regulation of both land and water in our primary field site, the Lau Lagoon. With the exception of a few relatively small parcels of land at urban and peri-urban sites across these islands, customary ownership dominates. Like Kula artifacts, resources are temporarily possessed in a highly flexible system. Take a palm tree, for example. The land on which it stands may be possessed by one lineage represented by individual or multiple leaders, typically men but, when it comes to usufructuary dimensions of this possession, at times also women (cf. Hobbis 2016). But the tree itself may be in the temporary possession of another lineage, and its coconuts of yet another. Each of these familial groupings is liable to fracture, whereupon each sub-lineage could make claims to possession. Land can be transferred in the course of reciprocal exchanges for almost any reason, from "scratching an older man's back" to welcoming "refugees," for instance in the wake of religious conversions. Conflicts about land tenure are resolved through reconciliation events that may involve complex feasting logistics, including the exchange of shell valuables and other ritually significant objects as well as lavish commensality. Miscalculation carries the risk of food poisoning ("Diarrhea Feasts"). Successful reconciliation events strengthen mutual economic entanglements.

The chaos of facts is difficult to discern without extensive longitudinal, on-site fieldwork and a comprehensive engagement with the complexities of social relations, digital and otherwise. That is where the logic of Lau lifeworlds, economic systems, and values is located. Greed is rejected (cf. Kahn 1987). In Island Melanesia, wealth is not accumulated but distributed through networks of relations, in which acts of giving and receiving "are the essential foundation upon which trust is built" (Hundleby 2017: 11), defining what makes a good enterprising person. Like Trobriand Islanders, the Lau spend considerable time exchanging goods within their social networks, even when these goods seem irrelevant to material livelihood, and thus, for the economist, the exchange is not "efficient," "productive," or "profitable." When Pierre Maranda (1969) attempted to measure the amount of time villagers spent on specific tasks, he found that relatively little was allocated to immediate livelihood activities. Instead, he found that the Lau (especially men but, to a lesser degree, also women) were preoccupied with ritually significant activities that served, above all, the maintenance and strengthening of social relations. These relations extended to dead, ancestral spirits who participated in exchange networks, for example, through the creation and eventual elaborate sailing of the *Barukwao* "white canoes" (see Maranda et al. 2022). By the time of our fieldwork, the ancestral religion had largely been effaced by Christianity, but a lot of time continued to be spent on social relations (including now the Christian God as broker of ancestral relations). Economic decisions were shaped by the connections they fostered (Hobbis and Hobbis 2022a, 2022b, 2023).

In short, a homogenizing global capitalism has yet to triumph in Island Melanesia (cf. Spann 2022; also Bird-David 1990 and Berger 2015 for other regions). Wherever the goals of social reproduction dominate over the self-interested, individual desire for "profit," we are likely to uncover an Internet that, like the Kula ring, does not fit the assumptions of the Western academy. Digital transformations cannot be adequately grasped from the armchair.

From Kula Ring to Bush Internet

A Malinowskian approach to digital ethnography in the Western Pacific offers insights into digitizing and firmly digital economic practices in, but critically also beyond, capitalism. The Pacific Ocean represents 50.1 percent of the world's ocean water, with over ten thousand islands representing a total land mass of 822,800 square kilometers. Humans have settled and sailed between these islands for millennia (on the southwestern border with Asia perhaps for as long as thirty thousand years). Although traditional forms of maritime mobility have declined following increased contact with "Western" sailors, missionaries, and traders, they have by no means disappeared.[10] By and large, the same or relatively similar maritime practices continue to be practiced into the present day by a significant number of communities across the region. The most sophisticated of these traditions can reliably navigate extreme distances, magnificently evidenced in the *Hōkūleʻa*, a Hawaii-based Polynesian double-hulled *waʻa kaulua* voyaging canoe. Sailors skilled in astronomy and at reading waves spread human settlement and connected communities across this region. The Oceanic wayfinder traverses vast seas seeking to create and maintain social ties, alongside the acquisition of personal prestige. The exchange of goods such as the shell ornaments of the Kula exchange is part of an effort to establish an ideally permanent relationship ("once in the Kula, always in the Kula" (Malinowski 1922: 83)). We argue that the same principles apply in Internet use: Melanesian islanders surf the world wide web to build, maintain, and strengthen relationships of perpetual mutual indebtedness. In doing so, they seek to acquire both relational fortune and fame without being assimilated into industrial-capitalist values and systems, as dominant digital economic theory wants us to believe.

We call this engagement with the Internet for relational, social reproduction the "Bush Internet." The "bush" metaphor is intended to invoke a vast spectrum of "other" places, from the harsh tundras of the Arctic to the dense rainforests of the Amazon, all of them conventionally dismissed as inconsequential "savage, untouched wilderness" (Graeber and Wengrow

2021: 150). Our goal is to bring to the fore "other histories of being with media [here: the Internet] that may not have entered—at least in any comprehensive way—our narration of media history in the (Western) academy" (Shome 2019: 306).

The materialities of the Bush Internet in Island Melanesia differ from what is commonly considered by the digital studies literature. The Internet is typically investigated as a global computer network, based on standardized communication protocols, interlinked and powered through infrastructures of grids and cables. This description is (with some caveats) accurate for describing the Internet as it functions in places like the UK or the Netherlands.[11] But it is not good enough to describe or analyze the Internet in places like Solomon Islands, or even remote areas of British Columbia, Canada, which continue to variously resist integration into industrial-capitalism (e.g., cf. Menzies 2016) while also presenting a deep history of anthropological investigation (e.g., Boas 1895).

To understand what is happening in places such as Solomon Islands, we need to take the widest possible frame available. At first glance, it would seem that computers are just devices such as laptops. But smartphones are also computers, globally perhaps the most significant type. What we are really talking about are electronic computers. Before electronic computers, and even for some time after their invention, critical computations were carried out by humans with some physical calculating tools. Some organizations called these people "computers" (NASA used human computers to verify early flight paths for first launches). Kula traders computed a social relation calculus in the exchange of items. Malinowski (1922: 18) noted that the ethnographer provided an observation-based counterpoint to those researchers whose work consisted in merely "computing documents."

The human computational element is still part of the operation of electronic computers everywhere. In combination, they yield a complex site that can provide great insights, particularly through the lenses of physical anthropology and studies of technique. Things get more complicated when we consider the materialities of "networks." In the Netherlands, as it is in many other places dominated by industrial capitalism, networks are materialized in servers linked together by fiberoptic cables (and also Wi-Fi routers and LAN cables). These material networks exist in Solomon Islands as well, but they are limited to urban areas and rarely involved in the last one hundred kilometers of delivery of the Internet network for most rural communities, which is where about 80 percent of the population continues to reside. It is true that some areas enjoy relatively reliable access to the Internet through satellite connections and broadcast towers. But these waves do not effectively blanket the countryside. They cannot penetrate steep valleys and they dissipate over water. And yet, we found that the Internet as a network covers these gaps. It does so through a human infrastructure, primarily through people downloading files in formal Internet cafes (and, but much less often, on private desktop computers and laptops) onto microSD cards and flash drives.[12] These microSDs and flash drives are then put into pockets and into bags and wallets. They are transported in ships across open oceans, moved overland on trucks, through mangrove swamps in dugout canoes, and between islands in lagoons by banana boat and between houses in pockets that pass through the jungle. Upon arrival, files are commonly transferred from microSD to microSD by means of Bluetooth or comparable applications. This is the materiality of the Bush Internet: a human–object non-grid communications network that brings the country into a new sort of "ring": a ring focused on exchange, in this case of digital files.

Similarly to the Kula ring, this "digital ring" is also, first and foremost, about the strengthening of social relations, and not about the acquisition of monetary wealth. Throughout our fieldwork we did not once encounter the "sale" of digital materials brought in pockets to rural environments. Instead, they were always given as gifts, grounded in broader networks of "giving and counter-giving" (Malinowski 1921: 8). Where this "digital ring" is different from the Kula ring is in its circulation of global materials for social reproduction, which is accompanied by particular moral challenges.

Contemporary digital argonauts are not passive transmitters of the foreign ideas and things brought to them via the cables and waves that connect their urban Internet cafes and desktop and laptop computers to the world wide web. Being a digital argonaut in the Bush Internet is also about being a broker in and of the Internet. Historically and today, Solomon Islanders have distinguished acutely between the objects and ideas that are integrated into day-to-day life and those that are not. Gatekeepers were adept negotiators of value between islanders and outsiders. This is what being a digital argonaut is all about: brokering connections in the network of the Bush Internet. One has to decide which digital objects (files) are valuable in the quest to maintain and strengthen social relationships and to extend one's own fame and fortune, as well as which ones are morally good.

As we discuss in detail elsewhere (Hobbis and Hobbis 2022b), digital brokers in the Bush Internet are often younger Solomon Islanders who have comparatively rare skills such as the ability to operate torrenting platforms for downloading multimedia files in formats that are resharable offline;[13] and they often have privileged access to the Internet and torrent-enabled computers, for instance as employees of Internet cafes. As brokers they use these unique positions to acquire digital "exchange valuables"—such as a movie from the *Rambo* franchise, which is popular across the region (Hobbis 2018; Kulick and Willson 1994)—and then modify them to fit local needs. This modification includes technological dimensions such as conversion to a file format that is easily readable on mobile phones and transference to microSD cards that can travel in pockets through the bush. Simultaneously, it includes sociocultural dimensions such as decisions to circulate particular movies only among particular family members. Solomon Islands digital brokers, as we have encountered them, often do not, for instance, bring digital entertainment files to their rural kin that depict extramarital sexual encounters; or they seek to restrict the circulation of such files to other men, with whom such files may increase their fame and the trust they receive from their social networks. As Stuart, one of the digital brokers we encountered, explained

> I downloaded most movies that my relatives are watching at home, and I know everyone else who can download and share movies at home. Some movies we do not share with them, like *Game of Thrones*. At home, they do not like TV shows anyways, and *Game of Thrones* is just not good. It fits town... If I bring a "bad" movie, no one will trust me anymore. Everyone trusts me because I bring only "good" movies. (Hobbis and Hobbis 2022b: 864)

Choosing which files to share is thus all about careful management of social networks, and as such immediately comparable to broader networks of exchange and circulation, which are essentially about the maintenance of morally good relations. As Joel Robbins and David Akin (1999: 7) suggest,

> Beneath the surface of any well-ordered Melanesian economy there always lurks the possibility that objects will begin to consort promiscuously, erasing in the shuffle the many boundaries between kinds of persons and kinds of relationships that people have worked hard to create through their exchange.

To understand the Internet in Solomon Islands and to understand how it is embedded in economic systems and values, it is, thus, necessary to focus on "tracing the history of a valuable [digital] object, and [gauging] the nature of its circulation" (Malinowski 1922: 12).[14] This can only be accomplished by moving beyond the nonhuman infrastructures that have been central to digital (ethnographic) research to date. Disconnected from the Internet in its dominant forms elsewhere in the world, the Bush Internet in Island Melanesia cannot be accessed remotely. It cannot be understood without engaging with the people whose pockets digital materials fill, and who as digital argonauts transport them, like Kula valuables, from one island to another. We need to follow the microSD cards as brokers pass them through the Bush Internet and discern how, when, and why particular digital files and practices are selected for their integration into this infrastructural assemblage. Tracing the interconnectedness of human and nonhuman actors, we see how digital brokers make choices as they move digital files, offline, over the sea, and through the jungle like sociotechnical tendrils.

Conclusion: Getting off the Desktop, Finding Algorithms

Island Melanesia, located beyond industrial modes of production as well as the state, exemplifies the possibilities for challenging dominant theoretical perspectives. Dave Elder-Vass (2016) has explored "the gift" in digitizing economies of "the West" with reference to classical anthropological texts, but much of this literature is ahistorical and poorly contextualized. Models of "gift economies" therefore resemble the "primitive economics" critiqued by Malinowski on the basis of his ethnographic evidence. By empirically engaging with the places that inspired theorizing of the gift, contemporary digital scholars can renew the Malinowskian impulse and thereby recognize the limitations of a dominant paradigm. In this context, a willingness to leave the veranda must mean leaving the desktop to open up the Bush Internet, thereby challenging definitions of the Internet itself and conventional postulates about digital economic transformations. Just as Malinowski did not find "Economic Man," we did not find an "average user" of the Internet absorbed into industrial capitalism. What we found was a flourishing system of exchange, centered around digital files, oriented toward fostering social reproduction and advancing the fame and relational fortune of those involved in the exchanges.

To understand digital transformations in places such as Island Melanesia, where industrial capitalism is present but not dominant, the need for Malinowskian ethnography is paramount. No other method will do. After all, what kind of algorithm could predict the offline movements of digital files we observed in Solomon Islands? The existence of these dimensions, hidden to other methodologies, in Melanesia begs the question of what is being missed elsewhere, whenever digital transformations are investigated using non-ethnographic methods. Even when the digital appears, at first sight, as more familiar, does it fit the "average" models that non-ethnographic approaches have assumed, or are there possibilities for diverse digital transformations? It is inadequate to rely on the "big data" statistical analyses that have informed so much digital research. Classical ethnography embraces inconvenience in the pursuit of accurate understanding through first-hand experience in an unfamiliar context. What could be more inconvenient for a privileged Western academic than to be dropped off on the beach somewhere, watching as "the launch or dingy which has brought you sails away out of sight" (Malinowski 1922: 4), having dropped you into a rapidly digitizing world in the Western Pacific?

Acknowledgments

We are grateful to numerous participants at the "Malinowski and the Argonauts" Centenary Workshop for their comments on an early draft of this chapter. We would also like to thank the attendees of the Friday Seminar Series at the Department of Anthropology of the London School of Economics, in particular Michael Scott, for the initial inspiration for this work.

Geoffrey Hobbis is an Assistant Professor at the Knowledge, Technology and Innovation Group, Wageningen University. His research has explored the digital transformations of long-standing other economies with a primary ethnographic focus on Solomon Islands. He is the author of *The Digitizing Family: An Ethnography of Melanesian Smartphones* (Palgrave, 2020) and principal investigator of an ERC Starting Grant on "Digitizing *Other* Economies" (grant agreement number: 101116741).

Stephanie Ketterer Hobbis is an Assistant Professor at the Sociology of Development and Change Group, Wageningen University, and a Senior Research Fellow at the Department of Knowledge Infrastructures, University of Groningen. With funding from the Dutch Research Council (NWO-Veni, 2022–25, VI.Veni.211S.062), she is currently investigating the resistance against digital extractivism in remote rural environments including Solomon Islands and British Columbia, Canada.

Notes

1. Like Malinowski, we too recognize the obstacles to obtaining a comprehensive holistic understanding, including, for example, encounters with and the study of "stereotyped manners of thinking and feeling" (Malinowski 1922: 23).
2. For more detailed ethnographic engagements with this material, see, among others, Geoffrey's monograph (Hobbis 2020) and various joint publications (Hobbis and Hobbis 2022a, 2022b, 2023).
3. Like each of us, Pierre Maranda was also one part of a husband-and-wife team; he conducted research in the Lau Lagoon with Elli Köngäs Maranda until her death in 1982.
4. The focus of digital studies on urban areas cannot solely be explained because of a heightened availability of digital infrastructures in these places. Instead, the sidelining of rural areas is indicative of an "urbanormativity" (Fulkerson and Thomas 2019) in much social scientific research, including media studies (cf. Hobbis et al. 2023).
5. Exceptions include Alan Howard and Jan Rensel's work on the digital transformation of Rotuma, Fiji, (e.g., Howard and Rensel 2004), David Lipset's investigation

of mobile phones among Murik men in Papua New Guinea (e.g., Lipset 2018), and Robert Foster's engagement with the digitization of nation-making, also in Papua New Guinea (Foster 2020; forthcoming). Hobbis (2020) is, as of January 2024, the sole ethnographic monograph to focus on digital transformations.

6. For example, ethnographic work is needed on the digital transformation of the North American potlatch, which is no less prominent in the literature of economic anthropology. It is also not necessary to remain within this subfield: what of the digital transformations of transactions between the witchcraft, oracles, and magic of the Azande, first investigated by Evans-Pritchard (1937) almost a century ago? The list of possibilities is long.
7. For a more detailed discussion of these interviews see Hobbis (2020).
8. However, we found, as Dalsgaard (2016) observed elsewhere in the Solomon Archipelago, online connections to be a boon to the maintenance of research relationships and their extension beyond the fieldwork location.
9. Like Malinowski, we recognize that terms such as "ownership" and "possession" are in various ways inadequate to describe the local practices and how they related to corresponding local words. However, again like Malinowski, we recognize that such analogies are indispensable for creating intelligibility (cf. de l'Estoile, this volume).
10. Malinowski noted a decline in canoe participation in the Kula exchange a century ago: "nowadays, other interests, such as diving for pearls, working on white man's plantations, divert the native attention, while many events connected with Missions, Government and trading, eclipse the importance of old customs" (Malinowski 1922: 155).
11. For more detailed analysis of these materialities, see Starosielski (2015) (on undersea cables) and Taylor (2021) (on data centers).
12. See Hobbis and Hobbis (2022b) for a more detailed ethnographic discussion of this process.
13. Torrenting refers to a process of downloading and uploading that is based on peer-to-peer (P2P) file-sharing and often used for unauthorized access to multimedia files or other software. Because this access is unauthorized, it is free (unlike, e.g., purchasing a movie on a platform such as Amazon or Apple) and the file is resharable, since no restrictions have been placed on the shareability of the file format by the platforms that sell the files.
14. See Bolt (this volume) for further exploration of the potential of Malinowski's approach to circulation.

References

Archambault, Julie Soleil. 2017. *Mobile Secrets: Youth, Intimacy, and the Politics of Pretense in Mozambique*. Chicago: University of Chicago Press.
Beaulieu, Anne. 2010. "Research Note: From Co-Location to Co-Presence: Shifts in the Use of Ethnography for the Study of Knowledge." *Social Studies of Science* 40(3): 453–70.
Berger, Peter. 2015. *Feeding, Sharing, and Devouring: Ritual and Society in Highland Odisha, India*. Berlin: De Gruyter.

Bird-David, Nurit. 1990. "The Giving Environment: Another Perspective on the Economic System of Gatherer-Hunters." *Current Anthropology* 31(2): 189–96.

Boas, Franz. 1895. "The Social Organization and the Secret Societies of the Kwakiutl Indians: Based on Personal Observations and on Notes made by Mr George Hunt." *Report of the United States National Museum for the Year Ending June 30, 1895*, 309–738. Retrieved from https://repository.si.edu/handle/10088/29967.

Burrell, Jenna. 2012. *Invisible Users: Youth in the Internet Cafes of Urban Ghana*. Boston: MIT Press.

Couldry, Nick, and Ulises A. Mejias. 2019. *The Cost of Connection: How Data is Colonizing Human Life and Appropriating It for Capitalism*. Stanford, CA: Stanford University Press.

Cupples, Julie, and Sara Kindon. 2003. "Far from Being 'Home Alone': The Dynamics of Accompanied Fieldwork." *Singapore Journal of Tropical Geography* 24(2): 211–28.

Dalsgaard, Steffen. 2016. "The Ethnographic Use of Facebook in Everyday Life." *Anthropological Forum* 26(1): 96–114.

De Kloet, Jeroen, Thomas Poell, Zeng Guohua, and Chow Yiu Fai. 2019. "The Platformization of Chinese Society: Infrastructure, Governance, and Practice." *Chinese Journal of Communication* 12(3): 249–56.

De Seta, Gabriele. 2020. "Three Lies of Digital Ethnography." *Journal of Digital Social Research* 2(1): 77–97.

Ebo, B. 1998. "Internet or Outernet?" In *Cyberghetto or Cybertopia? Race, Class, and Gender on the Internet*, ed. B. Ebo, 1–12. Westport, CT: Praeger.

Elder-Vass, Dave. 2016. *Profit and Gift in the Digital Economy*. Cambridge: Cambridge University Press.

Engelke, Matthew. 2004. "The Endless Conversation: Fieldwork, Writing, and the Marriage of Victor and Edith Turner." In *Significant Others: Interpersonal and Professional Commitments in Anthropology*, ed. Richard Handler, 6–50. Madison: University of Wisconsin Press.

Evans-Pritchard, E. E. 1937. *Witchcraft, Oracles and Magic among the Azande*. Oxford: Clarendon Press.

Foster, Robert J. 2020. "The Politics of Media Infrastructure: Mobile Phones and Emergent Forms of Public Communication in Papua New Guinea." *Oceania* 90(1): 18–39.

———. Forthcoming. *Uneven Connections: A Partial History of the Mobile Phone in Papua New Guinea*. Canberra: ANU Press.

Fulkerson, Gregory M., and Alexander R. Thomas. 2019. *Urbanormativity: Reality, Representation, and Everyday Life*. Lanham, MD: Lexington.

Garcia, Angela C., Alecea I. Standlee, Jennifer Bechkoff, and Yan Cui. 2009. "Ethnographic Approaches to the Internet and Computer-Mediated Communication." *Journal of Contemporary Ethnography* 38(1): 52–84.

Graeber, David. 2011. *Debt: The First 5000 Years*. New York: Melville House.

Graeber, David, and David Wengrow. 2021. *The Dawn of Everything: A New History of Humanity*. London: Allen Lane.

Hann, Chris, and Keith Hart. 2011. *Economic Anthropology: History, Ethnography, Critique*. Cambridge: Polity.

Hart, Keith. 2012. "Money in Twentieth Century Anthropology." In *A Handbook of Economic Anthropology, Second Edition*, ed. James G. Carrier, 166–82. Cheltenham: Edward Elgar.
Hine, Christine. 2007. "Connective Ethnography for the Exploration of E-Science." *Journal of Computer Mediated Communication* 12(2): 618–34.
Hobbis, Geoffrey. 2020. *The Digitizing Family: An Ethnography of Melanesian Smartphones*. London: Palgrave.
———. 2021. "Digitizing *Other* Economies: A Critical Review." *Geoforum* 126: 306–9.
Hobbis Geoffrey, and Stephanie K. Hobbis. 2021. "An Ethnography of Deletion: Materializing Transience in Solomon Islands Digital Cultures." *New Media & Society* 23(4): 750–65.
———. 2022a. "Beyond Platform Capitalism: Critical Perspectives on Facebook Markets from Melanesia." *Media, Culture & Society* 44(1): 121–40.
———. 2023. "Digitizing *Other* Markets: Lessons from the Bush Internet of Island Melanesia." *Journal of Cultural Economy* 16(4): 559-75.
Hobbis, Geoffrey, Marc Esteve-Del-Valle, and Rashid Gabdulhakov. 2023. "Rural Media Studies: Making the Case for a New Subfield." *Media, Culture & Society* 45(7): 1489-1500.
Hobbis, Stephanie K. 2016. "Shortages, Priorities and Maternal Health: Muddled Kastom and the Changing Status of Women in Malaita, Solomon Islands." In *Missing the Mark? Women and the Millennium Development Goals in Africa and Oceania*, 126–52. Bradford: Demeter Press.
Hobbis, Stephanie K., and Geoffrey Hobbis. 2022b. "Non-/Human Infrastructures and Digital Gifts: The Cables, Waves and Brokers of Solomon Islands Internet." *Ethnos* 87(5): 851–73.
Howard, Alan, and Jan Rensel. 2004. "Rotuman Identity in the Electronic Age." In *Shifting Images of Identity in the Pacific*, ed. Toon van Meijl and Jelle Miedema, 219–36. Leiden: KITLV Press.
Howard, Alan, and Alexander Mawyer. 2015. "Ethnography in the Digital Age." In *Emerging Trends in the Social and Behavioral Sciences*, ed. Robert Scott and Stephan Kosslyn, 1–15. Hoboken, NJ: Wiley.
Hundleby, Irene K. 2017. "Kwaimani ana liohaua gia: The Heart of Us." PhD thesis. Dunedin: University of Otago, New Zealand.
Kahn, Miriam. 1987. *Always Hungry, Never Greedy: Food and the Expression of Gender in a Melanesian Society*. Long Grove, IL: Waveland Press.
Kozinets, Robert V. 2010. *Netnography: Doing Ethnographic Research Online*. London: Sage.
Kulick, Don, and Margaret Willson. 1994. "Rambo's Wife Saves the Day: Subjugating the Gaze and Subverting the Narrative in a Papua New Guinea Swamp." *Visual Anthropology Review* 10(2): 1–13.
Leander, Kevin, and Kelly K. McKim. 2003. "Tracing the Everyday 'Sitings' of Adolescents on the Internet: A Strategic Adaptation of Ethnography across Online and Offline Spaces." *Communication & Information* 3(2): 211–40.
Lemonnier, Pierre. 1976. "La description des chaînes opératoires: Contribution à l'analyse des systèmes techniques." *Techniques & Culture* 1: 100–51.

Lipset, David. 2018. "A Handset Dangling in a Doorway: Mobile Phone Sharing in a Rural Sepik Village (Papua New Guinea)." In *The Moral Economy of Mobile Phones: Pacific Islands Perspectives*, ed. R. J. Foster and H. A. Horst, 19–38. Canberra: ANU Press.

Malinowski, Bronisław. 1921. "The Primitive Economics of the Trobriand Islands." *The Economic Journal* 31(121): 1–16.

———. 1922. *Argonauts of the Western Pacific: An Account of Native Enterprise and Adventure in the Archipelagoes of Melanesian New Guinea*. London: Routledge & Kegan Paul.

Maranda, Pierre. 1967. "Computers in the Bush: Tools for the Automatic Analysis of Myths." In *Essays on the Verbal and Visual Arts: Proceedings of the 1966 Annual Spring Meeting of the American Ethnological Society*, ed. June Helm, 77–83. Seattle: University of Washington Press.

———. 1969. "*Lau Markets: A Sketch*." *Working Papers in Anthropology*. Vancouver, University of British Columbia.

———. 2010. "Sea Peoples, Island Folk: Hypertext and People without Writing." In *Digital Cognitive Technologies: Epistemology and the Knowledge Economy*, ed. Bernard Reber and Claire Brossaud, 187–201. Hoboken, NJ: Wiley.

Maranda, Pierre, James Tuita Dede, and Ben Burt. 2022. *The Last White Canoe of the Lau of Malaita, Solomon Islands*. Hereford: Sean Kingston Press.

Markham, Annette. 2013. "Fieldwork in Social Media: What Would Malinowski Do?" *Qualitative Communication Research* 2(4): 434–46.

Menzies, Charles R. 2016. *People of the Saltwater: An Ethnography of Git lax m'oon*. Lincoln: University of Nebraska Press.

Miller, Daniel. 2017. "Anthropology is the Discipline but the Goal is Ethnography." *HAU: Journal of Ethnographic Theory* 7(1): 27–31.

Miller, Daniel, et al. 2016. *How the World Changed Social Media*. London: UCL Press.

Minter, Tessa, and Jan van der Ploeg. 2023. "'Our Happy Hour Became a Hungry Hour': Logging, Subsistence and Social Relations in Solomon Islands." *International Forestry Review* 25(1): 113–35.

Murthy, Dhiraj. 2008. "Digital Ethnography: An Examination of the Use of New Technologies for Social Research." *Sociology* 42(5): 837–55.

Pink, Sarah, Shanti Sumartojo, Deborah Lupton, and Christine Heyes La Bond. 2017. "Mundane Data: The Routines, Contingencies and Accomplishments of Digital Living." *Big Data & Society* 4(1): 1–12.

Pink, Sarah, Heather Horst, John Postill, Larissa Hjorth, Tania Lewis, and Jo Tacchi. 2015. *Digital Ethnography: Principles and Practice*. London: Sage.

Polanyi, Karl. 2001 [1944]. *The Great Transformation: The Political and Economic Origins of Our Time*. Boston: Beacon Press.

Ritter, Christian S. 2022. "Rethinking Digital Ethnography: A Qualitative Approach to Understanding Interfaces." *Qualitative Research* 22(6): 916–32.

Robbins, Joel. 2008. "Rethinking Gifts and Commodities: Reciprocity, Recognition, and the Morality of Exchange." In *Economics and Morality: Anthropological Approaches*, ed. Katherine E. Browne and B. Lynne Milgram, 43–58. Lanham, MD: Rowman & Littlefield.

Robbins, Joel, and David Akin. 1999. "An Introduction to Melanesian Currencies: Agency, Identity, and Social Reproduction." In *Money and Modernity: State and Local Currencies in Melanesia*, ed. David Akin and Joel Robbins, 1–40. Pittsburgh, PA: University of Pittsburgh Press.

Robinson, Laura, and Jeremy Schultz. 2009. "New Avenues for Sociological Inquiry: Evolving Forms of Ethnographic Practice." *Sociology* 43(4): 685–98.

Ross, Harold M. 1978. "Baegu Markets, Aereal Integration, and Economic Efficiency in Malaita, Solomon Islands." *Ethnology* 17(2): 119–38.

Sade-Beck, Liav. 2004. "Internet Ethnography: Online and Offline." *International Journal of Qualitative Methods* 3(2): 45–51.

Shome R. 2019. "When Postcolonial Studies Interrupts Media Studies." *Communication, Culture and Critique* 12(3): 305–22.

Spann, Michael. 2022. "'It's How You Live': Understanding Culturally Embedded Entrepreneurship; An Example from Solomon Islands." *Development in Practice* 32(6): 781-92.

Srnicek, Nick. 2017. *Platform Capitalism*. Cambridge: Polity.

Starosielski, Nicole. 2015. *The Undersea Network*. Durham, NC: Duke University Press.

Strathern, Andrew, and Pamela Stewart. 2012. "Ceremonial Exchange: Debates and Comparisons." In *A Handbook of Economic Anthropology, Second Edition*, ed. James G. Carrier, 239–56. Cheltenham: Edward Elgar.

Sykes, Karen. 2005. *Arguing with Anthropology: An Introduction to Critical Theories of the Gift*. London: Routledge.

Taylor, A. R. E. 2021. "Future-Proof: Bunkered Data Centres and the Selling of Ultra-Secure Cloud Storage." *Journal of the Royal Anthropological Institute* 27(S1): 76–94.

UNDP. 2022. "Solomon Islands." Human Development Reports. Retrieved from https://hdr.undp.org/data-center/specific-country-data#/countries/SLB .

Varis, Piia. 2016. "Digital Ethnography" In *The Routledge Handbook of Language and Digital Communication*, ed. Alexandra Georgakopoulou and Tereza Spiloti, 55-68. London: Routledge.

Zuboff, Shoshana. 2019. *The Age of Surveillance Capitalism: The Fight for a Human Future at the New Frontier of Power*. London: Profile.

 Afterword

REBECCA EMPSON

Today more than ever it is important to revisit the history of anthropology, to question its founders, and to look at how things can be done differently. It is a time when we need actively to separate ourselves from its colonial, racist, patriarchal, and imperial past. This book, based on a workshop celebrating the centenary of the publication of Bronisław Malinowski's first monograph *Argonauts of the Western Pacific*, both confirms and recasts knowledge about the history of the discipline. Reading the chapters, I learned about the complexity of Malinowski as a person, his own attempts to think beyond the canon that prevailed in his age, and his insistence on the need to rethink the idea of the economy. I learned about his unacceptable silences and omissions, but also about the hope and compassion that drove his research, impulses that fuel ways of rethinking anthropology today.

Malinowski (or Bronio as he was known within his family) was a very sickly child whose father died when he was 14. He grew up in Kraków, which at the time was part of the Austrian Partition of Poland. As Grażyna Kubica documents in her chapter, his mother struggled financially. To make ends meet, she managed a university student dormitory. Bronio's best friend was Staś, a painter and playwright who traveled with him to Australia, but then left to fight in World War I. As an Austrian citizen, Malinowski was unable to follow. His movements at the time were restricted, which led to an unplanned prolongation of his Trobriand fieldwork. On his return to the UK, Malinowski set out to show how the Melanesian Kula exchange system provided a different way of understanding what constituted the economy. To do so he had to write, with extensive assistance from his wife, in a language that was not his own, to gain entry to a British university system in which he had not been educated and with whose systems of power and authority he was largely unacquainted. Writing *Argonauts* unlocked this world for him. Once he was inside, his seminars at the LSE were attended by an extraordinary range of scholars from all over the world who drew on his training when they returned to their home countries. Yet, in many ways, Bronisław Malinowski remained an outsider throughout his life.

We learn from several of the chapters in this book that Malinowski clearly collaborated with the colonial government on labor and trade. The chapters by Freddy Foks and Rachel Smith both invoke Malinowski's testimony in Melbourne in 1916, when he addressed the problems experienced by the colonial plantation owners by arguing that the Trobrianders worked best through their local chiefs within their own economic systems, rather than through direct rule. In his published work, however, he seldom broached the effects of colonialism and its fundamental contribution to the very formation of the Kula exchange.

Argonauts was published in 1922 but it continues to captivate. The nuanced detail of everyday events and observations draws us in and takes us along as the broader theme unfurls. Malinowski's participant observation together with his diary (Malinowski 1967), which works as a kind of shadow of his more formal writing, hold our imagination. The Kula could not be explained by reference to maximizing individuals. Rather, the movement of material objects was determined by utterly different values. And while not an explicitly political text, *Argonauts* anticipates the arguments Malinowski elaborated in later publications in favor of "trusteeship" or "indirect rule" (Foks, this volume). By drawing attention to the existence of separate (or alternative) economic systems, Malinowski also anticipated what became known in the 1960s as the formalist–substantivist debate in anthropology. More recently, this has been largely superseded by the idea that, rather than postulate radically alternative economies, we need to recognize that differences flourish *within* capitalist economies. In fact, the economy is never a single "system." Seemingly central activities of production and consumption are often sustained, determined, or challenged by activities along the edges of what is conventionally considered to be economic. This is to attend to what Tsing (2015) calls the "arts of noticing"—to pay attention to the relationships and activities that flourish alongside the mainstream, giving rise to forms of resistance and critique that are shaped by specific historical conditions. In the spirit of Roelvink et al. (2015), Bear et al. (2015), Tsing (2015), and others, we can read Malinowski's deep commitment to ethnographic detail as a precursor of how to investigate contemporary encounters with structural forms of power. Malinowski's rejection of "economic man" accurately captures the limits of "capitalocentric" models of extraction and accumulation, thereby challenging hegemonic ways of describing and reproducing forms of power concealed within that paradigm.

Asking what our interlocutors value and what makes their lives worth living remains central to the discipline. Several chapters (perhaps most powerfully that of Benoît de L'Estoile) ask how we can learn from our interlocutors in order to imagine a better world. We also need to ask what has been left out of previous analyses. Steinmüller's chapter draws on ethnographic and archaeological research to uncover how colonial policies impacted on the Trobriand Islanders before Malinowski's arrival, something Malinowski's ahistorical account failed to take into consideration. This leads us to reflect on the production of anthropological knowledge itself. We need to question how contemporary research is shaped by the extractive neoliberal era we find ourselves in, and how we might think outside of these blinkers through ethnography. In doing so, we need to be careful that our work is not used to leverage existing inequalities and open the way for novel regimes of accumulation produced through racial capitalism and colonialism (cf. Ho 2023).

Malinowski was both freed and shackled by his personal history. In 1987 Marilyn Strathern identified a similar conundrum for the work of the anthropologist: "As anthropologists we have a technical problem at our fingertips, namely: 'how to create an awareness of different social worlds when all at one's disposal is terms which belong to one's own'" (Strathern 1987: 256). The terms used by Malinowski to describe the Kula were given context by showing that the idea of "the economy" could be stretched to include other forms of value. As Mark Mosko argues in his contribution to this volume, the spirits are an essential component of this enlarged notion. Strathern (1987: 257) goes on to highlight that "anthropology [is] not just about relating what other people think/believe, a way to affect what our readers think or believe. [It is not just] 'how to bring certain scenes to life' [by giving *context*], but about how to bring [new] life to ideas." While the idea of what the economy could mean was given a new life by Malinowski through his investigation of the Kula, Steinmüller succeeds in bringing new life to the idea of the Kula. Reciprocity, he shows, is never simply a tit-for-tat exchange, but is sustained by violence and creativity. Under colonial rule, Kula was reduced to "a noble substitute for actual warfare." The end of warfare meant that more people could participate in the Kula and more valuables could be included, thereby enabling more egalitarian forms of society. This new context takes us one step beyond seeing the Kula as an alternative economy out of time, to seeing it as a specific historical transformation of what had gone before. Malinowski's rendition was born out of the context that he gave it, influenced by the wider sociopolitical climate that he was working in. By omitting the concrete historical background, he overlooked the fact that rules were always malleable and had to be enforced. Similar objections can be made to many other theories developed in the Malinowskian "functionalist" paradigm. In this case, failure to capture the physical violence that was historically necessary to create "equivalence" has distorted our understanding of reciprocity and the gift. We need to think critically about the way that things are framed, and about the limited tools we have to apprehend and imagine the lives of others. Malinowski tried to do this within the context that he found himself, but our context is different, and we can do things differently.

Rebecca Empson is an anthropologist who works on economic anthropology and forms of ownership and possession in the UK, Mongolia, and the Baltic Sea. She is Head of Social Anthropology at University College London, where she has taught a long-standing course, "Anthropology of Capitalisms." In 2014 she gave the Malinowski Memorial Lecture at the London School of Economics and Political Science. She is author of *Harnessing Fortune: Personhood, Memory and Place in Mongolia* (Oxford University Press, 2011) and *Subjective Lives and Economic Transformations in Mongolia: Life in the Gap* (UCL Press, 2020).

References

Bear, Laura, Karen Ho, Anna Lowenhaupt Tsing, and Sylvia Yanagisako. 2015. "Gens: A Feminist Manifesto for the Study of Capitalism." *Fieldsights*, 30 March. Retrieved 10 November 2023 from https://culanth.org/fieldsights/gens-a-feminist-manifesto-for-the-study-of-capitalism.

Ho, Karen. 2023. "Afterword of 'Financial Frontiers': Towards Conceptualizing Finance That Engages Both Power and Contingency." *Journal of Cultural Economy* 16(3): 453–61.

Malinowski, Bronisław. 1967. *A Diary in the Strict Sense of the Term*. London: Routledge & Kegan Paul.

Roelvink, Gerda, Kevin St. Martin, and J. K. Gibson-Graham, eds. 2015. *Making Other Worlds Possible: Performing Diverse Economies*. Minneapolis: Minnesota University Press.

Strathern, Marilyn. 1987. "Out of Context: The Persuasive Fictions of Anthropology." *Current Anthropology* 28(3): 251–70.

Tsing, Anna Lowenhaupt. 2015. *The Mushroom at the End of the World: On the Possibility of Life in Capitalist Ruins*. Princeton, NJ: Princeton University Press.

Index

Aboriginal customs, 121
accumulation
   Laozi on, 229, 230
   within Kula, 231, 232
Africa
   forced labor and punitive expeditions in, 109
   Kenya, 256
   South Africa, 249, 250, 255–58, 259–67, 267n2
afterlife, Kula and, 197–99
The Andaman Islanders (Radcliffe-Brown), 63
anthropologists
   economics critiqued by, 89–90
   without price data, 86
anthropology, 66–67, 68–69, 219–20, 312, 314. *See also* economic anthropology
   Greco-Roman episteme influencing, 243
   social, 1, 2, 19n2
   sociology, collaboration with, 271
   tribal economy studied with, 163–64
apartheid, 257, 259
archaeological history, of Kula, 209–10, 213, 214–15, 219, 314–15
Argentina, 271
   money in, 17–18, 272, 273–85
   San Justo, 281
   soybeans in, 280, 281–83
   Villa Olimpia, 273–74, 276–79
Argentinian urban poor, monetary pluralism of, 273–79
Argentinian wealthy farmers, monetary pluralism of, 279–85

Argonauts of the Western Pacific (Malinowski, Bronisław). *See specific topics*
Aristotle, 181n19, 181n21
   on *oikonomia*, 181n20
   Politics by, 170, 181n23
Asad, Talal, 89
assentamento (settlement project), 172, 174, 180n15
astrology, of finance, 157n3
Australia, 71, 77–79, 313
Australia Interstate Commission, 90n2
Austro-Hungarian Empire, 1, 8
autocratic paternalism, 81
Axial Age, 228–29
axiomatic thought, Keynes on, 146–47

baloma (spirits of dead), 16, 118, 119, 187
   afterlife of, 197–98
   magical agency of, 188–90, 193, 201
   megwa spell involvement of, 192
Barton, Francis, 122, 123–24
Bellamy, Raynor L., 78, 130, 212
Bentham, Jeremy, 139, 142
Benthamite calculation/s, 153–54, 155–56
Black, Fischer, 154, 156
Black Administration Act, 259
blackbirding, 109, 112n2
Black families, Johannesburg township home inheritance for, 257–58, 259, 262
Bloch, Maurice, 270
Boas, Franz, 66
bodily fluids *(bubwalua)*, 190, 191
Bourdieu, Pierre, 165, 166

Brazil, 167–72, 175–77, 180n15
British and Australian Trade in the South Pacific in Melbourne Commission, 87–98, 101, 102–4
British Association for the Advancement of Science, 71
British Empire, 81. *See also* colonialism
bubwalua (saliva and bodily fluids), 190, 191
Bücher, Karl, 9, 65, 180n1
   on gift, 66
   Industrial Evolution by, 121, 134n1
   on labor, 98–99
   pre-economic stages argument of, 121, 162, 290
   principle of least effort, 10, 106, 113n6, 142, 145
burial, secondary, 212, 214, 215, 216
Bursa Akademicka
   Malinowska, Józefa, senior role at, 33–34, 312
   Malinowski, Lucjan, at, 29–30, 31
Burt, Ben, 292
bush internet, 18
   Kula compared to, 301–5
   materiality of, 302–3, 304–5
   Solomon Islanders brokers of, 303–5
butula (fame), 196–97, 231
bwekasa (sacrificial reciprocity), 188, 202n5
   baloma magical agency within, 189, 193
   Kula as, 193
   life and death in, 191–92
   in meals, 190

Cambridge Journal of Economics, 139–40, 157n1
Canary Islands, 34, 43
cannibalism, 208
canoes, 307n10
   descriptive ethnography on, 52
   Hōkūleʻa, 301
Capital (Marx), 158n7
caregiving money, of Argentinian urban poor, 276, 277–78, 279

Carpathian village, Poland, 70–71
Carrier, James, 166
Central and Eastern Europe, 26
Chałasiński, Józef, 25–26
chiefs, Trobriand, 199. *See also* dual chieftainship
   colonialism impacting, 80, 128, 130
   colonial pacification impacting, 212
   kobala of, 241
   Kula involvement of, 194, 196–97, 227
   land tenure system of, 237–38
China, 226, 229, 235–36, 237, 238
circuits, 254, 275
circulation, 254
   of Johannesburg township homes via inheritance, 250, 255, 260–61, 266–67
   of Kula valuables, 249, 250–51, 252–53, 266, 267
Clifford, James, 91n4
cold societies, 228, 242
colonialism, 77, 140–41, 313, 314
   depopulation impacted by, 132–33
   indigenous peoples influenced by, 74
   Labor Question of, 97–98, 100–101, 108–9, 111
   Trobriand chiefs impacted by, 80, 128, 130
colonial pacification, Kula and warfare impacted by, 209, 210–13, 220
colonial trade, 77–80
Conrad, Joseph, 61n21, 73
Cook, Scott, 7–8, 20n5
Coral Gardens and Their Magic (Malinowski, Bronisław), 10, 19n4, 74, 108–9, 127, 132
   "Confessions of Ignorance and Failure" in, 128
   "An Ethnographic Theory of the Magical World" in, 155
court judgments, 261, 264, 267n1
Cracow, Poland. *See* Kraków, Poland
cross-civilizational understanding (*wenming jiejian*), 226
cultural capital, 26, 37
cultural nationalism, 90n3

currency
  global, 283, 284
  soybeans as, 282, 283, 284

dala (matrilineages), 195, 203nn13–15, 233, 234–35, 236, 237, 239
Dali kingship (China), 235–36, 237, 238
Damon, Fred, 203n12, 215, 232, 252
Dao (the Way), 227, 230, 243
depopulation
  colonialism impacting, 132–33
  Labor Question relationship with, 103–4, 105
derivatives, 154, 156
descriptive ethnography, 52
deterritorialization, of ideas, 229
diaries, of Malinowski, Bronisław, 39n8, 72, 73
A Diary in the Strict Sense of the Term (Malinowski, Bronisław), 55–56, 61n22
digital ethnography, 291, 293–95, 305
  methods of, 296–98
  participant observation in, 296, 297
digital studies, 291–93, 295, 306n4
digital transformation, 289, 291, 293, 301, 305, 307n6
digitization, 289, 295
dividuality model, Melanesian, 193, 203n11
Dodd, Nigel, 271–72, 285
dollar, US
  Argentine peso relationship with, 272, 279–81, 282, 283
  as global currency, 283, 284
  monetary pluralism of, 271, 272, 279–81, 282, 283, 284
domestic government *(oikonomia)*, 167–72, 177, 178, 179, 181n18, 181n20
donas (masters), 169
dual chieftainship
  of Dali kingship, 235–36
  in Kiriwina, 234–36, 237–38, 240
  matrilineages transmission of, 234–35, 237
  quasi-incest of, 235, 236, 237

The Dual Mandate in British Tropical Africa, 74
Dumont, Louis, 167
Durkheim, Émile, 64, 201

earned money, of Argentinian urban poor, 276, 277, 278–79
eastern Massim islands, 216, 217, 221
Economica, 105, 120
economic anthropology, 1–2, 4–5, 77, 87, 129, 166, 178, 181n28, 270, 285
  on Brazilian peasantry, 168
  ethnographic, 7–12
  Firth on, 110, 164–65
  formalist-substantivist debate, 1, 8, 11–12, 87, 110, 313
  Mauss influence on, 201
  peasant economies, 164–68
  politics and, 81–83
economic institutions, 85
The Economic Journal, 66, 82, 83, 137, 138, 161
  and economic anthropology, 120
economic uncertainty and risk, distinction in, 140
economic man, 10. *See also* Homo economicus; Primitive Economic Man
economics, 121. *See also* primitive economics; uncertainty
  Bourdieu's critique of, 165
  economic anthropologists' critique of, 89–90
  embeddedness of, 1, 84, 88
  Firth on, 138, 140
  Keynes on, 137, 144
  neoclassical economics, 11, 138–39, 141–46
  new institutionalist, 12
  Nobel Prize for Economics, 158n8
  non-money, 86–87, 180n8
  Ökonomie, 9–10
  perfect knowledge assumptions in, 143–44
  Robbins, Lionel, on, 84–86
  time within, 144
Volkswirtschaftslehre, 10

economic sociology, 166, 285
economists, 164
　anthropologists, relationship with, 90
　ethnologists, mutual benefit with, 127
economization, 141
economy, 7–12, 313. *See also* economic anthropology; economics
　digital studies of, 295
　favela, 177
　moral, 19n4, 166
　national, 10, 131–32, 163
　ontological belief in, 167, 179
　psychic, of Malinowski, 53
　of thought, 126, 220
El Boquín (Tenerife villa), 43–44, 55
Elementary Forms of the Religious Life (Durkheim), 201
Eliot, T. S., 74
embeddedness, 1, 12, 167
　of economics, 84, 88
　of ethnographer, 129
empires, European, 79, 81, 82, 313
Engineer Islands, Tubetube Island, 122
entrepreneurs, uncertainty handled by, 152
epistemology
　of Mach, 126
　of Malinowski, 120
ethnographer, 55–57, 70, 129
ethnographic documentation, 53–54, 66–68
ethnographic economic anthropology, 7–12
ethnographic method, 5–7, 272, 273
ethnographic persona, 53–55
ethnographic present, 56
ethnographic writing, 56, 72–73
ethnography, 75
　descriptive, 52
　digital, 291, 293–95, 296–98, 305
　Rivers' intensive, 68–69
　Urry on, 61n17
ethnologists, 127
ethnology, 19n2, 57, 58
　on indigenous peoples, 59–60
　on Kula, 50

"Ethnology and the Study of Society" (Malinowski, Bronisław), 124, 132
evolutionist racism, 99, 107
export sales tax, soybean, 282–83

fame *(butula)*, 196–97, 231
family, Malinowski, 13, 19n3, 28–29, 31–32, 35, 37, 39n6
family houses, Johannesburg township home inheritance of, 257, 258, 259
famine, Solomon Islanders avoiding, 299
favelas, 175–76, 177, 181n27
Fei, Xiaotong, 226, 243
fieldwork. *See* ethnography; participant observation
finances, of Malinowski family, 28–29, 35, 37, 39n6
Firth, Raymond, 7, 52, 145
　on differential prices, 86
　on economic anthropology, 110, 164–65
　on economics, 138, 140
　on politics, 91n4
fishing traditions, Trobriand Islanders, 119, 149–50, 157n4, 192, 202n9
formalist-substantivist debate, 1, 8, 11–12, 87, 110, 313
fortune, 150–52, 157n5
Foucault, Michel, 181nn17–18
Frazer, James, 43, 44–45, 46–48
　The Golden Bough by, 63
　Totem and Taboo by, 70
Friedman, Milton, 145
functionalism, 3, 5–7, 53, 58, 65, 74–75, 83, 113n9, 134n2
　on colonial policy, 80
　indigenous perspective grasped with, 137
　of Wundt, 63–64
funerary rites, Kula influenced by, 216, 217

gainta (garden magician, of central India), 155, 156
garden magician *(towosi)*, 155–56
garden work, of Trobriand Islanders, 106, 108, 124, 150, 173

Gault, Wilhelm, 65–66
Gellner, Ernest, 66–67
genocide, 79, 81
German Empire, plantations of, 79
gift, 66, 305
gift-giving, tribal, 65–66, 180n2, 200, 219, 222n8. *See also* Kula
Ginsberg, Morris, 120
globalization, Solomon Islands resisting, 298
Godelier, Maurice, 200, 228, 242
gold standard, for money, 153
Goody, Jack, 256
The Great Transformation (Polanyi), 167
Greco-Roman episteme, 228–30, 243
Gudeman, Stephen, 166
Guyer, Jane, 199, 203n21, 271, 275

Hancock, Billy, 130–31
Herskovits, Melville, 11–12, 20n5
hiri expeditions, 122, 123–24
Hōkūle'a (Hawaii-based Polynesian double-hulled canoe), 301
Homo economicus, 139, 165
Honiara, Malaita (Solomon Islands, Melanesia), 296
hot societies, 228, 242
household *(oikos)*, 170, 171. *See also* oikonomia
houses, with gardens and fruit trees *(sittios)*, 172–73
Hubert, Henri, 200–201, 204n23

immortality, of spirits, 197–99, 203n19
imperialism. *See* colonialism
imponderabilia, ethnographic documentation of, 66–68
incest *(suvasova)*, 235, 237, 239
INCRA. *See* National Institute for Colonization and Land Reform
INDEC. *See* National Institute of Statistics and Censuses
indigenous peoples, 64. *See also* Kula; Trobriand Islanders
  Bücher pre-economic stages argument on, 121, 162, 290

  colonialism influence on, 74
  ethnology on, 59–60
  labor of, 82, 97, 99, 101–2, 103, 112n1
  living standards of, 88, 89
  perspective of, 129, 137, 180n14
  plantation labor of, 78–79, 102–3
  racism toward, 99, 100, 102–3, 105–6, 107, 112n1
  trade of, 123–24, 128
indirect rule, in European empires, 82, 313
Industrial Evolution (Bücher), 121, 134n1
inheritance, 256–57
inheritance, Johannesburg township homes, 249, 256, 267n2
  for Black families, 257–58, 259, 262
  circulation of, 250, 255, 260–61, 266–67
  court judgments on, 261, 264
  formality thresholds of, 263–64
  reversals of, 264–66
intellects, of Laozi, 238–42, 243
intelligentsia, Polish, 25, 26, 27, 29, 32, 37, 38
interpreters, payments to, 135n5
intestate succession law, 258, 259
Intichiuma ceremonies, 99, 108

Jagiellonian University, 8, 13, 25, 27, 28–29
James, William, 64
Joaquim, Zé, 172–75, 181n26
Johannesburg townships (South Africa)
  home inheritance in, 249, 250, 255–58, 259–67, 267n2
  Soweto, 259–60, 262

Keynes, John Maynard, 11, 15, 145
  on economics, 137, 144
  on economic uncertainty, 139–40, 141, 143, 146–49, 151–52, 154, 155
  The General Theory of Employment, Interest and Money by, 139, 154
  Marshall relationship with, 157n2
  on money, 152–53
  on probable knowledge, 147

A Treatise on Probability by, 139–40, 146
Keynesian revolution, 139
khrematistikè (necessities of life), 170, 171, 177, 178
Khuner, Paul, 130
Kiriwina (Trobriand Islands, Papua New Guinea), 10
   dual chieftainship in, 234–36, 237–38, 240
   Omarakana, 187, 234, 241
"Kiriwina" (Malinowski, Bronisław), 48–49
Knight, Frank
   on economic uncertainty, 139–40, 151–52
   The General Theory of Employment, Interest and Money critiqued by, 154
   on neoclassical economics revolution, 145
   Risk, Uncertainty, and Profit by, 139–40
kobala (subversion), 241–42
Koita peoples, Seligman on, 123
Kraków, Poland, 27–28, 30–31, 33, 35–38, 39n5, 40n23, 70–71, 111
Kula, 1, 5, 16–17, 49, 51, 79, 119–20, 201, 203n12, 203n16, 291
   accumulation within, 231, 232
   afterlife and, 197–99
   archaeological history of, 209–10, 213, 214–15, 219, 314–15
   Argonauts writing process on, 13, 44–46, 56
   bush internet compared to, 301–5
   as *bwekasa*, 193
   "Chronological List of Kula Events Witnessed by the Writer" on, 54–55
   circulation of, 249, 250–51, 252–53, 266, 267
   colonial pacification impacting, 209, 210–13, 220
   fame from, 196–97, 231
   funerary rites influencing, 216, 217
   Laozi lens on, 226, 227, 230–34
   Mauss on, 200
   plantation labor compared to, 80
   Primitive Economic Man dispelled by, 52–53, 290
   trade mixed with, 131
   Trobriand chief involvement in, 194, 196–97, 227
   Trobriand Islander magic in, 50, 57–58, 187–89, 235
   warfare replaced with, 220, 234, 314
Kula valuables, 6, 218, 220, 231, 233
Kuper, Adam, 13–14, 19n1
Kuper, Hilda, 35

labor, 100, 107, 111–12, 191. *See also* plantation labor; work
   Bücher on, 98–99
   depopulation impacting, 103
   of indigenous peoples, 82, 97, 99, 101–2, 103, 112n1
   in Kula valuables, 233
   sex impacting, 104, 113n4
   of Trobriand Islanders, 113n8
labor, forced
   in Africa, 109
   Blackbirding, 109, 112n2
   Pacific trade inquiry on, 78–79
Labor Question
   of colonialism, 97–98, 100–101, 108–9, 111
   depopulation relationship with, 103–4, 105
land, 157n6
   Lau Lagoon regulations of, 299–300
   Trobriand chiefs' tenure system for, 237–38
Landa, Janet Tai, 12
Laozi, 229
   intellects of, 238–42, 243
   Kula understood through, 226, 227, 230–34
The Laozi, 17, 229, 232, 240
Lau Lagoon, 291, 292, 293, 299–300
Lau peoples, 296, 300
Leach, Edmund, 64, 209
Leach, Jerry, 199
League of Nations, 81, 82, 91n5

lent money, of Argentinian urban poor, 278
Lévi-Strauss, Claude, 3, 228
linguistics, and pragmatism, 64–65
liquidation, Johannesburg home inheritance, 263, 265, 266
The Listener, 82, 83
living standards, of indigenous peoples, 88, 89
London School of Economics (LSE), 2–4, 7, 11, 120, 161, 164
Luo, of Kenya, 256

Mach, Ernst, 70
  epistemology of, 126
  "On the Principle of the Economy of Thought," 8–9, 114n10, 125
Macintyre, Martha, 210–11, 216
Macmillan (publisher), 46–49
Magic, Science and Religion (Malinowski, Bronisław), 149
magic, Trobriand Islander, 156, 203n20
  baloma agency in, 188–90, 193, 201
  functionalist linguistic analysis of, 137
  in Kula, 50, 57–58, 187–89, 235
  Mauss on, 200
  of *megwa* spells, 189, 192, 195, 199–201
  of *sosewa* and *tukwa* spells, 195–96
  spirits' agency with, 188–90
  within tribal economy, 149–50
  work influenced by, 99, 107, 113n7
Mailu, New Guinea, 67
Mair, Lucy, 83–84
Malaita (Solomon Islands, Melanesia), 18, 291, 292
Malinowska, Józefa, 27–28, 32, 33–34, 35, 312
Malinowski, Bronisław. *See also specific topics*
  Coral Gardens and Their Magic by, 10, 19n4, 74, 108–9, 127, 128, 132, 155
  diaries of, 39n8, 72, 73
  A Diary in the Strict Sense of the Term by, 55–56, 61n22

"Ethnology and the Study of Society" by, 124, 132
  family of, 13, 19n3, 28–29, 31–32, 35, 37, 39n6
  Magic, Science and Religion by, 149
  "On the Principle of the Economy of Thought" by, 8–9, 34, 40n19, 70, 114n10, 118, 125
  "The Primitive Economics of Trobriand Islanders" by, 121, 124, 161–62
  psychic economy of, 53
  Sex and Repression by, 113n4
Malinowski, Elsie, 13, 36–37, 45, 46, 48, 56, 67–68, 72, 73, 117
Malinowski, Lucjan, 33
  at Bursa Akademicka, 29–30, 31
  at Jagiellonian University, 13, 27, 28–29
  professorial income of, 28–29, 39n6
mana, 204nn22–23
management, economy as, 8
Maranda, Pierre, 293, 300, 306n3
Marett, R. R., 68, 69
marginal utility theory, 142–43. *See also* economics, neoclassical
maritime mobility, 301
Marshall, Alfred, 140, 144, 157n2
Marx, Karl, 138–39, 158n7, 276
Massim societies, 233
  600 BP great transformation of, 213–18
  Trobriand society compared to, 188, 193–94, 196, 208
masters *(donas)*, 169
Master's Office, 263, 264, 265, 266, 268n6
matrilineages *(dala)*, 195, 203nn13–15, 233, 239
  Kiriwina dual chieftainship transmission through, 234–35, 237
  quasi-incest of, 235, 236, 237
Mauss, Marcel, 1, 188, 199, 203n21, 204n23, 219, 221n6
  economic anthropology influenced by, 201
  on Kula, 200
  on money, 270

Mead, Margaret, 52
megalithic complexes, 214, 215, 232
megwa spells, 189, 192, 195, 199–201
Melanesia. *See also* Massim societies; Trobriand Islanders
digitization of, 289
dividuality model in, 193, 203n11
New Guinea, 67, 130, 211, 214, 215, 221n5
Papua New Guinea, 1, 4, 5–6, 10, 187, 217, 234–36, 237–38, 240, 241
Solomon Islands, 18, 291, 292, 296, 298
Melanesian islanders, bush internet use of, 301, 303–5
Melbourne, Australia, 77–79, 313
Merton, Robert C., 156, 158n8
methods, 51–53, 61n20
of digital ethnography, 296–98
ethnographic, 5–7, 272, 273
Mexico, Oaxaca Valley, 11, 12, 86–87, 180n8
Miller, Daniel, 294
Mitchell, Timothy, 166
Mond, Robert, 117–18
monetary pluralism, 271, 272
of Argentinian urban poor, 273–79
of Argentinian wealthy farmers, 279–85
money, 128
in Argentina, 17–18, 272, 273–85
caregiving, 276, 277–78, 279
circulation of, 253
currency, 282, 283, 284
hierarchies of, 275–76, 285–86
Keynes on, 152–53
Mauss on, 270
sociology of, 271–72, 273, 286
in Uganda, 83–84
moral economy, 19n4, 166
Mosko, Mark S, 16, 157n4, 234, 237–38, 239
Motu peoples, *hiri* expeditions of, 122
Murray, Hubert, 78, 83, 112n3
Museu Nacional, in Rio de Janeiro, 168
Muyuw (Woodlark) (New Guinea), 211, 214, 215, 221n5

Nam-Mit event, 238–39, 240–41
national economy, 131–32, 163. *See also* economic anthropology; economics
National Institute for Colonization and Land Reform (INCRA), 168, 180n16
National Institute of Statistics and Censuses (INDEC), 280
native persons. *See* indigenous peoples
ndap (shells), 217
necessities of life *(khrematistikè)*, 170, 171
neoclassical economics revolution, 138–39, 141–46. *See also* economics, neoclassical
New Guinea, 67, 130, 211, 214, 215, 221n5. *See also* Papua New Guinea
New Humanism, 58, 132–34
Nietzsche, Friedrich, 9, 33, 72
Notes and Queries on Anthropology (Royal Anthropological Institute), 67, 68
numericality, 153–56

Oaxaca Valley (Mexico), 11, 12, 86–87, 180n8
oikonomia (domestic government), 167–69, 171–72, 177, 178, 181n18
Aristotle on, 181n20
Polanyi on, 170
and primitive economics, 179
oikos (household), 170, 171
Ökonomie, 9
Omarakana (Kiriwina, Trobriand Islands), 187, 234, 241
online-centric digital ethnography, 297, 298
Osapola-Bwaydaga (OB), 234, 236, 237, 238–39
ownership, 307n9
in rural Pernambuco, 168
Trobriand Islanders' meaning of, 126–27, 162

Papua New Guinea. *See also* Trobriand Islanders
Rossel Island, 217

Trobriand Island monographs, 1, 4, 5–6
Trobriand Islands, 10, 187, 234–36, 236, 237–38, 240, 241
Paramount Chief, 234–35, 237
Parry, Jonathan, 270
participant observation, 3, 74, 219, 296, 297
patrilineal chieftainship, 242
patrilineal succession, of Johannesburg township home inheritance, 258
peasant economies, 164–65, 167, 168
Pernambuco, rural (Brazil), 167–72, 180n15
peso, Argentine, 272, 279–81, 282, 283
Petty, William, 253
Pickles, Anthony, 251–52
plantation labor, 14, 100, 108–9, 112n3
   of indigenous peoples, 78–79, 102–3
   Kula compared to, 80
   sex impacting, 104
   tribal economy impacted by, 83
plantations
   Bellamy encouraging, 78, 130, 212
   of German Empire, 79
   sugarcane, 172
platformization, 295
pokala (solicitory offerings, in Kula magic), 189, 235
Poland, 39n3
   Carpathian village, 70–71
   Jagiellonian University in, 8, 13, 25, 27, 28–29
   professors in, 28, 29, 39nn5–6
Polanyi, Karl, 1, 8, 19n3, 20n6, 178, 180n11, 181n19, 181n21, 270
   The Great Transformation by, 167
   on *oikonomia*, 170
police, *favelas* searched by, 175–76, 177
Polish gentry *(szlachta)*, 25, 36, 37
political money, 276, 277, 279
politics, 81–83, 91n4, 227
Politics (Aristotle), 170, 181n23
politikè, 169, 170, 171–72, 177, 179, 181n24
pragmatism, and linguistics, 64–65

Primitive Economic Man, 6, 10, 97, 105, 107, 126, 143
   garden work dispelling, 124
   Kula dispelling, 52–53, 290
   utilitarianism critique of, 106
primitive economics, 177–78, 220, 290
   oikonomia and *politikè* escaping, 179
   other economies from, 161–67
"The Primitive Economics of Trobriand Islanders" (Malinowski, Bronisław), 121, 124, 161–62
principle of least effort, 10, 106, 113n6, 142, 145
probability, continuum of, 147, 148–49
probable knowledge, Keynes on, 147
provisioning, 178
punitive expeditions, 109, 211

racism, toward indigenous peoples, 99, 100, 102–3, 105–6, 107, 112n1
Radcliffe-Brown, A. R., 3, 63, 113n9
reciprocity, 219–20
reconciliation events, of Lau peoples, 300
reincarnation, of spirits, 197–99, 203n19
rice production, 141–42, 155
Rio de Janeiro, Brazil, 168, 175–77
ritual. See *Intichiuma* ceremonies; magic
Rivers, W. H. R., 68–69, 74, 103
Robbins, Lionel, 84–86
Rossel Island, Papua New Guinea, 217

sacrificial reciprocity *(bwekasa)*, 188, 189–92, 193, 202n5
Sahlins, Marshall, 7, 8, 189, 234
saliva *(bubwalua)*, 190, 191
San Justo, Argentina, 281
Scholes, Myron, 154, 156, 158n8
Seligman, Charles, 47, 122, 123, 125
servants market, 31
settlement project *(assentamento)*, 172, 174, 180n15
sex, labor impacted by, 104, 113n4
Sex and Repression (Malinowski, Bronisław), 113n4
shells *(ndap)*, 217
Shipton, Parker, 256–57

shooting, Vânia's experience of, 176
Sienkiewicz, Henryk Józef, 36–37
Sinic perspectivism, 229
sittios (houses, with gardens and fruit trees), 172–73
slavery, 82
smartphone digital ethnography research method, 297
social anthropology, 1, 2, 19n2
social capital, 26, 274
sociology
    anthropology collaboration with, 271
    economic, 166, 285
    of money, 271–72, 273, 286
solicitory offerings, in Kula magic *(pokala)*, 189, 235
Solomon Islanders
    bush internet brokers, 303–5
    famine avoided by, 299
Solomon Islands (Melanesia), 18, 291, 292, 296, 298
sopi (thoughts and water), 190, 191, 202n7
sosewa spells, *tukwa* spells compared to, 195–96
South Africa, Johannesburg townships in, 249, 250, 255–58, 259–67, 267n2
Southern Massim, 122
Soweto (Johannesburg, South Africa), 259–60, 262
soybeans
    in Argentina, 280, 281–83
    as currency, 282, 283, 284
Spanish, 44
spirits. *See also baloma*
    ancestral, 16
    magical agency of, 188–90
    reincarnation and immortality of, 197–99, 203n19
Stocking, George, 54, 104, 113n4
stone markers, 215–16
Strathern, Marilyn, 6, 193, 203n11, 314
structural functionalism, 3
substantivists, 1, 7, 8, 11, 12, 87, 110, 111, 313
subversion *(kobala)*, 241–42

suvasova (incest), 235, 237, 239
Sykes, Karen, 295
synoptic charts, 53, 84
szlachta (Polish gentry), 25, 36, 37

Tabalu, 234, 236, 237, 238–39
tanerere ceremonies, 189–90
temporal autonomy, in rural Pernambuco, 169
Thurnwald, Richard, 20n6, 66, 112n1
time, within economics, 144
torrenting, 307n13
towosi (garden magician), 155–56
trade, 221n7, 251–52
    colonial, 77–80
    of indigenous peoples, 123–24, 128
    Kula mixed with, 131
trade inquiry, Pacific (Melbourne, Australia), 77, 78–79, 313
A Treatise on Probability (Keynes), 139–40, 146
tribal economy, 4, 5, 10, 66, 82, 120, 127–28, 134, 137, 138
    anthropology studying, 163–64
    and economics, 85–86
    economic uncertainty in, 149–51, 153
    national economy compared to, 163
    plantation labor impacting, 83
    Trobriand Islander magic within, 149–50
Trobriand Islanders, 64, 72, 118, 128–32. *See also* chiefs, Trobriand; magic, Trobriand Islander; tribal economy
    colonial influence on, 74
    fishing traditions of, 119, 149–50, 157n4, 192, 202n9
    garden work of, 106, 108, 124, 150, 173
    labor of, 113n8
    ownership meaning for, 126–27, 162
    plantation labor of, 102
    towosi of, 155–56
Trobriand Island monographs, 1, 4, 5–6, 10, 49–51. *See also* Kula
Trobriand Islands, Kiriwina (Papua New Guinea), 10, 187, 234–36, 237–38, 240, 241

Trobriand society, 37–38. *See also* Kula
  colonialism impacting, 128
  Massim societies compared to, 188,
    193–94, 196, 208
trusteeship, 81, 83, 88, 313
Tubetube Island, Engineer Islands, 122
tukwa spells, 195–96, 203n13
Tuma afterworld, 189, 191, 197, 198
Turing Test, 297

Uganda, Ngogwe, 83–84
uncertainty, economic, 15
  fortune influencing, 150–52
  Keynes on, 139–40, 141, 143, 146–49,
    151–52, 154, 155
  Knight on, 139–40, 151–52
  Marx on, 158n7
  in tribal economy, 149–51, 153
Urry, James, 61n17

Vânia *(favela* resident), 175–76, 177,
  181n27
verbality, 153–56
vida digna (worthy life), 174
Villa Olimpia (Buenos Aires, Argentina),
  273–74, 276–79
Völkerpsychologie (Wundt), 63–64
Volkswirtschaftslehre, 11

Wall Street, 158n8
warfare, 208
  colonial pacification impacting, 209,
    210–13, 220
  Kula replacing, 220, 234, 314
water *(sopi)*, 190, 191, 202n7
the Way (Dao), 227, 230, 243
Weiner, Annette, 222n8, 252
wenming jiejian (cross-civilizational
  understanding), 226
western Massim islands, 216–17, 221n5
white domination, Firth on, 86
Woodlark (Muyuw) (New Guinea), 211,
  214, 215, 221n5
work, 110, 111–12. *See also* labor
  garden, 106, 108, 124, 150, 173
  Trobriand Islander magic influencing,
    99, 107, 113n7
  of Vânia, 175, 176
World War I, 59, 71
worthy life *(vida digna)*, 174
Wundt, Wilhelm, 63–64

yolova offerings, 196, 202n3
Young, Michael, 4, 13, 210–11

Zelizer, Viviana, 253, 271, 275, 283, 286n1
Zola, Émile, 73

www.ingramcontent.com/pod-product-compliance
Lightning Source LLC
Chambersburg PA
CBHW051526020426
42333CB00016B/1800